DATING IN EXPOSED AND SURFACE CONTEXTS

DATING IN EXPOSED AND SURFACE CONTEXTS

edited by

CHARLOTTE BECK

University of New Mexico Press ∞ Albuquerque

Library of Congress
Cataloging-in-Publication Data
Dating in exposed and surface contexts/edited by Charlotte Beck.
  p.   cm.
  Includes bibliographical references and index.
  ISBN 0-8263-1523-2
  1. Archaeological dating.
   I. Beck, Charlotte, 1948–CC78.D38   1994
930.1'028'5—dc20   94–7113
                                                  CIP

© 1994 University of New Mexico
Press
All Rights Reserved.
First edition.

CONTENTS

Acknowledgments
xiii

Chapter 1
Introduction
Charlotte Beck
3

Chapter 2
Use of Rock Weathering Rinds in Dating Geomorphic Surfaces
Peter L. K. Knuepfer
15

Chapter 3
The Schmidt Hammer as a Measure of Degree of Rock Surface
Weathering and Terrain Age
Danny McCarroll
29

Chapter 4
Dating Surface Assemblages Using Obsidian Hydration
Charlotte Beck and George T. Jones
47

Chapter 5
Surface Exposure Dating with Rock Varnish
Ronald I. Dorn
77

Chapter 6
Thermoluminescence Dating of Surficial Archaeological Material
Robert C. Dunnell and James K. Feathers
115

Chapter 7
Surface Exposure Dating with Cosmogenic Nuclides
Mark D. Kurz and Edward J. Brook
139

Chapter 8
Surface Exposure Dating by Cosmogenic Chorine-36 Accumulation
Marek G. Zreda and Fred M. Phillips
161

Chapter 9
Lichenometric Dating: A Review with Particular Reference to 'Little Ice Age' Moraines in Southern Norway
John A. Matthews
185

Chapter 10
Using Dendrochronology for the Dating of Land Surfaces
Olavi Heikkinen
213

Index
237

FIGURES

2.1 Photograph of weathering rinds obtained from surface rocks exposed on postglacial river terraces of Branch River, South Island, New Zealand ... 16

2.2 Map of South Island, New Zealand, showing distribution of Torlesse Supergroup greywacke ... 20

2.3 Distribution of weathering-rind measurements from terraces of the Saxton River, South Island, New Zealand ... 21

2.4 Calibration curve of weathering-rind thickness of surface Torlesse greywacke rocks ... 21

2.5 Growth of surface rinds on moraines of Arikaree Cirque, Colorado Front Range ... 23

2.6 Growth of subsurface rinds in basalt and andesite clasts, western United States ... 25

3.1 The Schmidt hammer ... 31

3.2 Factors influencing Schmidt hammer rebound values ... 32

3.3 Variation in the mean R-value and the range of R-values obtained from samples of 50 blows on the test anvil during intensive field trials of three hammers ... 33

3.4 Comparison of mean calibrated values and mean original values obtained from 154 sites on seven glacier forelands in Norway ... 34

3.5 Schmidt hammer rebound values obtained from random and optimized placements on terrain of known age on the foreland of Storbreen, southern Norway ... 35

3.6 Frequency distributions of R-values obtained from boulders of mixed lithology on three sites at Leirbreen, southern Norway (A), compared with R-values obtained from boulders of specific lithologies on the outermost moraine ridge of the foreland (B) ... 37

3.7 The relationship between Schmidt hammer R-values and a measure of degree of weathering of a gabbro surface in Lerdalen, southern Norway ... 38

3.8 Comparison of mean R-values and surface roughness values obtained from boulders with differing transport histories on recently deglaciated terrain ... 39

3.9 Comparison of mean R-values and roughness values obtained from boulders grouped according to roundness ... 40

3.10 Mean roundness and mean R-values obtained from sites on the foreland of Storbreen ... 40

3.11 Mean R-values obtained from points of impact grouped according to roughness on boulders in recently deglaciated (fresh) and approximately 9,000-year-old terrain (weathered) ... 41

viii / FIGURES

4.1 Site locations in southern Butte Valley, Nevada 55
4.2 Known source locations of obsidians represented in the Butte Valley assemblages 58
4.3 Serial order of 13 Butte Valley assemblages, based on mean hydration values for the seven most prevalent obsidians 60
4.4 Distribution of hydration values for Butte Mountain and Browns Bench obsidians in each of the Butte Valley assemblages 63
4.5 Distribution of hydration values for "B," Panaca, and Topaz Mountain obisdians in each of the Butte Valley assemblages 64
4.6 Hydration values of Western Stemmed Tradition and Archaic projectile points for Browns Bench, "B," and Panaca obsidians 71

5.1 Representative barium concentration (A) in the types of varnishes that are appropriate for varnish dating, and (B) in different types of varnish microenvironments not appropriate for varnish dating 81
5.2 Examples of locations of high Ba concentrations in rock varnishes 82
5.3 Cation-leaching curves constructed by PIXE analyses of rock varnishes removed from surfaces of known age. 85
5.4 Laboratory leaching experiments comparing Death Valley rock varnishes still attached to the rock with varnishes that were scraped off the rock and cleaned of contamination 86
5.5 Laboratory leaching experiments on scrapings of Hawaiian rock varnishes 87
5.6 Electron microscope images of polished cross sections of rock varnishes 88
5.7 Generalized steps in the collection, laboratory evaluation, and analysis of samples for cation-ratio dating 90
5.8 Preferred method of assigning calibrated ages to rock varnish cation ratios 93
5.9 Scanning electron microscope images of subvarnish organic matter seen in rock varnish cross-sections 97
5.10 Organic matter in weathering rinds that are encapsulated by rock varnish formed over rock engravings from South Australia 98
5.11 Archaeological examples of varnish dating 102
5.12 Differential development of rock varnish layers formed over petroglyphs, examplified from two sites in South Australia: Wharton Hill and Panaramittee North 103
5.13 Geomorphological examples of varnish dating 105
5.14 Different scenarios in which rock has been exposed to cosmic rays before the most recent alteration event 107

6.1 Curve showing the relation between radiation dose and TL output 117
6.2 Spatial variation in ^{40}K at Cold Water Farm compared to the distribution of artifacts 120
6.3 Schematic of the environments of surface samples 122
6.4 Central Mississippi Valley, showing the location of the study area 123
6.5 Relation of variability in porosity and variability in mean age 132
6.6 Relation of the amount of disequilibrium and sample porosity 134

7.1 A spallation event found in an electron sensitive photographic emulsion, flown near the top of the atmosphere

	(15 g/cm²) by Le Prince-Ringuet et al. (1949)	141
7.2	Depth profiles in surficial rocks, found by Kurz (1986b) for ^{3}He (solid circles) in a Hawaiian lava flow and Brown, Brook, et al (1992) for ^{10}Be (squares) in an Antarctic sandstone	146
7.3	Calculated ^{3}He exposure ages from Hawaiian radiocarbon-dated lava flows compared to the ^{14}C ages for the same flows	149
7.4	^{3}He and ^{10}Be age distributions for a set of glacial moraine boulders in Arena Valley, Southern Victoria Land, Antarctica	150
7.5	^{3}He and ^{10}Be ages for a subsample of the samples shown in Figure 7.4, calculated with ^{3}He and ^{10}Be production rates of 191 and 7 atoms/g/yr, respectively	151
8.1	Normalized cosmogenic ^{36}Cl at atmospheric depths from 620 g/cm² (elevation 4,090 m above sea level) to 1,020 g/cm² (elevation 120 m)	164
8.2	Distribution of thermal and fast neutrons in the shallow subsurface, normalized to the surface values	166
8.3	Buildup of cosmogenic ^{36}Cl in the surface in rocks	167
8.4	Comparison of cosmogenic ^{36}Cl ages (Phillips et al. 1990; Zreda et al. 1990) with thermoluminescence (Sutton 1985a) selected ^{26}Al/^{10}Be ages (Nishiizumi et al. 1991) for Meteor Crater, Arizona	170
8.5	Distribution of cosmogenic ^{36}Cl boulder ages among the moraines at Bloody Canyon, Sierra Nevada, California (after Phillips et al. 1990 and Phillips et al. 1991)	172
8.6	Conceptual model for the cosmogenic ^{36}Cl buildup in boulders initially buried in soil and gradually exposed at the surface by erosion	173
8.7	Accumulation paths of cosmogenic ^{36}Cl in subsurface rocks in which half of the produced ^{36}Cl is due to spallation of ^{39}K and ^{40}Ca and half due to thermal neutron activation of ^{35}Cl	175
8.8	Relationship between erosion x_{max} and the coefficient of variation calculated for simulated ^{36}Cl buildup ages for sample MC-1 from Meteor Crater, Arizona	175
8.9	Simulation of ^{36}Cl buildup ages for Meteor Crater samples	176
8.10	Simulation of ^{36}Cl buildup ages in sample MC-1 from Meteor Crater, Arizona	176
8.11	Simulation of ^{36}Cl buildup ages for the Tioga moraine, Bloody Canyon, Sierra Nevada, California	177
8.12	Simulation of ^{36}Cl buildup ages for the Tenaya moraine, Bloody Canyon, Sierra Nevada, California	177
8.13	Distributions of apparent ^{36}Cl buildup ages for surfaces of actual ages of 10 ka and 100 ka with different values of erosion depth x_{max} and the erosion rate ε	178
8.14	Distributions of apparent ^{36}Cl buildup ages for a surface with an erosion depth x_{max} of 1,000 g/cm² and three sets of values of the actual age t and the erosion rate ε	178
8.15	Topographic correction calculated as a function of the angle θ between the sampling point and the top of the topographic feature partially blocking cosmic rays	179
9.1	Locations of lichenometric dating studies in southern Norway	187
9.2	Map of moraine ridges on the glacier foreland of Nigardsbreen	190
9.3	Lichen sizes on moraine surfaces of	

x / FIGURES

	known age at Nigardsbreen	191
9.4	Selected lichenometric dating curves from glacier forelands in southern Norway	192
9.5	Lichenometric dates for four moraines of unknown age on the Storbreen glacier foreland, Jotunheimen	193
9.6	The size of the "one in a thousand" lichen for different subplots on moraines of various ages at Nigardsbreen	196
9.7	Direct growth measurements of the *Rhizocarpon* subgenus at Nigardsbreen	198
9.8	Preliminary direct lichen growth curves for Nigardsbreen, based on the data in Figure 9.7, in relation to indirect lichenometric dating curves	199
10.1	Generalized anatomy of the base and upper root system of the tree	215
10.2	The bristlecone pine (*Pinus longaeva*), the longest-lived tree in the world, has been a treasure-house of information for dendrochronologists	216
10.3	Principle for constructing a long chronology by cross-dating and matching separate ring-width series	218
10.4	Under favorable conditions trees may invade new land surfaces in a matter of a few years	221
10.5	This mobile coastal dune has been burying pines on its slipface side	223
10.6	Idealized scheme depicting barrel-shaped growth of a pine buried in dune sand in three stages	224
10.7	Degradation has caused barrel-shaped growth in the exposed roots of a pine	225
10.8	The inclination of trees can be dated from the tree rings, which become eccentric after tilting	226
10.9	Schematic representation of the development and radial growth of adventitious roots	228
10.10	The development of layers and a candelabrum tree (A) and the formation of stem sprouts (B)	230
10.11	The age of a scar on a living tree can be determined by counting the annual rings of the callous margin	231

TABLES

2.1 Regression Coefficients for Surface-Rind Calibrations, Torlesse Greywacke — 21

4.1 Geochemical Obsidian Types Represented in the Butte Valley Assemblages — 57
4.2 Effective Hydration Temperature and Relative Humidity Calculations at Three Localities over a Period of Two Years — 59
4.3 Summary of Hydration Measurements over Seven Obsidian Types and the Thirteen Assemblages in the Serial Order — 62
4.4 Temporal Grouping of Assemblages within Each Obsidian Type — 65
4.5 Distribution of Projectile Points of WST, Early Archaic, and Mid-to-Late Archaic Periods across Seven Obsidian Types — 67
4.6 The Occurrence of 34 Geochemical Obsidian Types in Butte Valley Site and Offsite Assemblages — 68
4.7 Western Stemmed Tradition, Early Archaic, and Untyped Projectile Points Represented in Four Butte Valley Assemblages — 69
4.8 Material Composition of Four Butte Valley Assemblages — 69

5.1 Methods of Estimating the Age of Rock-Varnish Formation — 79
5.2 Different Types of Rock Varnishes — 80
5.3 Wavelength Dispersive Electron Microprobe Analyses of Points in Figure 5.2 — 83
5.4 Electron Microprobe (Wavelength Dispersive) Analyses along Transects of Porous and Layered Varnishes Delineated in Figure 5.6, as Compared to Bulk Samples of Varnish from the Same Site (from Dorn and Krinsley 1991) — 89
5.5 Factors Known to Influence a Cation Ratio of Black (Mn-rich) Rock Varnish Other Than Time — 91
5.6 Issues of Contention in Cation-Ratio Dating — 94

6.1 Woodland and Mississippian Radiocarbon Dates from the Malden Plain and Western Lowlands/Eastern Ozarks — 125
6.2 Woodland and Mississippian Thermoluminescence Dates from the Malden Plain and Western Lowlands/Eastern Ozarks — 126
6.3 University of Washington Woodland and Mississippian Thermoluminescence Dates from the Malden Plain — 128
6.4 Porosity and Depth Data for Table 6.3 Dates, with 100°C or Better Plateaus — 129
6.5 Means and Standard Deviations for Age and Porosity, by Locality — 130
6.6 Disequilibrium Data and Corrections — 133

7.1 Some Cosmogenic Nuclides Used for Exposure Dating — 142
7.2 Estimates of ^{3}He Production Rates Scaled to Sea Level and above 50° Geomagnetic

Latitude, Using Four Scaling Methods Discussed in Text   147

8.1 Scaling Formulation for Elevation and Geomagnetic Latitude in the Form of a Series of Cubic Polynomials ($y=a+bx+cx^2+dx^3$), Where x Is the Elevation Above Sea Level in km and y Is the Scaling Factor, Fitted to the Observed Thermal Neutron Data of Lal (1991)   163

8.2 Relative Contribution of Major Cosmogenic Reactions Leading to the Production of ^{36}Cl in the Top 100 g/cm² in Examples of Terrestrial Rocks (Granites, Basalts, Carbonates, and Shales) at Sea Level and High Geomagnetic Latitudes   165

8.3 Thermal Neutron Absorption Cross Section, σ, of the Elements Contributing Significantly to the Total Macroscopic Thermal Neutron Cross Section, $\Sigma\sigma N$ 168

8.4 Production Rates of ^{36}Cl from Its Main Target Elements and the Absorption Rate of Thermal Neutrons; Negative Muons are Included in the Spallation of ^{40}Ca 169

8.5 Concentration of Target Nuclides, Macroscopic Cross Sections, $^{36}Cl/CL$ Values, and ^{36}Cl Ages of Meteor Crater   169

8.6 Concentration of Target Nuclides, Macroscopic Cross Sections, $^{36}Cl/Cl$ Values, and ^{36}Cl Ages of the Bloody Canyon Samples   171

9.1 Lichenometric Dates for Moraine Ridges at Nigardsbreen, southern Norway   194

9.2 Applications of Lichenometric Dating Excluding Moraines   201

ACKNOWLEDGMENTS

I would like to thank Robert C. Dunnell for his suggestion several years ago that I begin this project and for his continuing support throughout. It is largely due to him and to Donald K. Grayson that I became involved in surface archaeology and have come to view the surface record as a valuable source of data and information. I would also like to thank my authors who have been so diligent and so patient throughout this long process. My greatest gratitude, however, goes to my husband George T. Jones, who has given me his continual support and encouragement and without whose help I would have never made it. Thanks Tom.

DATING
IN EXPOSED
AND SURFACE CONTEXTS

1
INTRODUCTION

Charlotte Beck

Department of Anthropology
Hamilton College
Clinton, New York

SCIENTISTS WHO DEAL WITH PAST PROCESSES that leave exposed and/or surficial records all share the problem of dating those records. As an archaeologist concerned with patterns of land use among prehistoric hunter-gatherers of the arid western United States, I am confronted by a primarily surficial archaeological record that is widely distributed over many kinds of topographic settings but that has proven very difficult to control chronologically. Most chronometric methods, such as radiocarbon dating, are considered inapplicable to surface deposits, since exposure potentially can contaminate or destroy the integrity of the datable sample. Thus archaeologists who are attempting to utilize surface data have had to turn to other, much less precise approaches that often lead to unsatisfactory results. Geomorphologists face a similar dilemma, in that many past physical processes have left their signatures in exposed rather than in stratigraphic contexts. In order to date these exposed features using standard methods such as radiocarbon dating, suitable datable material must be located in subsurface deposits, and the dates obtained must then be correlated in some way with the exposed features.

Such a state of affairs is unacceptable for scientists who need to study not just isolated points in the landscape but the evolution of the landscape itself; or in the case of the archaeologist, the distribution of cultural material across that landscape. Thus the difficulty lies not just in establishing an age estimate for a moraine or a soil, for an artifact or a site, but in developing chronologies for entire landscapes. For the geomorphologist whose aim is to understand the sequence and interaction of past processes that have produced the landforms we see today, focusing on stratigraphic sequences at isolated points is much too limiting; these land surfaces need to be seen in conjunction from a "horizontal" as well as a "vertical" point of view. For the archaeologist whose focus is the relation of humans to the environment, it is critical to understand the human past in the context of the contemporaneous landscape.

One of the difficulties for both geomorphologists and archaeologists has been that dating is generally applied not to the event of interest, or the "target event" (Dunnell and Readhead 1988), but to some other event that must be shown to be associated with the target event. As Dunnell and Readhead (1988) point out, the two are rarely synonymous in either geology or archaeology. What is desperately needed is a set of dating methods that are applicable directly to the exposed physical and cultural features about which chronological information is sought. Researchers will then not have to rely on arguments of association between material from subsurface deposits and the exposed features being studied.

Recently researchers in geology, archaeology, geography, chemistry, and physics have attempted too deal with the surface dating problem in several ways. First, methods used for some time in the dating of surface exposures, such as rock weathering, have been improved considerably, moving from simple relative-age estimates to the development of calibrated-age curves for particular weathering sequences. Second, methods such as obsidian hydration and thermoluminescence dating, originally applied only to subsurface deposits, have been applied with success to surface deposits. And finally, new methods have been developed specifically for application to exposed features, such as those based on the use of cosmogenic nuclides. Such efforts hold great promise for the development of landscape chronologies by both geomorphologists and archaeologists alike.

The aim of this volume is to present a number of these methods in systematic detail, while demonstrating their successful use in the dating of the surface artifact record and exposed features of the natural landscape. These approaches share not only their applicability to surface and exposed features, but also have the advantage of dating directly the target event, thus eliminating reliance on the associational argument. The treatment of methods that might be applicable in surface and/or exposed contexts is certainly not exhaustive, but is meant as a first cooperative effort among scientists of different backgrounds to address the real problem of dating in these contexts.

The methods presented here are applied in a variety of specific situations, both archaeological and geomorphological, but have the potential for more general cross-disciplinary application. For example Matthews in chapter 9 uses lichenometry to date newly deglaciated surfaces in Norway, but this approach can also be applied in archaeological contexts, where it has already seen limited use in the dating of features such as stone house rings (see Bettinger and Oglesby 1985) and hunting blinds (see Benedict 1975). Conversely thermoluminescence is used by Dunnell and Feathers (chapter 6) for the dating of ceramic artifacts from surface archaeological assemblages in Missouri, but the method can also be used for dating geological events, such as volcanic eruptions and loess deposition (see Huntley 1976).

Not only are these methods applicable in both geological and archaeological situations, but the dates obtained in one realm can also be useful in the other. For instance cultural material of known age can often provide an independent means of evaluating a method developed in other disciplines, such as geology or physics. When Libby needed material with which to test his new radiocarbon method, for example, he turned to archaeology. Furthermore, where the dating of natural landforms can provide maximum limiting dates for archaeological deposits and/or features, the dating of the cultural landscape can provide minimum limiting dates for natural landforms. Used in conjunction, then, the methods in this volume provide the opportunity for reconstructing paleolandscapes as well as the histories of those landscapes, including both physical and cultural elements.

A Note on Terminology

Over the past 50 years, a great deal of research has been undertaken in the dating of both geological and cultural events, and the methods that have been developed yield results that vary widely in precision and accuracy. The terminology that has evolved to categorize these methods is often confusing, if not inaccurate. The term *absolute,* for instance, is used by many researchers to refer to methods that yield quantitative results but most of which have degrees of uncertainty attached. Colman et al. (1987:315), in reviewing the situation for Quaternary dating methods, have suggested that the term *absolute* be abandoned altogether, since most quantitative dating methods yield results that are far from "absolute." They suggest four categories, based on the type of result produced (1987:317–318), and this terminology is followed in this volume. *Numerical-age* methods are those that produce results on a ratio (or absolute) scale, but that may have uncertainties attached; *calibrated-age* methods are those in which individual rates of particular processes must be calibrated by independent chronological control; *relative-age* methods produce sequences of events; and *correlated-age* methods are methods in which age estimates are produced through correlation (association) with independently dated events.

Geomorphological Dating

Quantitative chronological control of landforms has primarily been based on datable material from a stratigraphic sequence, using methods most appropriately applied in subsurface contexts, such as potassium-argon, fission-track, amino acid racemization, and radiocarbon dating (Dorn and Phillips 1991:303). Although some progress has been made in viewing landscapes not as stratigraphic points but as continuous spatial entities, "geomorphologists have been trained to think in terms of stratigraphic columns" (Dorn and Phillips 1991:304).

This is not to say that exposed geomorphological features have not been dated in the past; on the contrary, there is a long history of relative dating of these features, beginning in the 1930s with the dating of glacial moraines in the Sierra Nevada (see Blackwelder 1931; Matthes 1930) and continuing up to the present (McCarroll 1991). The geomorphological surface record has long been viewed as an important source of information, but as a record that is simply difficult to date. In fact many of the landforms of interest to geomorphologists occur in exposed or partially exposed contexts and must be studied if knowledge of the processes responsible for their formation is to be gained.

Most of the earlier relative dating studies were "semiquantitative," in that although they involved some measurement, they also relied on subjective decisions of the researcher (McCarroll 1991:175). After the mid-1960s, however, there was a gradual movement away from semiquantitative approaches, toward greater accuracy of measurement (McCarroll 1991:175). McCarroll (1991) recognizes two approaches in modern weathering-based dating that can be expanded more generally. In the chronosequence approach, a sequence in space is assumed to parallel a sequence in time; in raised shorelines, for instance, higher altitude often implies greater age. Time, however, may not be the only factor that varies in parallel with a spatial sequence. In the case of modern shorelines, there are environmental trends away from these shorelines that also parallel the trend in age, which, if they influence rock weathering rates, can result in misleading dates for these landforms.

A more reliable approach is found in the derivation of chronofunctions, since an independent dating method is involved. The chronofunction approach involves correlating the results of the prospective dating method with ages determined independently. It is still necessary, however, to control the effects of "other factors," such as environmental trends, in order to minimize potential error (McCarroll 1991). One way in which this has been done is through a determination of the degree of rock weathering, which can then be related to age. Two approaches to this type of study discussed in this volume involve the measurement of rind thickness (Knuepfer, chapter 2) and of rebound values from the Schmidt hammer (McCarroll, chapter 3).

Weathering studies were first used in the relative dating of glacial deposits in the Sierra Nevada (Blackwelder 1931; Matthes 1930). Since that time a number of techniques have been developed to obtain not only relative but also calibrated ages based on the degree of rock weathering (see Colman 1981). In chapter 2 Knuepfer, using examples from New Zealand and the western United States, reviews the use of weathering rind measurement for the calculation of relative and calibrated ages for landforms and surfaces such as talus, moraines, stream terraces, and deglaciated surfaces.

In chapter 3 McCarroll discusses a technique for the determination of the surface hardness of rock, which is a relative measure of the degree of weathering of that rock. This technique uses an instrument called the Schmidt hammer, which was originally developed to measure the surface hardness of concrete; its usefulness for geological applications, however, was quickly realized. Although Schmidt hammer results can be influenced by several factors other than the degree of weathering, as McCarroll discusses, the instrument provides an inexpensive, on-site technique that has been applied successfully to glacial moraines, landslide debris, and frost-shattered shorelines, among other features. McCarroll uses examples from his own work in the dating of glacial moraines in Norway.

Regarding quantitative age control, geomorphologists have suffered the same difficulties as archaeologists, in that most tried and true chronometric methods are not appropriate for exposed situations. As a consequence suitable material for dating, usually using isotopic approaches, must be located and then the date obtained must be correlated in some way with the landform under study. This approach is limited, in that datable material is often not available. If, however, such dates can be obtained, to apply the dates to most exposed landforms, the sedimentation rate must be known or assumed (Knuepfer, chapter 2). This problem can only be overcome by directly dating the landforms of interest.

Established Calibrated-Age and Numerical-Age Approaches

It is not quite accurate to say that there have been no calibrated-age or numerical-age dating methods in use for exposed features until recently. Lichenometry, for instance, was first used in 1950 (see Beschel 1950) and has seen considerable development since that time. Although its use has been limited for the most part to alpine and polar environments above the tree line, lichenometry has been widely applied to moraine ridges or recently deglaciated terrain in these environments. Matthews (chapter 9) discusses the method in detail and its application to Little Ice Age moraine sequences from southern Norway.

Dendrochronology is also a method that has been available for some time (see Douglas 1919, 1928, 1936); when it can be used, it provides potentially the most precise dates of any method available today. As Heikkinen notes in chapter 10, dendrochronology is used in climatological, hydrological, ecological, and archaeological studies. The approach that he discusses, dendrogeomorphology, is relatively recent in its development, however, and is used to study and date geomorphic processes such as flooding, volcanic eruptions, mass movements, and glacial retreat, through the dating of virgin soil development. Heikkinen demonstrates with his own work in Finland and the western United States how minimum ages for virgin soil development can be derived from the first trees to become rooted there.

Although Dunnell and Feathers (chapter 6) use thermoluminescence for the dating of archaeological materials, this approach saw its earliest uses in health physics, as a means of hazard detection in the vicinity of nuclear reactor sites and also to insure the safety of patients in radiotherapy (Fleming 1979:1). This work was followed shortly by geological applications, such as the identification of mineral sources, pressure and shock wave detection, the dating of marine invertebrates, and the dating of carbonate sediments (Fleming 1979:1). Dunnell and Feathers suggest that thermoluminescence is applicable to nearly all crystalline materials and thus has the potential to date physical events, such as loess deposition and alluviation, as well as some biological events, such as the formation of hydroxyapatite crystals in bone or calcite and/or aragonite crystals in shell.

Finally obsidian hydration (Beck and Jones, chapter 4), first presented in 1960 by Friedman and Smith, has been used primarily by archaeologists and almost exclusively in subsurface contexts. Obsidian hydration, however, has seen limited use in the dating of glacial and fluvial features (see Adams et al. 1992; Pierce et al. 1976) as well as events of vulcanism (see Friedman and Obradovich 1981). Obsidian hydration dating has wide applicability in situations where obsidian is present and could be used at least in a relative if not a calibrated-age or numerical-age manner for the dating of exposed geomorphological features.

New Calibrated-Age and Numerical-Age Approaches

Over the last decade or so, a number of new approaches have been developed for quantitative age measurement of exposed and surface geological features. These include cation-ratio and radiocarbon dating of rock varnish, accumulation of cosmogenic radionuclides ^{10}Be, ^{14}C, ^{26}Al, ^{36}Cl, and ^{41}Ca, and accumulation of the cosmogenic stable nuclides ^{3}He and ^{21}Ne (Dorn and Phillips 1991). Most of these methods are in various stages of development and thus still suffer from some degree of uncertainty; even so, they hold the greatest promise for numerical-age determinations of exposed geomorphological surfaces.

Although the occurrence and dating potential of rock varnish has been recognized for some time, only recently have methods been developed for quantitative age calculations of varnish accumulation (see Bard 1979; Dorn 1983, 1989; Dorn et al. 1989; Dorn and Oberlander 1982). Varnish dating yields minimum ages for the exposure of the underlying rock surface and thus can constrain ages of landforms that have no other source of quantitative age control. This approach is most effective in desert contexts, since varnish tends to dissolve in acidic environments (Phillips and Dorn 1991). In chapter 5 Dorn discusses the two most widely used approaches for dating black, manganese-rich varnishes: cation-ratio dating, which yields relative or calibrated ages, and accelerator radiocarbon dating, which yields numerical ages. Dorn discusses geomorphological applications, including the dating of glacial moraines, colluvium, exposed bedrock, and alluvial fans.

Dorn, in his final statements, suggests that in spite of the usefulness of varnish dating, the methods with the most promise for the future are those based on the accumulation of cosmogenic nuclides. In chapter 7 Kurz and Brook review several of these, while in chapter 8 Zreda and Phillips discuss ^{36}Cl in detail. These methods are based on the accumulation of cosmogenic nuclides, or nuclides produced by cosmic ray particles, in rocks exposed at the surface. If it is assumed that the cosmic ray flux in the atmosphere has been constant over time, then the concentration of these nuclides within surface rocks is directly related to the exposure time of those rocks (see Kurz and Brook, chapter 7). Kurz and Brook provide a description of the underlying principles of dating with cosmogenic nuclides and then address specific methods using ^{3}He, ^{21}Ne, ^{10}Be, and ^{26}Al.

In chapter 8 Zreda and Phillips detail the method that focuses on cosmogenic ^{36}Cl, first discussing the accumulation of ^{36}Cl in surface materials and then specifically outlining how this accumulation can be used for dating surface exposures. The method is then applied in two different contexts: a well-preserved meteor impact crater in Arizona and a set of late Pleistocene moraines in the Sierra Nevada. Although this method has been highly successful thus far, Zreda and Phillips caution that it is still under development.

Archaeological Dating

The dating of the surface archaeological record has been in many ways analogous to that in geology, but in equally many ways has been quite different. Like geomorphologists, archaeologists have been "trained to think in terms of stratigraphic columns" (Dorn and Phillips 1991:304), but unlike geomorphologists, many archaeologists continue to view the surface record as not particularly useful. The surface archaeological record can be viewed as consisting of two fairly distinct components, each with its own set of dating problems. The first of these comprises exposed features, such as cairns, rock circles and alignments, and rock art. These nonportable artifacts have proven most difficult to date when they are completely exposed, since their dating relies on arguments of association with datable adjacent artifact scatters or with dates obtained in stratigraphic context nearby. Associational arguments are more easily made between a diagnostic artifact, such as a projectile point, of known age and a debitage flake of the same material lying in close proximity, than between that same projectile point and an adjacent cairn, although such arguments are commonly made. It is even more problematic to apply a radiocarbon date from a stratigraphic sequence to a cairn near the stratigraphic cut.

Several of the methods discussed in this volume are applicable in precisely these situations. Lichenometry (Matthews, chapter 9) has been applied to exposed archaeological as well as natural features. Although the use of lichens to date archaeological features was first proposed in 1939 (see Renaud 1939), its use in this capacity has thus far been rather limited. Benedict (1975) used lichenometry to date a hunting blind and game drive system in the Rocky Mountains of Colorado. Some years later, Bettinger and Oglesby (1985) obtained lichenometric dates for 50 late-prehistoric house structures as well as for a number of other aboriginal and European features in ten alpine villages located in the White Mountains of eastern California (see also Broadbent and Bergquist 1986; Winchester 1988). For those features located in alpine situations, lichenometry has a great deal of potential, in that it provides artifact-specific dates for archaeological features that may otherwise be undatable.

Cation-ratio and radiocarbon dating of rock varnish (Dorn, chapter 5) are also applicable to exposed cultural features. Varnish dating yields a minimum age for the exposure of the underlying rock surface before the formation of the varnish on that surface. Both cation-ratio and radiocarbon dating have been successfully applied to petroglyphs in Australia (Nobbs and Dorn 1993) and the western United States (Dorn et al. 1992; Dorn and Whitley 1984; Whitley and Dorn 1987), as well as to the Nazca geoglyphs and subterranean irrigation aqueducts in Peru (Dorn et al. 1992).

Rock weathering can also be used to provide relative and calibrated age estimates for rock alignments, cairns, and house rings in the same way as it is used to date glacial moraines (Knuepfer, chapter 2; McCarroll, chapter 3; see Sjöberg 1987). The cosmogenic nuclide methods discussed by Kurz and Brook (chapter 7) and Zreda and Phillips (chapter 8) can potentially provide numerical estimates for these features, since these approaches have thus far been used to date a variety of minerals and rock types (e.g., olivine, quartz, basalt, and sandstone) in moraines and lava flows. And finally the use of dendrochronology (Heikkinen, chapter 10) to date virgin soil development might in fact be used to provide minimum dates for cultural features such as petroglyphs that are partially buried by these soils.

The second component of the archaeological surface record comprises scatters, both dense and sparse, of artifacts, such as lithics, pottery, and bone, across the land surface. This second component has an added disadvantage over the rock features discussed above, in that these artifacts are portable, and their original depositional position can easily be changed through natural and/or cultural disturbance (see O'Connell 1987).

Although the portable artifact record saw limited use throughout the first half of the twentieth century, its systematic use did not begin until the early 1950s, with the new interest in settlement and land use patterns (see Willey 1951, 1953). Subsequently archaeological focus began to change from the "site" to the "region," an approach that was strongly emphasized by the mid-1960s. Out of necessity the surface record came to play a major role in this approach, since the excavation of an entire region is an impossible task. It was not, however, until cultural resource management became so prevalent that researchers truly began to look at the surface record as a viable source of information (Dunnell 1979; Dunnell and Dancey 1983; Goodyear et al. 1978; Plog et al. 1978).

In a paper detailing the potential of the portable surface record in archaeology, Lewarch and O'Brien (1981b:311–312) outlined seven commonly cited reasons for not using surface data. These can be summarized as follows: (1) post-depositional disturbance due to natural forces, agricultural practices, and amateur artifact collecting; (2) the lack of congruence between patterned subsurface deposits and nonpatterned surface ones; and (3) the lack of analytical potential, especially chronological control.

Regarding the first two of these concerns, a great deal of evaluative work has been undertaken. For instance controlled studies of archaeological remains in plowed fields suggest that lateral movement due to plowing does not result in significant transverse and longitudinal displacement as a result of long-term tillage (Lewarch 1979; Lewarch and O'Brien 1981a; see also Roper 1976; Trubowitz 1978). Furthermore postdepositional disturbance of surface deposits due to natural factors is no greater than that experienced by many buried deposits (Schiffer 1972, 1987). Indeed buried deposits may once have lain on the surface (Dunnell and Dancey 1983) and may therefore have experienced disturbances common to both surface and subsurface contexts. Foley (1981) emphasizes that the depositional history of an artifact is not necessarily a simple one, even after burial. Once an artifact is buried, this situation cannot be assumed to be permanent; the artifact may be reexposed and subsequently reburied. This process may occur several times, and thus it cannot be assumed that "buried means *in situ*" (Foley 1981:170).

Many studies have also been performed concerning the relation between surface materials and the subsurface deposits they overlie (see Binford et al. 1970; Hole and Heizer 1973; Kirkby and Kirkby 1976; Redman and Watson 1970). This research has shown that the surface record is often patterned and that it is a good predictor of the structure of subsurface deposits, if they are present, although the degree of isomorphism between the two can be expected to diminish with increasing depth of the subsurface deposit (Lewarch and O'Brien 1981b:314). Dunnell and Dancey, however, contend that surface deposits constitute an appropriate source of archaeological data independent of subsurface remains (1983:270).

Although I am in full agreement with Dunnell and Dancey on this point, their contention can hold only if chronological control of the surface record can be obtained. The problem of dating the portable artifact record has not been treated in as systematic a manner as the first two concerns. Surface assemblages are most commonly dated using one or both of two methods: seriation and typological cross-dating. Both of these methods are based on the use of temporally sensitive artifact classes, such as pottery, basketry, or projectile points. These approaches rely on the principle of association: first that artifacts in close proximity are associated in space, and second that chronological information carried by associated time-sensitive artifacts can be transferred to all artifacts in an assemblage (Jones and Beck 1992). It is often the case, however, that few or no temporally sensitive artifacts are found in a surface assemblage, a problem that can be accentuated by the removal of such artifacts by amateur or professional artifact collectors (Lewarch and O'Brien 1981:316).

Even when diagnostics are present, both seriation and typological cross-dating are severely limited by the associational argument, especially in light of how the surface archaeological record accumulates. Artifact discard may be more or less a continuous process through time, and thus a heavily used landscape may at one point in time exhibit an artifact record with a tightly clustered appearance and then at some later time, after extended use, one that appears nonclustered and continuous across space (Foley 1981:159; see also, O'Connell 1987). In addition localities that tend to be reused by the same or different populations exhibit what has been termed the "palimpsest effect" (Aston and Rowley 1974:14); that is, an accumulation of many occupational events incorporating similar or differing activities over a long period of time. Such accumulations are more often than not impossible to separate and date using seriation or typological cross-dating.

A number of the methods discussed in this volume can be used to deal with both continuous, nonclustered distributions and palimpsests by dating individual artifacts. Beck and Jones (chapter 4), for instance, use obsidian hydration dating to demonstrate contemporaneity and association, as well as to establish a chronological order of assemblages. As noted above, obsidian hydration dating has been used in archaeology since the early 1960s, but its use has been almost exclusively in subsurface contexts (but see Michels 1967). Beck and Jones detail the hydration process and those factors affecting it in both subsurface and surface situations, concluding that obsidian hydration dating is as appropriate for use in the latter as in the former, at least for relative age control. The dating of surface artifacts by this approach is evaluated using an example from eastern Nevada.

The potential of thermoluminescence for the dating of archaeological ceramics was first suggested in 1953 by Farrington Daniels at the University of Wisconsin (Michels 1973:189). As Dunnell and Feathers (chapter 6) note, however, this method has been used primarily in Europe and in subsurface contexts; its lack of application to surface assemblages has been mainly due to distrust of the surface artifactual record. They describe the thermoluminescence dating method, suggesting that in fact it may be more accurate in surface than in subsurface contexts. Dunnell and Feathers use an example from southeast Missouri, in which thermoluminescence dating is applied to ceramics from the plowzone; they suggest, however, that the method is applicable to a wide range of materials, including heat-treated lithics, hearths, and, as noted earlier, possibly bone and shell.

Rock varnish dating has already been discussed as a method appropriate for the dating of archaeological rock features, such as stone circles and rock art. This approach has seen limited use in the dating of portable artifacts as well (see Bamforth and Dorn 1988), and thus can also be useful in dealing with the problems of surface mixing and contemporaneity. Other methods discussed in the volume, such as those used to measure rock weathering (Knuepfer, chapter 2; McCarroll, chapter 3) have the potential to produce at least relative-age, if not calibrated-age sequences for lithics. Although they have not yet been applied to archaeological data, the cosmogenic nuclide approaches also have potential in this direction, especially for dating such materials as basalt and quartz (Kurz, personal communication). All of the methods discussed by Kurz and Brook (chapter 7) and Zreda and Phillips (chapter 8) are applicable to at least mid-Holocene and earlier archaeological assemblages.

Conclusion

This volume represents a first combined effort among disciplines to address a major problem: the dating of surface and/or exposed features. Geomorphologists have been attempting to address this problem in a systematic way over the past few years, as evidenced by their participation in two recent conferences on the subject (see Dietrich and Monaghan 1987; Phillips and Dorn 1991). Archaeologists as well have been attempting to address the surface dating issue, although on more of an individual basis. It seems reasonable, then, that we should combine our efforts toward the single goal of dating the surface and exposed record. The methods presented here provide means of directly dating target events of different aspects of the exposed landscape; the development of various landforms, such as moraines, talus, soils, mass movements, beaches, terraces, and alluvial fans; as well as exposed archaeological features and artifact scatters, all of which go together to form the landscape.

References Cited

Adams, K. D., W. W. Locke, and R. Rossi
1992 Obsidian Hydration Dating of Fluvially Reworked Sediments in the West Yellowstone Region, Montana. *Quaternary Research* 38:180–195.

Aston, M., and T. Rowley
1974 *Landscape Archaeology: An Introduction to Fieldwork Techniques on the Post-Roman Landscape.* David and Charles, London.

Bamforth, D. B., and R. I. Dorn
1988 On the Nature and Antiquity of the Manix Lake Lithic Industry. *Journal of California and Great Basin Anthropology* 10:209–226.

Bard, J. C.
1979 *The Development of a Patination Dating Technique for Great Basin Petroglyphs Utilizing Neutron Activation and X-Ray Fluorescence Analyses.* Unpublished Ph.D. dissertation, University of California, Berkeley.

Benedict, J. B.
1975 The Murray Site: A Late Prehistoric Game Drive System in the Colorado Rocky Mountains. *Plains Anthropologist* 20:169–174.

Beschel, R. E.
1950 Flechten als Altersmassstab Rezenter Moränen. *Zeitschrift für Gletscherkunde und Glazialgeologie* 1:152–161.

Bettinger, R. L., and R. Oglesby
1985 Lichen Dating of Alpine Villages in the White Mountains, California. *Journal of California and Great Basin Anthropology* 7:202–224.

Binford, L. R., S. R. Binford, R. Whallon, and M. A. Hardin
1970 *Archaeology at Hatchery West.* Society for American Archaeology, Memoir No. 24.

Blackwelder, E.
1931 Pleistocene Glaciation of the Sierra Nevada and Basin Ranges. *Geological Society of America Bulletin* 42:865–922.

Broadbent, N. D., and K. I. Bergqvist.
1986 Lichenometric Chronology and Archaeological Features on Raised Beaches: Preliminary Results from the Swedish North Bothnian Coastal Region. *Arctic and Alpine Research* 18:297–306.

Colman, S. M.
1981 Rock Weathering Rates as Functions of Time. *Quaternary Research* 15:250–264.

Colman, S. M., K. L. Pierce, and P. W. Birkeland
1987 Suggested Terminology for Quaternary Dating Methods. *Quaternary Research* 28:314–319.

Dietrich, W. E., and M. C. Monaghan
1987 New Approaches to the Geochronometry of Earth Surface Processes. *Eos* 68:1286–1289.

Dorn, R. I.
1983 Cation-Ratio Dating: A New Rock Varnish Age Determination Technique. *Quaternary Research* 20:49–73.
1989 Cation-Ratio Dating of Rock Varnish: A Geographical Perspective. *Progress in Physical Geography* 13:559–596.

Dorn, R. I., Clarkson, M. F. Nobbs, L. L. Loendorf, and D. S. Whitley
1992 Radiocarbon Dating Inclusions of Organic Matter in Rock Varnish with Examples from Drylands. *Annals of the Association of American Geographers* 82:136–151.

Dorn, R. I., A. J. T. Jull, D. J. Donahue, T. W. Linick, and L. T. Toolin
1989 Accelerator Mass Spectrometry Radiocarbon Dating of Rock Varnish. *Geological Society of American Bulletin* 101:1363–1372.

Dorn, R. I., and T. M. Oberlander
1982 Rock Varnish. *Progress in Physical Geography* 6:317–367.

Dorn, R. I., and F. M. Phillips
1991 Surface Exposure Dating: Review and Critical Evaluation. *Physical Geography* 12: 303–333.

Dorn, R. I., and D. S. Whitley
1984 Chronometric and Relative Age Determination of Petroglyphs in the Western United States. *Annals of the Association of American Geographers* 74:308–322.

Douglas, A. E.
1919 *Climatic Cycles and Tree-Growth,* vol. I. Carnegie Institution of Washington, Washington, D.C.
1928 *Climatic Cycles and Tree-Growth,* vol. II. Carnegie Institution of Washington, Washington, D.C.
1936 *Climatic Cycles and Tree-Growth,* vol. III. Carnegie Institution of Washington, Washington, D.C.

Dunnell, R. C.
1979 Trends in Current Americanist Archaeology. *American Journal of Archaeology* 83:437–448.

Dunnell, R. C., and W. S. Dancey
1983 The Siteless Survey: A Regional Scale Data Collection Strategy. In *Advances in Archaeological Method and Theory,* edited by M. B. Schiffer, vol. 6, pp. 267–287. Academic Press, New York.

Dunnell, R. C., and M. L. Readhead
1988 The Relation of Dating and Chronology: Comments on Chatters and Hoover (1986) and Butler and Stein (1988). *Quaternary Research* 30:232–233.

Fleming, S.
1979 *Thermoluminescence Techniques in Archaeology.* Clarendon Press, Oxford.

Foley, R.
1981 Off-Site Archaeology: An Alternative Approach for the Short-Sited. In *Patterns of the Past, Studies in Honour of David Clarke,* edited by I. Hodder, G. Isaac, and N. Hammond, pp. 157–183. Cambridge University Press, Cambridge.

Friedman, I., and R. L. Smith
1960 A New Dating Method Using Obsidian: Part I. The Development of the Technique. *American Antiquity* 33:149–155.

Friedman, I., and J. Obradovich
1981 Obsidian Hydration Dating of Volcanic Events. *Quaternary Research* 16:37–47.

Goodyear, A. C., L. M. Raab, and T. C. Klinger
1978 The Status of Archaeological Research Design in Cultural Resource Management. In Contributions to Archaeological Method and Theory, edited by M. B. Schiffer. *American Antiquity* 43:159–173.

Hole, F., and R. F. Heizer
1973 *An Introduction to Prehistoric Archaeology.* Holt, Rinehart, and Winston, New York.

Huntley, D. J.
1976 Thermoluminescence as a Potential Means of Dating Siliceous Ocean Sediments. *Canadian Journal of Earth Sciences* 13:593–596.

Jones, G. T., and C. Beck
1992 Chronological Resolution in Distributional Archaeology. In *Place, Time, and Archaeological Landscapes,* edited by L. Wandsnider and J. Rossignol, pp. 167–192. Plenum Press, London.

Kirkby, A., and M. J. Kirkby
1976 Geomorphic Processes and the Surface Survey of Archaeological Sites in Semi-Arid Areas. In *Geoarchaeology,* edited by D. A. Davidson and M. L. Shackley, pp. 229–253. Westview Press, Boulder.

Lewarch, D. E.
1979 Controlled Surface Collection in Regional Analysis. In *The Cannon Reservoir Human Ecology Project: Recent Advances in the Archaeology of Northeast Missouri,* edited by M. J. O'Brien and D. E. Lewarch, pp. 42–51. Notebook No. 5, Department of Anthropology, University of Nebraska.

Lewarch, D. E., and M. J. O'Brien
1981a Effect of Short Term Tillage on Aggregate Provenience Surface Pattern. In *Plowzone Archaeology: Contributions to Theory and Technique,* edited by M. J. O'Brien and D. E. Lewarch, pp. 7–49. Vanderbilt University Publications in Anthropology No. 27.
1981b The Expanding Role of Surface Assemblages in Archaeological Research. In *Advances in Archaeological Method and Theory,* edited by M. B. Schiffer, vol. 4, pp. 297–342. Academic Press, New York.

Matthes, F.
1930 Geological History of the Yosimite Valley. *United States Geological Survey Professional Paper* 160.

McCarroll, D.
1991 Relative-Age Dating of Inorganic Deposits: The Need for a More Critical Approach. *The Holocene* 1:174–180.

Michels, J. W.
1967 Archeology and Dating by Hydration of Obsidian. *Science* 158:211–214.
1973 *Dating Methods in Archaeology.* Seminar Press, New York.

Nobbs, M. F., and R. I Dorn
1993 New Surface Exposure Ages for Petroglyphs from the Olary Province, South Australia. *Archaeology in Oceania* 18:407–425.

O'Connell, J. F.
1987 Alyawara Site Structure and its Archaeological Implications. *American Antiquity* 52:74–108.

Phillips, F. M., and R. I. Dorn
1991 New Methods for Dating Geomorphic Surfaces. Penrose Conference Report. *GSA Today,* May 1991, p. 102.

Pierce, K. L., J. D. Obradovich, and I. Friedman
1976 Obsidian Hydration Dating and Correlation of Bull Lake and Pinedale Glaciations near West Yellowstone. *Geological Society of America Bulletin* 76:703–710.

Plog, S., F. Plog, and W. Wait
1978 Decision Making in Modern Surveys. In *Advances in Archaeological Method and Theory,* edited by M. B. Schiffer, vol. 1, pp. 384–421. Academic Press, New York.

Redman, C. L., and P. J. Watson
1970 Systematic Intensive Surface Collection. *American Antiquity* 35:279–291.

Renaud, E. B.
1939 Report on Lichen of Spanish Diggings. Works Projects Administration, *Work Project* No. 885, Quarterly Report, October, November, December, 1939, p. 33.

Roper, D. C.
1976 Lateral Displacement of Artifacts Due to Plowing. *American Antiquity* 41:372–375.

Schiffer, M. B.
1972 Archaeological Context and Systemic Context. *American Antiquity* 37:156–165.
1987 *Formation Processes of the Archaeological Record.* University of New Mexico Press, Albuquerque.

Sjöberg, R.
1987 *Vittringsstudier med Schmidt Test-hammer, Tillämpningar inom Geomorfologi och Archeologi.* Center for Arctic Cultural Research, Umeå University, Research Reports No. 6.

Trubowitz, N. L.
1978 The Persistence of Settlement Pattern in a Cultivated Field. In *Essays in Northeastern Anthropology in Memory of Marian W. White,* edited by W. Englebrecht and D. K. Grayson, pp. 41–66. Occasional Publications in Northeastern Anthropology No. 5, Department of Anthropology, Franklin Pierce College.

Whitley, D. S., and R. I. Dorn
1987 Rock Art Chronology in Eastern California. *World Archaeology* 19:150–164.

Willey, G. R.
1951 Peruvian Settlement and Socio-Economic Patterns. In *The Civilization of Ancient America,* edited by S. Tax, pp. 195–200. The University of Chicago Press, Chicago.
1953 *Prehistoric Settlement Patterns in the Viru Valley, Peru.* Bureau of American Ethnology Bulletin No. 155, Smithsonian Institution, Washington, D. C.

Winchester, V.
1988 An Assessment of Lichenometry as a Method for Dating Recent Stone Movements in Two Stone Circles in Cumbria and Oxfordshire. *Botanical Journal of the Linnean Society* 96:57–68.

2

USE OF ROCK WEATHERING RINDS IN DATING GEOMORPHIC SURFACES

Peter L. K. Knuepfer

Department of Geological Sciences
State University of New York
Binghamton, New York

Abstract

Knowledge of the age of depositional and erosional *surfaces*, as opposed to the deposits underlying those surfaces, is of critical importance in many studies in Quaternary geology, geomorphology, and archaeology. The growth of weathering rinds, which are thin zones of oxidation or hydration products in a rock parallel to a clast surface, can be particularly useful for estimating ages of surfaces formed on coarse-grained deposits, due to the ubiquity of chemical weathering processes. Weathering rinds that have grown in clasts exposed at the ground surface (surface rinds) or clasts buried within the soil B horizon (subsurface rinds) can be used to differentiate relative ages of surfaces. The rate of weathering-rind growth can be quantified for a given rock type in a given climate, if sufficient independently dated calibration surfaces are available. Then weathering rinds can be used as a calibrated-age dating technique, although the precision of age estimates generally is much less than that from conventional radiometric dating techniques. Calibration of surface rinds in New Zealand allows high-precision dating of Holocene surfaces; calibration of subsurface rinds in the western United States allows differentiation of late Quaternary glacial and other surfaces. Applicability of these techniques to archaeological studies depends on achieving high-precision calibration of rind growth rates on local or regional bases, probably principally from surface rinds.

Introduction

A VARIETY OF STUDIES IN QUATERNARY GEOLogy, geomorphology, and archaeological geology depend on knowledge of the age of deposits and/or landscape surfaces. Such information can quantify rates of landscape development, tectonic activity (such as rates of fault slip or timing of prehistoric earthquakes), or occupational history. The conventional approach to age assessments is to use isotopic dating, especially radiocarbon (at least for surfaces and deposits less than about 40,000 years old), of deposits—an example of what Colman et al. (1987) call numerical-age dating. These techniques have the advantage of providing precise ages that are based on radioactive decay processes for which the physics are well understood and accepted by the earth-science and archaeological communities. Furthermore it is generally possible to interpret radio-

Figure 2.1. Photograph of weathering rinds obtained from surface rocks exposed on postglacial river terraces of the Branch River, South Island, New Zealand. Surface age increases clockwise from left. Note the sharp contrast between white weathering rind and dark unweathered greywacke. Scale in mm.

carbon dates in a stratigraphic context. However, isotopic techniques are limited in their applicability in at least two important respects: first, suitable material for radiometric dating is often absent from sites of interest; and second, in order to interpret the age of a surface from the age of deposits below that surface, the sedimentation rate must be known or assumed, which counterbalances the precision of the radiometric age. In addition charcoal and other materials datable by these methods are subject to contamination by older or younger carbon and may even be redeposited into a younger stratigraphic unit.

Regardless of the climatic setting, all landscape surfaces are subject to weathering processes that result in physical and chemical alteration of surficial deposits and the development of weathering and soil profiles. Soil formation and weathering begin immediately upon stabilization of a geomorphic surface. Modification of a surface by accretion (additions by streams or wind deposition) or removal (water or wind erosion) can be chronicled by careful analysis of soils and weathering (see Birkeland et al. 1991). Differences in the degree of rock weathering and soil development (among other properties) can assist the scientist in differentiating the relative ages of surfaces, as opposed to deposits. When the rates of these processes are calibrated at sites of known ages, the essence of a calibrated-age method (Colman et al. 1987), it is possible to estimate the ages of surfaces that lack datable materials or for which the relationship of deposit age to surface age is uncertain. Even though these techniques generally are not as precise as numerical-age methods, due to the greater variability in rates of the controlling physical and chemical processes, their applicability to all surfaces makes them of considerable utility in a wide variety of scientific studies.

One such technique, the development of weathering rinds, is particularly amenable to study in coarse-grained deposits, such as river gravels, alluvial-fan deposits, and glacial deposits. Under oxidizing conditions, most rocks weather inward from their surface, whether the rocks are exposed at the ground surface or are buried within the shallow parts of the soil. This produces a zone of oxidation within the rock that approximately parallels the outer rock surface and forms a discolored (typically whitened) ring or rind (Burke and Birkeland 1979)—a weathering rind (Figure 2.1).

This chapter reviews the utilization of rock weathering rinds as calibrated-age techniques. Examples of studies from New Zealand and the western United States emphasize the strengths and limitations of the technique for a variety of geologic problems. Weathering rinds formed on rocks buried beneath the surface ("subsurface rinds") and those formed on rocks at the ground surface ("surface rinds") are differentiated, because the applicability of these two populations to estimating ages of surfaces differs. To some degree this chapter updates the excellent review of rock weathering studies by Colman (1981), although here the emphasis is more strongly on the applications rather than on the rates of weathering.

Rock Weathering-Rind Formation

Rock weathering involves both physical and chemical processes. Physical processes, such as frost wedging and heat spalling, disintegrate the surface of rocks and operate principally at the ground surface. Chemical weathering processes, such as oxidation, hydrolysis, and dissolution, can occur wherever fluids (especially water) are in contact with a rock surface, in both the surface and the subsurface environments, to produce decomposition of the rock. The kinetics of these different rock and mineral weathering pathways strongly depend on the pH and Eh (redox or oxidation potential) of fluids that reach the rock surface. Chemical weathering of rocks produces weathering rinds, which develop as rings of discolored rock material migrating inward from the rock surface. Rinds tend to evolve in color and composition as weathering proceeds; however, Colman (1982) showed that all the minerals in rinds ultimately weather to amorphous clay-sized compounds, dominantly iron and aluminum hydroxides, as products of oxidation reactions.

The rate of chemical weathering depends on a variety of factors, analogous to the factors that control soil formation (Jenny 1941). In addition to time, these include climate, parent material (rock type), vegetation at the ground surface, and topographic position of a particular study site (Colman and Pierce 1981). The climate at a site (both temperature and precipitation, including the degree of seasonality of both) controls the overall availability of fluids in the weathering environment and strongly affects the kinetics of chemical reactions. Vegetation can have a strong impact on the acidity of waters available for weathering, although vegetation generally is strongly correlated with climate. Deciduous forests tend to produce high-acid soil environments, facilitating the chemical solution of aluminum and silicon; vegetation in deserts adds minimal acid to the soil environment. The position of a study site on the surface also can significantly affect the availability of moisture. A position at the crest of a hill tends to be well drained, whereas a position at the base of a hill is poorly drained; thus more fluids are available for weathering at the basal position.

The mineralogy, structure, and grain size of the parent material control what kinds of reactions can occur and the rates of such reactions. Rock mineralogy determines possible reaction pathways. For example feldspars in sandstone generally weather to clay minerals through hydrolysis; calcium carbonate in limestone dissolves; and quartzite, composed principally of quartz grains, is rarely weathered under most climatic conditions. The structure of a rock can strongly affect chemical weathering rates. For example weathering generally concentrates along the numerous planes of weakness in heavily jointed and foliated rocks such as schist, resulting in the disintegration of the rock more rapidly than inward weathering from the rock surface can proceed. Grain size offers two constraints on chemical weathering. First the smaller a rock, the larger the surface area/volume ratio, and the more rapidly the rock will weather (given that a rock with a high area/volume ratio has a greater percentage of its volume exposed to weathering fluids). Second the finer the size of the grains that make up the rock, the thinner the weathering rind from a given geologic deposit or surface. Colman and Pierce (1981) report that rinds formed in fine-grained andesite boulders are only 84 percent as thick as rinds from coarse-grained andesite boulders from the same deposit.

Rocks obtained from subsurface exposures generally have thinner weathering rinds than rocks obtained from the surface of the same deposit (Colman and Pierce 1981). This slower development makes subsurface rinds less useful in distinguishing among young Holocene surfaces than are surface rinds; conversely subsurface rinds are more useful in distinguishing Pleistocene surfaces. Weathering-rind growth in subsurface rocks is much more strongly dependent on variations in climate than is that of surface rinds. Soil moisture, which is dependent on precipitation, soil mineralogy, and depth of water table (among other factors); soil acidity, which depends both on precipitation and surface vegetation; and depth of rock burial all exert strong influences on rind growth.

Most weathering processes depend on time in a nonlinear fashion (Colman 1981). Empirical studies of rock weathering, as well as the few experimental studies that have been completed, show that the rates of most chemical weathering processes decrease with time. Early stages of weathering-rind growth probably follow a power-law increase (Chinn 1981), controlled by the kinetics of weathering reactions moderated by the permeability of the rock being weathered. Weathering rates slow down, however, commonly following a logarithmic growth curve, as the buildup of weathering residues (the rind) retards the movement of water into the rock (Colman 1981). In fact under some conditions (such as at the ground surface), removal of the weathered outer coating of a rock can ultimately balance the inward migration of the weathering front (Whitehouse et al. 1986), producing a constant rind thickness. Nonetheless, at least in the early stages of rock weathering, rind thickness can be used as a clear indicator of time since stabilization of a geomorphic surface.

Other complications to weathering-rind growth can occur due to physical weathering processes and rind inheritance. Surface rocks subject to high rates of frost shattering, as in alpine areas and cold-climate regions, as well as rocks on old (say, $> 50,000$ years in New Zealand or $> 200,000$ years in western North America) geomorphic surfaces, commonly lose much or most of the weathering rind that began to develop after deposition (cf. Colman and Pierce 1981). Frost-shattered rocks develop fresh surfaces, which then begin to weather and develop rinds, and it can be extremely difficult to recognize an "original" surface when frost-shattering is extreme. Rocks from old geomorphic surfaces have been subject to rejuvenation of the rock surface due to rind removal by abrasion and other processes. In principle rocks that are deposited through fluvial or other processes may already have been weathered prior to deposition. Thus rocks could be deposited with preexisting weathering rinds. However, Colman and Pierce (1981) found evidence that this is rarely the case among the hundreds of sites they sampled, and I obtained comparable evidence of lack of inherited rinds in New Zealand (Knuepfer 1988) and in modern stream deposits in Idaho (Knuepfer, unpublished data).

Field Sampling and Calibration

Field sampling techniques for weathering-rind studies vary from site to site, but several general principles must be followed. Sampling procedures may vary from study to study, but they must remain internally consistent for each study: similar parent materials, similar topographic settings, and similar depth of burial (for subsurface rocks). Grain size, both in terms of rock size and the grain size of the material comprising the rock, must be consistent among sites. In general at least fifty samples should be gathered at an individual site in order to obtain a useful distribution of the variations in rind thickness at a site. Rind measurements are most easily made on clasts of at least cobble, and preferably boulder, size. Rock types such as andesite, basalt, and medium- to fine-grained sandstone generally develop clear rinds with sharp inner edges, and these can be measured very precisely (even to the nearest 0.1 mm) using an optical comparator. Other rock types, such as granite and quartzite, commonly have less clear rind inner edges, and some rock types, such as schists and limestones, often display very poor rind formation, due to their mode of weathering (as discussed above).

The calibration of rind-thickening rates requires the independent dating of geomorphic surfaces from which rind samples are collected. The most precise rind-growth calibrations have been developed from radiocarbon dating of geologically instantaneous geomorphic surfaces, such as landslides (Whitehouse et al. 1986). Regional correlations of glacial deposits can also provide useful, but less precise, age control for rind-growth calibration (see Birkeland 1973; Colman and Pierce 1981). Calibration curves must be generated for each rock type and each study area, however, due to the strong dependence of rind growth on parent material and rock type (as demonstrated by Colman and Pierce 1981). Although this latter consideration can limit the ease with which dating from weathering rinds can be applied on a regional basis, well-established calibration curves, such as those from New Zealand, can have widespread applicability. Thus rock weathering rinds can provide highly reliable relative or calibrated dating (particularly compared to some other techniques, such as soil formation), because the type of material being weathered is clearly defined and limited, measurements can be made with high precision, and other factors that can affect weathering (such as climate, grain size and structure of the rock, and topographic setting) can be held constant or accounted for.

New Zealand Studies

Surface Rinds

The Torlesse greywacke, of Mesozoic age, is extremely widespread in the northern South Island and southern North Island of New Zealand (Figure 2.2). Some variations in rock chemistry are systematically related to age (Mackinnon 1983), but through most of its outcrop area it is remarkably homogeneous. As the principal bedrock type, it is the primary source for sediments deposited by rivers, deposited in moraines of active and Pleistocene glaciers, and deposited during rock avalanches and landslides or on talus slopes in the eastern South Island. All of these types of deposits commonly are very coarse-grained in New Zealand, resulting in abundant cobbles and boulders exposed at the surface. A substantial number of these surfaces have been radiocarbon-dated; in the case of rock avalanches, dating of trees buried by the landslides provides precise ages of the deposits and their surfaces.

Chinn (1981) has shown that the thickening of surface rinds developed in Torlesse greywacke sandstone clasts increases systematically with time. He measured weathering rinds on rocks from the surfaces of moraines and rock avalanche deposits that had been radiocarbon-dated. In his study and others from New Zealand, rinds were measured from faces of rock chips broken from fine- to medium-grained greywacke cobbles or boulders found at the ground surface. Individual rocks from surfaces of progressively greater age generally have progressively thicker weathering rinds (see Figure 2.1). Samples of many rocks from individual surfaces show an overall increase in rind thickness with age, although dispersion in the data also increases with age (Figure 2.3).

Chinn found that age of a surface with rinds of a given thickness can be estimated from a power-law function of the form

$$(1) \qquad t = kC_t^m$$

where C_t is the modal rind thickness, k and m are constants. The equation obtained (Table 2.1) can be used when estimating ages at least up to 10 ka (thousand years). A number of subsequent studies modified his equation. Whitehouse et al. (1986) argued that rind growth is more generally described by a relaxation law of the form

$$(2) \qquad C_t = C_\infty[1 - \exp(-t/\tau)]$$

where C_t is the rind thickness at some time t; C_∞ the equilibrium rind thickness that occurs when the rate of rind thickening is balanced by the rate of disintegration of boulders at their surface (less than 50 ka for Torlesse greywacke in New Zealand); and τ is the relaxation time (equivalent to a half-life). Such a curve is nearly equivalent to a power-law function for low t (up to about 10–15 ka). Knuepfer (1988) and Burrows et al. (1990) have modified Chinn's calibration still further (Table 2.1; Figure 2.4), adding or rejecting calibration sites and correcting radiocarbon dates for atmospheric variations in ^{14}C (following Klein et al. 1982 or Stuiver and Reimer 1986). Although these various studies slightly modify the rind-age relationship, the differences are of secondary importance to their applicability.

Each of these calibration equations has been determined using one or another technique of regression. In the calibration data, either time or rind thickness can be expressed as independent variables, as both are known. However, in applying the rind-growth curves to estimating ages of geomorphic surface, one knows only the rind thickness (expressed as an "average"; see below), which means that time must be treated as the dependent variable. Thus Table 2.1 lists regression coefficients for time varying as a function of (measured) rind thickness.

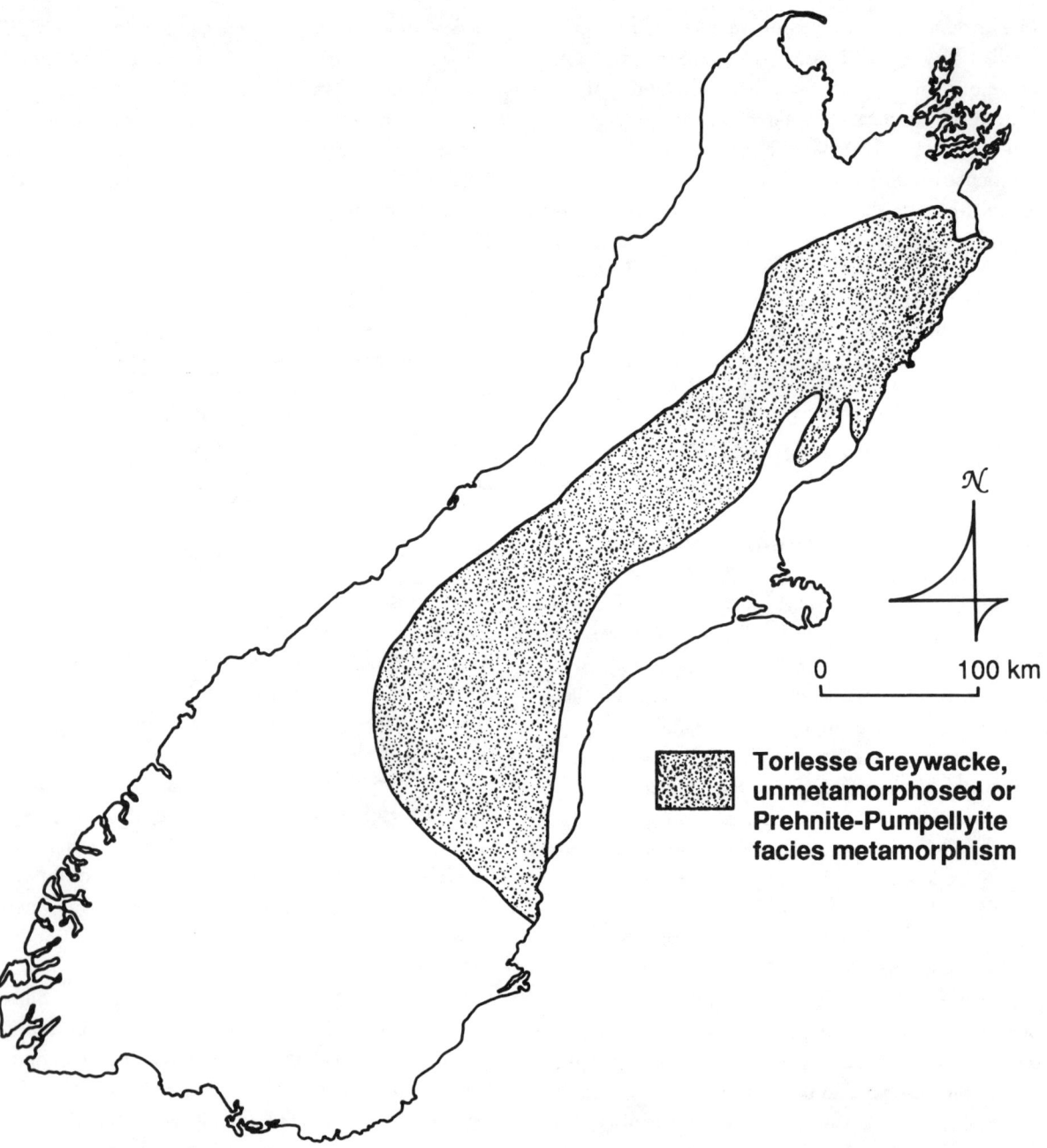

Figure 2.2. Map of South Island, New Zealand, showing distribution of Torlesse Supergroup greywacke.

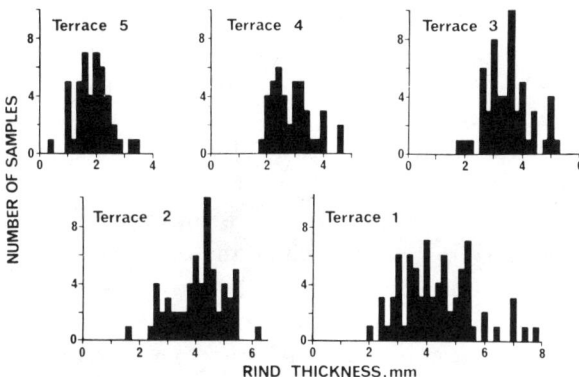

Figure 2.3. Distribution of weathering-rind measurements from terraces of the Saxton River, South Island, New Zealand. Terrace 1 is oldest; Terrace 5 is youngest. Modes at 5.4 mm for Terrace 1, 4.4 mm for Terrace 2, 3.6 mm for Terrace 3, 3.2 mm for Terrace 4, and 2.0 mm for Terrace 5 were chosen for age estimates by Knuepfer (1988).

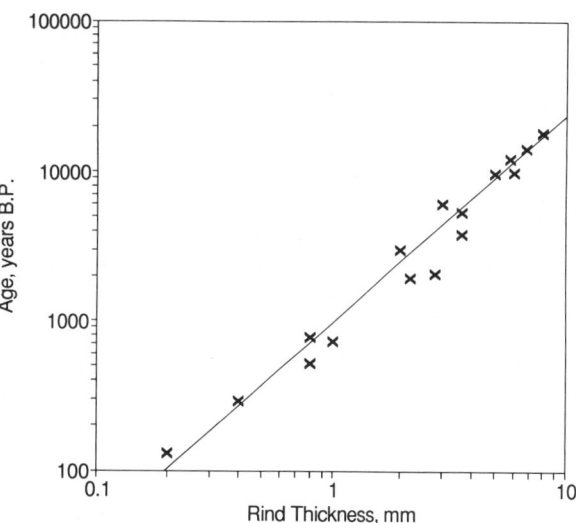

Figure 2.4. Calibration curve for weathering-rind thickness of surface Torlesse greywacke rocks; uncertainties in age are within the size of the asterisks. After Kneupfer (1988) with rind ages modified after Burrows et al. (1990). Best-fit regression is $t = 925 C_t^{1.36}$.

Table 2.1. Regression Coefficients for Surface-Rind Calibrations, Torlesse Greywacke.

Source	Exponent	Multiplier
Chinn (1981)	1.24	1030
Whitehouse et al. (1986)	1.33	1083
Knuepfer (1988)	1.33	973
Burrows et al. (1990)	1.433	876.2

There are many ways in which the "average" thickness of weathering rinds can be determined, such as by maximum (Birkeland 1973), mean (Birkeland 1982), and modal (Chinn 1981) rind thickness. Properties of the maximum and mean rind thickness argue against the use of these measures. For example maximum rind thickness is sensitive to individual clasts that may be more susceptible to rind development (Chinn 1981), perhaps because of subtle differences in permeability or fracturing of the rock. The fact that many of the weathering-rind distributions obtained from New Zealand surfaces are skewed and/or bimodal (Chinn 1981; Knuepfer 1988) argues against the use of rind mean, although Knuepfer (1988) computed a separate calibration equation for rind mean. These complex distributions of rind thickness, particularly common from older surfaces, imply multiple events such as frost shattering or partial burial or exhumation since deposition. Thus Chinn and most subsequent workers in New Zealand have utilized the mode as the "average" rind thickness. However, in populations with multiple peaks, choice of the "proper" mode is not obvious. Whitehouse et al. (1986) argue that in cases where more than one peak occurs in rind thickness, the largest (thickest) significant peak best represents the time since surface stabilization (i.e., surface age). They and Knuepfer (1988) used this thickest peak as the appropriate value for calibration and for age estimates (Figure 2.4).

The principal limitation in estimating surface ages from rinds involves the influence of factors other than time in determining rind growth, as previously discussed. Chinn (1981), Whitehouse et al. (1986), and Knuepfer (1988) found that despite a range in mean annual precipitation at calibration sites from 1200 mm to 5000 mm and a range in mean annual temperatures of some 5°C, precipitation and temperature explain little of the variation in rind thickness. Multiple regressions involving temperature, precipitation, vegetation, and aspect, as well as time, found that time explains nearly all of the variation in rind thickness (Knuepfer 1988; Whitehouse et al. 1986). By restricting analysis to greywacke clasts of consistent medium sand-sized grains and choosing sites with no obvious surface burial or erosion, influences on rind growth other than time can be minimized.

APPLICATIONS

Calibrated surface rinds have been used extensively in the South Island of New Zealand to date a wide variety of landforms. Whitehouse (1983) estimated ages of large rock avalanches in the Southern Alps of New Zealand, and later used the clustering of ages of avalanche events to infer the timing of large prehistoric earthquakes in the region (Whitehouse 1984). Whitehouse and McSaveney (1983) estimated the ages of talus surfaces in the Southern Alps, concluding that talus deposits decrease in age in the downslope direction. Chinn (1981) and Burrows et al. (1990), among others, have used rind thickness to estimate the ages of Holocene moraines and gain insights into variations in glacier advances and climates in New Zealand. Knuepfer (1988) used surface rinds as one criterion in estimating the ages of late-glacial and Holocene stream terraces, to gain insights into patterns of river incision (Bull and Knuepfer 1987) and rates of fault displacement of terrace surfaces (Knuepfer 1992).

Subsurface Rinds

The utilization of subsurface rinds in New Zealand has been less widespread than the use of surface rinds, in part because of the success of surface rinds in yielding age estimates for postglacial surfaces. Whitehouse et al. (1986) compared surface and subsurface rind modes from several surfaces and found a much less systematic variation in the rinds from subsurface rocks. Knuepfer (1988) established a rind-thickness relationship for slightly metamorphosed greywacke sandstones from the west coast of the South Island of New Zealand, where precipitation exceeds 3500 mm at all of the calibration sites. He sampled rocks at a consistent soil depth of 50 cm, which in general is within the B horizon of soils developed on postglacial and late-glacial surfaces. He concluded that estimated ages based on subsurface rinds have uncertainties of at least ±10 percent to more than ±50 percent, whereas uncertainties for surface rinds range from ±5 percent to ±40 percent (higher uncertainties for ages greater than 10 ka). The greater uncertainty in the age estimates from subsurface rocks probably reflects the variability in soil-moisture conditions among calibration sites.

Examples from the Western United States

Surface Rinds

Weathering rinds from rocks exposed at the surface have long been used as a relative dating tool in the western United States, principally in studies of glacial sequences (see Burke and Birkeland 1979; Porter 1975). These and many other studies have utilized rinds formed in a variety of different rock types, including basalt (Porter 1975) and granitic rocks (Burke and Birkeland 1979). Porter found that coarse-grained basalt and arkosic sandstone produced diffuse surface rinds of highly variable thickness; rinds formed in fine-grained basalt clasts have sharp inner boundaries and consistent thicknesses on surfaces of a given age. He found a mean surface rind thickness of 0.25 mm in fine-grained basalt clasts on moraines of presumed late-glacial (ca. 15–18 ka) age and a thickness of 0.5 mm on moraines of early last glacial age in the Yakima Valley of Washington. His ages were based on regional correlations rather than independent site-specific dating techniques. He also found that shallow subsurface rinds, taken from depths less than 20 cm, are of comparable thickness to rinds formed in similar rocks at the surface. Porter was able to produce a hierarchical classification of moraines of different relative ages, but he recognized that true age could be obtained only through calibration of the weathering rate by radiometric dating.

Birkeland (1973), Carroll (1974), and Anderson and Anderson (1981) are among many workers who have used surface weathering rinds as one relative-age technique in the Rocky Mountains, especially in differentiating late-glacial (Pinedale) surfaces from moraines of Holocene (Neoglacial) age. Carroll (1974) found maximum surface-rind thicknesses of 12 mm and 21 mm in granitic boulders from moraines of 3–5 ka and 10–12 ka ages, respectively (Figure 2.5). Birkeland (1973) found surface rinds as thick as 45 mm in granodiorite boulders from rock glacier deposits of late Pinedale age at Mt. Sopris in western Colorado; early Neoglacial surface rinds generally are less than 10 mm in thickness. Anderson and Anderson (1981) investigated surface rinds that have grown in fine-grained sandstones at Mount Timpanogos in Utah. They found surface rinds as thick as 13 mm, with a mean of five mm, from moraines of probable early Holocene age, and maxima of three mm, with a mean of one mm, from rock glacier deposits of Neoglacial age. Their study is the only one in the western U.S. of which I am aware that utilizes surface rinds in sandstones for relative dating. The precise ages of deposits are not known in these Rocky Mountain studies, as the age estimates rely on regional correlations. Assuming that the correlations are correct, however, they illustrate that substantially different rind thicknesses develop in different materials at different sites. Maximum rind thicknesses from late-glacial moraines range from 21 mm in granitic rocks of the Colorado Front Range to 45 mm in granodiorite in western Colorado. Maximum thicknesses in Holocene moraines range from three mm in the sandstones at Mount Timpanogos to 12 mm in the Front Range.

Butler (1982) investigated the potential for using surface rinds in quartzite boulders in the Lemhi Range of Idaho for the relative dating of moraines. He found few rinds, probably largely because the chemistry of

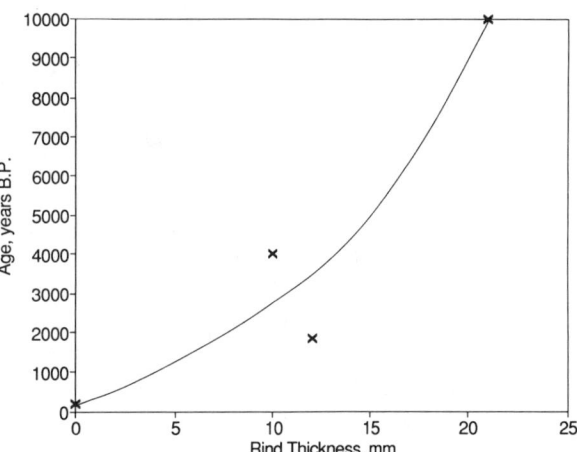

Figure 2.5. Growth of surface rinds on moraines of Arikaree Cirque, Colorado Front Range. Modified from Carroll (1974).

quartzite is not conducive to weathering-rind development. I examined weathering-rind growth in limestone and quartzite clasts on last-glacial and penultimate glacial moraines in the same area. Although progressive growth of weathering rinds with age occurs in the limestones, severe pitting of clast surfaces on older moraines obscures rind growth and has removed most rinds. The rate of rind growth in quartzite is slow enough that little rind development is seen on late-glacial surfaces.

None of these studies has provided the basis for a calibration of the rate of rind-thickness formation. Carroll (1974) presents a plot of maximum rind thickness on Holocene moraines from the Arikaree Cirque in Colorado against moraine age (Figure 2.5). The ages are based on radiocarbon dating of glacial deposits from other locations along the Front Range (Benedict 1973). The application of the radiocarbon dates, which constrain the ages but do not directly date the surfaces, is based on regional correlations (Benedict 1968; Carroll 1974); Carroll concludes that one of the correlations is wrong, because the weathering rinds are too large for the correlated age. Thus even at this site, the rind-growth curve is inadequately calibrated. Given this lack of calibration, as well as the wide variability in rind thickness as a function of rock type and among regions, the quantitative use of surface rinds for age estimates is not yet possible in the western United States.

Subsurface Rinds

Colman and Pierce (1981) gathered a large volume of data on subsurface rinds from basalt and andesite in the western United States. They examined glacial and glaciofluvial surfaces from 17 different areas, including surfaces correlated with the neoglacial events, the last glaciation and the penultimate glaciation. They argued that the use of surface rinds was unreliable, particularly for surfaces older than late Pinedale, because of the loss of rinds with increasing age due to abrasion, frost action, and flaking. Instead they examined subsurface rinds from B horizons of deposits, collected from depths generally around 50 cm.

Careful field-sampling experiments allowed Colman and Pierce (1981) to evaluate the effects of surface burial and erosion, minor differences in parent material chemistry, climate, and reproducibility of measurements by different workers on subsurface rind thickness. They found that only climate and time have significant effects on subsurface-rind growth. They computed the mean thickness of subsurface rind populations, arguing that rind distributions generally are log normal (although many of their published rind-distribution histograms are in fact multimodal).

Age control in their study is limited; relative-age methods and stratigraphic relationships were used to correlate glacial deposits in most of their study areas. However, they were able to calibrate one rind-growth curve with the well-dated glacial sequence from West Yellowstone, dated by the obsidian hydration technique (Pierce et al. 1976). Latest Pinedale (12–15 ka) deposits have a mean subsurface-rind thickness of 0.1 mm; early Pinedale (35 ka) deposits have a mean thickness of 0.4 mm; and Bull Lake (140 ka) deposits have a mean thickness of 0.8 mm. Climate dependence in rind thickening is demonstrated by the differences in mean rind thickness for a given (assumed) age. Penultimate (Bull Lake) deposits have a mean subsurface-rind thickness of 1.6 mm at McCall, Idaho, but only 0.93 mm at Donner Lake, California, and 0.78 mm at West Yellowstone.

Colman and Pierce investigated different mathematical fits to the Yellowstone data and concluded they are best fit by a logarithmic function of the form

$$(3) \qquad d = \log(a + bt)$$

where d is mean rind thickness and a and b are constants. Note that they expressed time as the independent variable; their data must be regressed with rind thickness as the independent variable in order to estimate the age of a deposit for which subsurface rinds have been measured. The growth curves vary from site to site, as shown in Figure 2.6, because of differences in climate and dependent on whether basalt or andesite cobbles were studied.

Other Weathering Studies

Numerous relative-dating studies in the western United States and elsewhere have relied on qualitative assessments of the degree of weathering of surface cobbles to differentiate apparent ages. For example Carroll (1974) and Burke and Birkeland (1979) used the amount of pitting on surface boulders as one indicator of relative surface age. Relative degree of cobble weathering and disintegration has been used by these and other workers extensively. Carroll (1974) found, however, that weathering rinds provide the single best overall relative-dating tool (although he and Burke and Birkeland caution against reliance on a single relative-dating method).

Two other types of weathering studies deserve particular mention. Obsidian hydration (Beck and Jones chapter 4 of this volume; Friedman and Long 1976; Pierce et al. 1976) has been used to date glacial, fluvial, and archaeological deposits. This technique actually involves the measurement of a weathering rind produced by hydration processes, as opposed to the oxidation rinds I have otherwise been discussing; it is dealt with

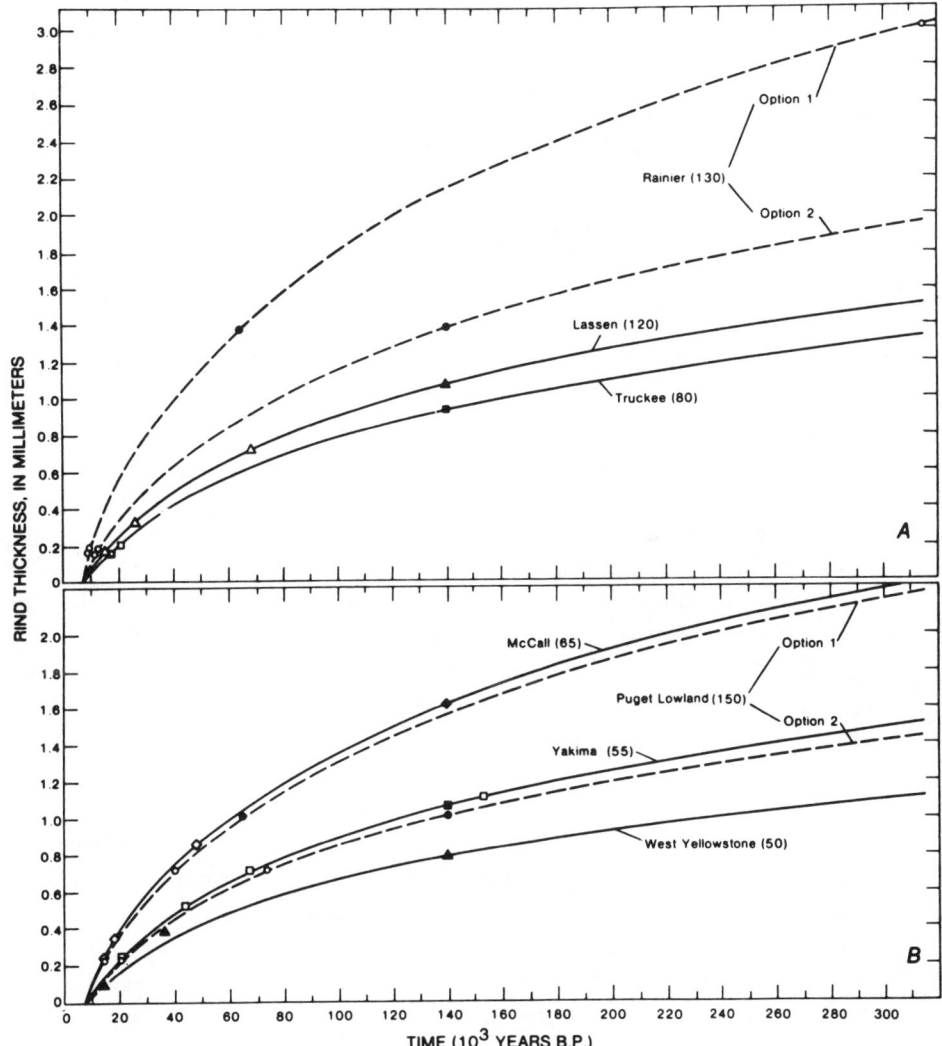

Figure 2.6. Growth of subsurface rinds in basalt and andesite clasts, western United States. From Colman and Pierce (1981).

in detail by Beck and Jones in chapter 4 of this volume. Thus I do not consider hydration rinds further.

A technique of more widespread applicability to dating geomorphic surfaces (though perhaps not artifacts), the clast-sound velocity method, has recently been developed by Crook (1986) and Crook and Gillespie (1986). They measure the compressional wave velocity for granitic clasts obtained from subsurface exposures into geomorphic surfaces. They have applied the technique to alluvial fan, fluvial terrace, and moraine deposits in southern and eastern California; deposit ages range from one ka to 130 ka (with one deposit having an estimated age of 730 ka). The principle is that microfractures develop in a clast as it weathers, causing an increase in rock compressibility and a concomitant decrease in compressional wave velocity. The method, although somewhat cumbersome in the field, successfully differentiates relative ages of deposits, and the change in velocity follows a logarithmic function similar to that used by Colman and Pierce (1981). This technique, like the other subsurface techniques, generally has poor resolution, however.

Discussion

Where the technique has been well calibrated by independent dating, such as in New Zealand for surface rinds or at West Yellowstone for subsurface rinds, the use of rock weathering rinds as a calibrated-age technique can provide extremely useful estimates of the age since formation of a geomorphic surface. Surface-rind development appears to be remarkably independent of climate, at least for New Zealand, but its applicability is effectively restricted to young geomorphic surfaces, due to the disintegration of the weathered surface of exposed clasts by frost, rainfall, and abrasion. In New Zealand the technique is best applied to surfaces with ages less than 20 ka; the drier climates in the western United States would allow its application over a longer time span, perhaps to surfaces with ages of 50 ka, although sufficient calibration is not currently available. Subsurface-rind development is strongly dependent on climate in all of the well-calibrated studies, and the relatively slow rate of rind growth in soil B horizons under a variety of climatic conditions makes this technique applicable to longer time intervals (at least 150,000 years, probably longer) before rind destruction approximates rind growth. However, resolution on the order of hundreds or even a few thousand years generally is not possible. Thus experience both in New Zealand and in the western United States clearly indicates that surface rinds are best suited for application to relatively short time intervals, such as the Holocene, whereas subsurface rinds can be utilized more successfully for longer time intervals, perhaps several hundred thousand years.

At the same time, the slow growth of subsurface rinds under most climatic and parent material conditions limits the resolution of this technique within the time frame in which surface rinds can best be applied.

The utilization of any weathering technique for quantitative age estimates (as opposed to the more typical relative dating application) is dependent on the availability of calibration data. The better the age of calibration deposits or surfaces is known by independent dating techniques such as radiocarbon, the better the rind-growth relationship can be determined. However, if available radiometric dates only constrain the maximum or minimum age of a surface or deposit, as is often the case, it may not be possible to develop a quantitative rind-growth relationship. Furthermore the precision of age estimates from weathering rinds is limited both by the uncertainties in calibration dates and the inherent variability in rind growth as affected by minor differences in grain size and chemistry of the clasts. Nonetheless age estimates of sufficient precision for a variety of applications can be obtained from calibrated rind-growth relationships, particularly in areas (such as New Zealand) where a relatively similar clast type is widely distributed.

Our experience in New Zealand suggests that similar detailed rind-dating relationships can be established in other regions where a single rock type is widely distributed and where geologically instantaneous coarse-grained deposits, such as landslides and debris flows, can be dated radiometrically. One region in the western United States that should be amenable to the development of a detailed weathering-rind curve is the Franciscan greywacke terrane of northern California.

I am unaware of any studies explicitly using weathering rinds as a dating tool in archaeological studies, despite the potential of the technique to supply easily obtained (if often imprecise) ages. The potential applicability to archaeology is, of course, dependent on calibration for a rock type within a region of consistent climate and on sufficiently rapid rind growth that resolution on the order of a few hundred to a thousand years is feasible for geomorphic surfaces no more than a few thousand to twenty thousand years old. This effectively limits the use of rinds to the surface-rind technique, such as has been established in New Zealand. The most likely settings for utilization of weathering rinds over the time frames of relevance to archaeology are in subhumid to humid climates (because weathering rates will likely be too slow in arid areas), and where a relatively homogeneous bedrock has provided clasts to young deposits.

References Cited

Anderson, L. W., and D. S. Anderson
1981 Weathering Rinds on Quartzarenite Clasts as a Relative-Age Indicator and the Glacial Chronology of Mount Timpanogos, Wasatch Range, Utah. *Arctic and Alpine Research* 13: 25–31.

Benedict, J. B.
1968 Recent Glacial History of an Alpine Area in the Colorado Front Range, U.S.A., II. Dating the Glacial Deposits. *Journal of Glaciology* 7: 77–87.
1973 Chronology of Cirque Glaciation, Colorado Front Range. *Quaternary Research* 3: 584–599.

Birkeland, P. W.
1973 Use of Relative-Age-Dating Methods in a Stratigraphic Study of Rock Glacier Deposits, Mt. Sopris, Colorado. *Arctic and Alpine Research* 5: 401–416.
1982 Subdivision of Holocene Glacial Deposits, Ben Ohau Range, New Zealand, Using Relative-Dating Methods. *Geological Society of America Bulletin* 93: 433–449.

Birkeland, P. W., M. E. Berry, and D. K. Swanson
1991 Use of Soil Catena Field Data for Estimating Relative Ages of Moraines. *Geology* 19: 281–283.

Bull, W. B., and P. L. K. Knuepfer
1987 Adjustments by the Charwell River, New Zealand, to Uplift and Climatic Changes. *Geomorphology* 1: 15–32.

Burke, R. M., and P. W. Birkeland
1979 Reevaluation of Multiparameter Relative Dating Techniques and Their Application to the Glacial Sequence along the Eastern Escarpment of the Sierra Nevada, California. *Quaternary Research* 11: 21–51.

Burrows, C. J., K. W. Duncan, and J. R. Spence
1990 Aranuian Vegetation History of the Arrowsmith Range, Canterbury, II. Revised Chronology for Moraines of the Cameron Glacier. *New Zealand Journal of Botany* 28:455–466.

Butler, D. R.
1982 Potential for Quartzite Weathering Rinds as a Quaternary Age Indicator, Central Lemhi Mountains, Idaho. *Journal of the Idaho Academy of Science* 18: 37–48.

Carroll, T.
1974 Relative Age Dating Techniques and a Late Quaternary Chronology, Arikaree Cirque, Colorado. *Geology* 2: 321–325.

Chinn, T. J. H.
1981 Use of Rock Weathering-Rind Thickness for Holocene Absolute Age-Dating in New Zealand. *Arctic and Alpine Research* 13: 33–45.

Colman, S. M.
1981 Rock-Weathering Rates as Functions of Time. *Quaternary Research* 15: 250–264.
1982 *Chemical Weathering of Basalts and Andesites: Evidence from Weathering Rinds.* U.S. Geological Survey, Professional Paper 1246.

Colman, S. M., and K. L. Pierce
1981 *Weathering Rinds on Andesitic and Basaltic Stones as a Quaternary Age Indicator, Western United States.* U.S. Geological Survey, Professional Paper 1210.

Colman, S. M., K. L. Pierce, and P. W. Birkeland
1987 Suggested Terminology for Quaternary Dating Methods. *Quaternary Research* 28: 314–319.

Crook, R., Jr.
1986 Relative Dating of Quaternary Deposits Based on P-Wave Velocities in Weathered Granitic Clasts. *Quaternary Research* 25: 281–292.

Crook, R., Jr., and A. R. Gillespie
1986 Weathering Rates in Granitic Boulders Measured by P-Wave Speeds. In *Rates of Chemical Weathering of Rocks and Minerals,* edited by

S. M. Colman and D. P. Dethier, pp. 395–417. Academic Press, Orlando.

Friedman, I., and W. Long
1976 Hydration Rate of Obsidian. *Science* 191: 347–352.

Jenny, H.
1941 *Factors of Soil Formation.* McGraw-Hill, New York.

Klein, J., J. C. Lerman, P. E. Damon, and K. E. Ralph
1982 Calibration of Radiocarbon Dates: Tables Based on the Consensus Data of the Workshop on Calibrating the Radiocarbon Time Scale. *Radiocarbon* 24: 103–150.

Knuepfer, P. L. K.
1988 Estimating Ages of Late Quaternary Stream Terraces from Analysis of Weathering Rinds and Soils. *Geological Society of America Bulletin* 100: 1224–1236.
1992 Temporal Variations in Latest Quaternary Slip across the Australian-Pacific Plate Boundary, South Island, New Zealand. *Tectonics* 11: 449–464.

Mackinnon, T. C.
1983 Origin of the Torlesse Terrane and Coeval Rocks, South Island, New Zealand. *Geological Society of America Bulletin* 94: 967–985.

Pierce, K. L., J. D. Obradovich, and I. Friedman
1976 Obsidian Hydration Dating and Correlation of Bull Lake and Pinedale Glaciations near West Yellowstone, Montana. *Geological Society of America Bulletin* 87: 703–710.

Porter, S. C.
1975 Weathering Rinds as a Relative-Age Criterion: Application to Subdivision of Glacial Deposits in the Cascade Range. *Geology* 3: 101–104.

Stuiver, M., and P. J. Reimer
1986 A Computer Program for Radiocarbon Calibration: *Radiocarbon* 28: 1022–1030.

Whitehouse, I. E.
1983 Distribution of Large Rock Avalanche Deposits in the Central Southern Alps, New Zealand. *New Zealand Journal of Geology and Geophysics* 26: 271–279.
1984 Large Rock Avalanches and Holocene Seismicity of Central Southern Alps (Abstract). *Abstracts for the International Symposium on Recent Crustal Movements of the Pacific Region,* p. 63. Royal Society of New Zealand, Wellington.

Whitehouse, I. E., and M. J. McSaveney
1983 Diachronous Talus Surfaces in the Southern Alps, New Zealand, and Their Implications to Talus Accumulations. *Arctic and Alpine Research* 15: 53–64.

Whitehouse, I. E., M. J. McSaveney, P. L. K. Knuepfer, and T. J. Chinn
1986 Growth of Weathering Rinds on Torlesse Sandstone, Southern Alps, New Zealand. In *Rates of Chemical Weathering of Rocks and Minerals,* edited by S. M. Colman and D. P. Dethier, pp. 419–435. Academic Press, Orlando.

3

THE SCHMIDT HAMMER AS A MEASURE OF DEGREE OF ROCK SURFACE WEATHERING AND TERRAIN AGE

Danny McCarroll

Department of Geography
University College Swansea
Swansea, United Kingdom

Abstract

The Schmidt hammer is a simple hand-held instrument, designed to measure the surface hardness of concrete. On natural rocks surface hardness and compressive strength are related to degree of weathering and thus surface age. Schmidt hammer results, however, are influenced by several factors other than degree of rock surface weathering and terrain age. Problems of calibration and spatial variations in lithology and rock surface texture can prove particularly problematic. If a critical approach is adopted, the Schmidt hammer provides a rapid, inexpensive, and nondestructive index of degree of rock surface weathering for use in the relative-age dating of inorganic landforms and deposits. It has been used successfully on glacial moraines, landslide debris, protalus ramparts, raised shorelines, and sorted circles. Although calibration curves could be constructed to allow numerical ages to be estimated, they would probably be valid only in a very restricted area.

Introduction

THE USE OF MEASURES OF DEGREE OF ROCK SURface weathering as indicators of terrain age is well established (Birkeland et al. 1979; Brookes 1982; Burke and Birkeland 1979; McCarroll 1991a). However, the degree to which some 'traditional' relative-dating (RD) parameters, such as boulder frequency, boulder roundness, and measures related to boulder surface texture, actually measure degree of rock surface weathering has been called into question (Benedict 1973; Dowdeswell 1984; McCarroll 1991a). More reliable measures of degree of weathering, such as weathering-rind thickness (Carrara and Andrews 1972; Cernohouz and Solc 1966, 1967; Chinn 1981; Colman and Pierce 1981; Gellatly 1984; Knuepfer 1988), or the microscopic relief of mineral grains (Hall and Michaud 1988; Locke 1979) are often time consuming and, where large samples of weathering rinds are required, may be unacceptably destructive. The Schmidt hammer, a simple handheld instrument, provides a relatively quick, inexpensive, and nondestructive field measure of rock surface hardness, and therefore provides a potentially valuable index of degree of rock surface weathering and terrain age. Schmidt hammer results, however, may be influenced by factors other than rock surface hardness and degree of weathering, and if reliable results are to be obtained, the technique must be applied critically. After reviewing chronological applications to date, this chapter aims to assess the problems in using the Schmidt hammer for relative-age dating, suggest a standard procedure and, finally, assess the potential for extending the technique to obtain numerical ages.

The Schmidt Hammer

The Schmidt hammer is a light, robust instrument that records the distance of rebound of a spring-loaded mass impacting a surface. The distance of rebound is related to the hardness and compressive strength of the surface. The instrument was originally designed as an on-site measure of the surface hardness of concrete, but it also provides a measure of the surface hardness of natural rocks (Augustinus 1991; Barton and Choubey 1977; Day 1980; Day and Goudie 1977; Deere and Miller 1966; Selby 1980; Sheorey et al. 1984; Summerfield and Goudie 1980; Yaalon and Singer 1974). The extent to which it provides a measure of the strength of a rock in three dimensions is disputed (Allison 1990, 1991; Augustinus 1991; Campbell 1991). Four sizes are available, with the same operating procedure but different impact energies (Day and Goudie 1977); most geomorphological applications have involved the intermediate model (type-N).

Operating Procedure

Pressing the instrument firmly against the surface extends a spring which, on automatic release, causes the hammer mass to impact and rebound from the steel plunger in contact with the rock surface (Figure 3.1). The rebound (R) values obtained are a measure of the distance rebounded by the hammer mass. The type-N hammer reads about 78 on a steel anvil; on hard unweathered rocks, values up to 75 can be expected. Softer or weathered rocks yield lower values. Where the rock is so soft that rebound values are below 30, it is advisable to use a hammer with a lower impact energy (type-L). As in the case of any measuring instrument, it is important that a Schmidt hammer be well maintained and suitably adjusted. Brief notes on maintenance and adjustment are presented in Figure 3.1.

Weathering Studies

The potential of the Schmidt hammer for recording the weakening of rock surfaces by weathering was demonstrated by Barton and Choubey (1977), who used it as a field measure of the compressive strength of joint surfaces. Because the surfaces were weathered, they yielded lower and more realistic estimates than laboratory tests on fresh samples. Day (1980) demonstrated that mean R-values are related to the degree of weathering of sandstones (classified using the criteria proposed by Fookes et al. 1971), while more recently McCarroll (1991b) demonstrated a close correlation with measures of the degree of weathering of gabbro. The instrument has been used to examine differences in degree of weathering inside and outside of caves in Sweden (Sjöberg 1991); on inselbergs in Sudan (Campbell et al. 1987); Bornhardts in Zimbabwe (Whitlow and Shakesby 1988); frost-shattered lake shorelines in Norway (Matthews et al. 1986); raised shorelines in Sweden (Sjöberg 1990; Sjöberg and Broadbent 1990, 1991); and snow patches in the European Alps, Scotland, and Norway (Ballantyne et al. 1989). It has also been used to obtain a relative measure of the degree of weathering of bouldery deposits including landslides (Dawson et al. 1986), protalus ramparts (Ballantyne 1986), sorted circles (Cook-Talbot 1991) and glacial moraines (Matthews and Shakesby 1984; McCarroll 1989a, 1989b, 1991c). It is this sensitivity to differences in degree of weathering that provides the potential for the instrument's use in dating.

Relative-Age Dating

The potential of the Schmidt hammer as an indicator of the relative age of landforms and deposits was first recognized by Matthews and Shakesby (1984). They

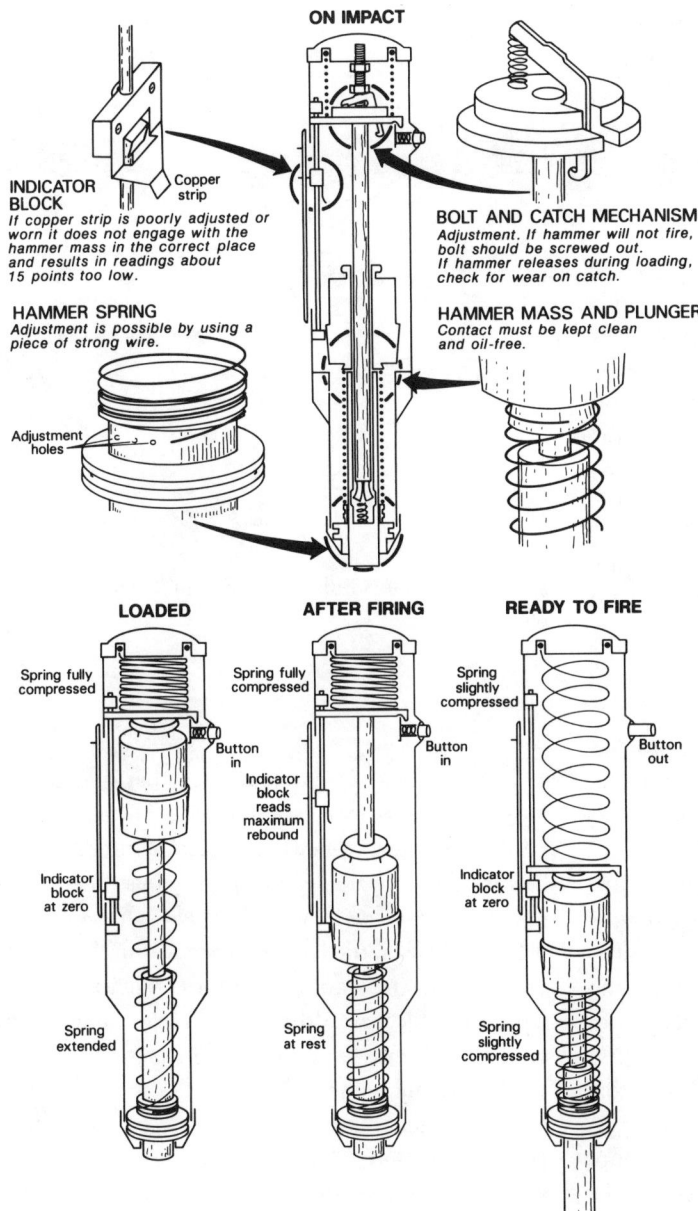

Figure 3.1. The Schmidt hammer: key parts and operation, including notes on dealing with some problems that may arise.

used the Schmidt hammer in conjunction with lichenometry to investigate the status of the "Little Ice Age" (Grove 1988) in southern Norway. At 38 glaciers they compared the mean R-value obtained from the outermost moraine with values obtained on recently deglaciated terrain (inside) and on terrain deglaciated about 9,000 years ago (outside). The results support the traditional model of a mideighteenth-century maximum extent for a large majority of the glaciers. Most moraines assigned by lichenometric dating (Innes 1985;

Matthews, chapter 9 of this volume) to the mideighteenth century yielded mean R-values much closer to those obtained on the young terrain inside than on the much older terrain outside the foreland. However, at a few glaciers the results were equivocal, with low mean R-values obtained on apparently young moraines.

The technique was further developed and refined in the same area by McCarroll (1989a, 1989b, 1991c), who adopted a critical approach, emphasizing possible sources of error. Detailed studies were carried out on the forelands of seven southern Norwegian glaciers. Low R-values were explained by several nontemporal controls on Schmidt hammer results (discussed below) or by the incorporation of previously weathered material during moraine formation.

Most subsequent chronological applications of the Schmidt hammer have also been conducted in cold, mountainous environments. Rebound values are now quite commonly used as evidence that adjacent deposits exhibit differing degrees of weathering and thus differ in age. Features that have been relatively dated in this way include rock glaciers (Shakesby et al. 1987), protalus ramparts (Ballantyne 1986; Shakesby et al. 1987), a catastrophic landslide (Dawson et al. 1986) and frost-shattered lake shorelines (Matthews et al. 1986).

It must be stressed, however, that the Schmidt hammer does not provide a direct measure of degree of rock surface weathering or terrain age. Rebound values are influenced by several interrelated factors, including lithology, rock surface texture, the transport history of boulders, and instrument errors (Figure 3.2). Rebound values are thus easily misinterpreted. Influencing factors other than degree of weathering and surface age represent potential sources of error and should be taken into account before any chronological inferences can be drawn.

Sources of Error

Calibration

Repeated testing of several Schmidt hammers, using the test anvil supplied by the manufacturers, revealed

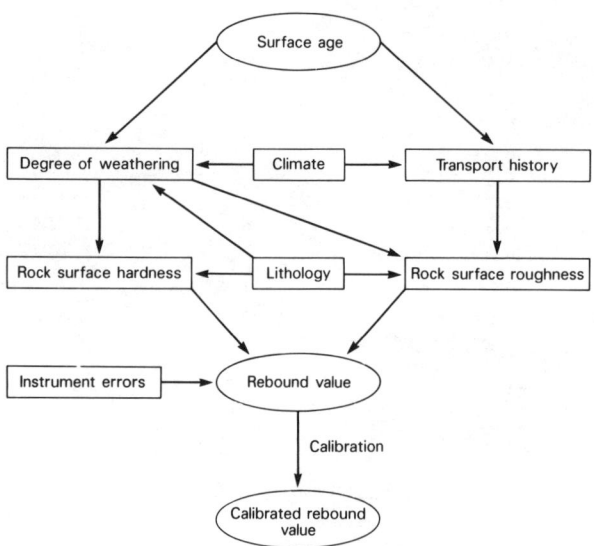

Figure 3.2. Factors influencing Schmidt-hammer rebound values.

several sources of instrument error that may seriously influence results (McCarroll 1987). The R-values obtained from new or newly adjusted hammers may not be directly comparable, and poor adjustment or wear may produce some anomalously low values (see Figure 3.1). In addition the R-values obtained in the field vary according to the amount of use to which the hammer has been subjected. Although the mean value obtained on the anvil tends to decline with increased use, the pattern of decline is unpredictable, and thorough cleaning and adjustment raises the mean value to varying degrees (Figure 3.3). The frequency distribution of results also varies with use, the spread of values tending to increase as the mean value declines.

In order to compare the results obtained from different hammers or even the same hammer at different times, it is essential that R-values be calibrated so that they represent the values that would be obtained from a "perfect" Schmidt hammer. The calibration procedure is simple and takes only a few minutes to perform. A "perfect" hammer would always record a value of 78 on the test anvil. Therefore 78 divided by the mean value obtained from several blows on the test

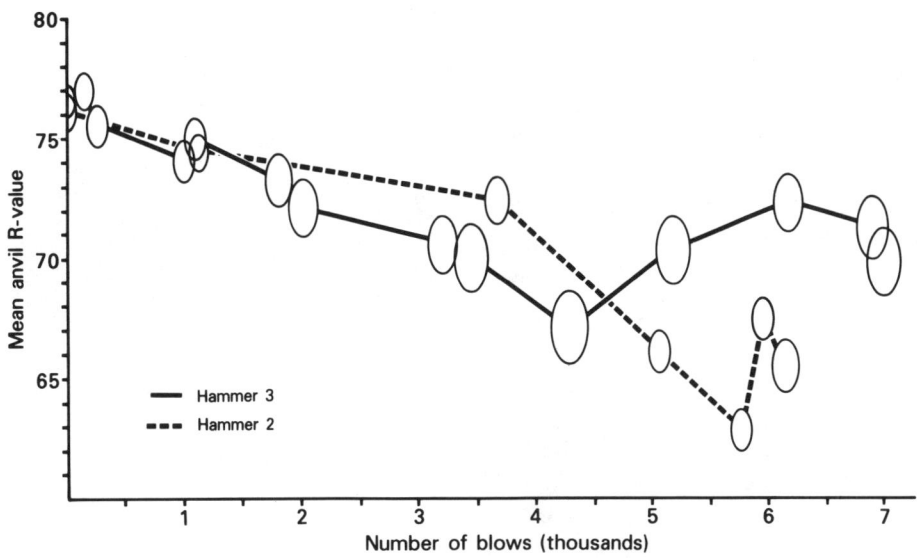

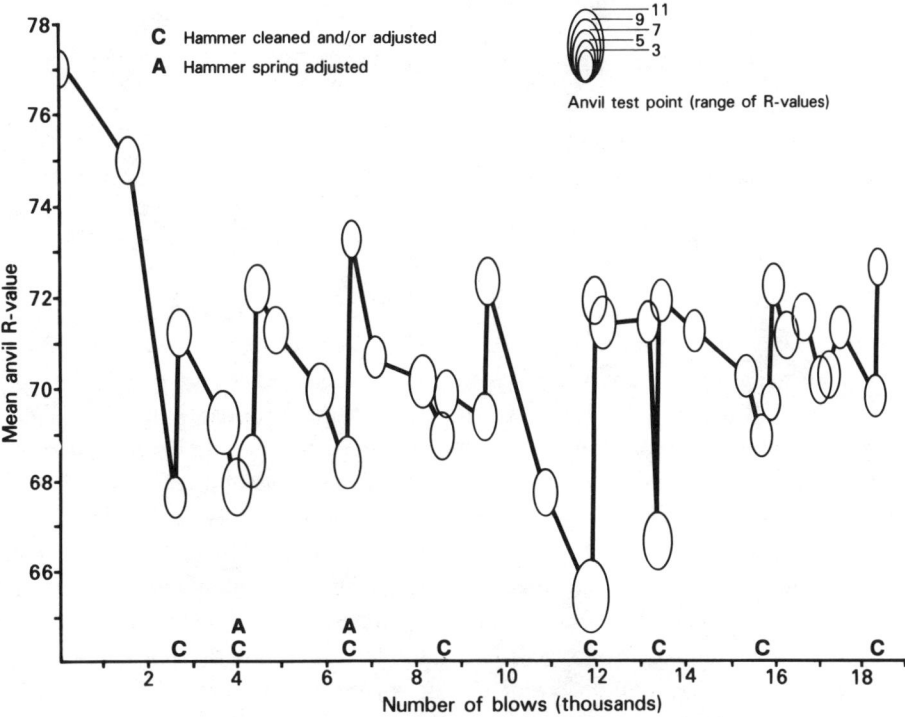

Figure 3.3. Variation in the mean R-value and the range of R-values obtained from samples of 50 blows on the test anvil during intensive field trials of three hammers. A hammer in perfect condition should read 78. Ellipses represent the range of values obtained.

anvil provides a ratio by which field values should be multiplied. Hammers should be tested at the beginning and the end of each day in the field and must be tested before and after any cleaning or adjustment (see Figure 3.3). If the mean value obtained on the anvil declines markedly between tests, calibration ratios can be calculated by assuming that the decline is linearly related to the number of blows recorded in the interval. As few as 10 blows on the anvil will provide a representative mean value, but a sample of 50 is preferable in order to display changes in frequency distribution and occasional anomalous values caused by poor adjustment or wear (see Figure 3.1).

The importance of calibration can be exemplified by comparing the calibrated and uncalibrated mean R-values obtained from 145 sites in Jotunheimen, Norway (Figure 3.4). The same calibrated values were obtained from uncalibrated values with a range of eight points. Matthews and Shakesby (1984) suggest that in Jotunheimen an age difference of up to 9,000 years results in a difference in mean R-values of only 12.7 points, so that a variability of ±8 points caused by not calibrating the results is clearly unacceptable.

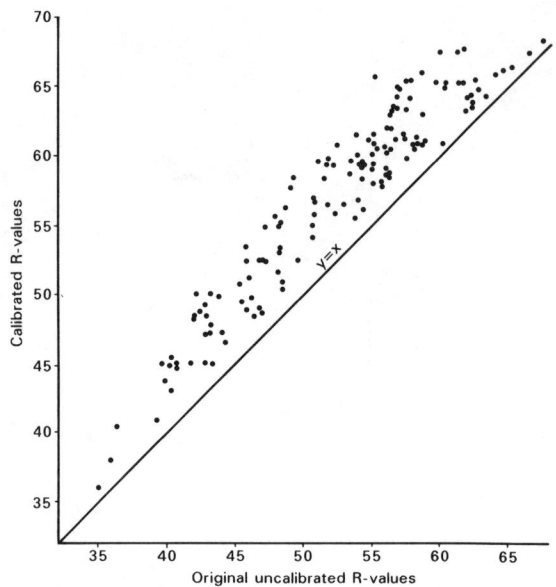

Figure 3.4. Comparison of the mean calibrated values and mean original values obtained from 145 sites on seven glacier forelands in Norway. Each site represents four blows on each of 30 boulders.

Sample Design

The sampling approach used can influence Schmidt hammer results, so it is important that the adopted design be appropriate to the aims of the study. In most studies three questions will require consideration. (1) Should impact points be located randomly or according to some optimizing criteria? (2) How many blows should be recorded from each boulder? (3) How many boulders should be included at each site?

The influence of random placements was tested on the foreland of Storbreen glacier in Jotunheimen, southern Norway. On six moraines of known age (Matthews 1974, 1975), R-values were recorded from 10 randomly located and 10 optimally located impact points on each of 12 boulders. Random points were located using a punctured drape; optimal points were defined as the smoothest available lichen-free surfaces away from joints and edges. The character of the surface at each random point was categorized as bare rock, yellow-green lichens (mainly *Rhizocarpon* spp.), other crustose lichens (mainly grey *Lecidea* spp.), lichen-attacked rock (surface broken by endolithic lichens), black lichens (*Umbilicaria* spp.), and points close to joints and edges (Figure 3.5).

This test produced three results. First, random blows produced consistently lower mean R-values than optimum blows; second, there was little correlation between the mean R-values obtained from optimized and random placements; and finally, whereas the mean R-values obtained from optimum placements displayed no correlation with terrain age over the range from 74 to 240 years, those obtained from random placements displayed a significant decline with increasing surface age over the same range ($p < 0.02$). At first glance these findings might be taken to suggest that, since they are correlated with terrain age, the results of random placements are the more suitable for use in dating studies. On closer examination, however, it is apparent that the

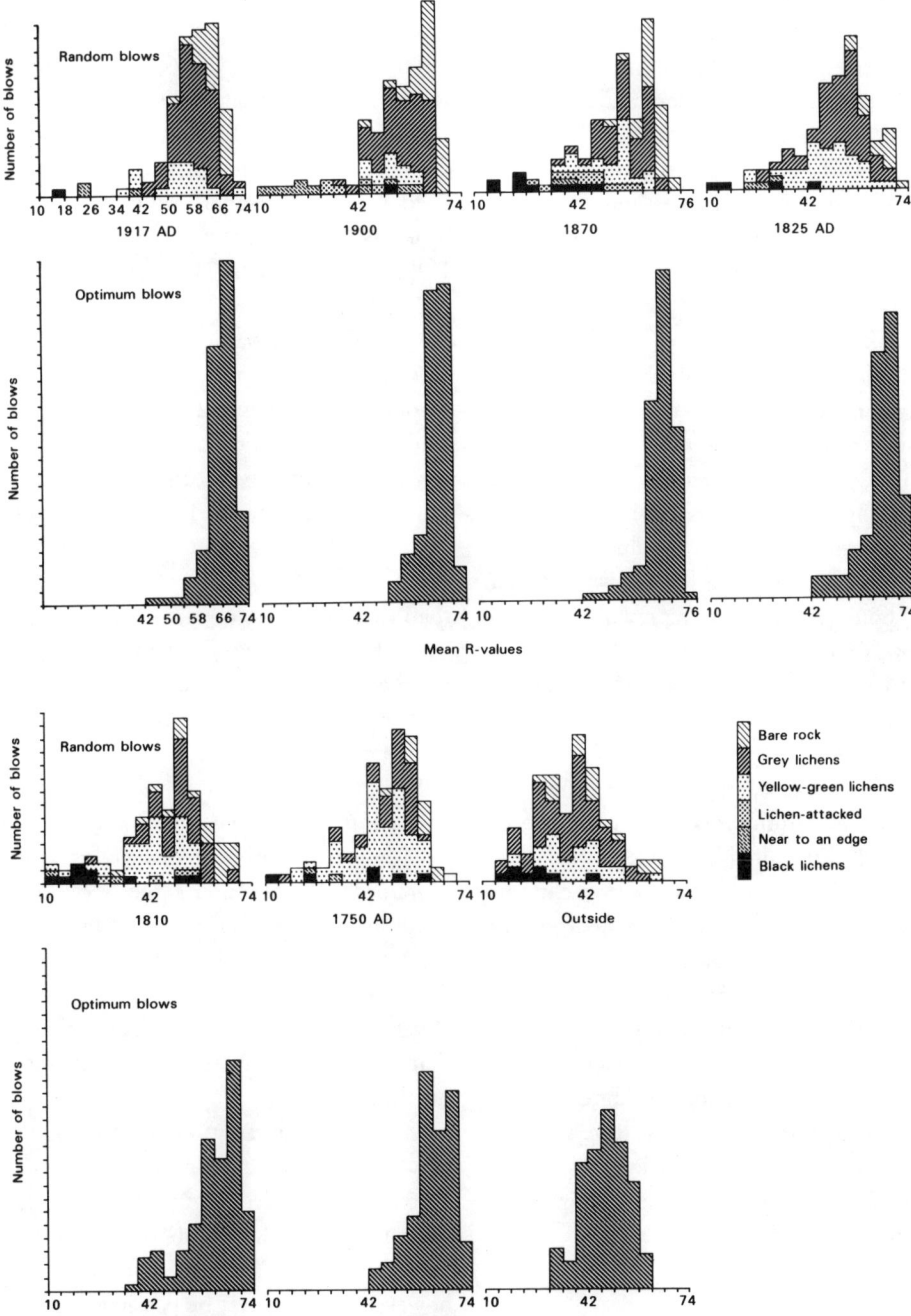

Figure 3.5. Schmidt hammer rebound values obtained from random and optimized placements on terrain of known age on the foreland of Storbreen, southern Norway.

decline in R-values is due not to increased surface weathering, but to changes in the percentage cover of different lichen species (Figure 3.5) and to the increasing thickness of older and larger lichen thalli (McCarroll 1986). Since the factors that control degree of weathering, principally terrain age and microclimate, are also the factors that control variations in lichen cover, R-values obtained by random placement of the Schmidt hammer will be subject to systematic errors, producing misleading results.

Two factors influence the optimum number of R-values to be recorded from each boulder. If too few are recorded, a large number of boulders is required to provide a representative sample. If too many are recorded, particularly on older, heavily lichen-covered surfaces, the choice of optimal points of impact is likely to be restricted, resulting in lower mean R-values. At Storbreen it was found that a sample of four blows recorded from each of 30 boulders provided a representative sample. If more blows were recorded from each boulder, the mean tended to decline. If more boulders were included, the mean remained stable and the standard error of the mean declined only very gradually.

Where boulders are sparse, an alternative procedure is to record several blows from the same point of impact (Ballantyne et al. 1989), but this is inadvisable (Day and Goudie 1977; McCarroll 1990a). The decline in R-values obtained from weathered surfaces incorporates a component due to declining hardness and a component due to increased surface roughness (McCarroll 1991b). Since the first blow is likely to crush the surface, subsequent blows on the same point will record only the first component, reducing the difference in mean values obtained from surfaces that have suffered differing degrees of weathering. Reducing this difference accentuate the (already considerable) impact of systematic errors.

Lithology

Lithology influences Schmidt hammer results through control of rock surface hardness, roughness, and resistance to weathering. It has been demonstrated that different rock types yield different R-values (Day 1980; Day and Goudie 1977; Deere and Miller 1966). Relatively small variations within a single lithology can also be important. On Glittertinden, Jotunheimen, for example, a heterogeneous glacial deposit of uniform age yielded a lower mean R-value for coarse-grained gabbroic rocks (41.84 ± 4.02) than medium- (47.72 ± 1.96) or fine-grained (51.27 ± 2.28) varieties (McCarroll 1989a).

Clearly spatial variations in lithology, even where they are relatively minor, such as a progression from medium- to fine-grained varieties of the same rock type, could cause significant differences in R-values that might be confused with differences in degree of weathering or terrain age. At Leirbreen in Jotunheimen, for example, the outermost moraine produced a lower mean and a more platykurtic distribution of R-values than sites elsewhere on the foreland (Figure 3.6). This could be interpreted as an indication of considerable weathering, and therefore antiquity, or the incorporation of previously weathered material during moraine formation (Matthews and Shakesby 1984; McCarroll 1989b). However, if the lithology of the boulders is examined, it is clear that the low R-values reflect spatial variation in the mixture of lithologies present on the moraines. On the outer ridge, a feldpathic rock that yields lower R-values is particularly common, accounting for the lower R-values. If only the more widespread gabbroic rocks are sampled (pyroxene granulites), the R-values obtained from the outer ridge are no lower than those obtained elsewhere on the foreland (see Figure 3.6)

Where spatial variations in lithology are known, it may be possible to avoid systematic error by adopting a scheme of stratified sampling to ensure that the assumed trend in degree of weathering and terrain age does not parallel a trend in lithology. In some cases, however, this may not be possible. Particular problems are likely to arise in attempting to distinguish the degree of weathering and relative age of locally sourced deposits or landforms, such as landslides, scree slopes, small cirque moraines and protalus ramparts, or archaeological features constructed from a uniform lithology, from

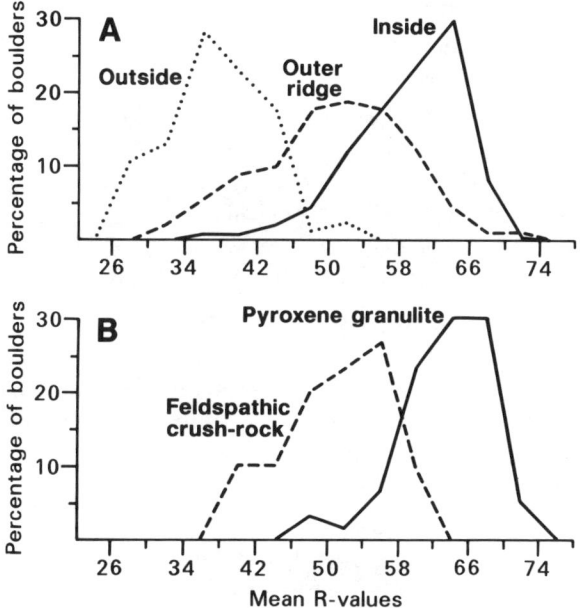

Figure 3.6. Frequency distributions of R-values obtained from boulders of mixed lithology on three sites at Leirbreen, southern Norway (A) compared with R-values obtained from boulders of specific lithologies on the outermost moraine ridge of the foreland (B).

more heterogeneous sediments such as extensive glacial deposits, beach gravels, or outwash. Using the figures obtained from Glittertinden, a locally sourced deposit of coarse-grained gabbro would yield a mean value (41.84) more than five points lower than a heterogeneous deposit of the same age but comprising equal proportions of the three grain sizes (46.94). In such circumstances, it may be necessary to restrict sampling to a narrowly defined lithology or to adjust the results obtained from different lithologies by comparing the results obtained within a heterogeneous deposit of uniform age. Using the example above, the results from coarse-grained gabbroic rocks would be multiplied by 1.14 (47.72 ÷ 41.84), and those from fine-grained rocks by 0.93 (47.72 ÷ 51.27) before comparison with results from medium-grained gabbro.

Weathering and Surface Roughness

Having controlled the influence of instrument calibration, sample design, and lithology, the major remaining factors influencing variability in R-values are degree of weathering and rock surface roughness (see Figure 3.2). It has been argued that rock surface texture exerts such a strong control on R-values that the use of the Schmidt hammer to measure relative intensities of weathering is doubtful (Williams and Robinson 1983). Rock surface roughness and degree of weathering, however, are not independent. On many lithologies, as weathering progresses, rock surface roughness is likely to increase. On gabbroic rocks in Norway, for example, weathering results in the differential relief of adjacent feldspar and pyroxene grains (McCarroll 1990b, 1991b). Differential relief declines with depth beneath the soil surface and provides a convenient measure of degree of weathering, which is strongly correlated with R-values (Figure 3.7).

Clearly differences in surface roughness cannot be viewed simply as a source of error. On the contrary, surface roughness reflects both initial texture and the influence of weathering. With increasing terrain age, increased surface roughness (developed as a direct result of weathering) is likely to contribute substantially to the decline in R-values. This suggests that it is valid to compare the R-values obtained from surfaces of varying roughness only where it is reasonable to assume that prior to the influences of weathering, the surfaces would have exhibited similar textures. The situation is similar to that encountered in attempting to control the influence of lithology. For example the boulders on a scree slope or protalus rampart are likely to be rougher than subglacially abraded boulders in a moraine or fluvially transported boulders in outwash. Stones that have been shaped before incorporation into archaeological structures may also have initial surface textures unlike those of natural rocks nearby. Even on a single glacier foreland, the surface texture of boulders varies spatially in response to the relative proportions of boulders transported by different mechanisms and differences in distance of transportation.

Using a purpose-built instrument, it is possible to re-

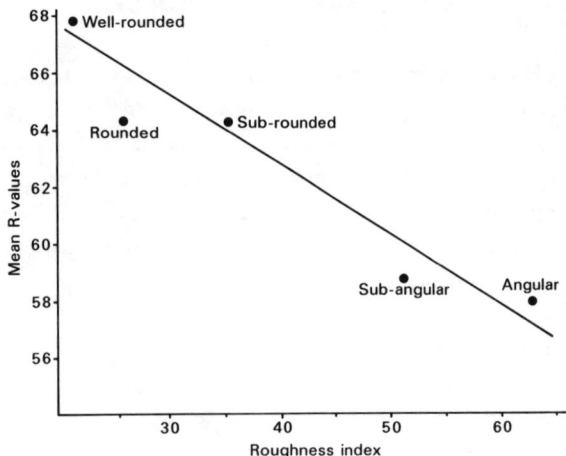

Figure 3.7. The relationship between Schmidt hammer R-values and a measure of degree of weathering of a gabbro surface in Leirdalen, southern Norway. The index of differential relief represents the mean height of pyroxene grains relative to adjacent feldspar grains on a transect. Bars represent two standard errors of the mean.

cord rock surface profiles at a small scale in the field and thus to quantify surface roughness (McCarroll 1992). On recently deglaciated terrain (< 240 years) at Storbreen, it can be demonstrated that boulder surface roughness is related to mode of transportation, with fluvioglacial boulders yielding lower values than subglacially abraded or supraglacially transported boulders (Figure 3.8). Since clast roundness is also related to distance and mode of transportation (Boulton 1978), roundness and roughness of fresh boulders are correlated (Figure 3.9). This relationship is particularly useful since, in glaciated terrain, it allows boulder roundness, estimated here using Powers's (1953) visual comparison technique, to be used as a surrogate of boulder surface roughness. Not only is roundness much easier to measure than roughness, but the former is related to surface roughness *at the time of deposition*. By comparing R-values obtained from boulders of similar roundness, therefore, it is possible to assume similar initial texture but to incorporate the decline in R-values due to increased roughness caused by weathering. The usefulness of this technique can be demonstrated at Storbreen. In Figure 3.10 mean R-values obtained from sites on the foreland are correlated with mean boulder roundness, with only one site falling below the 95 percent confidence limits of the regression line. This site proved to include previously weathered boulders incorporated by a push mechanism during moraine formation. It is notable that by using roundness as a surrogate of roughness it was possible to isolate a site comprising weathered material even though lower mean R-values were obtained elsewhere on the foreland.

Potential for Numerical-Age Dating

Although weathering-based relative-age dating techniques were originally viewed as only "semiquantitative" (Sharp 1969), increasing accuracy of measurement, together with the availability of radiometrically dated deposits that can be used to construct calibration curves, have allowed numerical ages to be estimated from weathering measurements (Carrara and Andrews 1972; Cernohouz and Solc 1966; Chinn 1981; Colman and Pierce 1981; Crooke 1986; Hall and Michaud 1988; Locke 1986; Peck et al. 1990). In theory it would be very straightforward to use Schmidt hammer results in the same way. For example Chinn (1981) used radiocarbon dates from wood buried by landslides to calibrate a rind/age curve; the mean R-value obtained on each landslide could be used to produce a similar R-value/age curve. Unfortunately, because of the range of nontemporal factors that can influence Schmidt hammer results, the curve would not be widely applicable and would probably encourage overconfidence in the accuracy of the technique. The closest approximation to R-value/age curves has been produced by Sjöberg and Broadbent (1990, 1991), who present mean R-values that are closely correlated with altitude on isostatically raised wave-washed moraines on the coast of

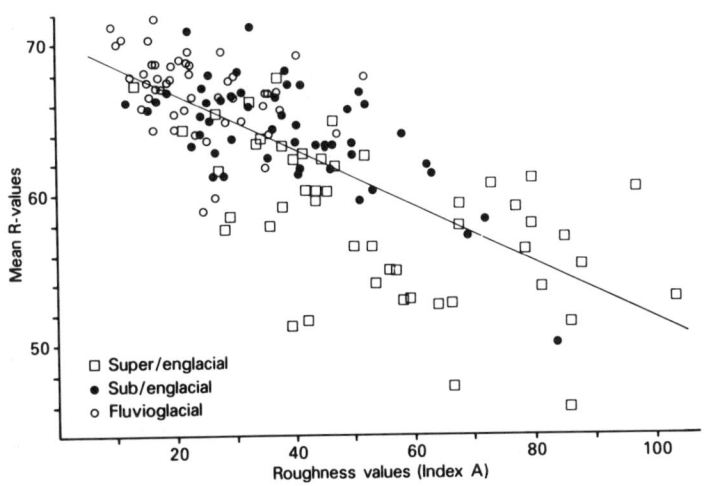

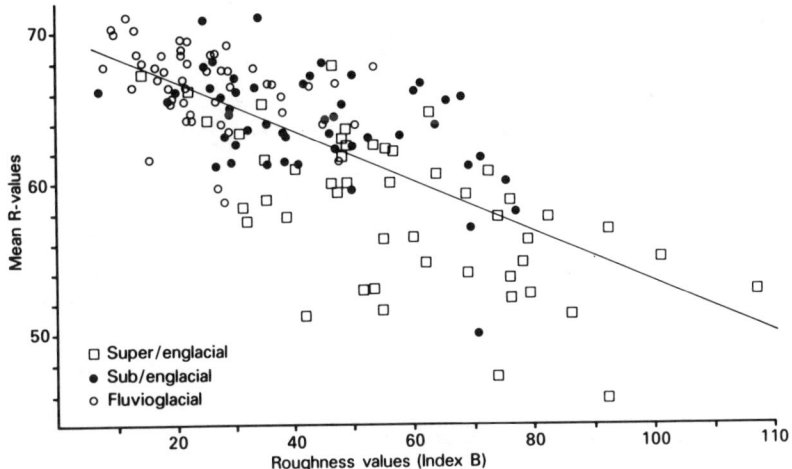

Figure 3.8. Comparison of mean R-values and surface roughness values obtained from boulders with differing transport histories on recently deglaciated terrain. The two indices of surface roughness are calculated from profiles measured using a purpose-built instrument (McCarroll 1992).

Sweden. The rates of present uplift which they quote are of little use in dating the terrain, but if an accurate uplift curve could be constructed, R-values might be of considerable value in dating associated archaeological features.

In glacial terrain, where variation in initial boulder surface texture is a potential source of considerable error, an alternative approach is to construct roughness/R-value curves for deposits of known age and use these to provide limiting dates. An instrument and techniques for measuring surface roughness in the field are described in detail elsewhere (McCarroll 1992). The curves can be constructed by plotting the mean R-values obtained from points of impact grouped according to roughness. Roughness/R-value curves calculated for sites in southern Norway suggest that the difference in R-values expected from smooth gabbro surfaces differing in age by approximately 9,000 years is about 12 points and on more common, slightly rougher surfaces about 10 points (Figure 3.11A). Similar results were obtained from a smaller sample on granitic rocks in Austerdalen, western Norway (Figure 3.11B). This

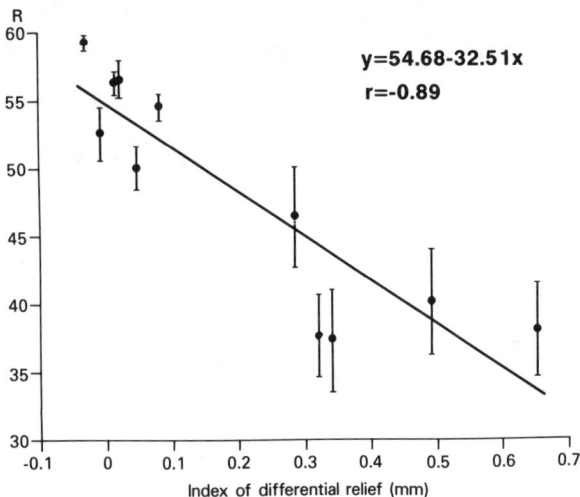

Figure 3.9. Comparison of mean R-values and roughness values (index A of Figure 3.8) obtained from boulders grouped according to roundness.

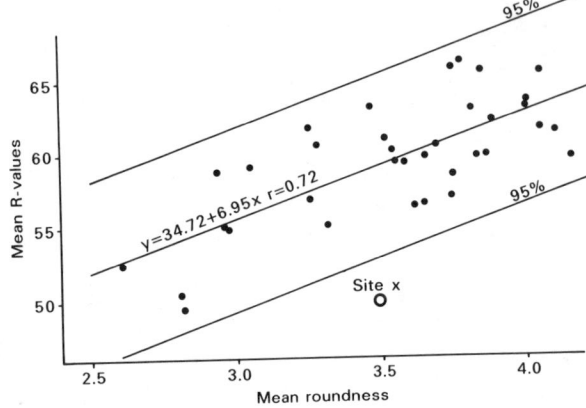

Figure 3.10. Mean roundness and mean R-values obtained from sites on the foreland of Storbreen. Each site represents four blows on each of 30 boulders. Mean roundness is calculated using an adaptation of Powers's (1953) index, where a value of six is assigned to well-rounded clasts, declining linearly to a value of one for very angular clasts.

relatively small difference in the results obtained from surfaces differing in age by 9,000 years leaves little room for error in recognizing deposits of intermediate age. At Storbreen a moraine dated as just 240 years old produced a curve intermediate between those obtained from the young and old ground, suggesting that the measurement of roughness is not accurate enough to allow such small differences in mean R-values to be assigned confidently to differences in terrain age (McCarroll 1989a).

Summary and Conclusions

The Schmidt hammer provides a rapid, inexpensive field measure of rock surface hardness, which is related to degree of weathering and therefore terrain age. It is easy to use and, compared with other measures of degree of rock surface weathering, a large volume of data can be collected relatively quickly. It must be stressed, however, that R-values are not a direct measure of terrain age, and considerable care in sampling design and data analysis is necessary if results are to be interpreted with confidence.

Like most scientific instruments, the Schmidt hammer requires regular maintenance. It seems, however, that it is rarely possible to maintain the instrument in perfect condition. To facilitate comparison of results from different studies, different hammers, and even the same hammer at different times, R-values must be calibrated (McCarroll 1987). The calibration procedure is simple, but has so far been studiously avoided (Ballantyne et al. 1989; Sjöberg and Broadbent 1990, 1991). Sampling schemes should be designed to identify the optimum number of blows on each boulder and the required number per site. Variations in lithology should be investigated and where there are systematic trends, stratified sampling or adjustment of values may be required.

In presenting the data obtained from each site, the mean R-value $\pm$ two standard errors ($\simeq p < 0.05$) provides a useful summary. Measures of deviation are best calculated using the mean R-value obtained from each boulder, rather than the total number of blows at a site.

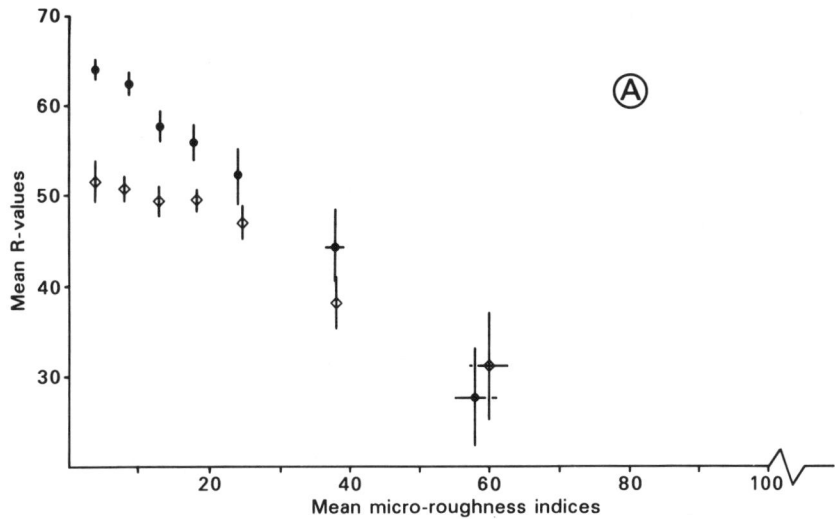

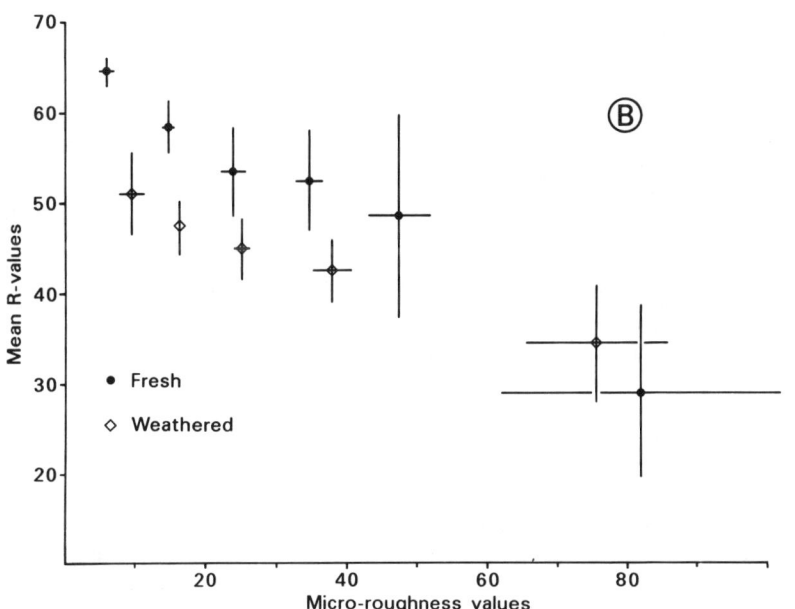

Figure 3.11. Mean R-values obtained from points of impact grouped according to roughness on boulders in recently deglaciated (fresh) and approximately 9,000-year-old terrain (weathered). Sites were located on gabbro at Storbreen in Jotunheimen (A) and on granitic rocks at Austerdalsbreen, western Norway (B). Bars represent two standard errors of the mean.

This reduces the influence of extreme values and stresses between-boulder variability, which is useful for recognizing the influence of variations in lithology or mixtures of fresh and weathered boulders.

The most important recommendation is that a critical, deductive approach be adopted. In weathering-based relative-dating studies, there has been too much emphasis on establishing chronosequences and not enough on the potential sources of error of the techniques used (McCarroll 1991a). That Schmidt hammer results decline in parallel with a presumed trend in surface age is not sufficient evidence that terrain age is the controlling factor. In particular the influence of systematic variations in lithology and initial surface texture should be investigated.

If a critical, deductive methodology is adopted, the instrument can be very useful for determining the relative age of inorganic landforms, deposits, and perhaps archaeological structures. Although calibration curves could be constructed to allow numerical ages to be estimated, they would probably be valid only in a very restricted area.

Acknowledgements

I would like to thank Louise Zelinka for assistance in the field and John Matthews for commenting on an earlier version of the manuscript. The figures were prepared in the cartographic office of the Department of Geography, University of Southampton. This work represents Jotunheimen Research Expeditions Contribution No. 97.

References Cited

Allison, R. J.
1990 Developments in a Non-Destructive Method for Determining Rock Strength. *Earth Surface Processes and Landforms* 15:571–577.
1991 Developments in a Non-Destructive Method of Determining Rock Strength: A Reply. *Earth Surface Processes and Landforms* 16:473–476.

Augustinus, P. C.
1991 Rock Resistance to Erosion: Some Further Considerations. *Earth Surface Processes and Landforms* 16:563–569.

Ballantyne, C. K.
1986 Protalus Rampart Development and the Limits of Former Glaciers in the Vicinity of Baosbheinn, Wester Ross. *Scottish Journal of Geology* 22:13–25.

Ballantyne, C. K., N. M. Black, and D. P. Finlay
1989 Enhanced Boulder Weathering under Late-Lying Snowpatches. *Earth Surface Processes and Landforms* 14:745–750.

Barton, N., and V. Choubey
1977 The Shear Strength of Rock Joints in Theory and Practice. *Rock Mechanics* 10:1–54.

Benedict, L. B.
1973 Chronology of Cirque Glaciation, Colorado Front Range. *Quaternary Research* 3:584–599.

Birkeland, P. W., S. M. Colman, R. M. Burke, and T. C. Mierding
1979 Nomenclature of Alpine Glacial Deposits, or, What's in a Name? *Geology* 7: 532–536.

Boulton, G. S.
1978 Boulder Shape and Grain-Size Distributions as Indicators of Transport Paths through a Glacier and Till Genesis. *Sedimentology* 25:773–799.

Brookes, I. A.
1982 Dating Methods of Pleistocene Deposits and Their Problems. VIII, Weathering. *Geoscience Canada* 99:188–199.

Burke, R. M., and P. W. Birkeland
1979 Re-Evaluation of Multiparameter Relative Dating Techniques and Their Application to the Glacial Sequence along the Eastern Escarpment of the Sierra Nevada, California. *Quaternary Research* 11:21–51.

Campbell, I. A.
1991 Comments on Allison's "Developments in a Non-Destructive Method of Determining Rock Strength." *Earth Surface Processes and Landforms* 16:471–472.

Campbell, M. D., R. A. Shakesby, and R. P. D. Walsh
1987 The Distribution of Weathering and Erosion on an Inselberg-Pediment System in Semi-arid Sudan. In *International Geomorphology* part II, edited by V. Gardiner, pp. 1249–1270. John Wiley and Sons, Chichester.

Carrara, P., and J. T. Andrews
1972 Quaternary History of Northern Cumberland Peninsula, Baffin Island, N.W.T. Part 1. The Late and Neoglacial Deposits of the Akudlermuit and Boas Glaciers. *Canadian Journal of Earth Science* 9:403–414.

Cernohouz, J., and I. Solc
1966 Use of Sandstone Wanes and Weathered Basalt Crust in Absolute Chronology. *Nature* 212:806–807.
1967 Vyuziti Piskovcovych Oblin a Zvetrale Cedicove Kury pro Absolutni Chronologii. *Ceskoslovensky Casopis pro Fysiku* 17:35–42.

Chinn, T. J. H.
1981 Use of Rock Weathering-Rind Thickness for Holocene Absolute Age Dating in New Zealand. *Arctic and Alpine Research* 13:33–45.

Colman, S. M., and K. L. Pierce
1981 *Weathering Rinds on Andesitic and Basaltic Stones as a Quaternary Age Indicator, Western United States.* United States Geological Survey, Professional Paper 1210.

Cook-Talbot, J. D.
1991 Sorted-Circles, Relative-Age Dating and Palaeoenvironmental Reconstruction in an Alpine Periglacial Environment, Eastern Jotunheimen, Norway: Lichenometric and Weathering-Based Approaches. *The Holocene* 1:128–141.

Crooke, R.
1986 Relative Dating of Quaternary Deposits Based on P-Wave Velocities in Weathered Granitic Clasts. *Quaternary Research* 25:281–293.

Dawson, A. G., J. A. Matthews, and R. A. Shakesby
1986 A Catastrophic Landslide (Sturtzstrom) in Verkilsdalen, Rondane National Park, Southern Norway. *Geografiska Annaler* 68(A):77–87.

Day, M. J.
1980 Rock Hardness: Field Assessment of Geomorphic Importance. *Professional Geographer* 32:72–81.

Day, M. J., and A. S. Goudie
1977 Field Assessment of Rock Hardness Using the Schmidt Hammer. *British Geomorphological Research Group Technical Bulletin* 18:19–29.

Deere, D. V., and R. P. Miller
1966 *Engineering Classification and Index Properties for Intact Rock.* Technical Report Number AFNL-TR-65-116. Air Force Weapons Laboratory, New Mexico.

Dowdeswell, J. A.
1984 Late Quaternary Chronology for the Watts Bay Area, Frobisher Bay, Southern Baffin Island, N.W.T., Canada. *Arctic and Alpine Research* 16:311–320.

Fookes, P. G., W. R. Dearman, and J. A. Franklin
1971 Some Engineering Aspects of Rock Weathering with Field Examples from Dartmoor and Elsewhere. *Quarterly Journal of Engineering Geology* 4:139–185.

Gellatly, A. F.
1984 The Use of Rock Weathering-Rind Thickness to Redate Moraines in Mount Cook National Park, New Zealand. *Arctic and Alpine Research* 16:225–232.

Grove, J. M.
1988 *The Little Ice Age.* Methuen, London and New York.

Hall, R. D., and Y. Michaud
1988 The Use of Hornblende Etching, Clast Weathering, and Soils to Date Alpine Glacial and Periglacial Deposits: A Study From Southwest Montana. *Geological Society of America Bulletin* 100:458–467.

Innes, J. L.
1985 Lichenometry. *Progress in Physical Geography* 9:187–254.

Knuepfer, P. L. K.
1988 Estimating Ages of Late Quaternary Stream Terraces from Analysis of Weathering Rinds and Soils. *Geological Society of America Bulletin* 100:1224–1236.

Locke, W. W.
1979 Etching of Hornblende Grains in Arctic-Soils: An Indicator of Relative Age and Paleoclimate. *Quaternary Research* 11:197–212.
1986 Rates of Hornblende Etching in Soils on Glacial Deposits, Baffin Island. In *Rates of Chemical Weathering of Rocks and Minerals,* edited by S. M. Coleman and D. P. Dethier, pp. 129–144. Academic Press, London.

Matthews, J. A.
1974 Families of Lichenometric Dating Curves from the Storbreen Gletschervorfeld, Jotunheimen,

Norway. *Norsk Geografisk Tidsskrift* 28:215–235.

1975 Experiments on the Reproducibility and Reliability of Lichenometric Dates, Storbreen Gletschervorfeld, Jotunheimen, Norway. *Norsk Geografisk Tidsskrift* 29:97–109.

Matthews, J. A., A. G. Dawson, and R. A. Shakesby

1986 Lake Shoreline Development, Frost Weathering and Rock Platform Erosion in an Alpine Periglacial Environment, Jotunheimen, Southern Norway *Boreas* 15:33–50.

Matthews, J. A., and R. A. Shakesby

1984 The Status of the 'Little Ice Age' in Southern Norway: Relative-Age Dating of Neoglacial Moraines with Schmidt Hammer and Lichenometry. *Boreas* 13:333–346.

McCarroll, D.

1986 *Relative-Age Dating of Neoglacial Moraines, Jotunheimen, Southern Norway: The Potential of the Schmidt Hammer.* Unpublished Ph.D. thesis, University of Wales.

1987 The Schmidt Hammer in Geomorphology: Five Sources of Instrument Error. *British Geomorphological Research Group Technical Bulletin* 36:16–27.

1989a Potential and Limitations of the Schmidt Hammer for Relative-Age Dating: Field Tests on Neoglacial Moraines, Jotunheimen, Southern Norway. *Arctic and Alpine Research* 21:268–275.

1989b Schmidt Hammer Relative-Age Evaluation of a Possible Pre-'Little Ice Age' Neoglacial Moraine, Leirbreen, Southern Norway. *Norsk Geologisk Tidsskrift* 69:125–130.

1990a A Comment on "Enhanced Boulder Weathering under Late-Lying Snowpatches" by C. K. Ballantyne, N. M. Black, and D. P. Finlay. *Earth Surface Processes and Landforms* 15:467–469.

1990b Differential Weathering of Feldspar and Pyroxene in an Arctic Alpine Environment. *Earth Surface Processes and Landforms* 15:641–651.

1991a Relative-Age Dating of Inorganic Deposits: The Need for a More Critical Approach. *The Holocene* 1:174–180.

1991b The Schmidt Hammer, Weathering and Rock Surface Roughness. *Earth Surface Processes and Landforms* 16:477–480.

1991c The Age and Origin of Neoglacial Moraines, Jotunheimen, Southern Norway: New Evidence from Weathering-Based Data. *Boreas* 20:283–295.

1992 A New Instrument and Techniques for the Field Measurement of Rock Surface Roughness. *Zeitschrift für Geomorphologie* 36:69–79.

Peck, B. J., D. S. Kaufman, and P. E. Calkin

1990 Relative Dating of Moraines Using Moraine Morphometric and Boulder Weathering Criteria, Kigluaik Mountains, Alaska. *Boreas* 19:227–239.

Powers, M. C.

1953 A New Roundness Scale for Sedimentary Particles. *Journal of Sedimentary Petrology* 23:117–119.

Selby, M. J.

1980 A Rock Mass Strength Classification for Geomorphic Purposes with Tests from Antarctica and New Zealand. *Zeitschrift für Geomorphologie* 24:31–35.

Shakesby, R. A., A. G. Dawson, and J. A. Matthews

1987 Rock Glaciers, Protalus Ramparts and Related Phenomena, Rondane, Norway: A Continuum of Large-Scale Talus-Derived Landforms. *Boreas* 16:305–317.

Sharp, R. P.

1969 Semiquantitative Differentiation of Glacial Moraines near Convict Lake, Sierra Nevada, California. *Journal of Geology* 77:68–91.

Sheorey, P. R., D. Barat, M. N. Das, K. P. Mukherjee, and B. Singh

1984 Schmidt Hammer Rebound Data for Estimation of Large Scale *in situ* Coal Strength. *International Journal of Rocks and Minerals Science and Geomechanics Abstracts* 21:39–42.

Sjöberg, R.

1990 Measurement and Calibration of Weathering

Processes on Wave Washed Moraine and Bedrock on the Upper Norrland Coast, Sweden. *Geografiska Annaler* 72A:319–327.

1991 Weathering Studies on Pseudokarst Caves along the Northern Swedish Coast. *Zeitschrift für Geomorphologie N.F.* 35:305–320.

Sjöberg, R., and N. Broadbent

1990 Measurement and Calibration of Weathering Processes on Wave Washed Moraine and Bedrock on the Upper Norrland Coast, Sweden. *Jeomorfoloji Dergisi* 18:19–23.

1991 Measurement and Calibration of Weathering, Using the Schmidt Hammer, on Wave Washed Moraines on the Upper Norrland Coast, Sweden. *Earth Surface Processes and Landforms* 16:57–64.

Summerfield, M. A., and A. S. Goudie

1980 The Sarsen Stones of Southern England: Their Palaeo-Environmental Significance with Regard to Other Silcretes. In *The Shaping of Southern England*, edited by D. K. C. Jones, pp. 71–100. Institute of British Geographers Special Publication 11.

Whitlow, R., and R. A. Shakesby

1988 Bornhardt Micro-Geomorphology: Form and Origin of Micro-Valleys and Rimmed Gutters, Domboshava, Zimbabwe. *Zeitschrift für Geomorphologie* 32:179–194.

Williams, R. B. G., and D. A. Robinson

1983 The Effects of Surface Texture on the Determination of the Surface Hardness of Rock Using the Schmidt Hammer. *Earth Surface Processes and Landforms* 8:289–292.

Yaalon, D. H., and S. Singer

1974 Vertical Variation of Strength and Porosity of Calcrete (nari), Shefala, Israel, and Interpretation of its Origin. *Journal of Sedimentary Petrology* 44:1016–1023.

4
DATING SURFACE ASSEMBLAGES USING OBSIDIAN HYDRATION

Charlotte Beck and George T. Jones

*Department of Anthropology
Hamilton College
Clinton, New York*

Abstract

Obsidian hydration dating, since its introduction in 1960, has been used extensively as both a numerical-age and a relative-age method, but almost exclusively with respect to subsurface artifacts. In this chapter the application of obsidian hydration dating in surface context is addressed, using nearly 700 dated artifacts from Butte Valley, Nevada. Following a detailed discussion of the method and its uncertainties, a serial chronological order of assemblages is constructed. Using this order, issues of contemporaneity among artifacts and duration of occupation are addressed.

Introduction

SINCE WILLEY'S PIONEERING WORK IN THE early 1950s (Willey 1951, 1953), prehistoric settlement and land use studies have become central to archaeological inquiry; this development was accompanied by a general shift in the focus of archaeological research design away from single-site studies to investigations of regions. In order to obtain data on a regional scale, however, researchers found it necessary to examine the potential of the surface record for providing the kinds of information generally believed attainable only through excavation (see Ahler and Benz 1980; Bettinger 1989; Dancey 1974; Foley 1981a, 1981b; Lewarch 1979; O'Brien and Lewarch 1982; Thomas 1972, 1973, 1975).

Several decades later the collection of surface data is now commonplace in archaeology, although concerns over the quality of these data remain. Arguments against their usefulness focus on several factors: (1) potential lateral movement as a result of postdepositional disturbance; (2) the mixing of assemblages due to reuse or overlapping use of areas; and (3) the inapplicability of most dating methods in surface contexts. Regarding the potential for lateral movement, Dunnell and Dancey (1983:269) have observed that most subsurface deposits originated on the surface and were subjected not only to surface disturbances but also to later subsurface disruptive processes, which can be considerable (see Schiffer 1972, 1987; Wood and Johnson 1978). Furthermore it has been shown that lateral movement due to postdepositional disturbance is not as great in many circumstances as one might expect (Lewarch 1979; Lewarch and O'Brien 1981; O'Brien and Lewarch 1982; Roper 1976; Trubowitz 1978). Thus the present problems with the use of the surface record lie in the second and third factors, which are inextricably related: assemblage mixing and dating.

The dating of surface artifact assemblages has traditionally been based on the use of temporally diagnostic artifacts such as ceramics, basketry, and projectile points, when such artifacts are present. This approach is dependent upon two major assumptions (Jones and Beck 1992): (1) that artifacts in close proximity are associated as if they were contained in a buried stratigraphic unit; and (2) that based on such associations, the chronological information carried by diagnostic artifacts can be extended to nondiagnostic artifacts in an assemblage. Stated in this way, such assumptions may seem unwarranted, but in the absence of other means of making chronological sense of surface assemblages, they have been made repeatedly.

It is often the case that surface assemblages lack diagnostic artifacts, making these assemblages virtually impossible to date. This is particularly vexing if there is reason to suspect that an assemblage represents multiple, overlapping occupations. Even more problematic, however, are artifactual remains that are widely dispersed (that is, "offsite" remains [Foley 1981a, 1981b]), for which no associational argument can be made even if diagnostics are present.

In this chapter we discuss one approach, obsidian hydration dating, that may be useful in separating temporally mixed assemblages, putting those assemblages into relative temporal order, and giving temporal context to the low-density artifact record. Although obsidian hydration dating is not a new approach, its use with regard to surface material is not widely practiced. It offers the potential, as does thermoluminescence dating (see Dunnell and Feathers, chapter 6 of this volume), for dating every artifact, which should lead us to think quite differently about how we organize the archaeological record for analytic purposes (Dunnell 1992).

The Obsidian Hydration Dating Method

First presented in 1960 by Friedman and Smith and evaluated archaeologically by Evans and Meggers (1960), obsidian hydration dating (OHD) has become widely used, especially in areas such as the American West and Mesoamerica, where obsidian is plentiful in the archaeological record. The method is based on the fact that a freshly broken surface of obsidian gradually absorbs moisture from its surroundings. The progress of this absorption is marked by a diffusion front that separates the hydrated glass (the hydration rind) from unaltered glass. This rind can be seen in thin section under a microscope when luminated by polarizing light. Measurement of the depth of the hydration rind, combined with knowledge of the rate at which the rind expands, provides a means of estimating the age of the artifact. The technique used to measure rind depth is detailed in Friedman and Smith (1960), Michels (1973), and Michels and Tsong (1980).

In their original presentation of the OHD method, Friedman and Smith (1960) suggested that the hydration of obsidian could be described as a simple diffusion process according to the following equation:

(1) $$x^2 = kt$$

where x is the depth of water penetration (thickness of hydration rind), k is the diffusion constant for a given temperature, and t is time in years. Although there has been some debate over whether this equation best describes the hydration process (see Clark 1964; Meighan et al. 1968; Meighan and Haynes 1970), most studies to date have supported its use.

Friedman and Smith discussed several factors that could have an effect on the hydration rate. Aside from burning and erosion, which actually damage the hydrated layer, three potentially influencing factors were discussed: chemical composition of the obsidian, temperature of the hydrating environment, and relative humidity of the hydrating environment. Because these factors are now known to affect OHD results substantially, we will discuss each of them in detail.

Chemical Composition

Obsidian is a glassy volcanic rock composed of eight major elements and a large number of minor, or trace, elements (Friedman and Smith 1960:484). Most artifact-quality obsidian is rhyolitic in composition, but as Hughes and Smith (1993) point out, such obsidians form in a number of different ways, and the conditions of formation directly affect the chemical composition of the flow. Friedman and Smith (1960:485) recognized from the beginning that obsidians of different compositions hydrate at different rates, pointing out that varying colors and different degrees of banding and mottling are due to differences in chemical composition or physical properties related to cooling. Because little was known, however, concerning the extent to which chemical composition could affect the hydration rate, their comparisons were of broad groups, such as "rhyolitic" versus "trachytic" obsidians. Although Friedman and Smith (1960:484) recognized that "there is some variation in the proportions of even the major components" of obsidians, such broad comparisons led other researchers to assume that there was little chemical variation among rhyolitic obsidians, and that it was temperature that caused the greatest differences in hydration rates (Michels and Tsong 1980). Thus although several early studies undertook geochemical analyses of the obsidian to be used in OHD (see Jack and Heizer 1968; Stross et al. 1968), it was not until the mid-1970s that chemical composition was recognized as a major factor affecting the hydration rate (Michels and Tsong 1980:424).

Today this effect is generally recognized, and source analysis is a routine procedure in any OHD project. The idea behind source analysis is that every obsidian flow can be characterized in terms of a distinct set of constituent trace elements and thus can be "fingerprinted." Once sources have been defined in terms of the relative proportions of these elements, an artifact can then be analyzed as to its constituent elements and identified with the source from which it came. A number of techniques are available for trace element analysis, such as atomic absorption spectroscopy, electron probe analysis, neutron activation analysis, and sputter-induced optical emission analysis; x-ray fluorescence spectrometry (XRF), however, appears to be the most commonly used for archaeological purposes.

Early source distinctions were based on the use of ternary diagrams using the three elements Rb, Sr, and Zr (see Jack and Heizer 1968; Stross et al. 1968). The approach served well when differences among sources were pronounced, but it tended to confuse sources with similar proportions of these elements (Hughes 1984). Later research employed the use of discriminant function analysis, distinguishing sources on a larger number of elements (see Hughes 1984 for a discussion of this approach).

Source characterizations generally proceed on the assumption that although separate rhyolitic flows may differ in their composition, individual flows should be chemically homogeneous throughout. Recently, however, it has been shown that this is not always the case, and that under some conditions, a source area might show a variety of chemical signatures (Hughes and Smith 1993).

Hughes and Smith (1993:81) suggest that most obsidian artifacts were probably manufactured from obsidians formed in the upper levels of very young lava flows or domes; such obsidians can show great variation in color, texture, and other physical properties, while most of the time retaining their chemical homogeneity. Some flows, however, have been shown to vary throughout in their chemical composition. Studies of the Casa Diablo source in Mono County, California (Hughes 1991), for example, suggest at least two and possibly three geochemical varieties of artifact-quality obsidian present. Such variation has led Hughes and Smith (1993:83) to designate Casa Diablo, as well as other sources such as Coso and Glass Mountain (also in California), as variable source areas, with each subarea within the source area being a coherent geochemical type.

Unfortunately Hughes and Smith's findings make the confidence we felt for a decade or more concerning our success in "sourcing" obsidian artifacts a bit premature. Although many, if not most, of the world's obsidian sources are believed to have been located and at least preliminarily surveyed, extensive studies of each source must be undertaken to ensure its chemical homogeneity.

Temperature

Since the inception of the OHD method, work has focused on effective hydration temperature as the primary factor influencing the hydration rate. It has been suggested by several researchers that an increase in temperature of 1°C can increase the hydration rate by as much as 10 percent (Ambrose 1976; Trembour and Friedman 1984). Furthermore Trembour and Friedman (1984:80) suggest that even short exposures to abnormally high heat, such as burning, can seriously affect the hydration process.

In their original paper, Friedman and Smith (1960) demonstrated that hydration rates for obsidians from tropical zones were very different from those in temperate zones, and that in fact there were smaller differences in rates within these zones. These differences were attributed by Friedman and Smith primarily to varying temperatures in the hydrating environments. They recommended and undertook experiments in measuring air, surface, and soil temperatures in an attempt to establish hydration rates for particular areas (see Friedman et al. 1966). These experiments, as well as those undertaken by others (see Friedman and Long 1976; Michels et al. 1983a; Michels et al. 1983b), have also investigated the utility of induced hydration of obsidians under laboratory conditions and elevated temperatures and pressures, for the purpose of establishing hydration rates for specific obsidians (that is, for specific source chemistries). Because investigations of temperature effects on the hydration process have been closely tied to induced hydration experimentation, we will first discuss induced hydration and then return to the estimation of effective hydration temperatures.

INDUCED HYDRATION

Induced hydration is an experimental approach that involves taking a piece of freshly broken obsidian and placing it in either a vapor (Friedman and Long 1976; Mazer et al. 1991) or hydrothermal (Michels et al. 1983a; Michels et al. 1983b) environment and heating it for an extended period of time.[1] Under high temperatures (100°–200°C) in such controlled environments, hydration rinds will form over the relatively short period of several weeks. Under these controlled conditions, the variables affecting the process (time, temperature, and chemical composition) are known and thus together with hydration-rind measurements can be used to calculate an experimental hydration rate. In the first experiments by Friedman et al. (1966), the samples were heated to 100°C and some samples were treated for as long as four years. Subsequent studies generally experiment at a range of temperatures and pressures for varying amounts of time.

As stated earlier, calculation of the hydration rate is based on the diffusion equation originally presented by Friedman and Smith 1960: $x^2 = kt$. In order to calculate an experimental rate for an obsidian (see the detailed discussion in Friedman and Long 1976:347–349), the hydration measurements for each effective hydration temperature are plotted against the square root of time, and the value of k (the diffusion constant at each temperature) is derived from the slope of each curve (see Friedman and Long 1976, Figure 3). These values are then plotted against 1/T to arrive at a solution for the Arrhenius equation, which relates the hydration rate to temperature:

$$(2) \qquad k = Ae^{-E/RT}$$

where A is a constant (coefficient dependent on physical or chemical properties of the glass), E is the activation energy of the hydration process (calories per mole), R is the universal gas constant (calories per degree per mole), and T is absolute temperature (degrees Kelvin). E and A are both dependent on the chemical composition of the glass, which is held constant in the experiment. Using the rates of hydration for each temperature, the Arrhenius equation can be solved for these variables: in the plot of k against 1/T, the slope of the line is equal to $-E/R$, while the intercept of the abscissa provides the value of 1nA.

Once the rate is computed, one need only determine

the natural effective hydration temperature for a specific location in order to apply the rate to obsidian of the same composition at that location.

Effective Hydration Temperature

Learning the thermal history of an obsidian artifact has proven to be the most difficult problem thus far in OHD studies. One approach is to use the average annual temperature and Lee's (1969) chemical temperature integration equation to approximate the effective hydration temperature (EHT). This equation was derived using the Pallman technique, which relates the reaction velocity of sucrose hydrolysis to temperature using an Arrhenius-type equation (Michels et al. 1983b:109; see also Friedman and Long 1976; Norton and Friedman 1981). Lee's equation makes use of the mean annual temperature (T_a) and the annual temperature range (R_t) to solve for the environmental effective mean (T_e):

(3) $\quad T_a = -1.2316 + 1.0645T_e - 0.1607R_t.$

Several studies have used this approach with general success (see Michels et al. 1983a; Michels et al. 1983b; Norton and Friedman 1981). Others, however, have suggested that average annual soil temperatures rather than average annual air temperatures should be used, since there can be great disparity between the two (Friedman and Long 1976; Ridings 1991; Zeier and Elston 1984). Furthermore not only is there disparity between air and soil temperature, but temperature also changes with depth. Soil temperature varies depending upon a number of factors (Hanks and Ashcroft 1980), such as color, moisture content, slope, aspect, vegetation, snow cover, cloud cover, and so on. Unless geothermal activity is present in the area, soil temperatures generally show a negative gradient from the surface, with changes becoming smaller with increasing depth. Thus the disparity between the temperature at 5 cm depth and that at 25 cm depth will be greater than the disparity between the temperature at 25 cm and 50 cm. As a consequence a piece of obsidian at a depth of 5 cm will hydrate at a faster rate than one 50 cm below the surface.

Friedman and Long (1976) measured soil temperatures at different depths at several sites. Measurements were made using a buried sensor, and temperature readings were taken every five days. Effective hydration temperatures were shown to vary considerably between air and soil, and then also to vary with depth. For instance, at Yellowstone National Park, effective air temperature was measured at 12°C, while effective soil temperature at 0.9 m depth measured only 6.9°C and at 1.8 m depth, 6.0°C. Mean annual air temperature was reported at 1.7°C, while mean soil temperature was reported at 6.0°C (at 0.9 m) and 5.7°C (at 1.8 m).

Other studies indicate that EHT not only varies with depth but can also vary in range at different locations. For instance, Ambrose's (1984) data indicate a 12°C difference between 0.05 m and 1.5 m in a dry lakebed setting. Leach and Hamel's (1984) study in New Guinea shows a 3.2°C difference between 0.18 m and 0.9 m. Such variation can also occur at different locations within a region. Zeier and Elston (1984) found different thermal gradients at each of nine stations measured over the period of a year in and around the Sugarloaf obsidian quarry, Inyo County, California, with some showing increased temperature with depth, due to geothermal activity.

Surface temperatures differ altogether from both air and subsurface soil temperatures. More recent data from Yellowstone show a difference of 14.2°C between surface temperature (19.7°C) and temperature at 1.8 m depth (5.5°C) (Friedman and Obradovich 1981). Such disparities have led Friedman and Obradovich (1981:41) to conclude that a sample exposed to the sun can be expected to hydrate five times faster than a sample buried 2 m below the ground (see also Friedman 1976).

These studies suggest that not only should soil temperature be measured at the site at which dating will be undertaken, but also that hydration rates will change with depth. A few researchers have attempted to do this (see Ridings 1991; Zeier 1986; Zeier and Elston 1984), although more often they compute a general obsidian-specific rate for all artifacts of that obsidian at a single location, regardless of depth of burial.

Relative Humidity

It was originally believed that relative humidity had no effect on the hydration process. Friedman and Smith's (1960) analysis of obsidian and perlite (thoroughly hydrated obsidian) showed that unhydrated obsidian contains between 0.1 percent and 0.2 percent water, while perlite contains 3.5 percent water. On a piece of hydrating obsidian, the diffusion front between hydrated and unhydrated portions is sharp, varying only on the order of 0.1 μm in depth. They concluded that the hydrated layer becomes "saturated" at 3.5 percent water, and that relative humidities of higher than this amount have no effect on the hydration rate.

Recently, however, researchers have begun to suspect that relative humidity is, in fact, an important factor in the hydration process (see Friedman et al. 1990; Leach and Hamel 1984; Mazer et al. 1991). In a recent study (Mazer et al. 1991), hydration was induced in obsidians from Coso (California), Mule Creek (New Mexico), and Orito Quarry (Easter Island), at 95 percent, 90 percent, and 60 percent relative humidity, using EHT's of 150°C and 175°C. The rate of hydration for each obsidian was constant at 60 percent and 90 percent relative humidity for each temperature; between 90 percent and 100 percent relative humidity, however, the rate changed significantly (between 10 percent and 30 percent), depending on the composition of the glass.

In order to understand these results, Mazer et al. considered the process of water sorption on a crushed sample of Coso obsidian. Sorption studies on glass indicate that the amount of sorbed water increases rapidly above 80 percent relative humidity, and this proved to be the case with the Coso obsidian (Ebert et al. 1991). Thus Mazer et al. (1991:510) conclude that obsidian hydration is a "relatively simple process of water diffusion that is controlled by the environmental variables temperature and relative humidity." They suggest that the combined effects of these two variables can cause extreme variations in the hydration rate. For instance, they suggest that the rate of hydration for Coso obsidian decreases by approximately 25 percent when relative humidity declines from 97 percent to 68 percent. Combined with the effects of EHT, their calculations show that the hydration rate "varied by nearly an order of magnitude within a 1-m soil profile" (1991:511).

Discussion

From the preceding discussion, it is obvious that the environmental variables of temperature and relative humidity are the controlling factors in any attempt to use OHD in either a numerical (see discussion of terminology, Introduction) or relative manner. Because these factors and their effects are still not completely understood, the use of OHD as a numerical-age method is limited to those circumstances in which artifacts are recovered from deeply buried, temperature- and humidity-stable environments. Even then a rate established in one locale will not be applicable to artifacts collected from another locale with different temperature characteristics (see Ridings 1991).

Furthermore different approaches to rate derivation will yield different chronometric estimates. For example, Zeier (1986) applied four different hydration rates derived from Medicine Lake obsidian to obsidian artifacts from Elk Creek in Oregon. Two of the rates (Ericson 1981; Johnson 1969) were derived archaeologically (that is, using the correlation of ^{14}C dates and hydration-rind measurements in associated stratigraphic context), a third was derived using Friedman and Long's (1976) chemical index, and the fourth was derived through induced hydration. Comparisons of the results suggested that the archaeologically derived rates were the least accurate, and that the induced rate gave the best results. Hall and Jackson (1989), however, although supporting in general the use of induced rates, argue that these rates should be verified against archaeological materials of known age before they are universally applied.

The effectiveness of OHD as a numerical-age method really depends on the precision sought in the research. For instance, Michels et al. (1983a), in applying OHD to subsurface artifacts from the Prospect Farm Site in Kenya, obtained reasonably good results. The 53 dates obtained (based on an induced rate and mean air temperature) correspond well with the four radiocarbon dates from the site. The obsidian dates, however, ranged from 119,646±1668 to 2,562±129 years B.P., where an error of a few thousand years at the oldest end and a few hundred years at the youngest end can be tolerated. Ridings (1991), however, applied the same approach to artifacts from Fort Bergwin, New Mexico, an area where dendrochronology is commonly used to yield very precise dates. Her comparisons of dates determined by OHD with those determined through dendrochronology yielded errors of 100 years or less, which in her case were unacceptable. Errors in both cases are undoubtedly due to differences in thermal and humidity histories of the artifacts, not only at different depths but also through time. The precision of the OHD method in any case will depend on the magnitude of these differences, and although variable thermal and humidity histories due to depth have been given considerable attention, such variation through time has not.

Artifacts at different stratigraphic levels have undergone different temperature histories and possibly different humidity histories, first simply as a function of depth, but also as a function of time and different depositional histories. As Dunnell and Dancey (1983) have pointed out, buried artifacts were once on the surface, and we have no way of knowing in many (if not most) cases how long they were exposed (see also Foley 1981b). For instance, if artifact A lies on the surface for 1000 years and is then buried, and then artifact B is deposited and buried relatively quickly, their hydration rinds will show too wide a difference, since the rate of hydration for A was accelerated during the first 1000 years. On the other hand, if artifact A is deposited under extremely cold conditions for 1000 years and then buried, and shortly afterward, during a warm period, artifact B is deposited and buried relatively quickly, their rind thicknesses will appear erroneously similar because of the slow rate of hydration for A during the cold period.

In addition artifacts may undergo a number of disruptive processes after burial (Schiffer 1972, 1987; Wood and Johnson 1978). Little attention, however, has been given to depositional histories and temporal variations in temperature and humidity in subsurface applications of OHD (but see Katsui and Kondo 1976; Zeier 1986). Hall and Jackson (1989:44) point out several factors concerning the depositional and environmental histories of deposits. First, "the thermal history of an obsidian artifact after it entered the archaeological record . . . is virtually impossible to ascertain in most instances"; second, "it thus cannot be assumed *a priori* that the respective stratigraphic positions of surface and subsurface debris have remained unchanged through time"; and third, "actual effects of varying effective temperatures are difficult to document and probably more relevant on an areal (elevational) basis." Interestingly these are generally the reservations expressed in applying OHD to surface artifacts. We now turn to a discussion of the use of OHD in surface contexts.

Obsidian Hydration Dating of Surface Obsidian

As stated earlier, surface temperatures are generally much higher than soil temperatures, even at 5 cm depth, and such differences can result in great disparities in the hydration of buried and surface obsidian. Several authors have suggested that an increase in temperature of 1°C can cause a change of 10 percent in the hydration rates; as a result obsidian on the surface can be expected to hydrate as much as five times as fast as subsurface obsidian (Friedman 1976; Friedman and Obradovich 1981). Studies comparing hydration measurements of surface and buried artifacts, however, do not appear to support these predictions. An early consideration of this issue by Michels (1965, 1969) showed no significant differences in hydration measurements of deeply buried artifacts and those on or near the surface. In a study of time-sensitive projectile points from northwestern Nevada, Layton (1973) suggested that surface artifacts hydrate at up to twice the rate of buried artifacts. Jackson (1984), however, cautioned that some of the variation in Layton's sample may be due to chemical composition, since this variable was not controlled in the study.

Origer and Wickstrom (1982:129), in a comparison of buried and surface projectile points from the Santa

Rosa Plain in California, concluded that while the range of hydration measurements for surface specimens was slightly larger than that for buried specimens, there were no statistical differences between them. Finally, in a 1989 study of projectile points of Casa Diablo glass in California, Hall and Jackson found "relatively minimal divergence between hydration values obtained on surface and subsurface specimens" (1989:44). In fact they found that within each projectile point type, with a few exceptions, hydration means were consistently larger for subsurface than for surface specimens, which one might expect in a stratigraphic relationship (1989:44).

Unlike most of the earlier cases, Hall and Jackson's results were based on the comparison of fairly large samples: 251 buried and 142 surface specimens. Their results have led Hall and Jackson (1989:44) to conclude that "while inter-sample variation in effective hydration temperature is certainly an important consideration, . . . excessive concern with surface/subsurface provenience on a local level may be inappropriate."

Theoretically, however, these studies should have shown large differences between the hydration results of buried and surface artifacts. Using the generalized hydration-rate curves presented by Friedman and Long (1976, Figure 4, based on their chemical index), a rate will increase on the order of 70 percent with an increase in temperature of 10°C, the average difference researchers have observed between surface and subsurface temperatures at about 25–50 cm depth. Not even Layton's (1973) results show this magnitude of difference between hydration measurements of surface and subsurface artifacts. There are likely several factors contributing to this situation.

The first may be the relative humidity of the hydrating environment. Although its effects are not yet well understood, Friedman et al. (1990) suggest that lower humidity levels experienced by surface artifacts may compensate to some extent for higher temperatures. As noted earlier, Mazer et al. (1991) suggest a 25 percent decrease in the hydration rate for Coso obsidian with a decrease from 97 percent to 68 percent relative humidity. Considering this decrease against the increase in the rate due to high temperature, the disparity is reduced from 70 percent to 45 percent, still quite a difference in magnitude, but more in line with Layton's results.

This factor does not, however, account for the much lower differences observed by Origer and Wickstrom (1982) and Hall and Jackson (1989). Their results suggest that depositional histories may be responsible in part; that is, that the traditional model of site formation (that deposition is followed shortly by burial, ensuring constant thermal histories at each successive depth) is not appropriate in these cases. In fact complex depositional and thermal histories may be more the rule than the exception. Tremaine (1991:288), for instance, notes that a number of factors other than temperature and relative humidity have been shown under experimental conditions to affect the hydration process, such as the flow rate of groundwater, element concentrations in groundwater solutions, and groundwater pH. Chris Stevenson (personal communication), however, points out that the effects of these factors are not well understood in archaeological contexts where the obsidian is not in solution.

These observations lead us to conclude that the application of OHD to surface artifacts is not so different from its application to buried artifacts. That is, if fairly good results can be obtained in buried contexts, where the depositional history and thus thermal history cannot be known, then they can be obtained in surface contexts as well. Until, all of the factors affecting the hydration rate are fully understood in isolation, however, as well as the effect of their combined interaction, we believe, along with others (Jackson 1984; Tremaine 1991; Tremaine and Frederickson 1988), that the method should be used as a relative-age approach when applied to surface specimens, which is how we use it here. We will now turn to our work in eastern Nevada, where we have been experimenting with the use of OHD to date surface artifact assemblages for the last five years.

Butte Valley Obsidian Project

Since 1986 we have conducted archaeological research in southern Butte Valley, located approximately

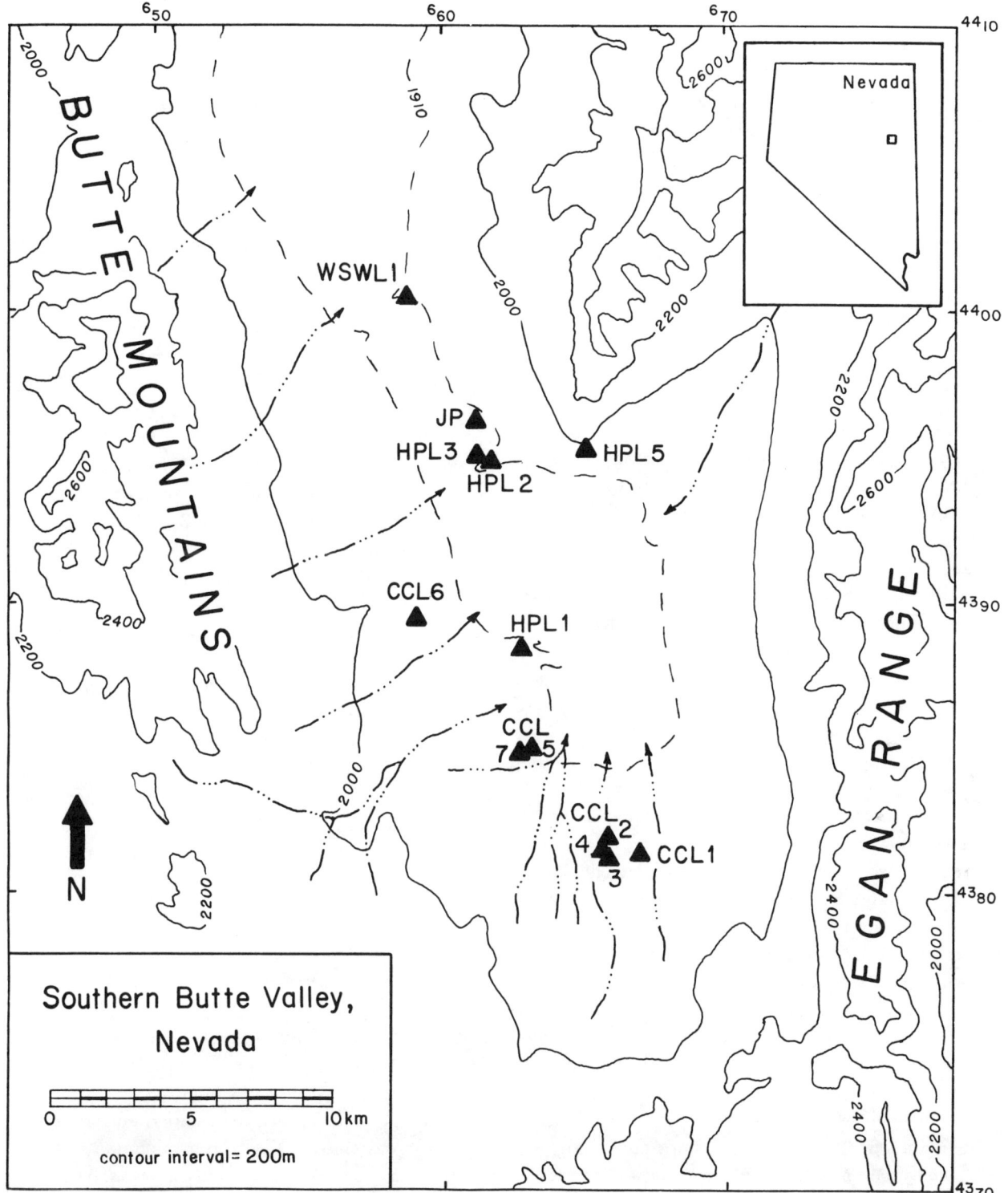

Figure 4.1. Site locations in southern Butte Valley, Nevada.

50 km north of Ely, Nevada (Figure 4.1) (see Beck and Jones 1990a). Our studies have documented a rich late Pleistocene/early Holocene surface record in that area, characterized by assemblages representative of the Western Stemmed Tradition (WST) (Willig and Aikens 1988), which is believed to date between ca. 11,500 and 8000 B.P. Later occupation (termed the Archaic), in contrast, is more poorly represented, limited largely to the earlier part of that period (ca. 8000–6500 B.P.). One consequence of this occupational history is the absence of significant temporal mixing at most sites. In contrast sites reported from nearby areas often evidence prolonged occupation, which creates serious analytic difficulties.

Because the large majority of the archaeological record of the Great Basin lines on the surface, the use of diagnostic projectile points has been the primary method of dating these assemblages. Although this approach has proven successful for Archaic assemblages (see Thomas 1981), such efforts have not yielded fine temporal discriminations among WST assemblages. This failure may relate to several factors, such as stylistic conservativeness, small sample numbers, component mixture on those surfaces, or inadequate typological evaluations. Whatever the case, WST assemblages are routinely attributed only to a very broad time period, encompassing as much as 3,500 years (ca. 11,500–8000 B.P.).

Because of the difficulty in making temporal distinctions among our Butte Valley collections, we began an obsidian hydration project in an attempt to construct a relative chronology of WST surface materials. Our long-term goals in this project were several. First, we wanted to assess contemporaneity among artifacts collected as a single assemblage; that is, do these assemblages represent single occupational events or more complex occupational histories? Second, using single-component assemblages, we hoped to create a serial order, based on average hydration readings. And finally, we wanted to assess the degree of occupational continuity in the study area during prehistoric times.

The project had three components: source characterizations, hydration analysis, and temperature/humidity studies. We discuss each in turn.

Source Analysis

The obsidian sample consists of 666 artifacts from Butte Valley and 29 from adjacent valleys. Trace element characterizations, performed by Richard Hughes using X-ray fluorescence spectrometry, revealed 34 different geochemical types represented in these collections (Table 4.1). Using four elements (Rb, Sr, Y, and Zr), comparisons were made with known sources in Nevada, Utah, Idaho, and California. These comparisons resulted in seven matches: (1) the Browns Bench source (and the "Browns Bench Source Area")[2] in northeastern Nevada/southern Idaho; (2) the Malad source in southern Idaho; and (3) the Topaz Mountain, Black Rock, Wildhorse, and Pumice Hole sources in western Utah (Figure 4.2). Additional matches were made with previously unidentified source areas: (1) a local pebble source we have named Butte Mountain; (2) Panaca Summit (ca. 200–225 km south-southeast of Butte Valley); (3) Pancake Mountains (ca. 100–125 km to the south-southwest); (4) South Pahroc Area (ca. 250 km to the south); and (5) Kane Spring (ca. 275 km to the south-southeast) (see Figure 4.2).

In all, 12 of our 34 chemical types have been identified with sources; chemical types not yet identified with sources are designated by the letters A–K and the numbers 1–14. Identification of an additional four may be forthcoming soon, however, since it is suspected that unknown sources 2, 3, 5, and 10 are from a source area in southern Nevada near Las Vegas (Hughes, personal communication).

Hydration Analysis

Hydration rind measurements, performed by Robert Jackson of Lithichron, have been made on a total of 666 artifacts from Butte Valley and four from adjacent Long Valley to the west. An average hydration value for each specimen was created, based on a minimum of four readings on two faces, measured to the nearest 0.01 μm (measurement error = ± 0.2 μm). Among the 670 artifacts sent for hydration analysis, 560 cases pos-

Table 4.1. Geochemical Obsidian Types Represented in the Butte Valley Assemblages

Geochemical Type	Number of Samples	Rb	Sr	Y	Zr
Butte Mountain	225	165.9±6.9	319.7±14.8	24.3±1.9	119.7±10.1
Browns Bench	130	211.9±10.7	46.2±4.6	65.6±5.9	439.6±42.8
"A"	17	189.7±16.0	61.3±10.9	71.2±8.4	543.8±59.5
"B"	97	196.6±8.4	123.6±5.2	35.4±2.4	162.4±5.4
Browns Bench Area	44	231.3±13.2	24.6±7.4	66.0±4.1	366.2±29.7
"D"	2	210.7±8.2	27.0±1.3	29.3±0.6	102.5±2.6
"E"	22	146.8±34.5	113.7±15.1	28.2±21.5	154.0±29.7
"F"	4	192.9±5.6	106.7±4.6	15.3±1.2	104.8±5.0
Panaca	46	197.2±8.1	75.9±3.6	30.3±3.0	122.2±7.9
"H"	1	194.1	43.1	25.2	111.8
"I"	2	336.6±4.8	5.7±2.6	40.0±1.1	113.6±15.6
"J"	2	437.2±12.4	7.3±0.1	46.8±0.2	148.0±2.6
"K"	1	170.6	89.6	25.4	145.0
Topaz Mountain	22	456.5±19.6	3.0±0.8	54.6±2.7	137.0±3.9
Wildhorse	10	188.1±7.5	35.8±2.8	27.3±7.1	113.8±14.0
Malad	5	119.8±2.2	68.0±2.9	33.8±1.8	85.6±2.9
Black Rock	3	262.3±3.2	6.7±0.6	61.7±3.1	92.7±0.6
Pumice Hole	1	183.0	55.0	30.0	130.0
Pancake Mts.	1	420.0	3.0	91.0	139.0
Kane Spring	1	205.0	42.0	42.0	156.0
"U1"	2	358.5±9.2	1.5±2.1	81.0±1.4	74.0±1.4
"U2"	6	199.0±7.3	74.8±2.3	28.7±2.0	212.7±5.4
"U3"	1	179.0	54.0	34.0	126.0
"U4"	1	181.0	12.0	53.0	167.0
"U5"	2	168.0±1.4	82.0±2.8	28.5±2.1	145.0±4.2
"U6"	2	320.5±7.8	1.0±0.0	46.0±1.4	95.0±5.7
"U7"	1	201.0	1.0	96.0	508.0
"U8"	2	225.0±15.6	6.5±2.1	27.0±2.8	92.5±0.7
"U9"	1	334.0	4.0	88.0	191.0
"U10"	2	203.0±17.0	0.5±0.7	93.5±7.8	1103.0±168.3
"U11"	2	166.5±6.4	0.0	67.5±0.7	370.0±2.8
"U12"	1	184.0	5.0	23.0	87.0
"U13"	6	103.0±4.6	153.5±4.8	27.3±2.0	80.2±36.7
"U14"	1	169.0	131.0	23.0	172.0

sess measurable hydration rinds, and of these, 65 have secondary rinds. The hydration rinds of several geochemical types, for example, "A," Browns Bench Source Area, and to a lesser degree, Browns Bench, proved difficult to measure, owing to their optical properties.

Temperature and Humidity Measurements

In early July of 1989 diffusion cells (Trembour et al. 1986; Trembour et al. 1988) were installed by Irving Friedman of the USGS at two locations in Butte Valley and one in neighboring Long Valley, to measure effec-

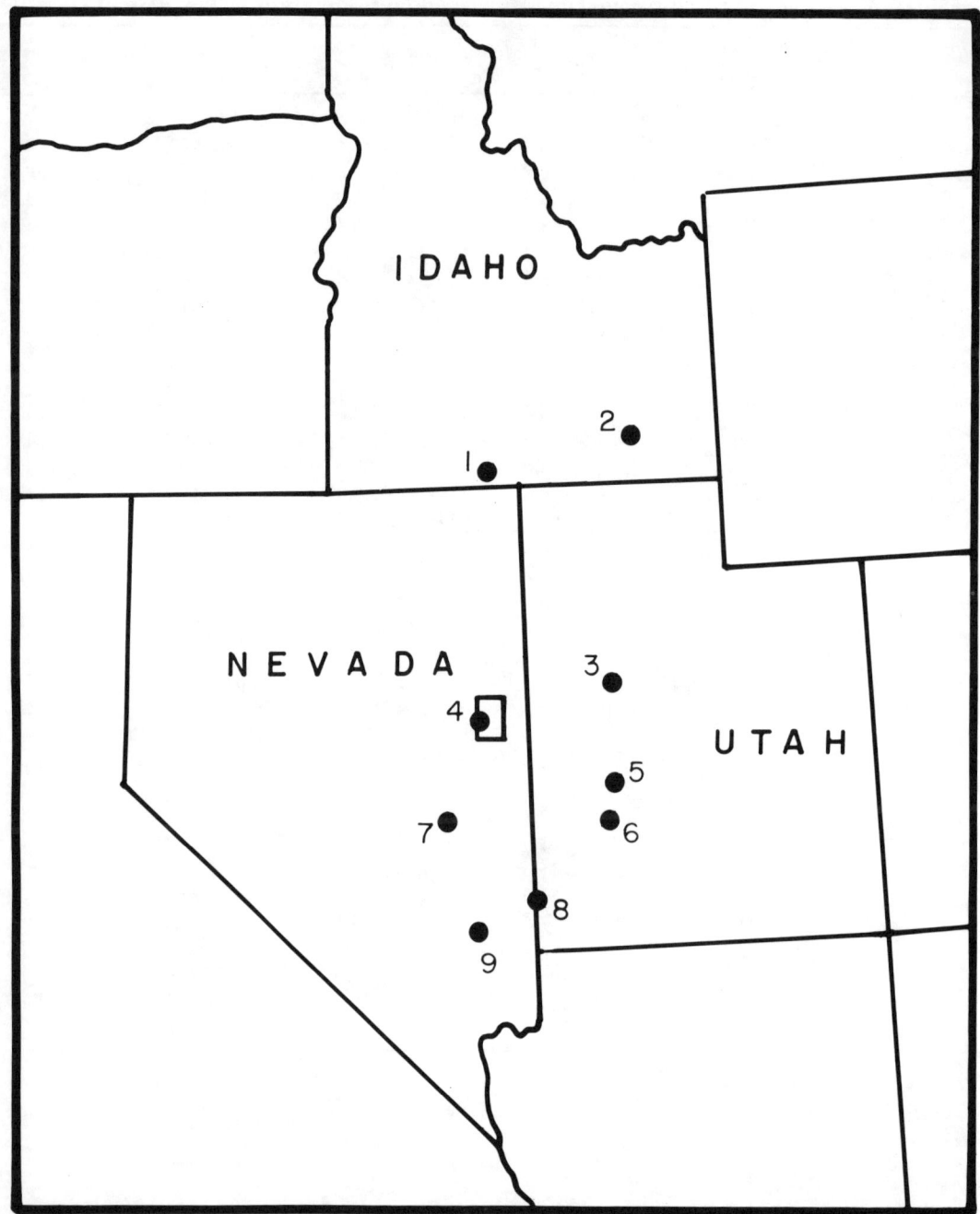

Figure 4.2. Known source locations of obsidians represented in the Butte Valley assemblages. (1) Brown's Bench, Brown's Bench Source Area; (2) Malad; (3) Topaz Mountains; (4) Butte Mountain; (5) Black Rock; (6) Pumice Hole, Wildhorse; (7) Pancake Mountains; (8) Panaca Summit; (9) South Pahroc, Kane Spring.

Table 4.2. Effective Hydration Temperature and Relative Humidity Calculations at Three Localities over a Period of Two Years[a]

Locality	Depth (m)	Temperature, °C		Percent Humidity	
		1989–90	1990–91	1989–90	1990–91
CCL1	0.12	15.2	17.1[b]	24.0	4.0[b]
	0.25	13.5	12.7	77.0	95.0
	0.50	12.6	12.6	87.0	97.0
	1.00	12.2	11.9	86.0	95.0
HPL2	0.12	—	12.6[c]	—	91.0[c]
	0.25	12.7	12.8	90.0	95.0
	0.50	13.2	12.3	93.0	97.0
	1.00	11.7	—	89.0	—
Sunshine Well	0.12	14.3	16.6[b]	98.0	5.3[b]
	0.25	13.7	13.0	97.0	96.0
	0.50	14.2	13.1	97.0	97.0
	1.00	12.6	12.4	99.0	98.0
	2.00	12.2	12.9	—	—

[a]All temperatures ± 0.2 degrees; all rH ± 5 percent.
[b]Cell found on the surface.
[c]Two-year average.

tive hydration temperature and relative humidity over a period of two years. These localities lie at about the same elevation, but represent different depositional environments, including fine-grained alluvial sediment (CCL1), coarse gravel on a pluvial spit feature (HPL2), and dunes (Sunshine Well).

Cells were placed at 0.12 m, 0.25 m, 0.5 m, and 1.0 m below the surface at each location, following procedures described by Trembour et al. (1986). Table 4.2 shows the results of the temperature and humidity readings over a two-year period; the topmost cells at CCL1 and Sunshine Well were found on the surface in 1991, and thus these readings reflect a combined surface/subsurface measurement. These results indicate that temperature is variable from locality to locality, but differences due to depth are not as great as might be expected. For example, Ambrose (1984) found a difference of 12°C between 0.05 m and 1.5 m depth, and Friedman and Obradovich (1981) found a 14.2°C difference between surface temperature and that at 1.8 m depth. Focusing on those two locations where cells were exposed on the surface, the difference between the surface reading and that at 1.0 m at CCL1 is only 5.2°C, while at Sunshine Well that difference is only 4.2°C. It is interesting to note that the temperature rose at 0.5 m at HPL2 during year one and at Sunshine Well during both years.

Relative humidity appears fairly constant at depths of 0.25 m and greater. However, the two cells that were exposed on the ground surface recorded far lower values, with as much as 90 percent difference between the exposed reading and that at 0.25 m. Such low humidity at the surface should significantly affect hydration rates, negating the effects of higher temperatures. In fact hydration at all depths will be influenced to some extent, since all readings but one are less than 99 percent. Effects at Sunshine Well, however, should be less pronounced that those at CCL1 and HPL2.

Serial Ordering of Assemblages

A serial order of 13 Butte Valley assemblages was created based on mean hydration values within seven of

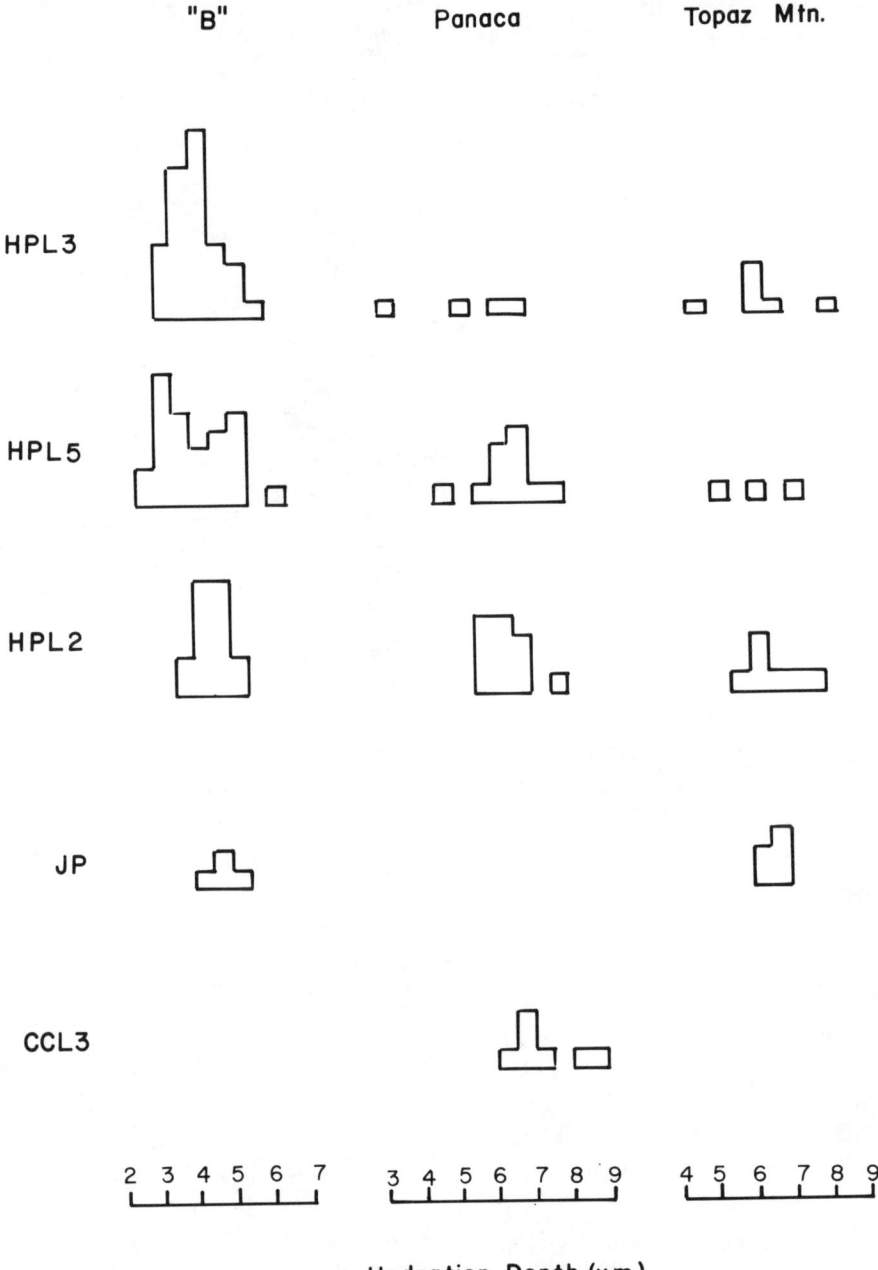

Figure 4.3. Serial order of 13 Butte Valley assemblages, based on mean hydration values for the seven most prevalent obsidians. Means based on three or more values are accompanied by standard deviations.

the most common geochemical types (Figure 4.3); cases in which there are more than three readings are presented with one-sigma error bars.[3] Although there is a good deal of overlap in the distribution of hydration values from case to case, mean hydration values in general tend to increase as one moves downward in the order, from CCL6 to CCL1. If we are to accept this order as chronological, however, two factors concerning the assemblages must be evaluated. First, the assemblages must be demonstrated to represent occupations of comparable duration, such that they can be meaningfully ordered in time; and second, they must represent continuous occupations, such that mean hydration values are good estimates of the time of occupation.

Continuity and Duration of Occupation

Creating an order based on means assumes that this statistic accurately describes the distribution of the values it represents. Raymond (1984–1985) has suggested that the continuous use of a locality should be manifested by symmetrical distributions of source-specific hydration measurements. All other things being equal, the length of such use will be expressed in the width of the range of values, with lengthy periods of use being represented by wide ranges and brief periods being represented by narrow ranges. Values that reference distinct manufacture/discard events should show multimodal distributions.

Table 4.3 summarizes the hydration data for the 13 Butte Valley assemblages over the seven geochemical types used in the serial order. These data illustrate that the ranges of some obsidians, e.g., Butte Mountain, Panaca, and Topaz Mountain, are more similar across assemblages than is true for other glasses, such as Browns Bench and "B." To explore factors that may account for these differences, we will focus our discussions primarily on the two most common obsidians, Butte Mountain and Browns Bench.

In the case of Butte Mountain obsidian, the range of hydration measurements in each of the assemblages varies between 2.0 and 2.7 μm in all but three assemblages, in which cases it is somewhat less, suggesting a shorter period of use at these localities. The distribution of hydration values for each assemblage is presented in Figure 4.4. Most of the distributions are fairly symmetrical, with similar ranges (except in cases of extremely small sample size). An examination of these graphs, however, reveals the similarity of these distributions in terms of modal occurrence. Although there is some shift upward as one proceeds from the first of the ordered assemblages (CCL6) to the last (CCL1), there is very little difference among HPL3, HPL5, CCL5, and HPL2, suggesting that use of these areas with respect to Butte Mountain obsidian is roughly contemporaneous.

Turning to the Browns Bench glass, the information in Table 4.3 suggests that distributions of hydration measurements are more variable across these assemblages than for Butte Mountain, with ranges varying from 0.7 to 3.9 μm. Those assemblages with small ranges, however, such as CCL3 and JP, have small sample numbers of this obsidian (n=2, n=3, respectively) compared with those that have wider ranges, such as CCL5 and HPL2, which have much larger numbers of items (n= 14, n=21, respectively). Histograms of the distribution of Browns Bench rind widths in each assemblage are also presented in Figure 4.4. The modes of this distribution do tend to shift upward from HPL3 to HPL1, suggesting that the use of these areas with respect to the Browns Bench glass is slightly different at each location. The distributions, however, are not symmetrical, and most are bimodal, both factors suggesting an uneven occupational history with respect to this glass. It is possible that differential depositional histories might account for these patterns, but if this is the case for Browns Bench, it must also be the case for other obsidians, including Butte Mountain. The distributions of Butte Mountain obsidian, however, do not show the same discontinuous pattern as do those of Browns Bench, and thus we believe that the patterns in these two materials represent somewhat different occupational histories. This raises an interesting question: were Butte Mountain and Browns Bench used at the same time, or might each glass reflect upon different occupation events at these sites? This is a point we will return to below.

Figure 4.5 shows the distributions of "B," Panaca,

Table 4.3. Summary of Hydration Measurements over Seven Obsidian Types and the Thirteen Assemblages in the Serial Order

Assemblage		Butte Mountain	Browns Bench	Source B	E	Panaca	Topaz Mountain	Wildhorse
CCL6	n	23						
	X̄	2.17±0.50						
	range	1.2–3.2						
CCL7	n	34	1		2			
	X̄	2.44±0.55	11.7		4.90±1.56			
	range	1.4–3.6			3.8–6.0			
HPL3	n	32	10	30		4	6	3
	X̄	3.42±0.73	10.48±0.95	4.28±0.58		5.53±1.51	6.53±1.08	5.70±2.93
	range	1.5–4.2	9.10–11.8	3.5–5.7		3.4–6.7	6.4–8.3	2.4–8.0
HPL5	n	17	13	27	3	9	3	4
	X̄	2.54±0.53	11.26±1.43	4.14±0.94	4.43±1.01	6.48±0.75	6.37±1.01	7.55±1.39
	range	1.3–3.3	7.8–12.8	2.6–6.5	3.5–5.5	5.0–7.6	5.3–7.3	6.3–8.9
CCL5	n	32	14	2	13	1		
	X̄	3.04±1.05	11.14±1.28	4.45±0.21	5.49±0.40	6.0		
	range	1.8–6.8	10.4–14.2	4.3–4.6	4.7–6.2			
HPL2	n	24	21	16	4	12	8	1
	X̄	2.74±0.61	11.55±1.31	4.58±0.43	5.80±0.86	6.38±0.58	6.81±0.70	9.6
	range	1.1–3.8	10.0–13.8	3.8–5.4	4.8–6.7	5.7–7.7	6.0–7.9	
JP	n		3	3		3	4	
	X̄		10.93±0.45	4.85±0.44		6.30±0.20	6.48±0.45	
	range		10.5–11.4	4.5–5.5		6.1–6.5	6.1–7.0	
WSWL1	n	5	4	1		1	1	
	X̄	3.30±0.65	11.68±0.79	4.80±0.85		5.9	7.3	
	range	2.4–4.2	10.9–12.5	4.2–5.4				
CCL4	n	3						
	X̄	3.10±0.57						
	range	2.7–3.5						
HPL1	n	3	5					
	X̄	3.43±0.06	12.94±1.27					
	range	3.4–3.5	11.7–14.5					
CCL3	n		2			7		
	X̄		13.85±0.50			7.33±0.91		
	range		13.5–14.2			6.5–8.8		
CCL2	n	2				2		
	X̄	3.40±0.85				7.70±1.56		
	range	2.8–4.0				6.6–8.8		
CCL1	n	15		7				
	X̄	3.78±0.66		5.79±0.34				
	range	2.6–5.2		5.3–6.3				

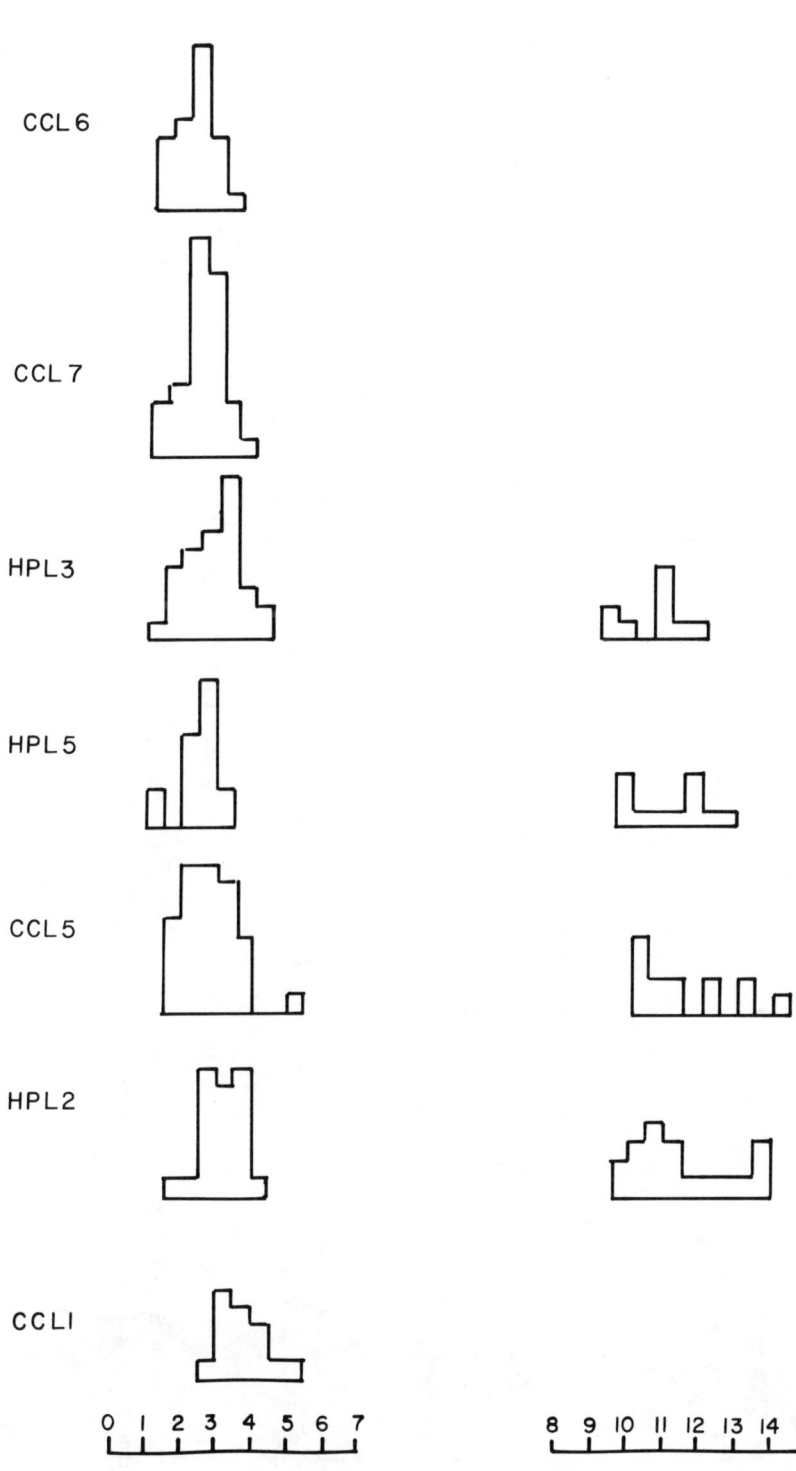

Figure 4.4. Distribution of hydration values for Butte Mountain and Brown's Bench obsidians in each of the Butte Valley assemblages. Only those assemblages with six or more values are graphed; values for remaining assemblages can be seen in Table 4.3

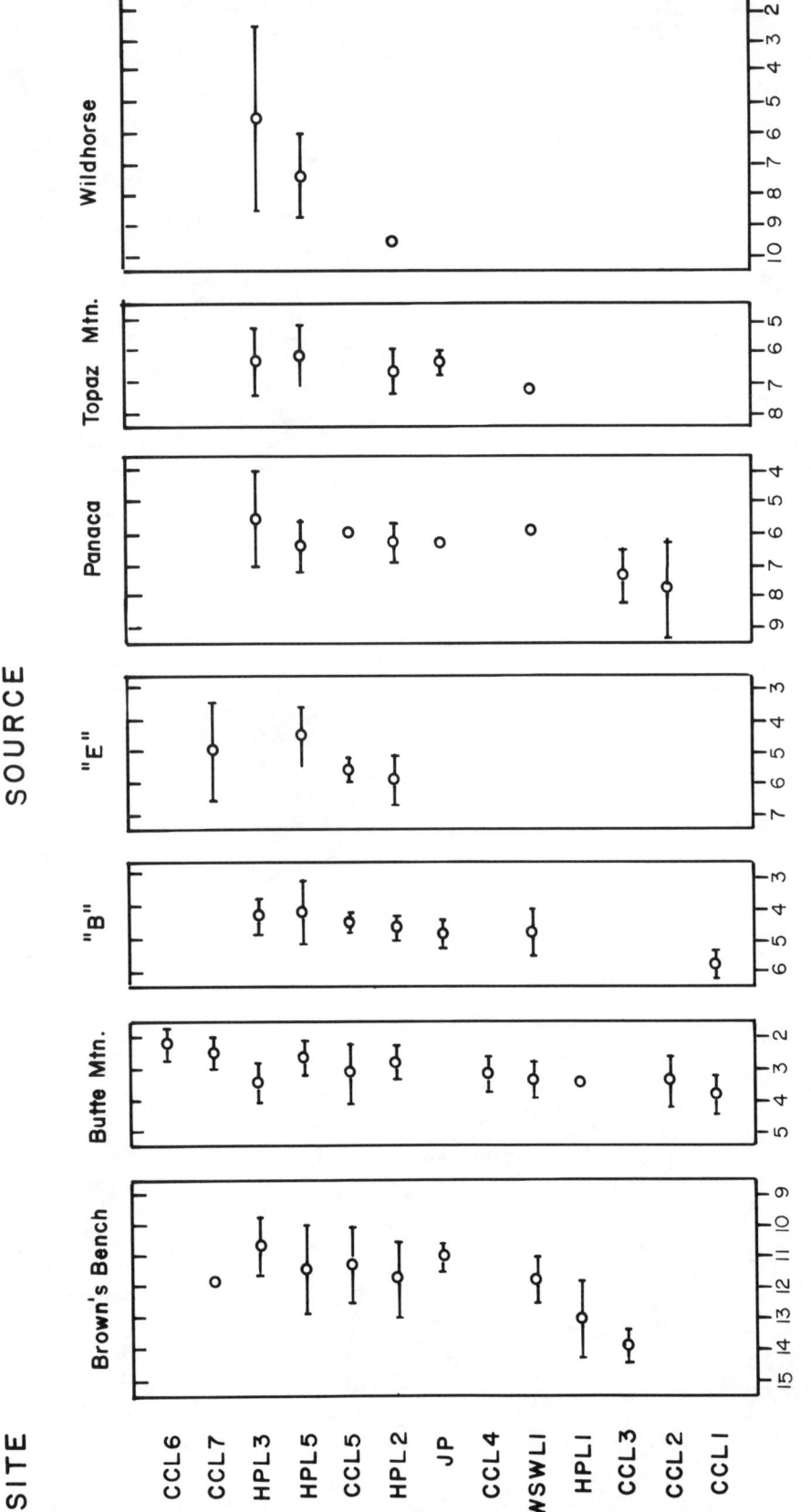

Figure 4.5. Distribution of hydration values for "B, Panaca, and Topaz Mountain obsidians in each of the Butte Valley assemblages. Only those assemblages with six or more values are graphed; values for remaining assemblages can be seen in Table 4.3

and Topaz Mountain obsidians in each assemblage. In the case of "B," areal use appears to be continuous at the four localities represented, although there is slight modality in its use at HPL5. Temporal use of these areas appears to be similar with respect to this glass, except that the duration of its use at HPL3 and HPL5 is greater than at HPL2 and JP, but this latter pattern may simply be a function of smaller sample size at these two localities.

The use of Panaca obsidian appears to be fairly continuous at all but HPL3; again, however, small sample size may be affecting the pattern. Although there is a good deal of overlap in values, the use of CCL3 and HPL2 begins a little earlier than at HPL3 and HPL5, while use of the latter two localities extends later in time.

Finally, the use of HPL3 and HPL5 is very uneven with respect to Topaz Mountain obsidian, but continuous at HPL2 and JP. The temporal span of use at all four of these localities, however, appears to be quite similar.

In summary, then, a general pattern can be extracted from the interassemblage comparisons within each obsidian. There are sets of assemblages where the distributions of hydration values are so similar as to suggest relative contemporaneity of use (perhaps on a large scale) with respect to that particular obsidian. (Table 4.4 shows these groupings of each of the five obsidian types). With respect to the obsidian component of these assemblages, there appear to be three periods represented in the serial order: the earliest is represented by CCL1, CCL2, CCL3, and possibly HPL1, while the latest is represented by CCL7 and CCL6. The other seven assemblages appear to represent rough contemporaneity, with the exception of the use of Browns Bench glass (and possibly Panaca). The use of Browns Bench obsidian is not continuous and appears to differ from assemblage to assemblage within this middle period. These results suggest that the order we have constructed is chronological, although only in a broad sense.

Table 4.4. Temporal Grouping of Assemblages within Each Obsidian Type

Butte Mountain	Browns Bench	"B"	Panaca	Topaz Mountain
CCL6	HPL3	HPL3	HPL3	HPL3
CCL7	HPL5	HPL5	HPL5	HPL5
		HPL2		HPL2
HPL3	CCL5	JP	HPL2	JP
HPL5	HPL2			
CCL5			CCL3	
HPL2	HPL1			
WSWL1	WSWL1			
CCL1				

Intra-assemblage Contemporaneity

Determining that all artifacts within an assemblage are in fact contemporaneous is a problem that often plagues researchers when dealing with surface deposits, primarily because of the possibility for reuse of an area over an extended period of time. Arguments of contemporaneity in subsurface deposits are based on the concept of association—that two or more artifacts residing in the same stratigraphic unit are associated (Jones and Beck 1992:168). Using associational arguments, we transfer chronological information for a particular unit to all items within that unit, and thus these items are considered to be contemporaneous. Contemporaneity, however, is relative, since any stratigraphic unit may represent a very narrow or a very wide timespan. When dealing with surface deposits, associations are based entirely on proximity—the closer artifacts are to one another in space, the stronger the case for their association. Associational arguments are confounded, however, by the possible reuse of localities over extended periods of time; such reuse can produce palimpsests of archaeological material that are difficult if not impossible to tease apart. Problems of contemporaneity can be at least partially solved using OHD. Two problems must be addressed: (1) the question of contemporaneous use of various chemical types within an assemblage, and (2) the transferrence of chronological information gained from OHD to other material types in the assemblage. This latter problem, however, is beyond the scope of this chapter and will be addressed at a later date. We will concentrate here on the contemporaneity of use among different obsidian types represented in the Butte Valley assemblages.

Contemporaneous Use of Obsidians

Unfortunately we know nothing about the rates at which each of these glasses hydrates; without this information we cannot know if, for example, a hydration reading of 3.0 μm in Butte Mountain is equivalent to one of 12.0 μm in Browns Bench. Given the range and modal values represented in each (see Table 4.3), it seems apparent that Browns Bench is a much more rapidly hydrating obsidian than Butte Mountain; the others appear to fall somewhere in between. Of course the differences in range and modal hydration values may not indicate different hydration rates at all, but that each obsidian was deposited in these localities during different time periods. That is, Browns Bench may have been used during the earliest occupations of Butte Valley, while Butte Mountain may have been used quite late. This would mean that sites where both occur represent at least two distinct and possibly widely different episodes of use. Expanding this argument to include other obsidians, we might hypothesize that each represents a use episode, so that an assemblage such as HPL3 is the result of at least six distinct episodes. This hypothesis, however, is weakened by the fact that mean hydration values in general increase from CCL6 to CCL1 in *every geochemical type*. If each obsidian represents a different temporal span of use, then it would be very difficult to explain why each locality was used in the same order during these different periods.

The actual pattern of use, however, probably lies between these two extremes. We have already noted differences in the distributions of hydration-rind widths across the different obsidian types, suggesting continuous and overlapping periods of use in some cases and discontinuous use in others. Furthermore the data in Table 4.4 indicate that the use of a particular obsidian from assemblage to assemblage may be temporally different in some cases, such as Browns Bench, and quite uniform in others, such as Butte Mountain. The solution to this problem must await additional analysis in the form of induced-hydration experiments, now underway.

Based on such experiments, Tremaine suggests that the relationship between the rates of hydration of two different obsidians remains constant at different temperatures (Tremaine 1991; Tremaine and Frederickson 1988). Thus ratios of temporally equivalent rim widths for different sources can be calculated based on induced experiments; that is, a rind thickness of x μm in obsidian A can be equated with a rind thickness of y μm in obsidian B. Using this approach, relative chronologies can be constructed using obsidians from different sources, without the introduction of error from translating microns into calendar years (Tremaine and Frederickson 1988:271).

Differential Source Use through Time

Although it is difficult to assess contemporaneity of use among obsidians within assemblages without knowledge of their relative rates of hydration, a temporal pattern of use does appear to exist with respect to source use through time. For instance, in Figure 4.3 it can be seen that the use of Butte Mountain, and to a lesser degree Browns Bench obsidian, spans the entire sequence of assemblages. The use of all others, on the other hand, appears to be concentrated in the middle of the sequence, although there is some use of "B" and Panaca early in the sequence. If it is accepted that the order in Figure 4.3 is chronological, then this pattern suggests that Butte Mountain, Browns Bench, Panaca, and possibly "B" were used early, and that the use of "E", Topaz Mountain, and Wildhorse did not begin until later. This pattern finds some degree of support in the pattern of diagnostic projectile points (see Beck and Jones 1992; Beck et al. 1992).

Table 4.5 shows the distribution of projectile points

Table 4.5. Distribution of Projectile Points of WST, Early Archaic, and Mid-to-Late Archaic Periods across Seven Obsidian Types

Obsidian Type[a]	WST[b]	Early Archaic[c]	Mid-to-Late Archaic[d]
Butte Valley			
BM	0	0	0
BB	23	6	1
B	1	6	4
E	1	0	0
PN	3	5	2
TM	0	0	1
WH	2	1	1
Other Valleys			
BB	10	0	0
B	6	1	0
E	0	1	0
PN	0	0	0
TM	0	0	1
WH	1	1	0

[a] BM = Butte Mountain, BB = Browns Bench, PN = Panaca, TM = Topaz Mountain, and WH = Whitehorse.
[b] Cougar Mountain, Parman, Silver Lake, Lake Mohave, Windust.
[c] Pinto.
[d] Elko, Humboldt, Desert Side-Notched.

representative of three general periods: WST (ca. 11,500–8000 B.P.), Early Archaic (ca. 8000–6500 B.P.), and Mid-to-Late Archaic (after ca. 6500 B.P.).[4] The use of Browns Bench and Panaca obsidians occurs primarily during the WST and Early Archaic periods, with over 80 percent of the points in each of these glasses representative of these two periods. The use of "B" appears somewhat later, with 87.5 percent of points made of this glass representative of the Early and Mid-to-Late Archaic periods.[5] The use of Topaz Mountain obsidian appears to date completely to the later period. Only one point of Topaz Mountain obsidian is identifiable with a known type (Elko Side-Notched), but five of the untyped points are small side-notched points and two are medium-sized corner-notched points, similar to those of "B" obsidian identified with the Mid-to-Late Archaic. If these points are all assumed to be Mid-to-Late Archaic in age, then all of Topaz Mountain points appear to be representative of this later period.

Overall the pattern suggests that Browns Bench and Panaca were utilized early, "B" somewhat later, and Topaz Mountain even later. This pattern is supported in part by data from other valleys (see Table 4.5), in which 10 out of 11 Browns Bench points are of WST types. On the other hand, six out of seven "B" points are also WST types, suggesting earlier use of that source than do data from Butte Valley. The one point of Topaz Mountain obsidian is a Late Archaic type. Thus, in a general way, these patterns support the pattern of obsidian use seen in the serial order.

Sample Size and Source Variability

Before we draw conclusions from these patterns, however, we must ask the question: if assemblages such as CCL1, CCL2, CCL3, and HPL1, which appear in the earlier portion of the serial order, had larger samples of obsidian, would more sources be represented at those localities? That is, is the occurrence of "E," Topaz Mountain, and Wildhorse obsidian at HPL3, HPL5, and HPL2 simply a function of sample size (see Jones et al. 1983)? Table 4.6 presents the occurrence of all 35 obsidian types in each of the 13 Butte Valley assemblages (offsite occurrence is shown as well). As can be seen from this table, with one exception (CCL5), those assemblages that have large numbers of obsidian artifacts also have large numbers of sources represented. In fact there is a strong correlation between the number of obsidian artifacts within an assemblage and the number of sources represented ($r=.882$).

Before concluding that samples containing large numbers of sources represent longer periods of use, it is important to examine the distribution of specific cases with respect to the general pattern of sample size and richness. For instance CCL5 has a fewer than expected number of sources represented, given the number of obsidian artifacts in the assemblage ($n=105$). We believe this is due to differences in the duration of use of the CCL5 locality as compared with the duration of oc-

Table 4.6 The Occurrence of 34 Geochemical Obsidian Types in Butte Valley Site and Offsite Assemblages

Assemblage	BM	BB	A	B	BBA	D	E	F	PN	H	I	J	K	TM	BR	WH	MA	PH	PM	P	KS	U1	U2	U3	U4	U5	U6	U7	U8	U9	U10	U11	U12	U13	U14
CCL1	X			X		X																													
CCL2	X							X																											
CCL3			X					X		X																									
CCL4	X											X																							
CCL5	X		X	X	X		X	X																									X	X	
CCL6	X																																		
CCL7	X		X				X																												
HPL1	X		X					X																											
HPL2	X		X	X	X		X	X					X	X	X	X						X	X	X	X										
HPL3	X		X	X	X			X					X	X	X	X	X	X				X				X	X								
HPL5	X		X	X	X		X	X					X	X	X	X						X				X		X	X	X	X	X			
WSWL1	X		X	X	X			X					X	X	X				X														X		
JP	X		X	X	X			X					X	X	X															X					
OFFSITE	X		X	X				X				X		X	X	X					X X														

Table 4.7. Western Stemmed Tradition, Early Archaic, and Untyped Projectile Points Represented in Four Butte Valley Assemblages[a]

Assemblage	WST	Early Archaic	Untyped	Total
CCL5	22	0	0	22
HPL2	12	6	2	22
HPL3	3	21	12	36
HPL5	15	20	14	49

[a]Projectile points of all materials included.

Table 4.8. Material Composition of Four Butte Valley Assemblages

Assemblage	Raw Material Type								Total N
	Chert		Obsidian		Basalt		Other		
	N	%	N	%	N	%	N	%	
CCL5	237	11.3	337	16.0	1,504	71.6	24	1.1	2,102
HPL2	203	20.9	246	25.3	516	53.1	6	0.6	971
HPL3	402	19.6	569	27.8	1,074	52.4	5	0.2	2,050
HPL5	2,260	53.6	621	14.7	1,305	31.0	27	0.6	4,213

cupancy at the Hunter Point localities (that is, HPL3, HPL5, and HPL2). This inference is supported by projectile point data in these assemblages (Table 4.7). As these data show, the entire projectile point assemblage at CCL5 consists of WST types, whereas Archaic (and untyped) points are also present in the other assemblages. Furthermore of the 22 points at CCL5, all are of the Cougar Mountain type, only one of many types assignable to the WST period. In a surface assemblage of over 2,000 artifacts, it is remarkable to find such uniformity among the projectile points, especially in an assemblage of this age. In contrast the 12 HPL2 WST points represent five different types (see Beck and Jones 1990b). There is also a variety of Archaic types represented in the Hunter Point assemblages, ranging from three different types at HPL5 to five at HPL2 and HPL3. Thus with respect to the projectile point data, there is much more uniformity within the CCL5 assemblage.

Turning to an examination of other aspects of the assemblages, Table 4.8 shows that over 71 percent of the CCL5 assemblage is basalt, with obsidian accounting for 16 percent and chert accounting for 11.3 percent. In the other three assemblages, obsidian and chert comprise much larger proportions. The reduced proportion of basalt in these assemblages is important, since at most of the Butte Valley sites, the use of this material during the WST period appears to have been primarily for the production of large stemmed projectile points (Beck and Jones 1988, 1990a, 1990b). At CCL5 98 percent of the bifaces are attributable to this reduction sequence, as compared with 58 percent of the bifaces from HPL2, 30 percent from HPL3, and 34 percent from HPL5.

These factors point to more variable occupational histories at the Hunter Point localities than at CCL5. If this is true and the Hunter Point sites saw more extended use, then there is simply a greater likelihood that those areas would accumulate a larger sample of the obsidian brought into Butte Valley. On the other hand, this does not entirely explain the pattern of obsidian use. For instance there are several types, such as "D,"

"F," and "H," that occur only in small assemblages (see Table 4.6). Furthermore types "J," "K," "U1," "U3," and "U4" occur at HPL2 but not in the other large assemblages; "U7," "U8," "U9," and "U11" occur only at HPL5, and "U13" and "U14" occur only at CCL5. Thus when the actual obsidian types that occur in each assemblage are examined, the patterns once again become complex. Consequently, although we believe that the Hunter Point localities represent more extended-use periods than other localities, we also believe there is a temporal pattern in the use of obsidian sources.

Conclusions

The results of obsidian hydration dating of artifacts recovered in surface contexts have been shown to be quite complex, owing (1) to the sensitivity of the hydration process to temperature, humidity, and chemical composition; and (2) to the often intricate nature of human settlement and locality reuse. In an extended example from our research in eastern Nevada, we have revealed a number of patterns in the source and hydration data that we attribute to occupational history in the study area. First, we have shown the occupational history at certain localities to be more complex than at other localities. Furthermore the use of particular obsidian types appears to have been fairly constant at most localities, while that of other obsidians was more erratic. While we were unable to evaluate whether the use of different obsidian types occurred simultaneously or at different times at specific localities, we were able to demonstrate differential source use through time. Finally, we have shown that a serial order of assemblages based on mean hydration readings among the seven most common obsidians is chronological in a broad sense.

Although we believe our analyses have revealed patterns in the Butte Valley data that are indeed chronological, we do not deny the influences of differing thermal and relative-humidity histories across microenvironments and through time. For instance it is widely accepted that following the close of the Pleistocene, there was a warming trend accompanied by decreased effective precipitation throughout the Great Basin. The effects of this trend, however, differ markedly from region to region. Accepting this overall trend as a given, it would be expected that hydration rates would increase during this period, due to increased effective hydration temperature; this increase was likely offset somewhat by decreasing relative humidity, but rates were still likely higher during the early to mid-Holocene than during the Pleistocene. These differences in hydration rates might be evident in the hydration readings of time-sensitive projectile points.

Earlier we compared source use through time, based on projectile points, from the WST, Early Archaic, and Mid-to-Late Archaic periods. Although we stated that Archaic points are not well dated in eastern Nevada, we would expect that if rates remained unchanged throughout the last 11,500 years, WST points would possess larger source-specific hydration readings than later Archaic points. Figure 4.6 shows the hydration measurements of typable projectile points manufactured from Browns Bench, "B," and Panaca obsidians. Pinto points are considered representative of the Early Archaic period, while, as has been previously noted, it is not known to what time periods the Archaic types of Elko and Humboldt date in eastern Nevada. Elsewhere in the Great Basin, Elko has been dated as early as 8000–7000 B.P. (Aikens 1970; Aikens et al. 1982; Bedwell 1973; Jennings et al. 1980), and possibly earlier (Aikens et al. 1977; Shutler and Shutler 1963), but most consider it representative of a much later time period. The Humboldt type, although not considered a particularly useful temporal type, is also believed to date to the mid-Holocene. The Desert Side-Notched type, however, is well dated in the Basin to about 1500 B.P. or later.

Figure 4.6 shows that the Archaic types do occur later than WST types, and in the case of the Desert Side-Notched point of Browns Bench obsidian, considerably later, which is the expected pattern. Close examination of the Browns Bench graph, however, shows that there is overlap between the lower end of the WST distribution with both Pinto and Elko. This could indicate that there was overlap in the manufacture and use of these points, or it could indicate changing environmen-

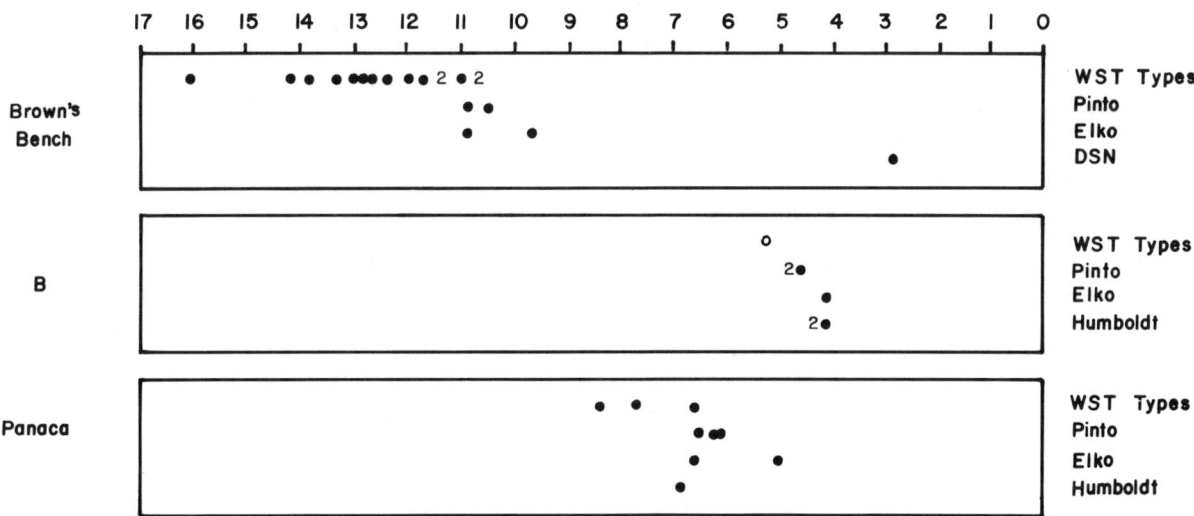

Figure 4.6. Hydration values of Western Stemmed Tradition and Archaic projectile points for Brown's Bench, "B," and Panaca obsidians. Numbers represent more than one occurrence of a value.

tal conditions that caused the Early Archaic points to hydrate at a faster rate than the WST points. This overlap can also be seen in Panaca obsidian but not in "B"; in the latter, the pattern is as would be expected, given unchanging hydration rates.

Because of the small sample size of typable points of each of these obsidians, these patterns are difficult to evaluate. But it does seem likely that changing environmental conditions may have influenced hydration rates, thus making Early Archaic types appear slightly older. The overall pattern, however, remains as expected, with WST types showing wider rind measurements than Archaic types, adding confidence to our discussions throughout this chapter.

The environmental trends considered here are general ones that affect all items lying on the surface in the same general way. Microvariation is certainly a factor, and it likely accounts for much of the complexity in the patterns observed. When OHD is used as a relative-age approach, however, such variation has fewer consequences for the results, and perhaps concern over its use in surface contexts has been excessive. We believe that our success in these analyses demonstrates that OHD is an effective dating method for surface assemblages, and that it shows great potential for solving many of the problems inherent in the dating of the surface-artifact record.

Acknowledgments

We wish to thank the Bureau of Land Management, Ely District, Nevada, and particularly Brian Amme, for their continuing support of the Butte Valley Archaeological Project. We also thank Chris Stevenson for his comments on an earlier version of this paper. Obsidian-source and hydration analyses were funded by a Faculty Research Grant from Hamilton College in 1987 and a grant from the National Science Foundation, BNS-8915392, in 1989.

Notes

1. More recent studies suggest that the vapor environment may be more appropriate, since it more clearly simulates the natural hydrating environment, and because experiments undertaken in the differing environments yield different results (Bates et al. 1988).

2. During the earliest stages of this project, matches were made only with the Browns Bench and local Butte Mountain sources (see Jones and Beck 1990). An additional 11 "unknown" sources were present, designated "A" thorough "K." Recent research on the Browns Bench ash-flow tuff by Hughes and Smith (1993), however, has revealed that this area shows a good deal of chemical variation. As a result of this research, Hughes has identified our unknown obsidian "C" with a subarea of this source, which he has named the Browns Bench Source Area. As more analysis is undertaken with respect to this flow area, it is likely that more of our unknowns may be identified with it. Hughes has suggested (personal communication) that our unknown type "A" might also be associated with this ash-flow tuff, since it is very similar in its concentrations of Rb, Zr, St, and Y to both Browns Bench and "C."

3. Extreme values were not included in the calculations of means for Figure 4.3 and Table 4.3. Extreme values are included, however, in the histograms in Figures 4.4 and 4.5.

4. At present no Archaic chronology exists for eastern Nevada, and thus it is not known exactly what time periods are represented by most Archaic projectile points in this area. Temporal ranges given for each of the three periods discussed are based on average dates suggested for these periods elsewhere in the Great Basin (see, for instance, Holmer 1986; Thomas 1981).

5. There are five additional points of "B" obsidian that are untyped; three of these have hydration measurements (4.7–5.5 μm) overlapping with those of the single WST point (5.3 μm) and the early Archaic points (4.6–4.7 μm), while two have smaller readings. If these are included in the two Archaic periods, then 50 percent of "B" points are representative of Early Archaic times, while 37.5 percent are representative of Mid-to-Late Archaic times.

References Cited

Ahler, S. A., and B. F. Benz
1980 *Analysis of Controlled Surface Artifact Collections from the Sakakawea (32ME11) and Lower Hidatsa (32ME10) Village Sites.* Department of Anthropology and Archaeology, University of North Dakota.

Aikens, C. M.
1970 *Hogup Cave.* University of Utah Anthropological Papers No. 93.

Aikens, C. M., D. L. Cole, and R. Stuckenrath
1977 *Excavations at Dirty Shame Rockshelter, Southeastern Oregon.* Miscellaneous Papers of the Idaho State Museum of Natural History No. 4.

Aikens, C. M., D. K. Grayson, P. J. Mehringer, Jr.
1982 *Final Project Report to the National Science Foundation on the Steens Mountain Prehistory Project.* Department of Anthropology, University of Oregon.

Ambrose, W. R.
1976 Intrinsic Hydration Rate Dating of Obsidian. In *Advances in Obsidian Glass Studies,* edited by R. E. Taylor, pp. 81–105. Noyes Press, Park Ridge, N.J.
1984 Soil Temperature Monitoring at Lake Mungo. Implications for Racemisation Dating. *Australian Archaeology* 19:64–74.

Bates, J. K., T. A. Abrajano, Jr., W. L. Ebert, J. J. Mazer, T. J. Gerding
1988 Experimental Hydration Studies of Natural and Synthetic Glasses. In *Materials in Art and Archaeology,* edited by E. Sayer, P. Vandiver, J. Druzik, and C. Stevenson. Materials Research Society Symposium Proceedings 123:237.

Beck, C., and G. T. Jones
1988 Western Pluvial Lakes Tradition Occupation in Butte Valley, Eastern Nevada. In *Early Human Occupation in the Arid West: The Clovis-Archaic Interface,* edited by J. A. Willig, C. M. Aikens, and J. L. Fagan, pp. 273–301. Nevada State Museum Anthropological Papers No. 21. Carson City.
1990a Late Pleistocene/Early Holocene Occupations in Butte Valley, Eastern Nevada: Three Seasons Work. *Journal of California and Great Basin Anthropology* 12:231–261.
1990b Toolstone Selection and Lithic Technology in Early Great Basin Prehistory. *Journal of Field Archaeology* 17:283–299.

1992 Paleoindian/Archaic Range Shifts in Eastern Nevada. *Current Research in the Pleistocene* 9:1–20.

Beck, C., G. T. Jones, and R. E. Hughes
1992 Late Pleistocene/Early Holocene Territorial Use in Eastern Nevada. Paper presented at the 23d Great Basin Anthropological Conference, Boise, Idaho, October 8–10, 1992.

Bedwell, S. F.
1973 *Fort Rock Basin: Prehistory and Environment.* University of Oregon Press, Eugene.

Bettinger, R. L.
1989 *The Archaeology of Pinyon House, Two Eagles, and Crater Middens: Three Residential Sites in Owens Valley, Eastern California.* Anthropological Papers of the American Museum of Natural History No. 67. New York.

Clark, D. L.
1964 Archaeological Chronology in California and the Obsidian Hydration Method. *Annual Report of the Archaeological Survey,* pp. 143–211. Department of Anthropology, University of California, Los Angeles.

Dancey, W. S.
1974 The Archaeological Survey: A Reorientation. *Man in the Northeast* 8:98–112.

Dunnell, R. C.
1992 The Notion Site. In *Place, Time, and Archaeological Landscapes,* edited by L. Wandsnider and J. Rossignol, pp. 21–41. Plenum Press, New York.

Dunnell, R. C., and W. S. Dancey
1983 The Siteless Survey: A Regional Scale Data Collection Strategy. In *Advances in Archaeological Method and Theory,* edited by M. B. Schiffer, vol. 6, pp. 267–287. Academic Press, New York.

Ebert, W. L., R. F. Hoburg, and J. K. Bates
1991 The Sorption of Water on Obsidian and a Nuclear Waste Glass. *Physics and Chemistry of Glasses* 32:133–137.

Ericson, J. E.
1981 Durability of Rhyolitic Obsidian Glass Inferred from Hydration Dating Research. In *Scientific Basis for Nuclear Waste Management 1,* edited by J. G. Moore, pp. 283–290. Plenum Press, New York.

Evans, C., and B. J. Meggers
1960 A New Dating Method using Obsidian: Part II. An Archaeological Evaluation of the Method. *American Antiquity* 40:344–348.

Foley, R.
1981a *Off-Site Archaeology and Human Adaptation in Eastern Africa: An Analysis of Regional Artifact Density in the Amboseli, Southern Kenya.* BAR International Series No. 97.
1981b Off-Site Archaeology: An alternative Approach for the Short-Sited. In *Patterns of the Past, Studies in Honour of David Clarke,* edited by I. Hodder, G. Isaac, and N. Hammond, pp. 157–183. Cambridge University Press, London.

Friedman, I.
1976 Calculations of Obsidian Hydration Rates from Temperature Measurements. In *Advances in Obsidian Glass Studies,* edited by R. E. Taylor, pp. 173–182. Noyes Press, Park Ridge, N.J.

Friedman, I., and W. Long
1976 Hydration Rate of Obsidian. *Science* 191:347–352.

Friedman, I., and J. Obradovich
1981 Obsidian Hydration Dating of Volcanic Events. *Quaternary Research* 16:37–47.

Friedman, I., and R. L. Smith
1960 A New Dating Method Using Obsidian: Part I. The Development of the Technique. *American Antiquity* 33:149–155.

Friedman, I., R. L. Smith, and W. D. Long
1966 Hydration of Natural Glass and Formation of Perlite. *Geological Society of America Bulletin* 77:323–328.

Friedman, I., F. Trembour, and F. Smith
1990 Obsidian Hydration Rate as a Function of Relative Humidity. Poster presentation at the Annual Meeting of the Society for American Archaeology, Las Vegas.

Hall, M. C., and R. J. Jackson
1989 Obsidian Hydration Rates in California. In *Current Directions in California Obsidian Stud-*

ies, edited by R. E. Hughes, pp. 31–58. Contributions of the University of California Archaeological Research Facility No. 48.

Hanks, R. J., and G. L. Ashcroft
1980   Applied Soil Physics. *Advanced Series in Agricultural Sciences* No. 8. Springer-Verlag, New York.

Holmer, R. N.
1986   Projectile Points in the Intermountain West. In *Anthropology of the Desert West, Essays in Honor of Jesse D. Jennings,* edited by C. J. Condie and D. D. Fowler, pp. 89–115. University of Utah Anthropological Papers No. 110. Salt Lake City.

Hughes, R. E.
1984   Obsidian Sourcing Studies in the Great Basin: Problems and Prospects. In *Obsidian Studies in the Great Basin,* edited by R. E. Hughes, pp. 1–19. Contributions of the University of California Archaeological Research Facility No. 45.
1991   Geochemical Description of the Various Flows of the Casa Diablo Obsidian Source, Inyo National Forest, Mono County, California. Ms. on file, Inyo National Forest, Bishop, California.

Hughes, R. E., and R. L. Smith
1993   Archaeology, Geology, and Geochemistry in Obsidian Provenance Studies. In *The Effects of Scale in Archaeological and Geological Perspectives,* edited by J. K. Stein and A. R. Binse, pp. 79–91. Geological Society of America Special Papers, No. 283.

Jack, R. N., and R. F. Heizer
1968   "Finger-Printing" of Some Mesoamerican Obsidian Artifacts. *Contributions of the University of California Archaeological Research Facility* 5:81–100.

Jackson, R. J.
1984   Current Problems in Obsidian Hydration Analysis. In *Obsidian Studies in the Great Basin,* edited by R. E. Hughes, pp. 103–115. Contributions of the University of California Archaeological Research Facility No. 45.

Jennings, J. D., A. R. Schroedl, and R. N. Holmer
1980   *Cowboy Cave.* University of Utah Anthropological Papers No. 104.

Johnson, L.
1969   Obsidian Hydration Rate for the Klamath Basin of California and Oregon. *Science* 165:1354–1356.

Jones, G. T., and C. Beck
1990   An Obsidian Hydration Chronology of Late Pleistocene/Early Holocene Surface Assemblages from Butte Valley, Nevada. *Journal of California and Great Basin Anthropology* 12:84–100.
1992   Chronological Resolution in Distributional Archaeology. In *Place, Time, and Archaeological Landscapes,* edited by L. Wandsnider and J. Rossignol, pp. 167–192. Plenum Press, New York.

Jones, G. T., D. K. Grayson, and C. Beck
1983   Sample Size and Functional Diversity in Archaeological Assemblages. In *Lulu Linear Punctated: Essays in Honor of George Irving Quimby,* edited by R. C. Dunnell and D. K. Grayson, pp. 55–73. University of Michigan, Museum of Anthropology, Anthropological Papers No. 72.

Katsui, Y., and Y. Kondo
1976   Variation in Obsidian Hydration Rates for Hokkaido, Northern Japan. In *Advances in Obsidian Glass Studies,* edited by R. E. Taylor, pp. 120–140. Noyes Press, Park Ridge, N.J.

Layton, T. N.
1973   Temporal Ordering of Surface-Collected Obsidian Artifacts by Hydration Measurement. *Archaeometry* 15:129–132.

Leach, B. F., and G. E. Hamel
1984   The Influence of Archaeological Soil Temperatures on Obsidian Dating in New Zealand. *New Zealand Journal of Science* 27:399–408.

Lee, R.
1969   Chemical Temperature Integration. *Journal of Applied Meteorology* 8:423–430.

Lewarch, D. E.
1979 Controlled Surface Collection in Regional Analysis. In *The Cannon Reservoir Human Ecology Project: Recent Advances in the Archaeology of Northeast Missouri,* edited by M. J. O'Brien and D. E. Lewarch, pp. 42–51. Notebook No. 5, Department of Anthropology, University of Nebraska.

Lewarch, D. E., and M. J. O'Brien
1981 The Expanding Role of Surface Assemblages in Archaeological Research. In *Advances in Archaeological Method and Theory,* vol. 4, edited by M. B. Schiffer, pp. 297–342. Academic Press, New York.

Mazer, J. J., C. M. Stevenson, W. L. Ebert, and J. K. Bates
1991 The Experimental Hydration of Obsidian as a Function of Relative Humidity and Temperature. *American Antiquity* 56:504–513.

Meighan, C. W., L. J. Foote, and P. V. Aiello
1968 Obsidian Dating in West Mexican Archaeology. *Science* 160:1069–1075.

Meighan, C. W., and C. V. Haynes
1970 The Borax Lake Site Revisited. *Science* 167:1213–1221.

Michels, J. W.
1965 *Lithic Serial Chronology through Obsidian Hydration Dating.* Unpublished Ph.D. Dissertation, University of California, Los Angeles.
1969 Testing Stratigraphy and Artifact Re-Use through Obsidian Hydration Dating. *American Antiquity* 34:15–22.
1973 *Dating Methods in Archaeology.* Academic Press, New York.

Michels, J. W., and I. S. T. Tsong
1980 Obsidian Hydration Dating: A Coming of Age. In *Advances in Archaeological Method and Theory,* vol. 3, edited by M. B. Schiffer, pp. 405–444. Academic Press, New York.

Michels, J. W., I. S. T. Tsong, and C. M. Nelson
1983a Obsidian Dating and East African Archaeology. *Science* 219:361–366.

Michels, J. W., I. S. T. Tsong, and G. A. Smith
1983b Experimentally Derived Hydration Rates in Obsidian Dating. *Archaeometry* 25:107–117.

Norton, D. R., and I. Friedman
1981 Ground Temperature Measurements, Part 1: Palman Technique. *United States Geological Survey Professional Paper* 1203:1–11.

O'Brien, M. J., and D. E. Lewarch
1982 *Plowzone Archaeology: Contributions to Theory and Technique.* Vanderbilt University Publications in Anthropology No. 27.

Origer, T. M., and B. P. Wickstrom
1982 The Use of Hydration Measurements to Date Obsidian Materials from Sonoma County, California. *Journal of California and Great Basin Anthropology* 4:123–131.

Raymond, A. W.
1984–1985 Evaluating the Occupational History of Lithic Scatters: Analysis of Obsidian Hydration Measurements. *North American Archaeologist* 6:115–133.

Ridings, R.
1991 Obsidian Hydration Dating: The Effects of Mean Exponential Ground Temperature and Depth of Artifact Recovery. *Journal of Field Archaeology* 18:77–85.

Roper, D. C.
1976 Lateral Displacement of Artifacts Due to Plowing. *American Antiquity* 41:372–375.

Schiffer, M. B.
1972 Archaeological Context and Systemic Context. *American Antiquity* 37:156–165.
1987 *Formation Processes of the Archaeological Record.* University of New Mexico Press, Albuquerque.

Shutler, M. E., and R. Shutler, Jr.
1963 *Deer Creek Cave, Elko County, Nevada.* Nevada State Museum Anthropological Papers No. 11.

Stross, F. N., J. R. Weaver, G. E. A. Wyld, R. F. Heizer, and J. A. Graham
1968 Analysis of American Obsidians by X-Ray Fluorescence and Neutron Activation Analysis. *Contributions of the University of California Archaeological Research Facility* 5:59–79.

Thomas, D. H.
1972 A Computer Simulation Model of Great Basin Shoshonean Settlement and Subsistence Patterns. In *Models in Archaeology,* edited by D. L. Clarke, pp. 275–308. Methuen, London.
1973 An Empirical Test for Steward's Model of Great Basin Settlement Patterns. *American Antiquity* 38:155–176.
1975 Nonsite Sampling in Archaeology: Up the Creek without a Site? In *Sampling in Archaeology,* edited by J. W. Mueller, pp. 61–81. University of Arizona Press, Tucson.
1981 How to Classify the Projectile Points from Monitor Valley, Nevada. *Journal of California and Great Basin Anthropology* 3:7–43.

Tremaine, K. J.
1991 A Relative Dating Approach for Bodie Hills and Casa Diablo Obsidian Derived from Accelerated Hydration Experiments. In *Archaeological Evaluation of CA-Mno-2456, -2488, and -564, near Bridgeport, Mono County, California.* Ms. on file at California Archaeological Inventory, NW Information Center.

Tremaine, K. J., and D. A. Frederickson
1988 Induced Obsidian Hydration Experiments: An Investigation in Relative Dating. *Materials Research Society Symposium Proceedings* 123: 271–278.

Trembour, F., and I. Friedman
1984 Obsidian Hydration Dating and Field Site Temperature. In *Obsidian Studies in the Great Basin,* edited by R. E. Hughes, pp. 79–90. Contributions of the University of California Archaeological Research Facility No. 45.

Trembour, F., I. Friedman, F. J. Jurceka, and F. L. Smith
1986 A Simple Device For Integrating Temperature, Relative Humidity or Salinity over Time. *Journal of Atmosphere and Ocean Technology* 3:186–190.

Trembour, F., F. Smith, and I. Friedman
1988 Diffusion Cells for Integrating Temperature and Relative Humidity over Long Periods of Time. In *Materials Issues in Art and Archaeology,* edited by E. Sayre, P. Vandiver, J. Druzik, and C. Stevenson. Materials Research Society Symposium Proceedings 123:245–251.

Trubowitz, N. L.
1978 The Persistence of Settlement Pattern in a Cultivated Field. In *Essays in Northeastern Anthropology in Memory of Marian W. White,* edited by W. Englebrecht and D. K. Grayson, pp. 41–66. Occasional Publications in Northeastern Anthropology No. 5, Franklin Pierce College.

Willey, G. R.
1951 Peruvian Settlement and Socio-Economic Patterns. In *The Civilization of Ancient America,* edited by S. Tax, pp. 195–200. University of Chicago Press, Chicago.
1953 *Prehistoric Settlement Patterns in the Viru Valley, Peru.* Bureau of American Ethnology Bulletin No. 155, Smithsonian Institution, Washington, D.C.

Willig, J. A., and C. M. Aikens
1988 The Clovis-Archaic Interface in Far Western North America. In *Early Human Occupations in Far Western North America: The Clovis-Archaic Interface,* edited by J. A. Willig, C. M. Aikens, and J. L. Fagan, pp. 1–40. Nevada State Museum Anthropological Papers No. 21.

Wood, W. R., and D. L. Johnson
1978 A Survey of Disturbance Processes in Archaeological Site Formation. In *Advances in Archaeological Method and Theory,* vol. 1, edited by Michael B. Schiffer, pp. 315–381. Academic Press, New York.

Zeier, C. D.
1986 Obsidian Studies. In *Data Recovery at Sites 35-JA-102 and 35-JA-107, Elk Creek Lake Project, Jackson County, Oregon,* by E. E. Budy and R. G. Elston, pp. 371–394. CRM Report for U.S. Army Corps of Engineers, Portland, Oregon.

Zeier, C. D., and R. D. Elston
1984 An Analysis of Obsidian Hydration Processes at the Sugarloaf Obsidian Quarry, Inyo County, California. Ms. on file at Intermountain Research, Silver City, Nevada.

5
SURFACE EXPOSURE DATING WITH ROCK VARNISH

Ronald I. Dorn

Department of Geography
Arizona State University
Tempe, Arizona

Abstract

The exposed surfaces of landforms, rock engravings, geoglyphs, and surface artifacts in drylands develop a coating of rock varnish that is often amenable to dating. Numerical ages for exposure of the underlying rock surface are obtained by radiocarbon dating of organic matter buried by rock varnish, and calibrated ages are obtained by cation-ratio dating. Rock varnish ages are always minimums, because varnish forms after the exposure of the underlying rock. Although still experimental, rock varnish dating has been replicated by different laboratories world-wide and has performed well in rigorous blind tests. Archaeological and geomorphological examples of rock varnish ages are presented for material from the deserts of Australia, North America, and Peru. In contrast to dating material in stratigraphic sequences, rock varnish provides an opportunity to obtain chronological information on surface material with a spatial distribution.

Introduction

THE SYSTEMATIC STUDY OF ROCK SURFACES HAS a long history, perhaps starting with the first humans who engraved rock art into natural blackboards blackened by manganese-rich rock varnish. The fascination for these rock surface changes, called patina or patination by archaeologists, is shared by earth and human scientists alike, because alterations can provide useful information on the history of a rock surface.

Rock-surface weathering and rock coatings are distinct phenomena. Weathering is the breakdown of minerals and rocks, and chapters by Knuepfer, McCarroll, and Beck and Jones in this volume illustrate the potential for extracting valuable data from the results of these processes. Rock coatings, in contrast, are accretions, not derived from the underlying rock. Some coatings are purely biogenic, such as lichens (see Matthews, chapter 9 of this volume). Many coatings found on rock surfaces have a biogenic origin but are composed of an inorganic matrix with pieces of organic material. These include rock varnish that is catalyzed by manganese-concentrating bacteria (Dorn and Oberlander 1981) and oxalate-silica skins that may be initiated by lichens and other oxalate-producing organisms (Watchman 1991). Other coatings, such as amorphous silica, probably have an abiotic origin (Curtiss et al. 1985). However, even amorphous silica (Dorn, Phillips, et al. 1991;

Watchman 1990) and carbonate rinds (Hooke and Dorn 1992) have bits of organic material trapped in a largely inorganic matrix.

Most archaeologists and earth scientists have been trained to think in terms of stratigraphic columns. The whole notion of obtaining age information from a surface context adds a spatial dimension (of examining the distribution of surfaces of different ages) that is vastly different from the traditional stratigraphic perspective (of excavating and dating layers). Yet coatings on rocks have great potential to yield unique information. Layers within coatings can record environmental changes experienced by that rock surface (see Dorn 1986, 1988, 1992b, 1994; Reheis 1987; Watchman 1990). Dating the coating provides a minimum age for the exposure of the underlying surface.

The focus of this chapter is how the age of exposure of a rock surface can be constrained by dating the dark coating called rock varnish. Rock varnish has been of interest to archaeologists and earth scientists because it accretes on stone surfaces that have been worked by both natural geomorphic processes and humans. Within the past decade, over a dozen new approaches to the dating of rock varnish have been explored (Table 5.1). Of these only two have seen widespread application and are the subject of this chapter: cation-ratio dating and accelerator-radiocarbon dating. As is the case in all Quaternary dating methods, the most important step is collecting the right type of sample in the field. Before proceeding with details on these methods, the critically important matter of sampling will be discussed first.

Sampling

Not All Rock Varnishes are Alike

Rock varnish is a dark coating on rocks, typically less than 200 μm thick. It is composed of clay minerals cemented to the underlying rock by oxides of manganese and/or iron (Potter and Rossman 1977, 1979). It is an accretion with chemical and morphological characteristics distinct from the underlying substrate (Dorn and Oberlander 1982; Perry and Adams 1978; Potter and Rossman 1977).

Beyond these characteristics, rock varnishes differ greatly in structure and chemistry at all scales from kilometers to micrometers. Even at the scale of cubic millimeters, great differences exist between varnishes of different colors, between black varnishes found in subaerial environments and nonsubaerial environments and between varnishes found in different types of subaerial environments. Table 5.2 presents a field- and laboratory-based classification of rock varnishes. Because this paper concerns the dating of black (manganese-rich) varnishes found in a subaerial environment in drylands, the table is most detailed for these varnishes.

DIFFERENT COLORS

Black varnishes are greatly enriched in manganese (which provides the dark coloration) in the upper few microns, typically greater than 10 percent MnO (Dorn and Oberlander 1982). Orange varnishes (Munsell 10R4/8, 2.5YR4/6 to 5/6, 5YR7/6 to 7/8) generally have MnO concentrations of less than 0.2 percent throughout the entire varnish. Dusky-brown varnishes (Munsell 10R3/3 to 4/4) are those intermediate in surface chemistry; they have enough manganese to darken the color (in the range of ca. 0.5–5 percent), but not enough manganese to give the varnish a black appearance.

SUBAERIAL VS. NON-SUBAERIAL BLACK VARNISHES

Manganese-rich varnishes that do not form at the surface have different structures than varnishes that form at the air/rock interface (Dorn 1986; Dorn and Oberlander 1982). Trace element chemistries also differ. For example, varnishes that originally developed in rock crevices but have been exposed by rock spalling have much higher levels of barium than varnishes formed exclusively in a subaerial environment (Figures 5.1 and 5.2).

Distinguishing different types of manganese-rich

Table 5.1. Methods of Estimating the Age of Rock Varnish Formation

Method	Theory	Indicator	Precision Level[a]	Comments
Appearance	Varnish darkens over time	Subjective appearance	Relative	Controlled by factors other than time
Thickness	As varnish gets older, it grows vertically	Measurement with microscope	Relative	Also controlled by microenvironment
Cover of black surface varnish	Varnish grows laterally away from nucleation centers	Visual estimate of percent cover on exposed clasts	Relative	Derbyshire et al. 1984
Orange bottom varnish growth	As age increases, the undersides of clasts are coated with Fe-clay rock varnish (Mn-poor)	Percent of clasts in desert pavement that have cover of orange bottom varnish	Relative	Derbyshire et al. 1984
Trace element trends	Assumes varnish derived from underlying rock. Trace element profiles with depth reflect time	Scraped layers of varnish and underlying rock. Measured by neutron activation analysis	Relative	Bard 1979
Metal scavenging	Zn, Cu, Ni and other metals increase over time as they are scavenged by Mn-Fe oxides	Concentration of trace heavy metals relative to Mn and Fe	Relative	Dorn, Jull, et al.1992
Paleomagnetism	Magnetic field aligned when Fe-oxides precipitate	Profiles of paleomagnetic properties with depth	Correlative	Clayton et al. 1990
Tephra-chronology	Glass fragments from known volcanic eruptions might be identifiable in rock varnish	Possible tephra found in varnish, but requires glass identification and geochemical correlations	Correlative	Harrington 1988
Varnish layers	Sequences of chemical and textural changes correlated from site to site.	Mn:Fe, Pb, $\delta^{13}C$, and textures	Correlative	Dorn 1988, 1992b, 1994
Stratigraphy	Dating material on or under varnish constrains varnish age	Radiocarbon dating of carbonate formed over varnish	Correlative; and Numerical	Dragovich 1986
Cation ratio	Mobile cations are leached faster than immobile cations.	Elemental ratio of $(K+Ca)/Ti$	Calibrated	Dorn 1989; Dorn, Cahill, et al. 1990
K-Ar dating	As varnish clays accumulate, they may undergo a diagenesis that refixes K; or date K in Mn-oxides	K-Ar dating of radiogenic argon in varnish clays; ^{40}Ar-^{39}Ar of Mn-oxides	Numerical	Dorn 1989; Vasconcelos et al. 1992
Uranium-series	Uranium precipitates with Mn-oxides and then decays.	U/Th measurements	Numerical	Knauss and Ku 1980
Radiocarbon	Accreting varnish encapsulates underlying organic matter	Accelerator Mass Spectrometry radiocarbon dating	Numerical	Dorn, Clarkson, et al. 1992b

[a] *Relative, correlative, calibrated,* and *numerical* are Quaternary dating terms developed by Colman et al. (1987); *absolute* is no longer advocated as a dating term.

Table 5.2. Different Types of Rock Varnishes

I. BLACK (Mn-rich) VARNISH
  A. *In drylands*
    1. Subaerial positions that occur:
      interdigitated with silica skins
      where water runoff occurs
      where water collects
      with microcolonial fungi
      with lichens
      with filamentous fungi
      with cyanobacteria
      where organic matter collects
      where dust collects
    2. Subaerial varnishes that contain:
      infilled erosional pits
      fractures refilled with Mn-Fe
      internal deformation of layers
      evidence of aeolian abrasion
      anomalous concentrations of K, Ca, Ti, Ba
      pH values <6 and >9
      abundant botryoids
    3. At or within 10 cm of soil surface
      ground-line band in pavement
      with cryptogamic soils
      where soil has been eroding
      where soil has accumulated
    4. Crack varnish
    5. Former crack varnishes exposed by recent spalling on talus
      by cm-scale flaking
      by granular disintegration
    6. Fractures in bedrock
    7. Underside of pavement cobbles
    8. Paleosols
  B. *Outside drylands*

II. ORANGE (Mn-poor) VARNISH
(Munsell 10R4/8, 2.5YR4/6 to 5/6, 5YR7/6 to 7/8)
  A. *In drylands*
    1. Crack varnish
    2. Underside of pavement cobbles
    3. Subaerial position
    4. Fractures in bedrock
    5. Paleosols
  B. *Outside drylands*

III. DUSKY BROWN VARNISH
(Munsell 10R3/3 to 4/4)
  A. *In drylands*
    1. Crack varnish
    2. Underside of pavement cobbles
    3. Subaerial position
    4. Fractures in bedrock
    5. Paleosols
  B. *Outside drylands*

varnishes can be tricky. The author has been in the field with experienced desert geomorphologists who have confused varnishes developed only in a subaerial position with varnishes originally developed in a subsurface position. It is an easy but crucial error. Varnishes on hillslopes and talus typically start out in a crevice but are later exposed by rock spalling along a joint plane. Similarly, ground-line band varnishes, which originally form at the soil-rock-atmosphere interface, are often found in exposed desert pavements that have experienced soil erosion.

Many varnish researchers are drawn toward crack and ground-line varnishes because of their darker and shinier appearance. Crack varnish and ground-line band varnish are almost always darker, smoother, and better looking than adjacent varnishes that have only experienced a subaerial environment. This is due to their development in protected environments that favor the concentration of manganese (see Dorn and Oberlander 1982).

The location of original varnish formation is of concern to varnish dating, because what is of interest is when varnish started to form over a surface that was abraded by humans (such as petroglyph manufacturing) or a physical process (such as transport by floods or glaciers). If a rock surface has spalled or been exposed by soil erosion, the newly exposed varnish would not date the event of interest. The temptation is strong to collect the best-looking varnishes, but it is often the wrong type of varnish and will yield incorrect results.

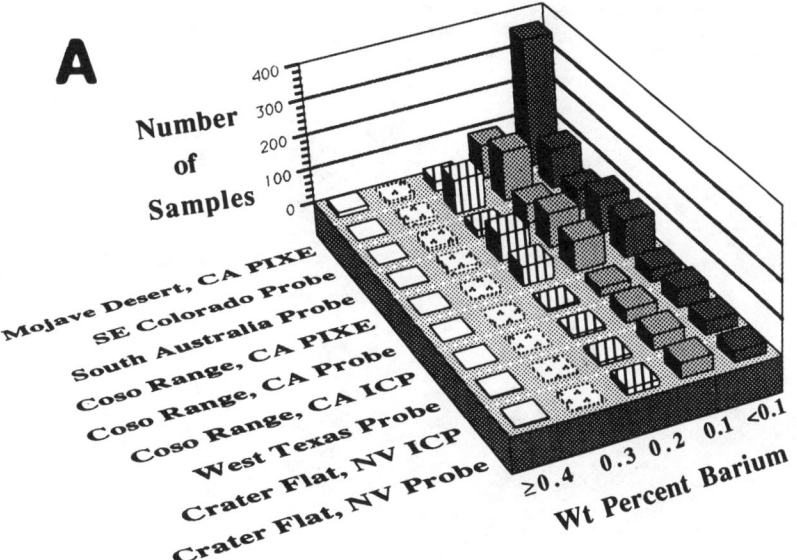

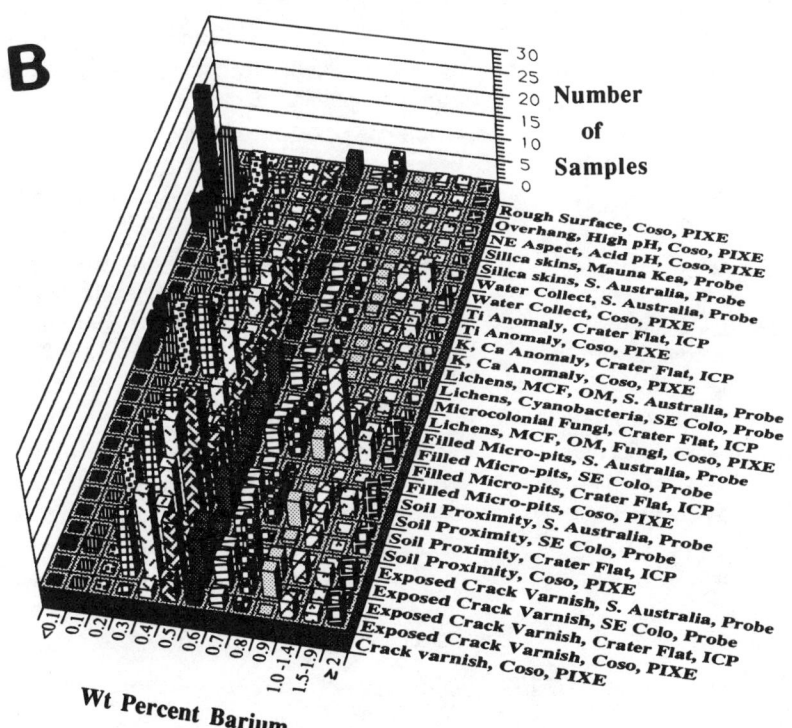

Figure 5.1. Representative barium concentrations (A) in the types of varnishes that are appropriate for varnish dating, and (B) in different types of varnish microenvironments not appropriate for varnish dating. Barium measurements are rounded off to the nearest 0.1 percent to assist in the graphical portrayal of over a thousand analyses. Sampling criteria, sample assessment criteria, sample preparation, and sample analysis methodologies are detailed elsewhere (Dorn 1989; Dorn, Jull et al. 1990; Krinsley et al. 1990). Chemical-analysis methods are abbreviated as follows: proton induced X-ray excitation (PIXE), wavelength dispersive electron microprobe (Probe), and inductively coupled plasma (ICP). Samples were collected from the Coso Range, eastern California; Crater Flat, southern Nevada; southeastern Colorado; South Australia; and Mauna Kea, Hawaii. A more complete description of the different types of microenvironments is elaborated in Table 5.5.

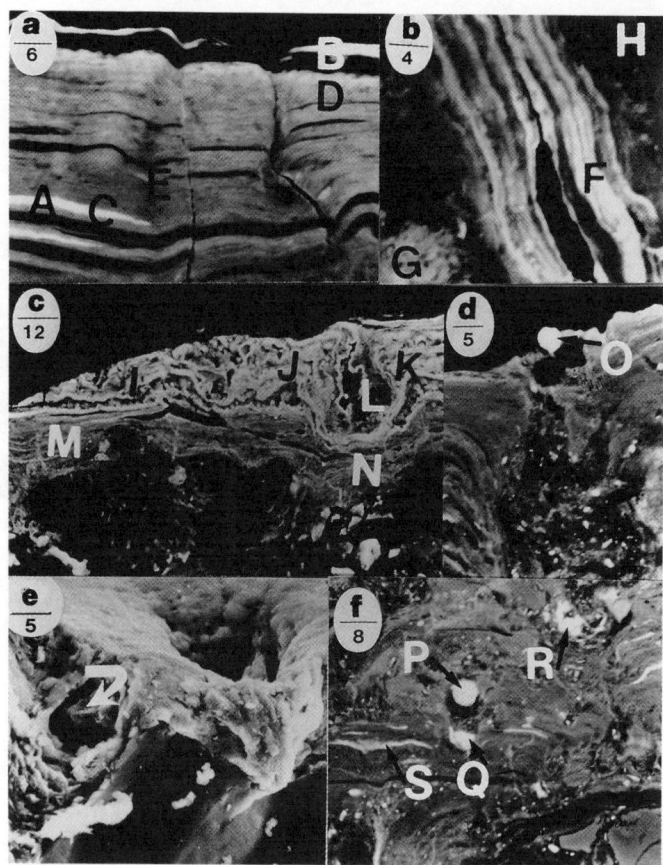

Figure 5.2. Examples of locations of high Ba concentrations in rock varnishes. Letters refer to wavelength dispersive electron microprobe analyses in Table 5.3 Scale bars in microns. All micrographs imaged by backscatter, except that 2E is by secondary electron microscopy.

A through C show black crack varnishes with high barium levels, Mn-Ba association, and a surface layer enriched in Mn. (A) From Little Cones basalt flow in Crater Flat, southern Nevada, where the crack was opened in sampling. Dust was not in contact with the varnish. (B) From eroding hillside near Mannahill, South Australia, on silicified dolomite, exposed by sampling. Dust was not in contact with the varnish. (C) From Lone Pine Creek alluvial fan, Owens Valley, California with microcolonial fungi found on ca. 15 percent of the varnish surface. The lower layer is Mn-poor, typical of orange crack varnish. The brighter manganese-rich layer is black crack varnish, formed as the crack widened enough to wash away alkaline dust. The bright lines running through the lower layer are Ba and Mn that have been remobilized from the upper layer. After the crack varnish was exposed by natural spalling, the varnish was truncated, probably by the aeolian abrasion that commonly erodes the varnish in this part of the Owens Valley.

D through F show micron-scale pits in subaerial black varnishes, filled with barium-rich detritus that is associated with sulfur (probably as barium sulfate). (D) Ba-S rich detritus (letter O) trapped in a surface depression, from varnish with a concentration of microcolonial fungi ca. 10 percent, from Chiatovich Creek, White Mountains, Nevada (E) The erosional hollow on the left has been refilled by younger varnish, including a barium sulfate crystal (arrow), according to semiquantitative energy-dispersive analysis. Sample from varnish with a concentration of microcolonial fungi ca. 10 percent Death Valley. (F) Eroded pits refilled by barium-sulfate (letters P, Q, S), with some of the barium remobilized in Ba-Mn rich stringers (such as letter S), collected from Cima basalt flow #29.

Table 5.3. Wavelength Dispersive Electron Microprobe Analyses of Points in Figure 5.2[a]

Point	Na2O	MgO	Al2O3	SiO2	P2O5	K2O	CaO	TiO2	MnO	Fe2O3	BaO	Total	CR
From Figure 5.2a:													
A	0.37	1.05	10.48	22.41	1.36	0.92	1.03	0.45	21.54	13.24	3.55	76.40	5.58
B	0.40	1.09	10.67	23.37	1.15	1.59	0.95	0.48	28.02	7.34	3.09	78.15	6.97
C	0.23	1.84	13.82	29.33	1.20	1.01	0.71	0.49	22.93	8.41	1.97	81.94	4.60
D	1.02	1.06	12.77	33.30	2.32	1.42	1.28	0.71	19.10	11.14	0.84	84.96	4.94
E	2.44	0.78	8.87	32.33	1.92	1.07	0.86	0.36	18.75	17.91	0.56	85.85	6.99
From Figure 5.2b:													
F	2.04	1.08	11.02	31.52	0.26	1.59	1.85	0.51	20.63	14.28	2.13	86.91	8.68
G	0.05*	1.26	12.56	26.25	1.90	0.46	0.74	0.76	17.59	13.63	0.97	76.12	2.01
H	1.88	1.16	10.90	23.24	1.86	1.65	1.07	0.53	8.14	17.56	0.44	68.43	6.74
From Figure 5.2c:													
I	0.92	0.21	9.97	33.50	1.13	0.49	0.80	0.24	11.78	7.98	0.88	67.90	6.84
J	0.92	0.99	12.29	19.44	1.02	1.39	0.96	0.45	14.70	11.43	0.97	64.56	6.85
K	1.02	1.04	12.48	20.13	3.38	1.36	1.46	0.53	15.81	10.71	1.16	69.08	6.87
L	2.47	0.77	8.74	24.25	1.88	1.06	0.98	0.36	9.29	16.99	0.42	66.79	7.35
M	1.96	1.03	10.78	31.10	2.52	1.44	1.12	0.45	8.16	18.67	0.81	78.04	7.43
N	2.33	1.41	11.52	32.06	1.22	0.86	1.18	0.35	0.89	12.30	0.72	64.84	7.46
From Figure 5.2d:[b]													
O	0.05*	0.04*	2.13	6.77	0.05*	0.03*	0.89	0.27	1.01	2.49	24.07	37.63	nc
From Figure 5.2f:[c]													
P	0.03*	0.37	3.49	11.35	0.05*	0.24	1.53	0.83	3.47	14.27	17.13	52.68	2.62
Q	0.27	0.89	8.38	18.97	0.72	1.49	0.82	0.65	5.87	19.75	14.06	71.87	4.69
R	0.86	0.94	10.98	18.91	1.26	0.05*	0.61	0.51	1.85	9.78	20.72	66.42	nc
S	1.24	1.63	11.76	24.67	1.08	1.65	0.76	0.65	28.67	10.76	3.57	86.44	4.93

[a]Beam width ~ 2 microns. Counting time 30 seconds. Analyses below limit of detection indicated by *. nc = CR cannot be calculated. Points correspond to locations in Figure 5.2.
[b]High concentrations of sulfur in point O indicated by energy dispersive X-ray analysis.
[c]High concentrations of sulfur in P, Q, and R indicated by energy dispersive X-ray analysis.

For example, a very well developed crack varnish collected from an *unexposed* fracture on Ayers Rock, Australia, yielded an AMS^{14}C age of 27,100 ± 400 B.P. (Beta 19893; ETH 2809), indicating that *unexposed* varnishes can have considerable antiquity. The identification of nonsubaerial varnishes should be verified in the laboratory with studies of cross sections (see Krinsley and Dorn 1991; see also Figure 5.2 and Table 5.3).

Subaerial Black Varnishes

Even different types of subaerial black varnishes have very different stable-isotope compositions (Dorn and DeNiro 1985), different manganese concentrations (Dorn 1990; Jones 1991), different micromorphologies (Dorn 1986), different degrees of interdigitation with silica skins (Dorn, Jull, et al. 1992), different backscatter textures (Krinsley et al. 1990), and different trace element concentrations (see Figure 5.1)

Subaerial varnishes must be avoided where deposition has been interrupted by mechanical or biogeochemical erosion (Krinsley et al. 1990). Samples with discontinuous layers should not be processed for dating. Discontinuities can be produced, for example, by organisms that bore holes into the varnish (Figure 5.2E).

These hollows are then filled in with much younger material, leading to inaccurate ages, as demonstrated in prior tests (Dorn 1989; Dorn, Jull, et al. 1989). Other cross-sectional characteristics that disqualify a sample for further processing are explored in the cation-ratio dating section of this paper.

Collection Procedures

The sample collection philosophy followed here is to avoid specific varnish characteristics and microenvironments that have produced results inconsistent with independent age controls.

Only subaerial varnishes are sampled, and then only the subaerial varnishes that do not have the characteristics listed in Table 5.2. Also implicit in this approach is collecting and analyzing large volumes of sample; typically cubic millimeters to cubic centimeters. This is because the extreme microchemical variability that occurs at the scale of microns (see Dorn 1989; Dorn and Oberlander 1982; Dragovich 1988; O'Hara et al. 1989, 1990; Raymond et al. 1991; Reneau and Raymond, 1991) is vastly reduced when greater volumes are analyzed.

A critical factor in sampling is the realization that any spot of varnish will not do. Varnish should be sampled from micropositions where varnish first starts to grow. Ongoing studies of historical rock engravings and stones faced during historical construction reveal that colonization occurs first in specific types of places on different lithologies. For example, varnish first colonizes vesicles in basalt, impurities in chert, fractures in quartz and silicified dolomite, and grain boundaries in granitic rocks and sandstones.

When a new method develops, different investigators often have their own approaches to sample collection. This is the case in rock varnish research. Unfortunately, not all varnish researchers specify the type(s) of varnish they have analyzed, so the author is unable to compile a chart comparing different sampling procedures. A few investigators have noted avoidance features, such as lichens or places where aeolian abrasion occurs (Glazovskiy 1985; Zhang et al. 1990). Others simply indicate that "the darkest varnish is sampled because, in comparing spots with similar settings, relative darkness may be the best field criteria for relative age. The smoothest varnishes are sampled to minimize surface roughness effects in SEM analyses of natural surfaces" (Reneau et al. 1991: 54). Or they may state that varnish is collected from "outcrops possessing the darkest, most consistent varnish at each site" (Raymond et al. 1991: 38). Still others do not specify what type of varnishes are collected or analyzed (Harrington et al. 1991; Harry et al. 1992).

The lack of quality control in sample collection has led to inaccurate comparisons in the published literature. Certainly there is no evidence to indicate that any two varnish investigators have analyzed the same type(s) of varnishes. This is not to suggest that data from any particular investigator(s) is invalid or unrepresentative for the type(s) of varnish analyzed. On the contrary, when varnish type is factored in, results among different groups appear to be fairly consistent. Until investigators specify the different type(s) of varnish analyzed, however, readers interested in varnish studies need to be aware that 'apples and oranges' are being compared, often unknowingly.

The Cation-Ratio Dating Method

Cation-ratio (CR) dating is a method that assigns relative or calibrated ages to rock varnishes (Dorn 1983, 1989). The ratio of cations (positive ions) of (potassium + calcium)/titanium decreases with age. If this CR is measured at sites with known exposure ages in a region, a calibration called a cation-leaching curve can be constructed. The CRs in unknown samples are then compared with this curve and a CR age is assigned. CR dating is similar to obsidian hydration analysis (see Beck and Jones, chapter 4 of this volume), in that both techniques attempt to extract a time signature from a chemical change.

Since its discovery the trend of decreasing CRs with age has been replicated by several researchers around the world (see Bull 1991; Glazovskiy 1985; Harrington and Whitney 1987; Pineda et al. 1988; Pineda et al. 1990; Zhang et al. 1990). Figure 5.3 presents examples of cation-leaching curves. Differences among curves may

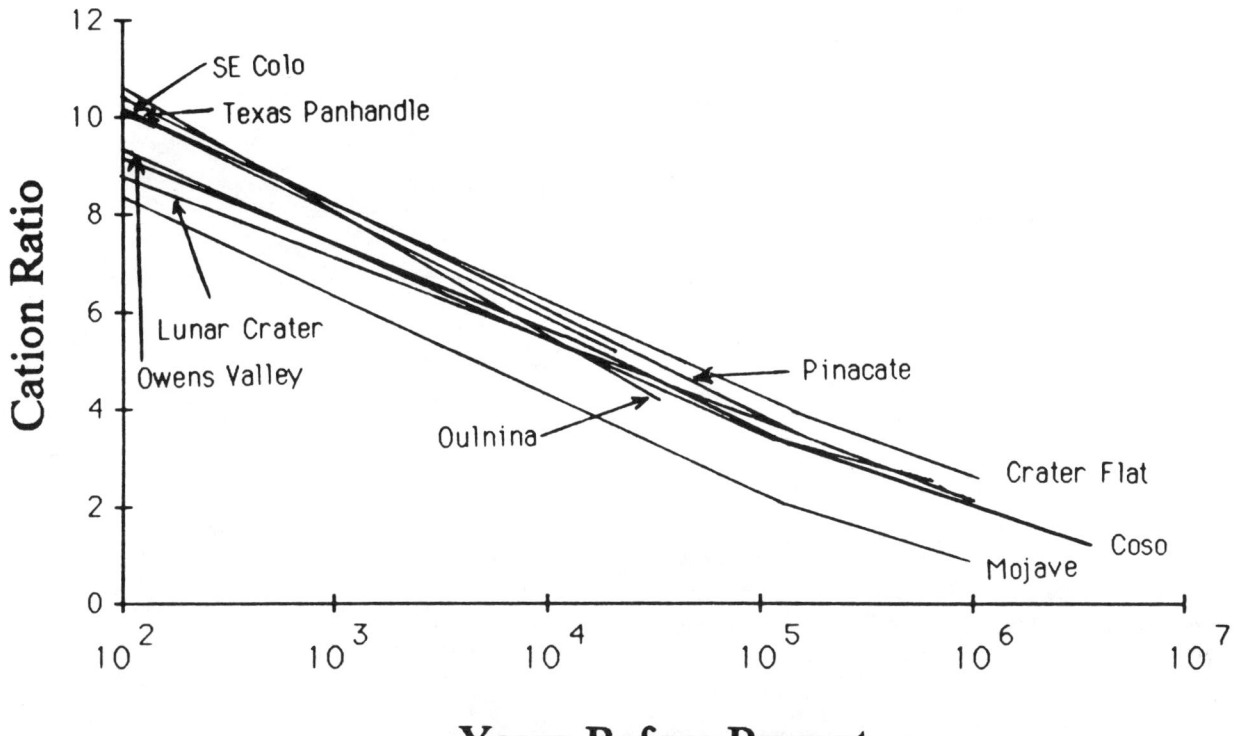

Figure 5.3. Cation-leaching curves constructed by PIXE analyses of rock varnishes removed from surfaces of known age. Sites for the different curves are described in Dorn, Nobbs, et al. (1988) for the Oulnina curve in South Australia and in Dorn (1989) for the other sites in western North America.

be due to variations in the chemistry of airborne fallout, temperature, precipitation, the seasonality of temperature and precipitation, and micromorphological characteristics of the varnish.

The simplest hypothesis to explain the lowering of the CR of $(K^+ + Ca^{2+})/Ti^{4+}$ with time is cation leaching (Dorn 1983), where potassium and calcium are more mobile than titanium in the geochemical environment where varnish forms. The following two sections present evidence from two different types of studies to support the hypothesis of cation leaching.

Laboratory Studies of Cation Leaching

Two types of laboratory leaching experiments were conducted by Dorn and Krinsley (1991): exposure of varnish scrapings to leaching solutions and exposure of varnishes still attached to the rock to leaching solutions. These laboratory tests were carried out in less than a year; hence they cannot be completely analogous to natural processes taking thousands of years. The goal was simply to assess if cation leaching occurred and then to better understand some of the variables that influence it.

One boulder on the Q3a surface of Hanaupah Canyon Fan in Death Valley (Dorn 1988) was cut into pieces in order to examine the influence of temperature on the leaching process and to compare the leaching process involving varnish scrapings with that involving varnishes attached to the rock. Exposed *rock* surfaces were coated with epoxy, leaving about 80 cm² of rock varnish exposed to deionized water. Four subsamples were kept at 5°C, four at 25°C, and four at 40°C. Subsamples within each temperature group were agitated for five days, 20 days, 50 days, and 100 days. At the end of each period, the water was analyzed by inductively coupled plasma atomic emission spectroscopy (ICP-AES). Twelve additional 20-mg subsets of varnish were also scraped from the same Death Valley boulder; the scrapings were cleaned of rock contaminants as described by Dorn (1989). These were subjected to the same conditions as the *in situ* samples (varnish still attached to the rock).

Figure 5.4 presents the results of this experiment. The rate of Ca and K leaching from rock varnish appears to increase with time and higher temperatures. Varnish scrapings were leached of Ca and K faster and more extensively than varnish still attached to the rock, which is probably because scraped varnish has much more surface area than varnish still attached to the rock. This emphasizes the importance of internal fracture systems in varnish (Figures 5.2A–C) in opening up internal volumes of varnish to leaching solutions.

In order to assess the influence of interdigitation of rock varnish with coatings of amorphous silica, samples were collected from the Puu Waawaa Ranch lava flow of Hualálai, Hawaii (Dorn, Jull, et al. 1992). One group of samples was of varnish interlayered with silica skin (see Curtiss et al. 1985). Another group of samples from the same site was Mn-rich rock varnish without any silica skin. Each group was divided and split into subsamples exposed to deionized water for 20, 40, 60, 80, 100, and 120 days. Ti concentrations were usually below the limit of detection for ICP-AES (0.2 mg/l), so CRs could not be calculated for these samples. Figure 5.5 illustrates that coatings of amorphous silica appear to slow the leaching of K and Ca. This sealing effect can be seen in the micrographs.

In Situ *Observations of Sites of Cation Leaching*

Backscatter electron microscopy (BSE) images chemistry along with texture (Krinsley and Manley 1989). Figure 5.6 presents BSE textures of leached rock varnish, compared to adjacent varnish that has not been leached. The brighter (unbleached) material has a higher atomic number, and the darker-porous (leached)

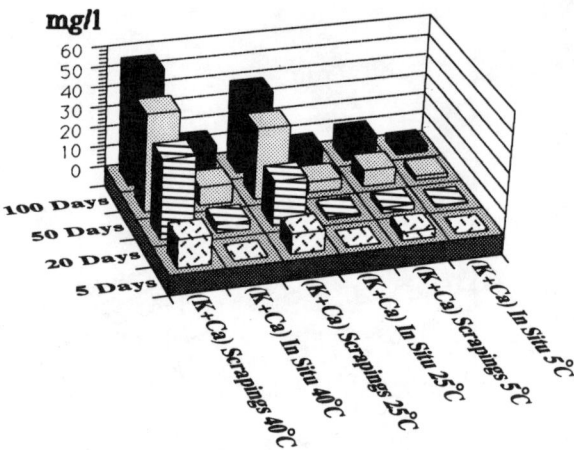

Figure 5.4. Laboratory leaching experiments comparing Death Valley rock varnishes still attached to the rock with varnishes that were scraped off the rock and cleaned of contamination. See Dorn and Krinsley (1991) for more methodological details.

material has a lower atomic number. BSE imaging is critical to the detection of zones of cation leaching; a more conventional form of electron imagery, from secondary electrons (Figure 5.6B), does not record the leaching zones that are evident in the corresponding BSE image (Figure 5.6A).

Table 5.4 presents the results of wavelength dispersive electron microprobe (probe) analyses of the different textures in Figure 5.6. Table 5.4 is keyed by numbers that identify the locations of the probe analyses in Figure 5.6. For most numbers there are two sets of analyses: on layered varnish (identified by dark lines); and on porous varnish (identified by white lines). Porous varnish has lower CRs than adjacent layered varnish; cation leaching is taking place from these porous zones, which are laterally and horizontally discontinuous.

The generalized explanation for the decline in the rate of CR change at progressively older sites is that it becomes increasingly difficult to remove fewer and fewer Ca and K cations, while all Ti remains (Dorn 1989). This has been found in the leaching experiments (see Figures 5.4 and 5.5). Sometimes K, Ca, and Mg are lowered. In other cases, however, Ti is increased rela-

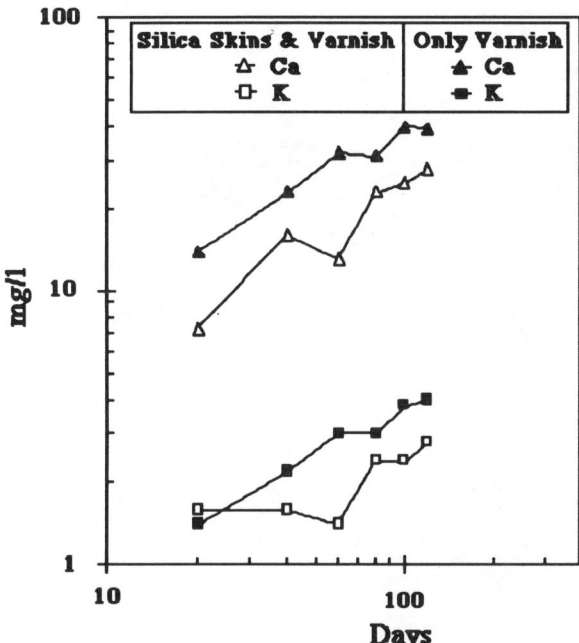

Figure 5.5. Laboratory leaching experiments on scrapings of Hawaiian rock varnishes. Two types of scrapings were leached: varnishes interdigitated with amorphous silica (see Curtiss et al. 1985) and just rock varnish. See Dorn and Krinsley (1991) for more method details.

tively in the porous zones. Morad and Aldahan (1986) reported that as detrital Fe-Ti oxides weather, Ti oxides replace the Fe-Ti phases. A soil analogy may be appropriate here. Titanium may be present as nonexchangeable clay-sized anatase (see Bain 1976). Harden (1988) found a net influx of Ti into finer fractions of soil with time; Akimoto et al. (1984) explained this by the low-temperature oxidation of titanomagnetites, resulting in the depletion of mobile cations such as Mn^{2+} and the relative enrichment of the highly stable Ti^{4+}.

Bulk CRs on cubic millimeters to cubic centimeters of varnish scraped from these sites is provided for comparison in Table 5.4. Bulk methods of CR analysis use enough volume to incorporate both leached and unleached textures (see Dorn 1983, 1989; Pineda et al. 1988; Zhang et al. 1990); the larger the sample, the greater the likelihood that the areas of cation leaching are being picked up. The bulk CRs in Table 5.4 indicate a mixture of leached and unleached regions, but these defocused microprobe measurements are nowhere near as representative as the bulk measurements.

The small pieces of detritus in the porous areas are most often Fe-rich and Ti-rich grains that are present in layered varnish but are more noticeable after leaching has occurred. In addition to these small pieces of detritus, there is a 'detritus-rich' texture of a chaotic mix of large pieces of rock detritus (>10 μm) and Mn-Fe-clay varnish (see Figure 5.6I, 5.6J). These detritus-rich textures are not formed in the same way as the leached zones. The pieces of detritus are larger, and the texture is probably the result of larger pieces of dust being trapped in larger depressions in the varnish. Although some leaching does appear to occur in these regions, the topic of a detrital texture is beyond the scope of this chapter.

An alternative explanation for the porous textures seen in Figure 5.6 is a constructional origin, but Dorn and Krinsley (1991, 1992) rejected this explanation for several reasons. (1) A constructional origin would imply that this texture would be forming actively on the surface of varnish in some environment, somewhere. Hundreds of varnish cross sections have been examined with BSE in samples ranging from tropical rainforest streams to hyperarid southern Peru (see Krinsley and Dorn 1991; Krinsley et al 1990; Krinsley and Manley 1989). Yet a leached, porous texture has been found only at the surface of one sample, and in this sample it appears that the layered varnish is disintegrating in discrete pockets into a porous texture (Dorn and Krinsley 1991). (2) There is a gradient of increased porosity away from the layered varnish. (3) Islands of layered varnish are found in the middle of porous zones. (4) Fossilized bacteria and other discrete clasts are often left largely unsupported in a geometry that could not be produced by a constructional mechanism. (5) Fractures that channel capillary water have coatings of Mn-Fe similar to those identified by Krinsley et al. (1990) as deposits of remobilized material (see Figure 5.6G). The deposition of at least some remobilized material would be expected if leaching occurred. (6) No depositional process has been proposed that could explain the characteristics of this texture (Dorn and Krinsley 1992; Watchman 1992).

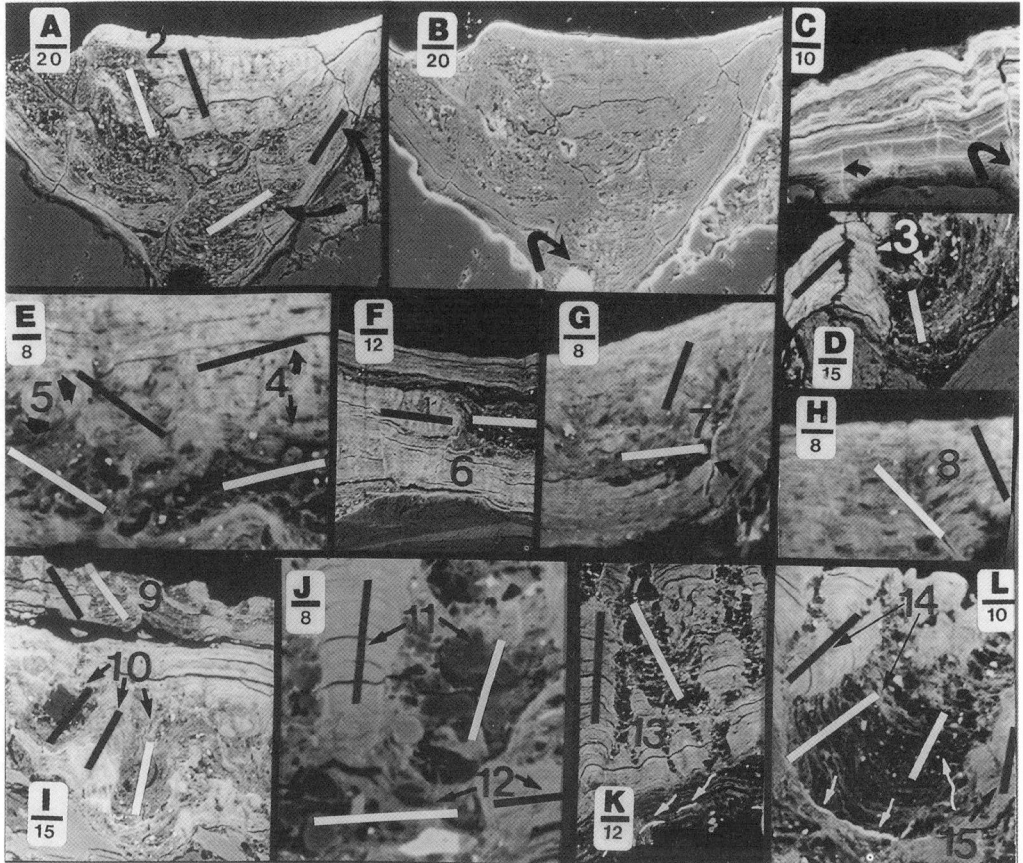

Figure 5.6. Electron microscope images of polished cross sections of rock varnish. All micrographs except B use backscattered electron microscopy, where material with higher net atomic numbers appears brighter (Krinsley and Manley 1989). Scale bars under letters in microns. Numbers identify pairs of transects, where electron microprobe analyses were made on layered textures (black lines), leached textures (white lines), and detritus-filled hollows (Figures 5.6I, J).

(A) Wharton Hill Petroglyph 5, South Australia, showing layered and leached textures. (B) Secondary electron (SE) image (showing topography instead of chemistry) of same frame as Figure 5.6A. The porous, leached texture is almost impossible to identify with SE. The black particle trapped at the base of the varnish in Figure 5.6A is white, charging in SE, and appears to be "cracking"; all typical characteristics of organic matter.

(C) Wharton Hill Petroglyph 5, illustrating layered texture appropriate for paleoenvironmental analysis, but no areas of leaching. Arrows identify cracks refilled with mobilized and reprecipitated Mn and Fe oxides. Analysis by 2-μm probe on spot identified by large arrow has 53 percent MnO and 31 percent Fe_2O_3; the small arrow has 44 percent MnO and 27 percent Fe_2O_3. (D) Yunta Springs Petroglyph 2, South Australia. (E) Karolta Petroglyph K23, South Australia (Dorn, Nobbs, et al. 1988). (F) Desert pavement on Pampa de Los Chinos, near Nazca, southern Peru. (G) Petroglyph WP17, Wyoming. (H) Petroglyph WP12, Wyoming. (I) Artifact, Mojave Desert. (J) Makanaka till, Hawai'i (Dorn et al. 1991). (K) Little Cone basalt flow, Crater Flat, southern Nevada. (L) Perry Aitken till, Chiatovich basin, White Mountains, Ca-Nev (Elliott-Fisk 1987).

Table 5.4. Electron Microprobe (Wavelength Dispersive) Analyses along Transects of Porous and Layered Varnishes Delineated in Figure 5.6, as Compared to Bulk Samples of Varnish from the Same Site (from Dorn and Krinsley 1991)[a]

Transect[b]	Layered Textures			Leached Textures			Bulk CR[d] (method)
	MnO(%)	Fe2O3(%)	CR	MnO(%)	Fe2O3	CR	
1	23.86 ± 8.22[a]	16.87 ± 3.71	5.12 ± 0.86	10.26 ± 3.31	13.69 ± 4.26	3.46 ± 0.55	4.33 (Probe)
2	28.76 ± 5.95	16.16 ± 2.20	5.28 ± 0.61	11.77 ± 2.97	14.20 ± 5.24	3.53 ± 0.47	4.33 (Probe)
3	25.43 ± 1.32	9.47 ± 0.73	6.74 ± 0.22	8.76 ± 1.73[c]	7.90 ± 1.56[c]	4.10 ± 0.54[c]	5.88 (Probe)
4[c]	12.81 ± 2.20	13.37 ± 0.49	7.14 ± 0.99	2.32 ± 1.20	9.93 ± 1.68	3.32 ± 0.44	4.85 (Probe)
5[c]	16.86 ± 4.20	13.87 ± 1.85	5.74 ± 1.52	10.25 ± 1.62	11.46 ± 2.39	2.93 ± 0.60	4.85 (Probe)
6	12.73 ± 0.73	22.00 ± 5.15	24.14 ± 9.06	2.75 ± 1.17	14.79 ± 10.37	10.11 ± 3.71	13.24 (Probe)
7[c]	29.17 ± 4.30	17.08 ± 0.94	10.18 ± 0.01	11.23 ± 3.27	15.37 ± 0.81	6.61 ± 1.68	8.80 (Probe)
8[c]	28.79 ± 1.86	17.52 ± 3.13	10.54 ± 0.41	10.80 ± 3.34	9.75 ± 3.54	7.97 ± 0.98	8.18 (Probe)
9[c]	10.16 ± 1.28	12.89 ± 0.29	6.71 ± 0.19	3.05 ± 1.33	11.95 ± 1.99	4.09 ± 1.55	3.81 (PIXE)
10	27.83 ± 6.19	16.02 ± 1.03	7.99 ± 0.84	10.84 ± 4.63	16.04 ± 3.00	4.12 ± 0.16	3.81 (PIXE)
11[c]	16.27 ± 2.53	13.63 ± 1.60	7.04 ± 0.55				6.51 (PIXE)
12[c]	9.87 ± 4.00	14.51 ± 1.18	6.89 ± 1.11				6.63 (Probe)
13	13.37 ± 3.77	13.37 ± 5.69	2.73 ± 0.18	10.27 ± 2.96	10.90 ± 1.19	1.85 ± 0.37	2.71 (ICP)
14	27.19 ± 2.08	13.44 ± 1.08	5.87 ± 1.28	4.28 ± 2.14[c]	10.34 ± 1.39[c]	4.83 ± 0.35[c]	5.05 (Probe)
15	21.20 ± 4.61	15.36 ± 3.01	5.22 ± 0.17	10.40 ± 2.27[c]	13.79 ± 0.82[c]	2.54 ± 0.22[c]	5.05 (Probe)

	Detritus-Rich Textures		
	MnO(%)	Fe2O3(%)	CR
10	5.12 ± 1.17[c]	11.43 ± 7.64[c]	4.90 ± 2.16[c]
11	1.20 ± 1.01	12.35 ± 11.20	6.45 ± 5.46
12	2.28 ± 0.98	16.32 ± 3.81	1.78 ± 0.78

[a] Note: Errors are ±1 sigma. Dorn and Krinsley (1991) data repository gives complete details of analysis methods.
[b] Numbers correspond to transects in Figure 5.6. Five analyses were made per transect with 10-micrometer spot size, except where not possible due to limited area.
[c] Only three analyses possible, due to minimal length of transect. Overlap was not desired, due to loss of K and Na.
[d] Bulk CRs are analyses of varnishes from the same sites as the microprobe transects, only on cubic millimeters of varnish.

Methods of Determining Cation Ratios

Figure 5.7 presents the general approach that I use in cation-ratio (CR) dating, which starts with sample collection. Table 5.5 presents a list of variables that can influence a CR other than time; these influences can be avoided with proper sampling.

Once samples are collected in the field, cross sections are examined to avoid factors that would interfere with a varnish date (see Krinsley et al. 1990; Nobbs and Dorn 1993). This is a critical filtering step. Unlayered varnishes and other textures are known to produce erroneous ages; these samples can be rejected for further analysis by simple textural tests. Ideally the author

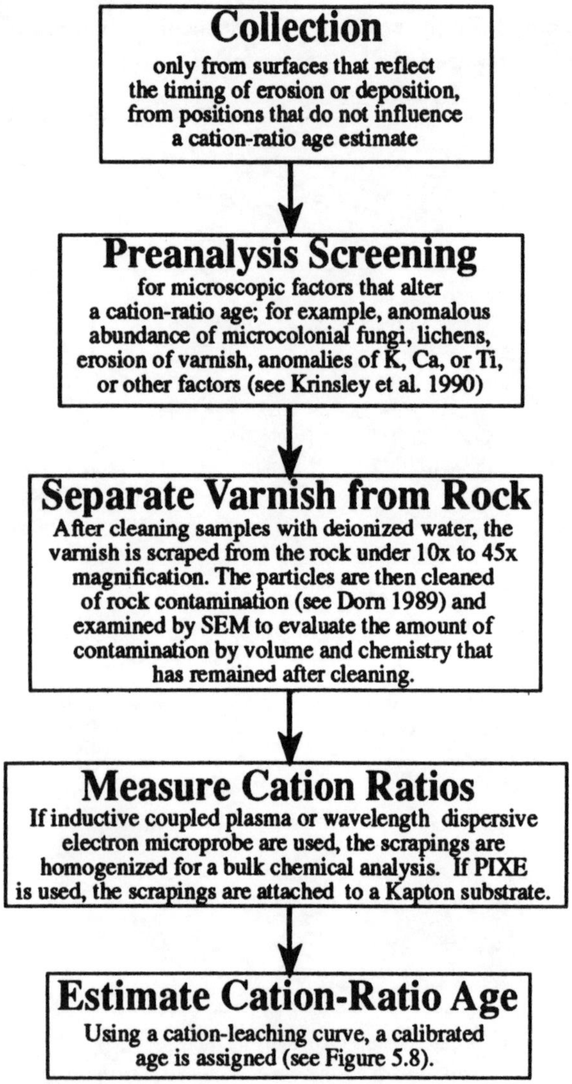

Collection
only from surfaces that reflect the timing of erosion or deposition, from positions that do not influence a cation-ratio age estimate

Preanalysis Screening
for microscopic factors that alter a cation-ratio age; for example, anomalous abundance of microcolonial fungi, lichens, erosion of varnish, anomalies of K, Ca, or Ti, or other factors (see Krinsley et al. 1990)

Separate Varnish from Rock
After cleaning samples with deionized water, the varnish is scraped from the rock under 10x to 45x magnification. The particles are then cleaned of rock contamination (see Dorn 1989) and examined by SEM to evaluate the amount of contamination by volume and chemistry that has remained after cleaning.

Measure Cation Ratios
If inductive coupled plasma or wavelength dispersive electron microprobe are used, the scrapings are homogenized for a bulk chemical analysis. If PIXE is used, the scrapings are attached to a Kapton substrate.

Estimate Cation-Ratio Age
Using a cation-leaching curve, a calibrated age is assigned (see Figure 5.8).

Figure 5.7. Generalized steps in the collection, laboratory evaluation, and analysis of samples for cation-ratio dating.

would present a table of how different groups who conduct cation-ratio dating preselect the particular area of varnish for chemical analysis, but other varnish researchers (see Harrington et al. 1991; Harry et al. 1992) do not provide information on how they preselect samples for chemical analysis.

Once samples are preselected, there are two major issues on how the chemistry of rock varnish is measured. The first concern is whether to mechanically remove the varnish from the rock or to analyze it *in situ,* still attached to the rock. The other decision is whether to use an analytical method that analyzes a small volume of sample or a larger volume of sample.

The approach favored here is the mechanical removal of a large volume (mm^3 to cm^3) of varnish from the underlying rock (Dorn 1989; Dorn, Cahill, et al., 1990; Zhang et al. 1990). The philosophy behind analyzing large samples is to average enough varnish to obtain a representative CR. The analysis of bulk samples can be done by a variety of techniques. The author has used PIXE, wavelength dispersive electron microprobe (probe), and inductively coupled plasma (ICP) methods. These techniques are elaborated in Dorn, Cahill, et al. (1990).

The mechanical removal of the varnish from the underlying rock and its analysis by a bulk-chemical method has several advantages. Scraping does not destroy archaeological material. Scrapings can be cleaned of most rock contamination; what rock material is left can be determined quantitatively and independently by an analysis of varnish scrapings (Dorn 1989). The same scrapings can be analyzed by different chemical methods. Greater volumes of varnish can be analyzed less expensively and more rapidly. Lastly, variability in varnish thicknesses and the irregular rock/varnish boundary make it extremely difficult and time consuming to rule out the generation of X-rays from the underlying rock, especially on a routine basis (Dorn 1989: 575; Reneau and Raymond 1991).

In situ analysis by a scanning electron microscope, in contrast, involves the analysis of only cubic micrometers of varnish still attached to the underlying rock. This is a tiny fraction of the amount of material analyzed by bulk methods (Dorn 1983:58; Glazovskiy 1985; Harrington and Whitney 1987). Since the SEM technique analyzes only the very surface layer (<5 microns) of the varnish (Dorn 1989: 575; Reneau et al. 1991) the CR is derived from a measurement of X-rays generated in the upper few cubic microns by the SEM beam.

The last step is to use a cation-leaching curve (see

Table 5.5. Factors Known to Influence a Cation Ratio of Black (Mn-rich) Rock Varnish Other Than Time

Variable	Effect and Probable Cause
Lichens	Lower cation ratio from acidification
Microcolonial fungi	Lower cation ratio when they actively erode into varnish. Do not alter cation ratios when adventitious
Water runoff	Lower cation ratio, unless source of water runoff is locale where alkaline dust collects
Basin of water collection	Lower cation ratio due to enhanced leaching effect of longer water contact
Organic matter in contact with varnish	Lower CRs due to secretion of organic acids
Aspect	Northeast-facing aspects in North American deserts tend to have slightly lower cation ratios than varnish on boulder tops or south-southwest aspects; this is probably due to the cumulative effect of more mesic conditions
Filamentous fungi	Lower CRs when surface area greater than ca. 5%, due to secretion of organic acids
Varnish has low pH values	When varnishes have acidic pH values (<6), cation ratios tend to be lower than near neutral varnishes
Ground-line band varnish	Sites where dust collections in a depression have a cumulic aeolian (loess) soil; a ground-line band is created at the soil-varnish-atmosphere interface that has slightly lower cation ratios than adjacent varnishes
Titanium anomaly	Local environments can contain abundant titanium detritus, which once incorporated into varnish decreases the cation ratio
Cryptogamic soil	Varnishes collected near a soil surface of cryptogamic algae, fungi, lichens, and mosses have lower cation ratios
Varnish that interlayers with oxalate skins	Although quite rare, when rock varnish interlayers with films of oxalate, cation ratios decrease
Crack varnish	Varnish that starts out in rock crevices and is exposed by spalling of the overlying rock tends to have much higher CRS than adjacent subaerial varnishes
Soil proximity	Varnishes collected within a few centimeters of a soil surface have higher cation ratios due to capillary flow of salts
Calcium anomaly	Local environments can contain abundant calcium carbonate detritus; once incorporated it increases the cation ratio
Potassium anomaly	Local environments can contain abundant potassium-rich detritus; once incorporated it increases the cation ratio
Varnish has high pH values	When varnishes have alkaline pH values (>9), cation ratios increase
Overhang	Where varnishes are collected from the underside of overhangs, cation ratios increase, probably due to less leaching
Abundant botryoids	Varnishes with uncommonly great abundance of botryoids have slightly lower cation ratios, due to greater leaching between stromatolitic-like structures

Table 5.5. Continued.

Variable	Effect and Probable Cause
Irregular topography of underlying rock	Varnishes collected from lava flows that have a very rough and irregular surface have higher cation ratios
Varnish that interlayers with amorphous silica	The interdigitation of amorphous silica skins greatly decreases the rate of leaching and increases the cation ratio
Rock weathering	When a rock surface weathers by spalling, flaking, granular disintegration, or block breakage, the newly exposed rock surface has higher cation ratios than unweathered surfaces of the same landform
Time transgressive growth	If sampled from locations where varnish does not grow initially (see text for further discussion), CRs are higher for the varnish that spreads out from the initial colonization point

Figure 5.3) to assign CR ages (Dorn 1989; Dorn, Cahill et al., 1990). CRs are typically calibrated by K-Ar dates or radiocarbon, depending on the time scale. Each CR is treated as an independent indicator of age (Figure 5.8). If the material being dated has definitely not experienced erosion, for example a petroglyph or the flake scar of an artifact, these separate CR ages for a given surface are averaged to assign a mean age for the surface; the uncertainty is derived from the standard deviation of these ages. If the substrate being dated may have experienced erosion, for example in the case of an alluvial-fan boulder, the oldest CR age is considered to be a minimum age for surface exposure.

An alternative approach to calculating CR ages, suggested by Bierman et al. (1991), uses the mean and variation of multiple CR measurements. This implies that the different samples that are being grouped together have the same exposure history. For example, if a petroglyph were to be dated with this approach, different collections of varnish from different parts of a petroglyph would be treated as a mean with a variation. However, varnish growth is time-transgressive, starting first in one place and growing vertically and horizontally. By treating each CR as a separate time indicator, intersample variability can easily be treated as indicating time-transgressive growth. Treating each CR as a separate time signal requires fewer assumptions: only that the calibration curve is the best estimate of CR age and that CR ages are normally distributed. In essence this approach keeps the assignment of calibrated ages as close to the raw data as possible.

Controversies in Cation-Ratio Dating

Table 5.6 presents a summary of issues under contention in the CR dating literature. Most of these differences result from different investigators analyzing different types of varnishes. The discussion over the cause of CR change with time shows this nicely.

All parties agree that CRs lower over time. At issue is why the cation-ratio dating method works. One hypothesis is cation leaching (Dorn 1983; Dorn and Krinsley 1991, 1992), also supported by O'Hara et. al (1990) and Krinsley et al. (1990), who found ubiquitous textural and geochemical evidence of cation mobility. The alternative hypothesis is contamination from the underlying rock (Reneau and Raymond 1991). After collecting "darkest, best developed varnishes" Reneau and Raymond (1991:937) found a "lack of evidence for leaching."

These discrepancies are due to different researchers examining different types of varnishes. "Dark," "smooth varnishes," and "best developed" are the sole published sampling criteria of the Los Alamos varnish group (Raymond et al. 1991; Reneau et al. 1991; Re-

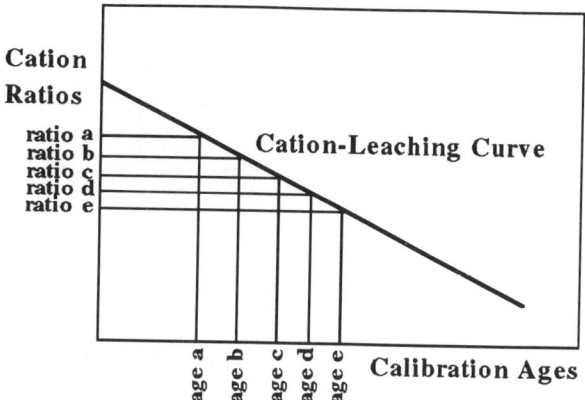

Figure 5.8. Preferred method of assigning calibrated ages to rock varnish cation ratios. First, the semilog least-squares regression (cation-leaching curve) is constructed from CR's on surfaces of known age. Second, individual CR's are obtained for different pockets of varnish on the surface of unknown age (ratios a, b, c, d, e). Third, each individual CR is assigned a calibrated age, based on the cation-leaching curve. Fourth, the average of the individual ages comprises a mean age for the surface, and the standard deviation of these ages forms the uncertainty estimate.

neau and Raymond 1991). Recently exposed crack varnishes are usually the "darkest," due to high Mn concentrations in the outermost layers, and the "smoothest" due to formation on a planar fracture surface. Ground-line bands are typically the darkest, best developed, and smoothest varnishes, because growth occurs in such a favorable microenvironment (see Dorn and Oberlander 1982:359–360). The texture and chemical profiles in Raymond et al. (1991) are remarkably similar to those of varnishes collected from former crevices.

While subaerial positions are exposed to alternating conditions of dust deposition, water flow, and acid-producing organisms, crack varnishes formed in rock crevices and exposed by later spalling provide an environment of wetting and drying buffered by long-term contact with collected alkaline dust. The crack varnish environment promotes superior varnish cementation, while avoiding exposure to the acidity of rainfall and rock-surface organisms in the subaerial environment. The tight layering found in crack varnish does not open itself to leaching the way subaerial varnishes do.

The barium controversy reported in Table 5.6 may also be explained by comparing different varnishes. Some varnishes have high levels of barium, while others have virtually none. Crack varnishes contain a Ba-Mn oxide romanechite (Potter and Rossman 1979:1221). Varnishes that originally developed in rock crevices have relatively high barium levels, strong Mn-Ba correlations, and a surface layer enriched in Mn (see Figures 5.1B, 5.2; Table 5.3; see also Harrington et al. 1991). In contrast the manganese mineral found in subaerial varnishes is birnessite (Potter and Rossman 1979), which does not contain barium. This is consistent with observations of low barium concentrations in varnishes formed only at the air/rock interface (see Figure 5.1A).

In summary apparently contradictory findings move toward a convergence of views when the types of varnish analyzed are factored in. To avoid future confusion, varnish researchers should specify as explicitly as possible: (1) the type of environment where the sample was collected (see Dorn 1989: 568–569; Dorn and Oberlander 1992: 359–360; Dragovich 1984, 1987, 1988; Jones 1991; Potter and Rossman 1979; Whalley et al. 1990; White 1990; Zhang et al. 1990); (2) cross-sectional textures and surface micromorphologies of varnishes selected for chemical analysis (see Krinsley et al. 1990); and (3) the volume of material analyzed.

There is one controversy, however, that cannot be resolved easily. It regards the accuracy of CR measurements made by PIXE (proton-induced X-ray emission) by the Air Quality Group at Crocker Nuclear Lab (CNL) at the University of California at Davis. Bierman and Gillespie (1991a) claimed that PIXE analyses by this group were invalid. They sent "artificial varnish" of known composition for PIXE analysis. Cahill (1992) informed Bierman and Gillespie in writing that the analyses would only be qualitative, because a dedicated run on geological material was not feasible for only a few samples. The samples were analyzed and qualitative data were sent. Bierman and Gillespie (1991a) then published these measurements as absolute values, used

Table 5.6. Issues of Contention in Cation-Ratio Dating

Issue	Los Alamos Weapons Lab & University of Washington	Arizona State University	Resolutions
Theory to explain reductions in cation ratios over time	Cation ratios are reduced over time, but it is not due to cation leaching. Samples analyzed show no evidence of elemental mobility. The reduction must, therefore, be due to changes in the primary composition of the surface layers in varnish for the SEM method (Reneau and Raymond 1991). The reduction as measured by scraped samples is probably due to less contamination from the underlying rock over time as varnish thickens.	Cation ratios are reduced over time in subaerial varnishes due to cation leaching, as documented in this paper. However, the places of cation leaching occur below the very surface of the varnish. Since the SEM method only analyzes the top of the varnish, cation leaching cannot explain why the SEM method works. The SEM method may work because of the different length of time since the crack varnishes analyzed by Los Alamos have been exposed.	(1) Have an independent laboratory replicate the leaching experiments reported in this chapter. (2) Have proponents of the SEM method develop a theory to explain why the chemistry in the very surface layer of the varnish would change over time.
Contamination from the underlying rock exists in the analysis of varnish samples	The SEM method only analyzes the upper few microns of varnish (Dorn 1989: 575; Reneau et al. 1991), so contamination is unlikely in well-developed, thick varnishes. Scraping the varnish produces fragments from the underlying rock that cannot be 'picked out.'	No method has been proposed to independently evaluate the amount of contamination in the X-rays generated by the SEM. The presence of a topographic high in the underlying rock under the area of analysis cannot be tested. In contrast, the amount of rock contamination in scrapings is evaluated by an independent means (Dorn 1989).	Run an experiment on shared samples.
Destruction of archaeological samples	No discussion of this issue	The SEM method must take fragments of archaeological samples, requiring mechanical breaking or coring. Scraping varnish for bulk chemical analysis can be done in the field and does little to influence the appearance of the cultural artifact.	There is no argument at present that the preservation of archaeological samples is more important than using experimental methods that are destructive.
Chemical analyses by different analytical methods	No discussion of this issue	The SEM method cannot be replicated by other analytical methods (Dorn 1989).	Varnish scrapings can be analyzed by a number of different methods (Dorn, Cahill, et al. 1990).
Volume of material analyzed	Enough volume can be analyzed by the SEM method to be representative of the chemistry of varnish on a given surface.	Micron-scale chemical variability is too extreme to use an SEM to obtain representative chemistries, especially since the depth of penetration is only a few microns. The philosophy behind the approach of removing material is to analyze as much volume as possible, to obtain the most representative chemistry.	A clear determination of how much volume of material is necessary to dampen the variability seen in micron-scale analyses.

Topic			
Young samples	The SEM method can analyze pockets of varnish that are just starting to form, whereas removing this material is too difficult.	SEM results on a few spots of varnish are not as representative as collecting varnish from hundreds of pockets. Working with young varnishes is easier, because the places where varnish starts to grow first are easily identified. Furthermore blind tests on late-Holocene samples indicate this approach yields valid results (Loendorf 1991).	Share samples from the same young surface. Young varnishes will have best potential for comparing results from the different methods, because they are relatively thin.
Statistical determination of CR ages	The statistics of assigning an error term to cation ratios should be based on expected variation of a mean CR (Bierman et al. 1991).	CR ages should not be assigned based on an average and error term of the CRs. Each CR should be assigned a separate single age, using the least-squares regression. Age uncertainty should be based on variability in the individual age assignments, because each location of varnish has a separate history.	They are based on different assumptions. Using an expected variation of a mean assumes that all the subsample CRs belong to the same population. Using individual CRs assumes only that each CR represents the age signal of that varnish.
Surface stability	Fire spalling can restart the varnish clock (Bierman and Gillespie 1991b); desert pavements are too unstable to warrant the use of cation-ratio dating of artifacts (Harry et al. 1992).	It is relatively simple to avoid fire spalling by careful field selection. Artifacts are dated from stable pavements. Sources of surface degradation other than fire spalling need to be considered in sampling (Dorn 1989).	Avoid surface textures produced from weathering. Avoid unstable geomorphic contexts.
Blind tests of results	No blind intercomparisons are reported for the SEM method of CR dating.	Several blind tests of varnish radiocarbon and varnish CR dating by bulk methods are presented in the text.	Have proponents of the SEM method agree to participate in a series of blind tests.
Barium in rock varnish can interfere with the measurement of titanium by energy dispersive X-ray detectors (Dorn 1989: 575)	Harrington et al. (1991) acknowledged that prior SEM-EDS measurements of Ti were influenced by Ba, but they claim that a new SEM method deconvolutes the X-ray signal in polished cross-sections. They also claim that Dorn's PIXE measurements were also affected by Ba, based on indirect reasoning. This claim was supported by Bierman and Gillespie (1991a), who report PIXE data from PIXE and SEM-EDS data on standards.	(1) Bierman and Gillespie misrepresented PIXE data given to them by U.C. Davis (Cahill 1992). (2) Reanalysis of varnish samples previously measured by PIXE with ICP and the microprobe show similar results (Dorn, Cahill, et al. 1990). (3) Ba concentrations in varnishes used for CR dating are low (see Figure 5.1). (4) Bierman and Gillespie (1992) contradict themselves by first claiming that the PIXE method does not measure barium, then citing barium data from PIXE to show that barium is present in rock varnish. (5) Blind tests of PIXE-based CRs match control ages.	(1) An offer by Dorn (1992a) to share samples previously analyzed by PIXE was rejected by Bierman and Gillespie (pers. comm., Oct. 1990). (2) Sharing of samples previously analyzed by the SEM method would permit claims of accurate deconvolutions to be tested by an independent party. (3) All parties avoid energy dispersive detectors. For example, all new CRs are determined by methods not susceptible to a Ba-Ti overlap: ICP and wavelength dispersive electron microprobe techniques.

to claim that PIXE data from the Air Quality Group were inaccurate. In response Cahill (1992:469) wrote:

> The data in Bierman and Gillespie (1991a) Table 1, described as "PIXE UCD" did not in fact come from us. They appear to have been prepared by Bierman and Gillespie from "reduced" and "raw" X-ray spectra that was clearly labelled "*The Raw Values In These Tables Are Incorrect*" (written communication to Bierman, June 18, 1990). I deeply regret that they were used to generate Table 1, since we notified Bierman and Gillespie in the memo that "there is no way to obtain absolute *or* relative values" without particle size or proper standards, and "Ba is not in the tables we used for this run. These data were provided to Bierman and Gillespie for "evaluatory" purposes," with an explicit written prohibition against their publication . . .

Bierman and Gillespie (1992) responded that oral permission was given to publish these data. One side is misrepresenting information. Cahill's case makes sense for two reasons. First, when I started submitting samples for analysis, I was also told the data would be qualitative, not publishable, and only useful to assess whether a dedicated run would be warranted. Second, I have seen the extensive written documentation available at the Air Quality Group, and it is quite clear that Bierman and Gillespie were told in great detail why the PIXE data were qualitative, just as Cahill (1992) indicates.

Varnish Radiocarbon Dating

In an initial evaluation of the potential for radiocarbon dating varnish, Dorn, Jull, et al. (1989) extracted organic matter (OM) from the lowest layer of rock varnishes collected from sites of known age. Although this research demonstrated the feasibility of radiocarbon dating varnish, there was no clear understanding of where the dated OM was actually located in rock varnish. They assumed that the OM was dispersed throughout the varnish, perhaps in oxides of manganese and iron. Subsequently this assumption has been shown to be false. Transmission electron microscope studies have shown that varnish oxides do not contain OM

Figure 5.9. Scanning electron microscope images of subvarnish organic matter seen in rock-varnish cross-sections. Scale bars in microns. Underneath is the organic matter–rock boundary. In A, B, D, E, and H, the upper line separates the varnish from the subvarnish organic matter. In I and J, the line separates varnish and rock. Organic matter (OM) was distinguished by morphology, low counts with energy-dispersive analysis of X-rays (WDS), very low characteristic varnish peaks (such as Mn, Fe, Si, Al) in spot analyses by EDAX, and the similarity of these spectra to OM resting on the surface of rock varnishes. Sample numbers correspond with the radiocarbon ages in Dorn, Clarkson et al. (1992) and Nobbs and Dorn (1993).

(A) OM under varnish on cobble from geoglyph in Nazca, Peru (see Figure 5.11B). (B) OM under varnish from South Australian petroglyph K24 (Dorn, Nobbs, et al. 1988). (C) Mat of subvarnish organic matter removed from South Australian petroglyph WH5 (see Figure 5.11A). (D) OM under rock varnish (upper right) and on top of rock (lower left), from cobble in Colorado River geoglyph CRG-2 (see Figure 5.11C). (E) From Mojave Desert artifact 85-8, where the OM and varnish formed in a vesiclelike feature (Figure 5.11D). The letter *i* indicates organic matter (perhaps pollen grains) imbedded in varnish, whereas the letter *d* identifies a grain that may have become detached during sample preparation and may not be *in situ*. (F) Subvarnish OM attached to fragment of rock scraped from South Australian petroglyph K23 (Dorn, Nobbs, et al. 1988). Arrow indicates organic filament attached to organic mat. (G) Subvarnish OM scraped from South Australian petroglyph K26. Arrow points to fragment of underlying rock still attached to OM. (H) Backscatter electron (BSE) micrograph of polished cross section of varnish, from South Australian petroglyph WH1. In BSE brighter material has a higher atomic number (Krinsley et al. 1990) and the subvarnish OM (arrow) is black. (I) BSE of polished cross section of South Australian petroglyph K15, illustrating abundant silica skin (electron microprobe measurements indicate content of ca. 91 percent SiO_2), interlayering with brighter rock varnish. (J) BSE of polished cross section of South Australian petroglyph WH5 (see Figure 5.10A), illustrating a rare example of OM that is not subvarnish (indicated by arrow), but has been incorporated as varnish has accreted in layers.

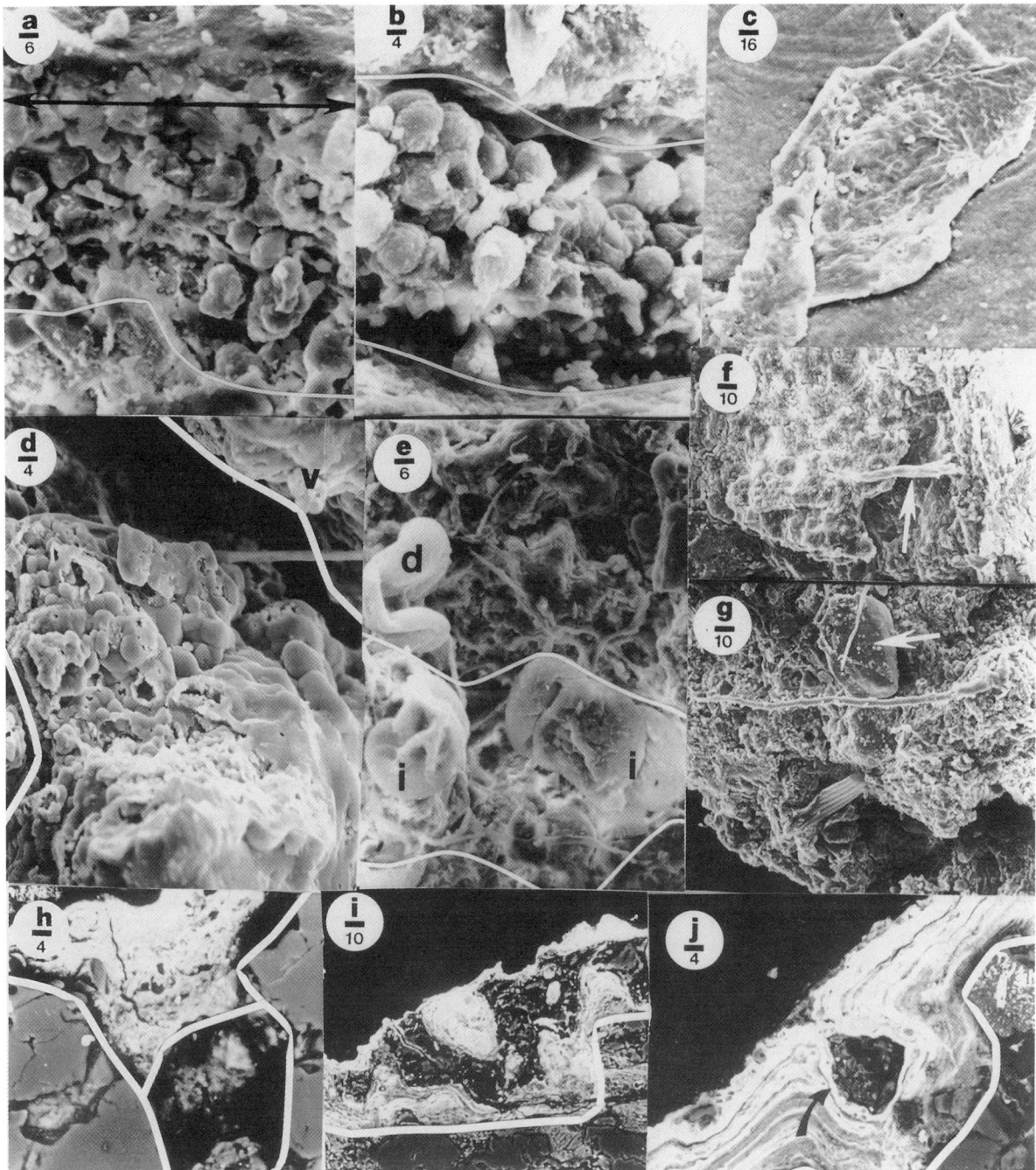

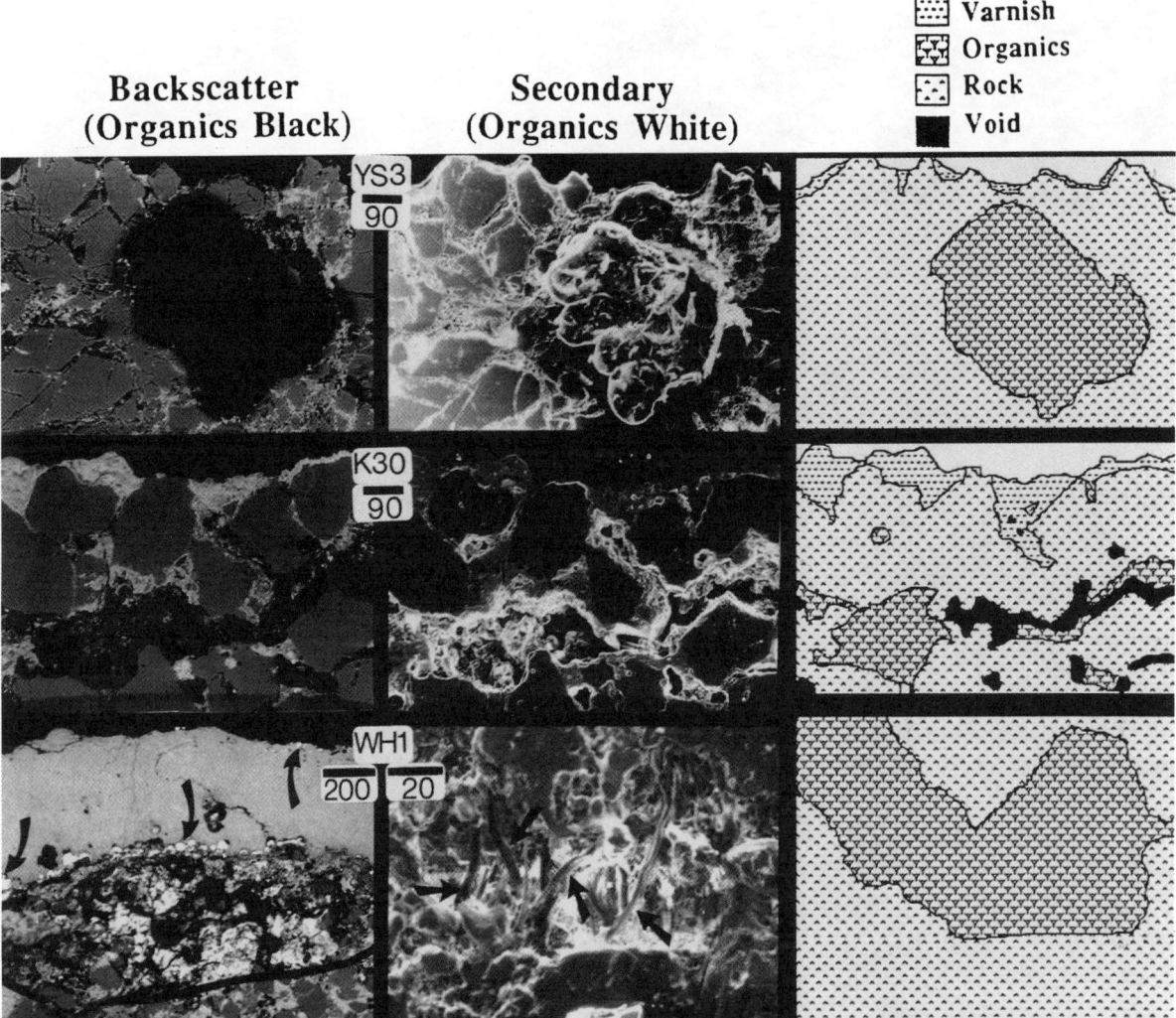

Figure 5.10. Organic matter in weathering rinds that are encapsulated by rock varnish formed over rock engravings from South Australia (Nobbs and Dorn 1993). The three examples from top row to bottom row are petroglyphs: YS3, K30, and WH1. The left column is entirely by backscatter imagery. The middle column is the corresponding secondary image (except bottom row). The right column is a "map" of the middle secondary image. YS3 shows a pocket of unidentified organic matter under a thin varnish cover. Organic matter from the weathering rind yielded an AMS ^{14}C age of ca. 1500 B.P. (Nobbs and Dorn 1993). K30 shows scattered pockets of weathering-rind organics under motif K30 that yielded an AMS ^{14}C age of ca. 20,000 B.P. (Nobbs and Dorn 1993). Many of these scattered pockets have bits of calcium mixed with the organics, perhaps calcium oxalate, which is often found associated with lichens. WH1 shows a relatively thick layer of amorphous silica coating the petroglyph. Arrows in the BSE image identify bright pockets of rock varnish that interdigitate with the silica. The SE image of WH1 is a close-up of the weathering rind under the amorphous silica. The corresponding map was drawn from the BSE image, where the indicated organic mat is black in BSE, yet clearly present in SE, with filaments (arrows) running throughout the mat. The ^{14}C age for the encapsulated organics was ca. 14,900 B.P. (Nobbs and Dorn 1993).

(Krinsley et al. 1990), and preliminary amino acid studies suggest that OM is not well preserved in the middle rock varnish (Nagy et al. 1991).

The fundamental methodological advance of Dorn, Clarkson, et al. (1992) was a determination of where OM occurs in rock varnish. Detrital fragments of organic material are almost always found either at the very surface of the varnish or trapped under the varnish at the rock interface (Figure 5.9A–H). Also quite common are organics trapped in voids in the weathering rind that are subsequently entombed by the overlying varnish (Figure 5.10). Intravarnish inclusions of OM are usually trapped in unlayered varnish; in only a few cases has intravarnish OM been trapped in layered varnish (see Figure 5.9J).

Radiocarbon ages extracted from subvarnish organic matter are interpreted according to the following sequence of events. (1) A cultural or natural process exposes a new surface to the atmosphere; this is the event that is of interest for dating. (2) Organisms such as lichen, cyanobacteria, or fungi grow in surface hollows and voids in the weathering rind. (3) Rock varnish growth encapsulates these organics (see Figures 5.9 and 5.10). (4) Accelerator radiocarbon dating this subvarnish OM, therefore, provides a minimum age for the exposure of the underlying surface.

The first stage in isolating subvarnish OM starts with field sampling. The objective is to collect varnish that starts to colonize a surface exposed by human or geomorphic processes. The procedure used is basically the same as for CR dating.

The second stage of sample preparation is collecting organic microinclusions entombed by the varnish. The top layer of the varnish is abraded away with a tungsten-carbide needle. This is to remove organics on the surface of the varnish. Then the needle is used like a microbulldozer to turn over the varnish. Sifting through this material under 45x magnification with microsurgical tools, students and I find fragments of OM still attached to the underlying rock (see Figure 5.9F, G). Contamination of OM from the middle of the varnish is certainly possible but unlikely, because OM is rarely found in the middle of varnish and because OM is still attached to the underlying rock. If contamination of younger OM does occur, the age is still interpreted as a minimum.

Third, after the microinclusions are isolated, the collection of organic fragments attached to rock is then treated with 20 percent HCl to remove carbonate and concentrated HF to remove loose organics absorbed to clays. If samples in the terrestrial-weathering environment that contain clays are not treated with HF, organic molecules loosely adsorbed onto the clay minerals can contaminate a sample and produce too young an age (Dorn, Jull, et al. 1989; Gillespie 1991).

Lastly, the sample is submitted for AMS^{14}C measurement (see Linick et al. 1989).

Blind Tests of Varnish Dating

There are several blind tests available for varnish dating, where the independent age control was not available until after the varnish results were reported.

The author was asked by L. Loendorf to provide CR ages on rock varnish formed on petroglyphs in southeastern Colorado. Some of the sites already had preexisting radiocarbon age control, but this information was not revealed by Leondorf. It was learned after the fact that Loendorf was skeptical of the CR method. In all blind tests, the CR ages were consistent with the independent controls. In one example Loendorf (1991:253) writes:

> A meandering line petroglyph on the wall of a small rockshelter has two CR dates, 1750 ± 300 and 1900 ± 250 BP. Covering this petroglyph were cultural deposits containing chipped stone tools and flakes, ground stone fragments, burned and unburned bone, freshwater shell, and charcoal. A ^{14}C determination on charcoal for the deposit of 1220 ± 130 BP, consistent with the cultural debris, is in a correct relative order to the CR date.

In other cases, the test was double blind, where neither Loendorf nor I knew of the independent age control until after the CR age was given. Loendorf (1991:253) writes:

Of further interest is a radiocarbon date for a circular pit, about 2 m in diameter and 1 m deep, adjacent to the rectangular petroglyphs on site 5LA5598. Test excavations did not reveal its function, but a carbon sample from the lowest levels was determined at 2290 ± 140 BP (Beta 26793); the calibrated age of this sample, 2340 ± 140 BP (Stuiver & Becker 1986:907), is within the statistical overlap of the cation-ratios, which were measured before the radiocarbon age of the charcoal was determined . . . Another important site, on the Purgatoire River canyon rim, is the Zookeeper site, 5LA5993, where a single human figure is surrounded by 36 animal figures. Four CR dates in the main panel range from 900 ± 150 to 1000 ± 250 BP, and one CR date for a second panel is 1200 ± 150 BP. The Zookeeper site is within 100 m of the Point site, 5LA6028, situated on a protruding canyon rim remnant that is isolated from the remainder of the canyon wall. At least seven house rooms were constructed on the site by stacking slabs of sandstone in vertical and horizontal tiers. A test excavation into one of the rooms produced chipped stone debitage and charcoal, uncalibrated radiocarbon determination of 1030 ± 90 BP (Beta 37703). The series of CR dates overlap with the ^{14}C date, and the dates are again consistent with the chronology suggested by seriation. Prior to obtaining the ^{14}C date for the Point site, no two archaeologists offered the same guess as to its age; estimates ranged from 600 to 1750 BP. All the CR dates were reported before any of the ^{14}C dates reported above were known. . .

The first study comparing different surface exposure dating methods was on the glacial polish and moraines of Mauna Kea, Hawaii (Dorn, Phillips, et al. 1991). Five different methods were compared: varnish CR dating; varnish radiocarbon dating; radiocarbon dating of organic matter in amorphous silica; ^{36}Cl dating (see Zreda and Phillips, chapter 8 of this volume), and *in situ* ^{14}C dating. The first analyses were conducted by PIXE on varnish CRs. Then varnish and silica radiocarbon measurements were made; next ^{36}Cl and lastly *in situ* ^{14}C ages. With the exception of two *in situ* ^{14}C measurements, different methods yielded similar ages.

CR ages and varnish radiocarbon ages for glacial moraines in the western Great Basin of North America have also been validated by subsequent results. According to varnish ^{14}C dating, the last glacial maximum occurred about 19,000–20,000 B.P. and left recessional moraines about 13,000–14,000 B.P. at Pine Creek in the eastern Sierra Nevada (Dorn, Cahill, et al. 1990; Dorn, Turrin, et al. 1987). These varnish ages closely match new ^{10}Be and ^{26}Al exposure ages for material taken from the same boulders (Nishiizumi et al. 1993). Then after these ^{26}Al and ^{10}Be ages were known, a conventional ^{14}C age of ca. 19,500 B.P. on charcoal collected from Tioga till matrix was determined (Bach et al. 1991). This conventional radiocarbon date corresponds with both the varnish and the ^{10}Be–^{26}Al ages.

A similar validation occurred for the glacial chronology at Bishop Creek, where varnish CR and ^{14}C ages were obtained before ^{36}Cl measurements; the different methods correspond well (Phillips et al. n.d.). Across the Owens Valley, in the White Mountains of California-Nevada, varnish radiocarbon ages were determined for glacial till in the Chiatovich and Middle Creek basins (Dorn, Jull, et al. 1990; Elliott-Fisk 1987). ^{36}Cl measurements subsequently obtained from these sites correspond well with the previously published varnish ages (Zreda et al. 1991).

Other tests include Crater Flat in southern Nevada, where varnish CR ages and varnish radiocarbon ages are consistent with uranium-series ages on pedogenic carbonate (Bell et al. 1991). Similarly, varnish CR ages on Johnson Canyon fan in Death Valley (Dorn 1988) correspond with uranium-series ages for the same alluvial surface (Hooke and Dorn 1992). Varnish radiocarbon and CR age for deposits in the Cima volcanic field (Dorn, Bamforth, et al. 1986) are similar to soil, thermoluminescence, and ^{3}Ne dating (Wells et al. 1990; Wells et al. 1991). Previously published CR ages on petroglyphs at the Karolta site (Dorn, Nobbs, et al. 1988) were verified by new varnish radiocarbon ages on the same petroglyphs (Nobbs and Dorn 1993).

An independent assessment of the precision of CR dating was provided by flakes and cores sampled from surfaces in the central Mojave Desert. The CR ages determined from PIXE measurements of the varnish scrapings were provided to D. Bamforth, project archaeologist. The design of the study was to analyze material that could be refitted back together, like pieces of a puzzle. The assumption of the test of precision is that the pieces in a sequence were flaked at the same time. The CR ages assigned to the different refitted flakes and cores within a given sequence had standard deviations of about 10 percent (Bamforth and Dorn 1988; Dorn, Bamforth, et al. 1986). This means that there is reasonable confidence that the CR age assigned to an individual artifact will have the same age as a different artifact made at the same time.

Selected Applications of Varnish Dating

Archaeological Examples

Rock engravings are an ideal system to work with; this section will emphasize the dating of petroglyphs. The artists have chosen to use a natural blackboard of a well-varnished natural surface. This provides a pool of bacteria to quickly colonize the newly exposed engraving. Petroglyphs are readily distinguished from natural rock weathering. They are also characterized by small hollows that collect organic fragments, which are in turn encapsulated by rock varnish.

One of the most exciting applications of varnish has been dating rock engravings in the arid Olary Province of South Australia (Nobbs and Dorn 1993). Three different age-dependent signals were used: radiocarbon, cation-ratio, and a paleoenvironmental method involving fluctuations in alkalinity (Dorn 1992b). Over two dozen radiocarbon ages were obtained, including replicate radiocarbon measurements on subvarnish organic matter for several petroglyphs. Two of the petroglyphs were quite old: an oval petroglyph, WH5 Figures 5.11a and 5.12); and set of curved lines, PN6 (Figure 5.12). Four ^{14}C measurements on WH5 were older than 35,000 B.P., with the oldest being >42,000 B.P. Two ^{14}C measurements on PN6 were older than 40,000, with the oldest being ca 43,000 B.P. The cation ratios measured for these petroglyphs also indicate that they are the oldest in the region. Similarly, the most complex varnish layers were found on the engraved surfaces of WH5 and PN6 (see Figure 5.12). These results indicate that humans migrated into what is now the "arid zone" of Australia at least 14,000 years earlier than previously thought. These results are presented in detail in Nobbs and Dorn (1993).

CR dating of petroglyphs has seen widespread application in the western United States. The method was initially applied in the Coso Range (Dorn and Whitley 1984; Whitley and Dorn 1988) and the Cima volcanic field (Whitley and Dorn 1987), both in eastern California. These results showed that individual panels can have a history of use lasting several thousands of years, and that the time sequence of curvilinear abstract, rectilinear abstract, and representational that had been assumed by some individuals is not necessarily correct.

Southeastern Colorado has been an area of extensive use for CR dating. In addition to the CR ages reported by Loendorf (1991) and discussed earlier, Dorn, McGlone, et al. (1990) presented results on controversial motifs in this same area. Although the paper simply presented the analytical results, the designs that were dated are considered by some to be ancient forms of writing. W. R. McGlone, P. M. Leonard, and their colleagues are commended for supporting a study that could have falsified their hypothesis. Interested individuals now at least have some independent time framework by which to consider these controversial hypotheses.

Extensive CR and radiocarbon dating work is in progress in two parts of Wyoming. J. Francis, M. Beis, and L. Loendorf have selected dozens of motifs for analysis in the Bighorn Basin area. The petroglyphs all appear to be mid- to late-Holocene in age, and details of these analyses are in preparation. The author has also been working with A. Tretebas in the western Black Hills of Wyoming, where initial results suggest the petroglyph record may be one of the longest in North America. When these projects are completed, we will have a much better idea of the behavior of the CR system in this region, as well as having estimated the radiocarbon and CR ages of over a hundred motifs in Wyoming.

It is also possible to use the principal of dating encapsulated organics in other contexts. The first direct age control on Nazca geoglyphs and subterranean irrigation aqueducts in southern Peru indicate probable manufac-

Figure 5.11. Archaeological examples of varnish dating. Radiocarbon ages and lab numbers are presented in Dorn, Clarkson, et al. (1992).

(A) South Australian petroglyph WH5, from the Wharton Hill site, with a minimum ^{14}C age of ca. 36,400 B.P. on subvarnish organic matter (Dorn, Clarkson, et al. 1992a). (B) Aerial photograph of Nazca geoglyphs, bird (wide arrow), and line (narrow arrow), with minimum varnish ^{14}C ages of 1,520±60 B.P. and 1,460±60 B.P., respectively. (C) Colorado River, California, geoglyph with minimum varnish ^{14}C age of 1,195±65 B.P. (Photo used with permission of H. Casey). (D) Mojave Desert flake and corers constrained by AMS ^{14}C dating of OM trapped under varnish. Artifacts number 16, 8, and 12 have minimum ^{14}C ages of about 3,700 B.P., 14,800 B.P., and 26,000 B.P., respectively.

ture during the early Early Intermediate period ca. 1,400–2,200 B.P. (see Figure 5.11B). Geoglyphs along the Colorado River in the United States were made before 1,100 B.P. (see Figure 5.11C). Artifacts from a quarry site in the Mojave Desert, California, yield ^{14}C ages from 3,700 B.P. to 26,000 B.P. (see Figure 5.11D). These examples are detailed in Dorn, Clarkson, et al. (1992).

Physical Geography Examples

Ocean cores provide an opportunity to obtain lengthy records of paleoclimatic fluctuations. They have a continuous and often well dated stratigraphic record. Marine cores can also be taken at a variety of locations, allowing spatial variations to be assessed along with temporal changes. Assessing terrestrial pa-

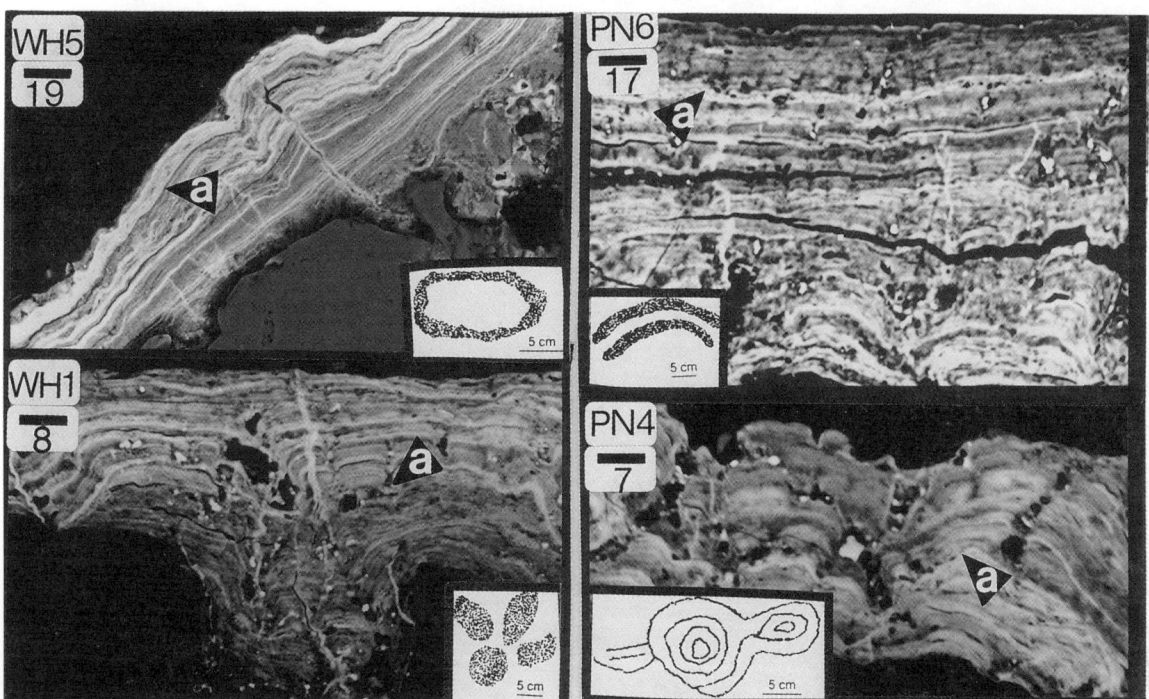

Figure 5.12. Differential development of rock varnish layers formed over petroglyphs, exemplified from two sites in South Australia: Wharton Hill (WH) and Panaramittee North (PN). Images are organized from top to bottom: older to younger petroglyphs. WH5 versus WH1 shows the complexity of layering in WH5 with a ^{14}C age that is greater than 42,000 B.P., compared with a ^{14}C age of ca. 14,900 B.P. Similarly, PN6, with a ^{14}C age of ca. 43,000 B.P., has far more layers than younger petroglyphs, such as PN4, with a ^{14}C age of ca. 5,600 B.P. The letter a on an arrow identifies the contact between the darker (less Mn) surface layer and the underlying brighter (more Mn) layer. Please note porosity in many of the layers; this indicates cation leaching (Dorn and Krinsley 1991). The bright lines that crosscut the layers are fractures lined with MnO ad Fe_2O_3, probably leached from the porous zones and reprecipitated in the fractures. Scale bars for the micrographs are in microns. The different motifs are inset with a scale bar of 5 cm.

leoclimatic changes is also possible, using lake cores and ice cores. In contradistinction many continental regions display landforms that hold clues to past climate systems. But these landforms are difficult to date, because they exist at the surface. Varnish dating methods have been applied to a variety of geomorphic contexts in continental interiors. This section illustrates how varnish radiocarbon dating can play an important role in dating paleoclimatic events in a terrestrial context.

Prior to the varnish radiocarbon minimum age of ca. 19,000 B.P. at Pine Creek, eastern Sierra Nevada (Dorn, Turrin, et al. 1987), there was no numerical age for the last glacial maxima in this region. Subsequently Phillips et al. (1990) established two maxima from ^{36}Cl ages of ca. 20,000 and ca. 24,000 B.P. for moraines at Bloody Canyon, Sierra Nevada. As elaborated above, new ^{10}Be, ^{26}Al, and charcoal radiocarbon ages verified the Pine Creek age of ca. 20,000 B.P.

Figure 5.13. Geomorphological examples of varnish dating.

(A) Shoreline of Lake Lahontan at the north end of Pyramid Lake, where varnish radiocarbon date on the high stand (arrow) indicates that the lake desiccated before 12,680±105 B.P. (Dorn, Jull, et al. 1990). This is consistent with other evidence indicating that the lake dropped from its high stand ca. 13,000–14,000 B.P. (B) Hillslope about 500 m in elevation in the Panamint Range above Death Valley, California. Late Pleistocene ages (in thousands of years B.P.) indicate varnish radiocarbon and CR ages on fossil colluvium deposits. More recent ages on debris-flow levees and exposed bedrock indicate that these hillslope remnants have been eroding throughout the Holocene. The white debris-flow chutes yield varnish CR ages < 500 B.P. (C) Oblique aerial photo and corresponding generalized map of Ingenio-1 alluvial fan, southern Peru (from Dorn, Clarkson et al. 1992). Ages are based on single varnish radiocarbon dates. While older units have Nasca pottery, the post-Nasca age for unit 5 is indicated by the lack of Nasca-style pottery observed on the surface. There was also no Nasca pottery found in the "active" channel that was delineated by the presence of withered vegetation.

One interesting aspect of the paleoclimatology of the western United States is that the paleolakes in the region last had high stands ca. 13,000–14,000 B.P., according to radiocarbon ages on rock varnish (Figure 5.13A; Benson et al. 1990; Dorn, Jull, et al. 1990). Varnish radiocarbon and ^{10}Be–^{26}Al ages (Nishiizumi et al. 1993) on recessional moraines at Pine Creek indicate there may have been a small glacial advance (or still stand) at the same time when lake levels were high, but the entire glacial system was largely in retreat after about 20,000 B.P.

Since the water melted from glaciers would have been insufficient to create a high stand in these lakes (see Gilbert 1890), the more positive water balance to create high stands must have come from more precipitation, less evaporation, or both. Glacial retreat implies an increase in the elevation of the snow line (Dorn, Jull, et al. 1990), suggesting warmer temperatures and more evaporation. This constrains paleoclimatic models to explain both higher snow lines and higher lake levels at the close of the Pleistocene.

Paleoclimatology also interfaces with slope evolution. W. B. Bull's (1991) model of slope development is that the climatic change from more humid to more arid conditions at the close of the Pleistocene devegetated slopes, leading to the erosion of colluvium off hillslopes. Varnish observations provide independent support for Bull's model. Figure 5.13B illustrates varnish ages for colluvium, exposed bedrock, and debris-flow levees in Death Valley. There is a pattern of slope deposits that stabilized during the late Pleistocene, when vegetation was more developed. These deposits of colluvium have been gradually eroding by the process of debris-flow erosion throughout the Holocene.

An alluvial fan near the Nazca geoglyphs of southern Peru exemplifies how varnish radiocarbon dating can be used to constrain the ages of desert landforms that have had no other source of numerical age control (Dorn, Clarkson, et al. 1992). The Ingenio-1 fan exits a small basin that faces west (see figure 5.13c). varnish radiocarbon dating indicates that alluvial units range in age from before ca. 22,000 B.P. to latest Holocene surfaces lacking Nasca-age pottery (see Figure 5.13C). The existence of the debris-flow and braided-stream deposits on Ingenio-1 demand a mechanism to produce intense precipitation, but the drainage basin is in the rainshadow of the Andes Mountains. One possibility is that paleo–El Nino events played a role in producing high-magnitude floods (Dorn, Clarkson, et al. 1992).

The Future of Varnish Dating

The ideal way to apply rock varnish dating is through the use of multiple methods in tandem. The cross-sectional analyses needed to evaluate sample suitability also provide information about relative age through the degree of layering (see Dorn 1992b; Figure 5.12). Cation-ratio dating provides an inexpensive way to estimate calibrated ages, but there is no question that radiocarbon dating is the method of choice in constraining the age of rock varnish. It has a proven record of providing numerical age control where no other method will work.

Although CR dating suffers from the inherent limitation of being susceptible to a multitude of environmental influences that can interfere with the time signal (see Table 5.5), and it has been plagued by controversy (see Table 5.6), it can play an important role in a unified dating effort. First, it can access time beyond the ca. 40,000 B.P. cap of the radiocarbon method. Second, some varnishes do not contain encapsulated organics for radiocarbon dating. Third, it is much less expensive than radiocarbon dating. Fourth, where CR dating has been subject to blind tests, CR ages are consistent with ages available from independent controls. Lastly, it can be used to preselect the best samples to analyze by more expensive analytical methods, such as varnish radiocarbon or cosmogenic isotopes.

Of the remainder of the varnish methods (see Table 5.1), I believe that uranium-series (Knauss and Ku 1980) combined with varnish layers (Dorn 1990, 1994) will be the most likely methods to see widespread use. There are new approaches to dealing with "dirty" samples, such as rock varnish that contains detrital thorium, and there are new mass spectrometry and laser methods that facilitate working with small samples.

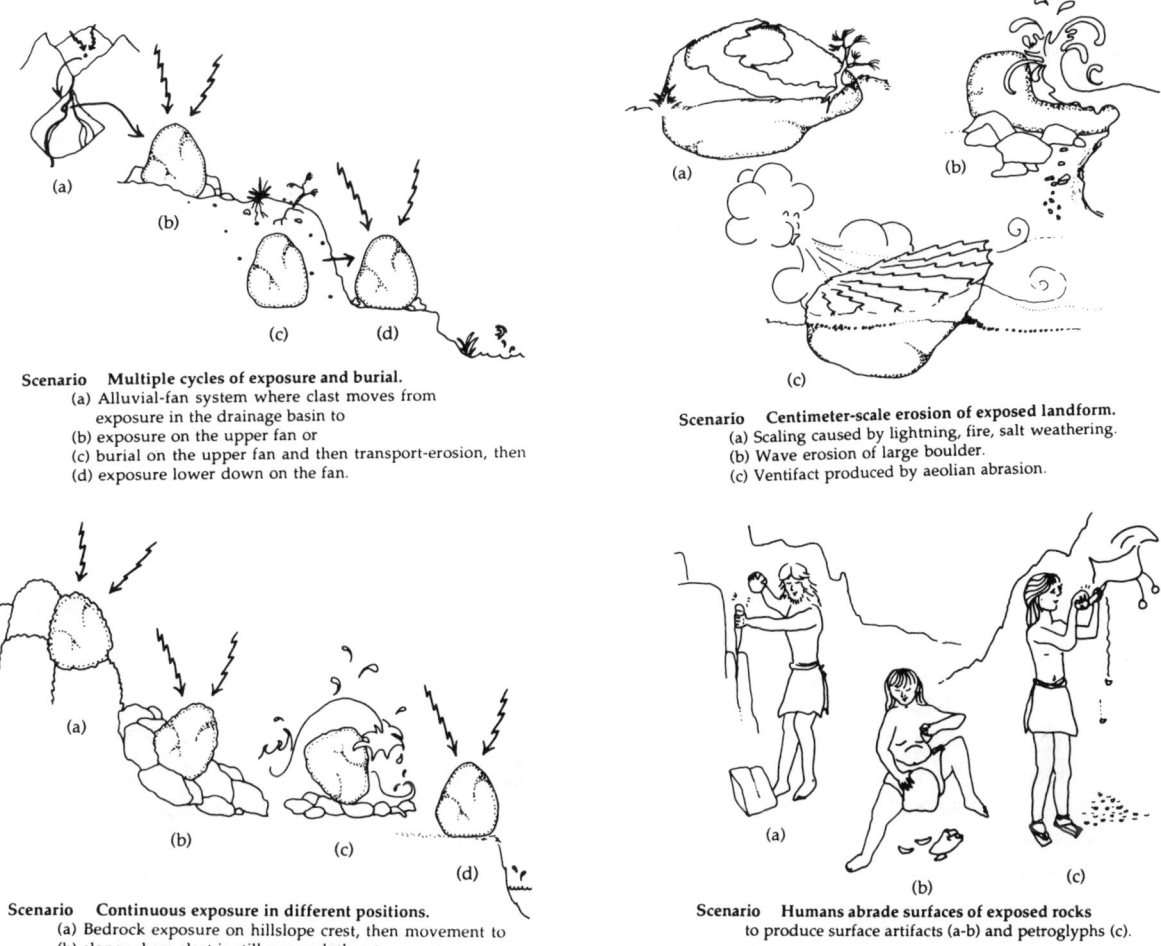

Figure 5.14. Different scenarios in which rock has been exposed to cosmic rays before the most recent alteration event.

A key variable in the future of varnish dating is the development of cosmogenic isotopes such as ^{3}He, ^{10}Be, ^{26}Al, and ^{36}Cl as dating tools (cf. Cerling 1990; Kurz et al. 1990; Nishiizumi et al. 1993; Phillips et al. 1990). The *in situ* buildup of cosmogenic isotopes has a number of advantages over rock varnish, the most important being: (1) if the very surface of the rock spalls, the varnish clock is reset, but centimeters of erosion would have little effect on the cosmogenic age signal; (2) varnish is unstable in acidic environments that would not influence the buildup rates of isotopes; and (3) cosmogenic isotopes are based on physics, not biogeochemistry, which varies in different environments.

Cosmogenic isotopes provide more accurate, more precise, and more reliable ages for most geomorphic situations than rock varnish. In contrast, for archaeological applications in dryland regions, rock varnish is an inherently superior tool. Cosmogenic isotopes have the greatest inherent problems in circumstances where the rocks being sampled have an exposure history that precedes the event of interest. Figure 5.14 illustrates several examples where the surface of a rock was exposed recently, but the rock material had a prior exposure history. Yet even a prior exposure history does not rule out the use of cosmogenic isotopes, because multiple isotopes with different half-lives (some stable, such as ^{3}He) can be used to sort out the history of a rock that has seen burial and reexposure.

The long-term future of varnish age determination rests in dating processes that alter the very skin of a rock. Wind abrasion, for example, will blast off varnish, but it will not alter the cosmogenic signal of the rock. So if what is of interest is discovering when aeolian abrasion ceased, only the post-abrasion development of varnish will inform on this topic (see Figure 5.14). Similarly, archaeological features such as petroglyphs, geoglyphs, and artifacts that were made from surface materials cannot be dated by cosmogenic isotopes, because what is of interest is not the exposure history of the rock material, but when the rock surface was last abraded by humans (see Figure 5.14).

The challenge is to continue to refine varnish-dating methods with the aid of blind tests. The key to the use of varnish as a chronometric tool is understanding the limitations imposed by how the varnish was formed.

Acknowledgments

Supported by NSF PYI award and SES 89-00403. Thanks to A. Bach, M. Bees, J. Bell, L. Benson, J. Clark, D. Dragovich, D. Elliott-Fisk, J. Francis, T. Liu, L. Loendorf, N. Meek, R. Moore, M. Nobbs, F. Phillips, D. Tanner, P. Trusty, D. Whitley, E. Wolfe, and M. Zreda for comments and field and lab assistance; John Chappell for suggesting variations on leaching experiments; and B. Trapido and S. Clark for graphical assistance. The ASU microprobe was purchased, in part, by NSF EAR 8408163.

References Cited

Akimoto, T., H. Konoshita, and T. Furuta
1984   Electron Probe Microanalysis Study on Processes of Low-Temperature Oxidation of Titanomagnetite. *Earth and Planetary Science Letters* 71:263–278.

Bach, A. J., D. Elliott-Fisk, T. Liu, R. Dorn, F. Phillips, and M. Zreda.
1991   Pleistocene Glacial Moraine Complexes at Pine and Bishop Creeks, East-Central Sierra Nevada, CA. *Geological Society of America Abstracts with Programs* 23:223–224.

Bain, D. C.
1976   A Titanium-Rich Soil Clay. *Journal of Soil Science* 27:68–70.

Bamforth, D. B., and R. I. Dorn
1988   On the Nature and Antiquity of the Manix Lake Lithic Industry. *Journal of California and Great Basin Anthropology* 10:209–226.

Bard, J. C.
1979   *The Development of a Patination Dating Technique for Great Basin Petroglyphs Utilizing Neutron Activation and X-ray Fluorescence Analyses.* Unpublished Ph.D. dissertation, Department of Anthropology, University of California, Berkeley.

Bell, J. W., F. F. Peterson, R. I. Dorn, A. R. Ramelli, and T. L. Ku
1991   Late Quaternary Surficial Geology in Crater Flat, Yucca Mountain, Southern Nevada. *Geological Society of America Abstracts with Programs* 23:6.

Benson, L. V., D. R. Currey, R. I. Dorn, K. R. Lajoie, C. G. Oviatt, S. W. Robinson, G. I. Smith, and S. Stine.
1990   Chronology of Expansion and Contraction of Four Great Basin Lake Systems During the Past 35,000 years. *Palaeogeography, Palaeoclimatology, Palaeoecology* 78:241–286.

Bierman, P., and A. Gillespie
1991a Accuracy of Rock-Varnish Chemical Analyses: Implications for Cation-Ratio Dating. *Geology* 19:196–199.

1991b Range Fires: A Significant Factor in Exposure-Age Determination and Geomorphic Surface Evolution, *Geology* 19:641–644.

1992 Reply to Comment on Accuracy of Rock-Varnish Chemical Analyses: Implications for Cation-Ratio Dating. *Geology* 20:471–472.

Bierman, P., A. Gillespie, and S. Kuehner

1991 Precision of Rock-Varnish Chemical Analyses and Cation-Ratio Ages. *Geology* 19:135–138.

Bull, W. B.

1991 *Geomorphic Responses to Climatic Change.* Oxford University Press, London.

Cahill, T. A.

1992 Comment on "Accuracy of Rock-Varnish Chemical Analyses: Implications for Cation-Ratio Dating." *Geology* 20:469.

Cerling, T. E.

1990 Dating Geomorphic Surfaces Using Cosmogenic He-3. *Quarternary Research* 33:148–156.

Clayton, J. A., K. L. Verosub, and C. D. Harrington

1990 Magnetic Techniques Applied to the Study of Rock Varnish. *Geophysical Research Letters* 17:787–790.

Colman, S. M., K. L. Pierce, and P. W. Birkeland

1987 Suggested Terminology for Quaternary Dating Methods. *Quaternary Research* 28:314–319.

Curtiss, B., J. B. Adams, and M S. Ghiorso

1985 Origin, Development and Chemistry of Silica-Alumina Rock Coatings from the Semiarid Regions of the Island of Hawaii. *Geochimica et Cosmochimica Acta* 49:49–56.

Derbyshire, E., L. Jijun, F. A. Perrott, X. Shuying, and R. S. Waters

1984 Quaternary Glacial History of the Hunza Valley, Karakoram Mountains, Pakistan. In *The International Karakoram Project,* vol. 2., edited by K. J. Miller, pp. 456–495. Cambridge University Press, Cambridge.

Dorn, R. I.

1983 Cation-Ratio Dating: A New Rock Varnish Age Determination Technique. *Quaternary Research* 20:49–73.

1986 Rock Varnish as an Indicator of Aeolian Environmental Change. In *Aeolian Geomorphology,* edited by W. G. Nickling, pp. 291–307. Allen and Unwin, London.

1988 A Rock Varnish Interpretation of Alluvial-Fan Development in Death Valley, California. *National Geographic Research* 4:56–73.

1989 Cation-Ratio Dating of Rock Varnish: A Geographical Perspective. *Progress in Physical Geography* 13:559–596.

1990 Quaternary Alkalinity Fluctuations Recorded in Rock Varnish Microlaminations on Western U.S.A. Volcanics. *Palaeogeography, Palaeoclimatology, Palaeoecology* 76:291–310.

1992a Comment on "Accuracy of Rock-Varnish Chemical Analyses: Implications for Cation-Ratio Dating." *Geology* 20:470–471.

1992b Paleoenvironmental Signals in Rock Varnish on Petroglyphs. *American Indian Rock Art* 18:1–15.

1994 Rock Varnish as an Indicator of Climatic Change. In *Desert Geomorphology,* edited by A. Abrahams and A. Parsons, pp. 539–552. Chapman Hall, London.

Dorn, R. I., D. B. Bamforth, T. A. Cahill, J. C. Dohrenwend, B. D. Turrin, A. J. T. Jull, A. Long, M. E. Macko, E. B. Weil, D. S. Whitley, and T. H. Zabel

1986 Cation-Ratio and Accelerator-Radiocarbon Dating of Rock Varnish on Archaeological Artifacts and Landforms in the Mojave Desert, Eastern California. *Science* 223:730–733.

Dorn, R. I., T. A. Cahill, R. A. Eldred, T. E. Gill, B. H. Kusko, A. J. Bach, and D. L. Elliott-Fisk

1990 Dating Rock Varnishes by the Cation Ratio Method with PIXE, ICP, and the Electron Microprobe. *International Journal of PIXE* 1:157–195.

Dorn, R. I., P. B. Clarkson, M. F. Nobbs, L. L. Loendorf, and D. S. Whitley

1992 Radiocarbon Dating Inclusions of Organic Matter in Rock Varnish, with Examples from Drylands. *Annals of the Association of American Geographers* 82:136–151.

Dorn, R. I. and M. J. DeNiro

1985 Stable Carbon Isotope Ratios of Rock Varnish

Organic Matter: A New Paleoenvironmental Indicator. *Science* 227:1472–1474.

Dorn, R. I., A. J. T. Jull, D. J. Donahue, T. W. Linick, and L. T. Toolin
1989 Accelerator Mass Spectrometry Radiocarbon Dating of Rock Varnish. *Geological Society of America Bulletin* 101:1363–1372.
1990 Latest Pleistocene Lake Shorelines and Glacial Chronology in the Western Basin and Range Province, USA: Insights from AMS Radiocarbon Dating of Rock Varnish and Paleoclimatic Implications. *Palaeogeography, Palaeoclimatology, Palaeoecology* 78:315–331.

Dorn, R. I., A. J. T. Jull, D. J. Donahue, T. W. Linick, L. J. Toolin, R. B. Moore, M. Rubin, T. E. Gill, and T. A. Cahill
1992 Rock Varnish on Hualálai and Mauna Kea Volcanoes, Hawaii. *Pacific Science* 46:11–34.

Dorn, R. I., and D. H. Krinsley
1991 Cation-Leaching Sites in Rock Varnish. *Geology* 19:1077–1080.
1992 Reply. *Geology* 20:1051–1052.

Dorn, R. I., W. R. McGlone, and P. M. Leonard
1990 Age Determination of Petroglyphs in Southeast Colorado. *Southwestern Lore* 56:21–36.

Dorn, R. I., M. Nobbs, and T. A. Cahill
1988 Cation-Ratio Dating of Rock Engravings from the Olary Province of Arid South Australia. *Antiquity* 62:681–689.

Dorn, R. I., and T. M. Oberlander
1981 Microbial Origin of Desert Varnish. *Science* 213:1245–1247.
1982 Rock Varnish. *Progress in Physical Geography* 6:317–367.

Dorn, R. I., F. M. Phillips, M. G. Zreda, E. W. Wolfe, A. J. T. Jull, P. W. Kubik, and P. Sharma
1991 Glacial Chronology of Mauna Kea, Hawaii, as Constrained by Surface-Exposure Dating. *National Geographic Research* 7:456–471.

Dorn, R. I., B. D. Turrin, A. J. T. Jull, T. W. Linick, and D. J. Donahue
1987 Radiocarbon and Cation-Ratio Ages for Rock Varnish on Tioga and Tahoe Morainal Boulders of Pine Creek, Eastern Sierra Nevada, California, and their Paleoclimatic Implications. *Quaternary Research* 28:38–49.

Dorn, R. I., and D. S. Whitley
1984 Chronometric and Relative Age Determination of Petroglyphs in the Western United States. *Annals of the Association of American Geographers* 74:308–322.

Dragovich, D.
1984 Desert Varnish as an Age Indicator for Aboriginal Rock Engravings: A Review of Problems and Prospects. *Archaeology in Oceania* 19:48–56.
1986 Minimum Age of Some Desert Varnish near Broken Hill, New South Wales. *Search* 17:149–151.
1987 Desert Varnish and Problems of Dating Rock Engravings in Western New South Wales. In *Archaeometry: Further Australasian Studies* edited by W. R. Ambrose and J. M. Mummery, pp. 28–35. Australian National University, Canberra.
1988 Desert Varnish and Environmental Change near Broken Hill, Western New South Wales. *Earth-Science Reviews* 25:399–407.

Elliott-Fisk, D. L.
1987 Glacial Geomorphology of the White Mountains, California and Nevada: Establishment of a Glacial Chronology. *Physical Geography* 8:299–323.

Gilbert, G. K.
1890 Lake Bonneville. *U.S. Geological Survey Monograph* 1:1–438.

Gillespie, R.
1991 Charcoal Dating—Oxidation is Necessary for Complete Humic Removal. *Radiocarbon* 33:199.

Glazovskiy, A. F.
1985 Rock Varnish in the Glacierized Regions of the Pamirs [in Russian]. *Data of the Glaciological Studies* (Moscow) 54:136–141.

Harden, J. W.
1988 Genetic Interpretations of Elemental and Chemical Differences in a Soil Chronosequence, California. *Geoderma* 43:179–193.

Harrington, C. D.
1988 Recognition of Components of Volcanic Ash in Rock Varnish and the Dating of Volcanic Ejecta Plumes. *Geological Society of America Abstracts with Programs* 20:167.

Harrington, C. D., S. L. Reneau, R. Raymond, and D. J. Krier
1991 Barium Concentrations in Rock Varnish: Implications for Calibrated Rock-Varnish Dating Curves. *Scanning Microscopy* 5:55–62.

Harrington, C. D., and J. W. Whitney
1987 Scanning Electron Microscope Method for Rock Varnish Dating. *Geology* 15:967–970.

Harry, K. G., P. Bierman, and L. Fratt
1992 Lithic Procurement and Rock Varnish Dating: Investigations at CA-KER-140, a Small Quarry in the Western Mojave Desert. *Statistical Research Technical Series* 36.

Hooke, R. L., and R. I. Dorn
1992 Segmentation of Alluvial Fans in Death Valley, California: New Insights from Surface Exposure Dating. *Earth Surface Processes and Landforms* 17:557–574.

Jones, C. E.
1991 Characteristics and Origin of Rock Varnish from the Hyperarid Coastal Deserts of Northern Peru. *Quaternary Research* 35:116–129.

Knauss, K. G., and T. L. Ku
1980 Desert Varnish: Potential for Age Dating Via Uranium-Series Isotopes. *Journal of Geology* 88:95–100.

Krinsley, D. H., and R. I. Dorn
1991 New Eyes on Eastern California Rock Varnish. *California Geology* May: 107–114.

Krinsley, D. H., R. I. Dorn, and S. Anderson
1990 Factors That May Interfere with the Dating of Rock Varnish. *Physical Geography* 11:97–119.

Krinsley, D. H., and C. R. Manley
1989 Backscattered Electron Microscopy as an Advanced Technique in Petrography. *Journal of Geological Education* 37:202–209.

Kurz, M. D., D. Colodner, T. W. Trull, D. E. Sampson, R. B. Moore, and K. O'Brien
1990 Cosmic Ray Exposure Age Dating with in situ Produced Cosmogenic He-3: Results from Young Hawaiian Lava Flows. *Earth and Planetary Science Letters* 97:177–189.

Linick, T. W., P. E. Damon, D. J. Donahue, and A. J. T. Jull
1989 Accelerator Mass Spectrometry: The New Revolution in Radiocarbon Dating. *Quaternary International* 1:1–16.

Loendorf, L. L.
1991 Cation-Ratio Varnish Dating and Petroglyph Chronology in Southeastern Colorado. *Antiquity* 65:246–255.

Morad, S., and A. A. Aldahan
1986 Alteration of Detrital Fe-Ti Oxides in Sedimentary Rocks. *Geological Society of America Bulletin* 97:567–578.

Nagy, B., L. A. Nagy, M. J. Rigali, W. D. Jones, D. H. Krinsley, and N. A. Sinclair
1991 Rock Varnish in the Sonoran Desert: Microbiologically Mediated Accumulation of Manganiferous Sediments. *Sedimentology* 38:1153–1171.

Nishiizumi, K., E. L. Winterer, C. P. Kohl, J. Klein, R. Middleton, D. Lal, and J. R. Arnold
1989 *In situ* Be-10 and Al-26 in Granitic Rocks with Glacially Polished Surfaces. *Journal of Geophysical Research* 94:17,907–17,915.

Nishiizumi, K., C. P. Kohl, R. Dorn, J. Klein, D. Fink, R. Middleton, D. Lal, and J. R. Arnold
1993 Role in *in situ* Cosmogenic Nuclides Be-10 and Al-26 in the Study of Diverse Geomorphic Processes. *Earth Surface Processes and Landforms* 18:407–425.

Nobbs, M. F., and R. I. Dorn
1993 New Surface Exposure Ages for Petroglyphs from the Olary Province, South Australia. *Archaeologia in Oceania* 28:18–39.

O'Hara, P., D. H. Krinsley, and S. W. Anderson
1989 Elemental Analysis of Rock Varnish Using the Ion Microprobe. *Geological Society of America Abstracts with Programs* 21:165.

1990 Microprobe Analysis of Rock Varnish—Cation Ratios and Elemental Variance. *Geological Society of America Abstracts with Programs* 22:271.

Perry, R. S., and J. B. Adams
1978   Desert Varnish: Evidence of Cyclic Deposition of Manganese. *Nature* 276:489–491.

Phillips, F. M., M. G. Zreda, S. S. Smith, D. Elmore, P. W. Kubik, and P. Sharma
1990   Cosmogenic Chlorine-36 Chronology for Glacial Deposits at Bloody Canyon, Eastern Sierra Nevada. *Science* 248:1529–1532.

Phillips, F. M., M. Zreda, D. Elmore, R. I. Dorn, T. Liu, A. Bach, D. Elliott-Fisk, and J. Clark.
n.d.   Glacial Geology of Lower Bishop Creek, Eastern Sierra Nevada: Cosmogenic Cl-36 and Rock Varnish Chronology. *Manuscript in preparation..*

Pineda, C. A., L. Jacobson, and M. Peisach
1988   Ion Beam Analysis for the Determination of Cation-Ratios as a Means of Dating Southern African Rock Varnishes. *Nuclear Instruments and Methods in Physics Research* B35:463–466.

Pineda, C. A., M. Peisach, L. Jacobson, and C. G. Sampson
1990   Cation-Ratio Differences in Rock Patina on Hornfels and Chalcedony Using Thick Target PIXE. *Nuclear Instruments and Methods in Physics Research* B49:332–335.

Potter, R. M., and G. R. Rossman
1977   Desert Varnish: The Importance of Clay Minerals. *Science* 196: 1446–1448.
1979   Mineralogy of Manganese Dendrites and Coatings. *American Mineralogist* 64:1219–1226.

Raymond, R. J., S. L. Reneau, and C. D. Harrington
1991   Elemental Relationships in Rock Varnish Determined by Scanning Electron Microscopy and Energy Dispersive X-Ray Elemental Line Profiling. *Scanning Microscopy* 5:37–46.

Reheis, M. C.
1987   Climatic Implications of Alternating Clay and Carbonate Formation in Semiarid Soils of South-Central Montana. *Quarternary Research* 27:270–282.

Reneau, S. L., R. C. Hagan, C. D. Harrington, and R. J. Raymond
1991   Scanning Electron Microscopic Analysis of Rock Varnish Chemistry for Cation-Ratio Dating: An Examination of Electron Beam Penetration Depths. *Scanning Microscopy* 5:47–54.

Reneau, S. L., and R. J. Raymond
1991   Cation-Ratio Dating of Rock Varnish: Why Does it Work? *Geology* 19:937–940.

Vasconcelos, P. M., T. A. Becker, P. R. Renne, and G. H. Brimhall
1992   Age and Duration of Weathering by ^{40}K–^{40}Ar and ^{40}Ar/^{39}Ar Analysis of Potassium-Manganese Oxides. *Science* 258:451–455.

Watchman, A.
1990   What are Silica Skins and How Are They Important in Rock Art Conservation. *Australian Aboriginal Studies* 1:21–29.
1991   Age and Composition of Oxalate-Rich Crusts in the Northern Territory, Australia. *Studies in Conservation* 36:24–32.
1992   Comment on "Cation-Leaching Sites in Rock Varnish". *Geology* 20: 1050.

Wells, S. G., L. D. McFadden, C. E. Renault, and B. M. Crowe
1990   Geomorphic Assessment of late Quaternary Volcanism in the Yucca Mountain Area, Southern Nevada: Implications for the Proposed High-Level Radioactive Waste Repository. *Geology* 18:549–553.

Wells, S. G., L. D. McFadden, and C. T. Olinger.
1991   Use of Cosmogenic He-3 and Ne-21 to Understand Desert Pavement Formation. *Geological Society of America Abstracts with Programs* 23:206.

Whalley, W. B., A. F. Gellatly, J. E. Gordon, and J. D. Hansom
1990   Ferromanganese Rock Varnish in North Norway: A Subglacial Origin. *Earth Surface Processes and Landforms* 15:265–275.

White, K.
1990   Spectral Reflectance Characteristics of Rock Varnish in Arid Areas. *School of Geography University of Oxford Research Paper* 46:1–38.

Whitley, D. S., and R. I. Dorn
1987   Rock Art Chronology in Eastern California. *World Archaeology* 19: 150–164.

1988 Cation-Ratio Dating of Petroglyphs using PIXE. *Nuclear Instruments and Methods in Physics Research* B35:410–414.

Zhang, Y., T. Liu, and S. Li
1990 Establishment of a Cation-Leaching Curve of Rock Varnish and its Application to the Boundary Region of Gansu and Xinjiang, Western China. *Seismology and Geology* [Beijing] 12:251–261.

Zreda, M. G., F. M. Phillips, D. Elmore, P. W. Kubik, P. Sharma, and R. I. Dorn
1991 Cosmogenic Chlorine-36 Production Rates in Terrestrial Rocks. *Earth and Planetary Science Letters* 105:94–109.

6
THERMOLUMINESCENCE DATING OF SURFICIAL ARCHAEOLOGICAL MATERIAL

Robert C. Dunnell and James K. Feathers

Department of Anthropology
University of Washington
Seattle, Washington

Abstract

Thermoluminescence dating has suffered, particularly in the United States, from a number of misconceptions that have tended to relegate it to a minor role in archaeological research. The circumstances that have led to this condition are examined. We argue that thermoluminescence dating ought to be the absolute dating method of choice in the surficial context, because of the close congruence between the dated event and the archaeological target event. We conclude the paper with a brief account of ongoing surface research in the central Mississippi Valley, which demonstrates the effectiveness of thermoluminescence dating on old surfaces.

Introduction

THE PRESUMED INABILITY TO DATE ALL BUT A small fraction, the so-called diagnostics, of surface finds (Jones and Beck 1992; Tingle 1987) and the common assumption that the surface almost always represents a "disturbed" context (Dunnell and Dancey 1983) have combined to relegate the surface record to one of secondary importance. Until quite recently (Lewarch and O'Brien 1981), its principal use was as a means to predict (erroneously, see Dunnell and Simek 1994) locations that could properly be investigated by excavation. Even today surface remains are not accorded the same degree of legal protection as their buried counterparts.

This slight of the surface record had minimal impact on archaeological results, so long as the principal interest was in chronology. From the 1960s on, however, a new emphasis was placed on functional questions, and these, in turn, demand a representative sampling of the archaeological record. The vast bulk of the archaeological record lies on the surface or is incorporated in a tillage zone partly exposed on the surface; the buried record is a product of rather special geomorphic conditions. It is obvious that if a spatially representative record is required, archaeologists must cope with surficial deposits.

The prejudice against the use of surface materials is ameliorating, however. More sophisticated understandings of formation processes have called into question concepts such as "*in situ*" and "disturbed" (see Dunnell and Dancey 1983; Schiffer 1987). Cultural resource management (CRM) has forced the use of the surface, even when plowed.

Nevertheless the problem with dating surface remains persists, largely because common techniques such as seriation and ^{14}C dating rely upon association; the former because it employs type frequencies in assemblages, and the latter because it dates a nonarchaeological event (Dean 1978; Dunnell 1981; Tingle 1987). The inability to associate nondiagnostic surface artifacts into assemblages is therefore seen as a barrier to dating. (It must also be emphasized, however, that these acknowledged "problems" with surface deposits must, contrary to archaeological practice, also characterize most subsurface deposits, because subsurface deposits are simply buried surface deposits.) The potential of thermoluminescence (TL) dating arises from the fact that the event dated, usually a heating event, is very often the archaeological target event, thus mitigating the need for "associations."

TL dating has been sparingly employed by archaeologists in the United States, relative to its use elsewhere in the world. In part this relates to the simple fact that much of the basic research was done in Europe (see Aitken 1985). Here TL dating is usually regarded as a supplemental, less-desirable method, to be employed only when materials suitable for ^{14}C dating are absent. Furthermore, because TL dating is technically much more complex than ^{14}C dating, it is substantially more expensive and inherently less precise. Its complexity arises from the fact that the "clock" used in TL dating is local rather than global.

However, as Dunnell and Readhead (1988) point out, the precision in measuring ^{14}C cannot normally be translated into an archaeological chronology of similar precision, because of the difficulties and uncertainties in linking the measured event (the isolation of the sample's carbon from the atmospheric carbon reservoir) to an archaeologically relevant event. Thus not only is TL applicable to a much wider range of substances (nearly all crystalline materials) and over a longer time span (Aitken 1985), but it may be routinely capable of producing more precise archaeological chronologies for many periods (for instance, the last millenium, where variation in ^{14}C production produces multiple age intercepts for any given concentration of ^{14}C) and depositional contexts. That TL dating has not been exploited to solve the problem of dating in surficial contexts is largely a function of the archaeological prejudice against the use of surface materials and of the idea that only objects with good associations can be, or should be, dated, as well as the physicists' general lack of appreciation of formation processes (see Lalou and Valladas 1989). We attempt to show that TL dating not only can be applied in the surface context, but that it represents potentially the most robust dating method in this arena.

TL Dating

There are several excellent recent summaries of TL dating (Aitken 1985, 1989; Lalou and Valladas 1989), most of which are directed toward nonspecialist audiences. Thus we need only to sketch the general principles on which it operates, emphasizing those elements that relate to its deployment in the surface context.

General Principles

The TL phenomenon, the production of photons of light upon heating (or other inputs of energy), arises in crystalline solids as a result of environmental radiation. Ionizing radiation detaches (increases the energy state of) some electrons in the material. While many return to their original sites (return to a ground state), some become trapped in defects (such as impurities, chemical substitutions, broken bonds) in the crystal lattice. An

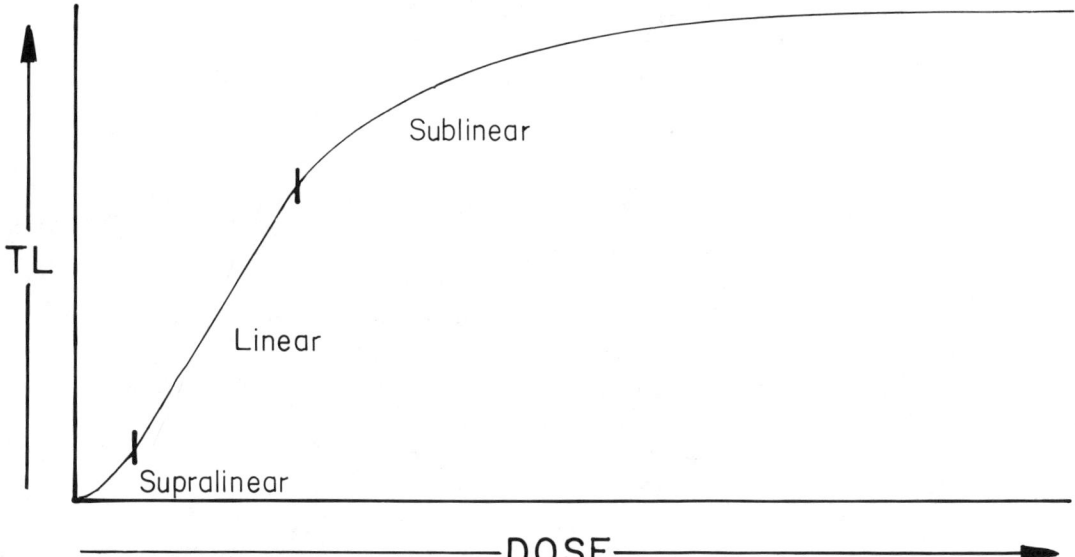

Figure 6.1. Curve showing the relation between radiation dose and TL output. Note the supralinear, linear, and sublinear portions of the curve.

additional input of energy is required to eject electrons from the traps, the exact amount varying with the specific trap. Such trapped electrons and holes (locations vacated by electrons) thus accumulate over time as a more or less constant rate, in proportion to the radiation dose being received from the immediate environment, until a saturation point is reached (all defects are occupied). As this point is approached, the ratio between dose and age is no longer linear, but rather sublinear (Figure 6.1). The saturation point, the point at which so many defects are occupied by trapped electrons that the accumulation of TL is no longer linear, varies with the material. Fortunately the saturation points of common materials such as quartz and calcite are so high in relation to typical levels of environmental radiation as to allow dating over several hundreds of thousands of years (Aitken 1985). The initial development of thermoluminescence is also nonlinear with respect to dose; in fact, it is parabolic (Lalou and Valladas 1989). "Competition" for electrons among superabundant traps has been theorized as the cause of the slow growth of TL initial (Chen and Bowman 1978), the so-called supralinearity effect (see Figure 6.1). TL dating must correct for supralinearity; for old samples approaching the saturation point, complex curve fitting is required.

Dating Events

Trapped electrons begin to accumulate with the formation of the crystal structure; thus the formation of the crystal is a datable event. This is actually the basis for some geological applications. Crystal formation also has the potential to date biological events, as in the formation of hydroxyapatite crystals in bone or calcite and/or aragonite crystals in shell. Other events are datable as well, however. An additional input of energy (such as heat, UV, X-rays) can "bleach" or "zero" a particular specimen by emptying all of the traps and letting the electrons return to a ground state. The amount of energy required varies with the particular trap. For example, there are four well-defined TL output peaks roughly associated with 110°C, 230°C, 325°C, and 375°C in quartz, the temperature representing the amounts of energy required to empty particular traps (often spoken of as the "depth" of the trap). The 110°C trap is very "leaky" at ambient temperature, with a half-life of only about 3.5 hours (and thus is of no direct value in dating), whereas the 375°C trap has a half-life of about 40×10^6 years (Aitken and Flemming 1972). Traps in calcite and plagioclase have traps of even greater stability (Lalou and Valladas 1989). Whenever a sample is heated above the temperature needed to empty its traps, the TL clock is reset to zero; TL begins to accumulate from that point on.

Archaeological heating is thus the usual TL dating event. The manufacture of ceramics, both intentional, as in vessel construction, or accidental, as in the burning of a wattle-and-daub house or building a fire on the ground or in a pit, is a typical datable event. Depending upon vessel function, vessel use might also be a datable event. Likewise, the heating of many rocks (e.g., quartz, felspars), as in the heat treatment of lithics in manufacture or accidental/incidental heating in other contexts, has the same potential. Work under way at the University of Washington promises to extend dating to the use of steatite vessels and the manufacture of some kinds of mortar. Biogenic crystals such as hydroxyapatite are also potentially datable, as noted earlier, but technical difficulties have largely prevented the realization of the potential (McCutcheon n.d.); electron spin resonance (ERS) has been employed to circumvent some of these problems (Ikeya 1978). Fluorine dating (see Callaghan 1986) can be used to create local relative chronologies for bone as well.

In finely divided aeolian sediments, ultraviolent light can partly bleach the particles, allowing loess deposition to be dated (see Huntley 1976). The same kind of zeroing event may prove datable in some alluvial situations as well (Berger, personal communication). The exposure of coarse-grain opaque solids is of no consequence, as the outer 2 mm of solids are usually removed to simplify dose-rate calculations. Thus the amount of time a particular object has been resident on the surface does not influence its datability, since it does not bleach the archaeological event clock.

Measurement of Trapped Electrons

Two approaches, ESR and TL, have been extensively employed to measure the number of trapped electrons in solids for the purposes of dating. ESR is inherently several orders of magnitude less precise than TL (Poupeau and Rossi 1989:275). Consequently ESR is normally used only on materials where heating to produce luminescence is problematic or for very ancient materials where the inherent imprecision is of less concern. In TL dating, heating supplies the energy to empty the traps of their electrons, and in the process some electrons combine with luminescence centers and give off a photon, the light measured in TL. More recently lasers have been used to supply the energy needed to allow the electrons to escape (optical stimulation), and the more general term, luminescence dating, is coming into vogue as a result (see Aitken 1989). In TL the light production of a sample is recorded by a photomultiplier as the sample is heated from ambient temperature to 500°C or more, filters being used to exclude extraneous light (such as blackbody radiation) to the extent possible. The measurement of TL is the least problematic component in TL dating.

Dose Rate

To convert the measurement of natural TL to an estimate of age requires two additional pieces of information: a measurement of the specimen's sensitivity to ionizing radiation and the annual influx of radiation coming from the sample and its surroundings. The first parameter is relatively easy to measure, by laboratory-controlled irradiation of the sample and measurement of the TL thus induced (Aitken 1985), and is of no further concern here. Measurement of the annual dose rate, however, is fraught with problems and introduces the largest uncertainty into TL dating.

The radioactivity of the sample itself is measured in the laboratory. Alpha, beta, and gamma radiation have different effective penetration distances in solids, ranging from a few microns in the case of alpha particles to over 30 cm for gamma radiation. To simplify the estimation of annual dose rate, the outer 2 mm of samples are removed under darkroom conditions. This effectively eliminates the need to measure the alpha and beta contribution from the surrounding environment. It also removes the material that has been exposed to sunlight and thus bleached to a variable degree.

Two different approaches have been taken in measuring environmental contributions to the annual dose. The first of these is the placement of dosimeters in the field for a year or more, to measure the local radiation directly. While this may seem like an effective and uncomplicated technique for determining the annual dose, it is seriously flawed in practice. First, even within the same geological stratum, there is often substantial variability in K, Th, and U, the principal sources of radiation in natural settings. At Cold Water Farm, a locality within the study area developed later in this paper, we investigated the distribution of K in an area 98 m × 48 m, from which many samples were to be dated. Not only did K vary significantly over distances of a few meters, but this variation was also patterned (Figure 6.2) and negatively correlated with the presence of prehistoric cultural material. Thus for the dosimeter approach to be effective, one would have to place the instrument in virtually the same location as the sample. Since many samples are acquired by excavation, it is clearly not possible to insert a dosimeter in the sample location, as most if not all of the sample environment is destroyed in the process of discovery. For surface locations there are major difficulties in ensuring the integrity of the dosimeter for a period long enough to secure a reliable measurement. Consequently, for these and other reasons, we abandoned the use of field dosimeters early in our research.

The second approach, measurement of sample radiation in the laboratory from a sample of matrix, has the advantage of allowing the use of more sophisticated measurement devices. Unlike the field dosimeter, which measures radiation from all sources, laboratory measurement allows one to separate different components in the radiation if need be. This is essential data for assessing whether the uranium and thorium decay chains are in equilibrium, and thus that contemporary measurements of radiation are relevant to the time the sample has been in its find location.

Certain unknowns plague both approaches, principal among which is the need to estimate the water content of the sample and the matrix over the period of time since burial. The frequently employed procedure of sealing samples at the time of collection and measuring the actual water content is clearly of little relevance, as the amount of moisture in most samples undergoes enormous variation seasonally, if not daily.

This is to say nothing at all of climate change over archaeological time. Of course there are some special contexts that do admit a more simplified approach. Permanently dry rock shelters or extreme desert conditions reduce moisture to insignificance; conversely, a permanently waterlogged condition also simplifies calculations on this account (although it may present other problems, as noted below). But the key point is that the typical buried sample will have been subjected to variable degrees of saturation over the period of burial, and a significant element of uncertainty arises because of this imprecision.

Standard wisdom in TL dating (see Aitken 1985:264–265) seeks samples from homogeneous contexts, so that a single sediment sample may be used to characterize the radioactivity of the matrix. This is of obvious concern when using the laboratory approach to estimate environmental contributions to the annual dose rate but is of no moment if in-place dosimeters are used. While satisfying this condition of a homogeneous matrix certainly does simplify the calculations, it is neither realistic nor debilitating if not met. Few archaeological contexts provide homogeneous deposits in a 60-cm sphere surrounding a potential dating sample. On the other hand, if two or more strata lie within 30 cm of the sample, the condition can be accommodated

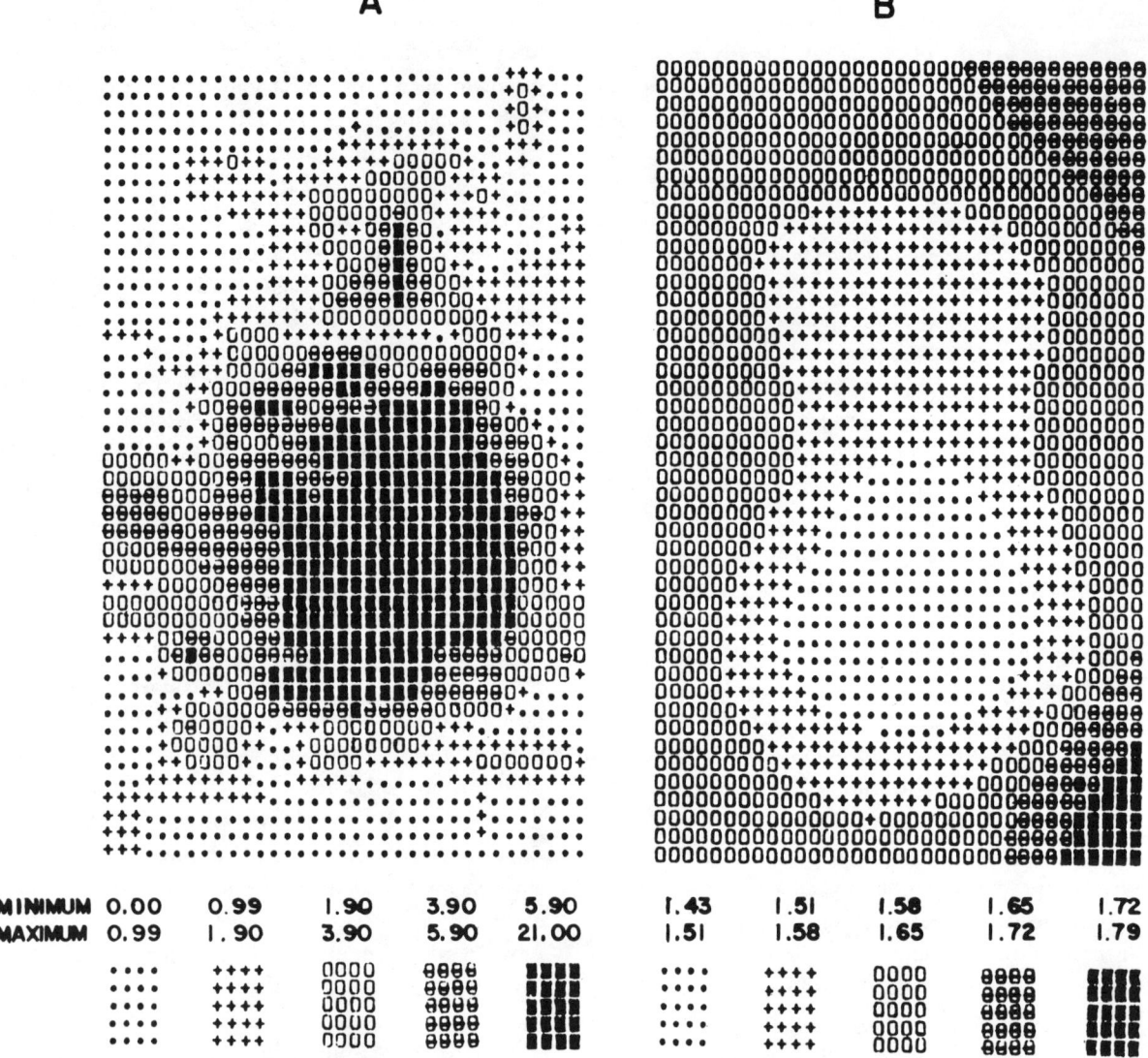

Figure 6.2. Spatial variation in ^{40}K at Cold Water Farm (A), compared to the distribution of artifacts (B). The ^{40}K distribution was determined by gamma spectrometry. The difference in resolution of the two maps arises from the sample nature of ^{40}K data, contrasting with the continuous coverage for artifacts.

simply by measuring the radioactivity of each component and calculating its contribution to the TL of the sample.

Partly in consequence of the desire to simplify estimates of the environmental dose and partly because of the view that buried samples are somehow more "pristine" than materials found on the surface, conventional wisdom has sought dating samples that were buried at least 30cm deep (see Aitken 1985:264). This prejudice is misplaced. Almost all archaeological materials were originally deposited on the surface, and they remain at or near the surface unless covered by natural or artificial deposits at a later, unspecified, date. Thus buried artifacts have more complex environmental histories than those that have remained on the surface since deposition (Dunnell and Dancey 1983). Of course some surface deposits have been buried and then later uncovered by erosion, but this is usually a readily detectable condition. The time at which burial took place, or may have begun to have taken place, and the thickness of the overburden at any given time, are almost always unknown in precise terms, since it is dating such events that summons the use of TL dating in the first place.

Furthermore, even if a sample had been buried catastrophically at some known time in the past, the idea that measurements of the contemporary radioactivity of the sample matrix can be generalized to represent the entire time of burial is not well founded. This idea also ignores soil-formation processes and the illuviation and alluviation of ions, molecules, and even macroparticles. The downward translocation of clays, for example, is a typical soil-forming process and one that would directly influence the concentration of K, an important contributor to environmental radioactivity, because K is frequently part of the clay. Uranium compounds are frequently quite leachable under a wide range of conditions (Kabata-Pendias and Pendias 1984:19), and their gradual removal would have an important impact. In saturated settings leaching may be virtually complete. The point is not that x, y, and z soil-forming processes affect the relation between contemporary radioactivity and that which characterized the sample matrix in the past, but that such processes go on, are largely impossible to reconstruct, and act to make it difficult to estimate annual dose rates for buried samples. These kinds of concerns have gone largely unnoticed by both archaeologists and TL practitioners. Much to their credit, Lalou and Valladas (1989:246) explicitly recognize this class of problem and conclude: "The problem raised in "d" [soil formation processes], which is one of the most important, is quite impossible to solve definitely." Their only practical advice is to select samples that have not been subjected to such changes. This is not strictly possible, although samples from dry caves, extremely arid, and permanently frozen environments approach this ideal, because the absence of liquid water greatly retards chemical reactions and limits mechanical transport. Of course the vast bulk of potential samples will not originate in such environments.

It is in this respect that surficial samples may actually be preferable to buried materials. While it is true that calculations of the environmental dose are complicated by having to consider two environments (Figure 6.3), the atmospheric component is a constant for all intents and purposes over the range of the dating method. Furthermore, for items deposited on old surfaces, there are no uncertainties introduced by variable depths and timings of burial episodes. Even the difficulties introduced by the uncertainties of water saturation are reduced, as the surface moisture levels are largely controlled by the moisture capacity of the soil (in mesic environments again), something that can be measured and is less likely to be influenced by climatic factors such as changes in the water table.

In sum, then, the lion's share of error that arises in TL dating occurs in estimating the environmental dose, partly because of the number of different parameters that must be measured, and partly because we typically lack the means to estimate several of the parameters accurately. In general, however, these uncertainties are larger for buried samples, because of their complex and typically unknown histories, than for surficial samples. The only real way to avoid these errors is to employ single crystals, such as zircon and apatite, that because of high radioactivity are essentially self-dosing. While these techniques may be important in the future of TL dating, there are formidable problems that currently prevent their implementation (Aitken 1989:154).

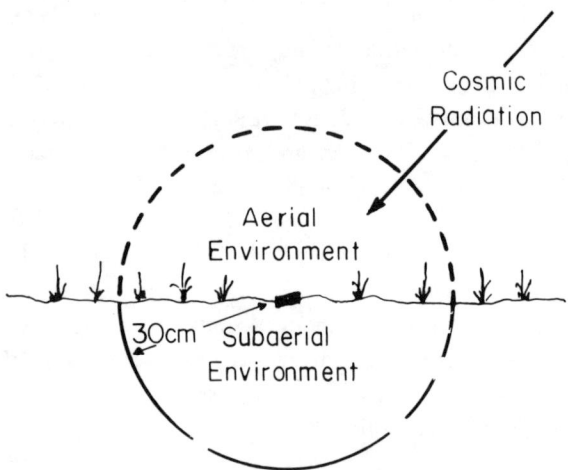

Figure 6.3. Schematic of the environments of surface samples.

TL Dating on the Malden Plain, Southeast Missouri

There is nothing inherent in TL dating that precludes its use with surface samples. As we have just argued, TL dating is particularly robust, because the event dated is typically and securely an archaeological event. Since TL dating does not require "good associations" for its use, it can play a major role in sorting surficial palimpsests into archaeologically meaningful components. Moreover surface samples are preferred, because many of the sources of imprecision attributable to estimating the environmental dose rate are minimized by the simplicity of their environmental history. The prejudice against dating surface artifacts is so deeply engrained in archaeological circles, however, that it is important to show that these arguments can be realized empirically. Our ongoing chronological work in southeast Missouri provides evidence of variable quality on two key points. (1) The agreement in age among sherds on the surface is at least as close as it is among buried sherds, when there is a reason to suppose that all of the sherds originate in a short set of historically related depositional events (for instance, low diversity in historical types, simple uninodal spatial distributions). (2) The difference in TL ages between surface and subsurface samples originating in the same depositional event are of the same order of magnitude as they are among surface sherds alone or subsurface sherds alone and generally lie within the range exhibited by multiple dates on the same object. Furthermore these outcomes are realized in typical archaeological contexts—very old surfaces in mesic climates that have been subjected to agricultural tillage for more than 150 years. While hardly constituting a definitive case in the present state of development, these demonstrations are consistent with the theoretical arguments advanced earlier.

The Malden Plain

The Malden Plain is a physiographic feature located in the central Mississippi Valley (Fisk 1944; Saucier 1974). At this point the Mississippi flows in a structural feature called the Mississippi embayment, which is 130 km wide. Today the Mississippi itself is situated along the eastern margin of the valley, adjacent to the loess-covered Paleozoic rocks of western Tennessee. The valley is divided along its north-south axis by a linear monadnock of Tertiary age, called Crowley's Ridge. In the Pleistocene the Mississippi flowed west of Crowley's Ridge, and the Ohio, which today joins the Mississippi at Cairo, Illinois, flowed east of the ridge. In terminal Pleistocene times, meltwater from the retreating glaciers first flushed most deposits from the valley and then, in its final stages, became a braided stream choked with sediment. The Mississippi and Ohio rivers assumed their present configuration during the late Pleistocene (Royall 1988). With higher sea level and more modest sediment loads, the Mississippi became a meandering stream and removed or reworked much of the sediment laid down by the Ohio east of Crowley's Ridge. The remaining Ohio sediments deposited east of the ridge are today exposed as the Malden Plain, a narrow strip abutting the east flank of Crowley's Ridge (Figure 6.4). The Malden Plain is bounded on the east by an erosional escarpment, representing the westward boundary of Mississippi's meandering.

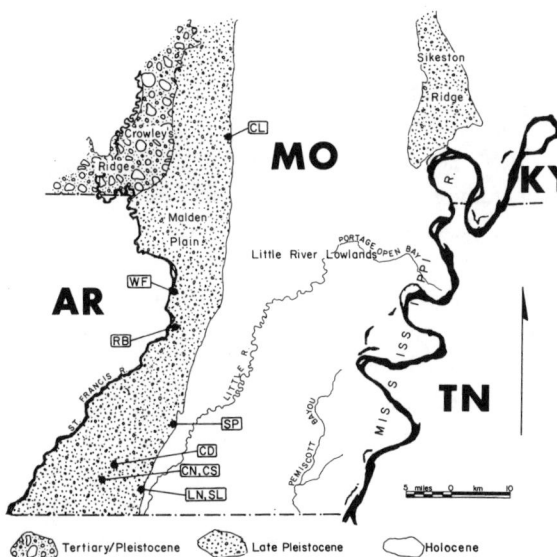

Figure 6.4. Central Mississippi Valley, showing the location of the study area.

The surface of the Malden Plain is latest Pleistocene/earliest Holocene in age. The loess of the late Pleistocene is absent, indicating that these deposits were not in place by 13,000 B.P. or so (see Guccione et al. 1988). Recently a well-preserved *Paleolama*, found by W. A. Long in the uppermost part of the braided-stream sands, has been dated by ^{14}C at 11,890 ± 130 B.P. (Morse, personal communication). There is an abundant megafauna, mostly elephants (*Mammut americanum*), in these sediments. At the time of European settlement in the middle of the nineteenth century, the Malden Plain was a series of seasonal islands, the former point bars of the braided stream surface, separated from the Mississippi River by a vast backswamp occupying the Mississippi meander belt. This swamp, along with the higher Malden Plain, was drained in the early years of this century, and today more than 90 percent of the surface is in agriculture (the remaining 10 percent being roads, drainage ditches, and buildings), bearing no resemblance to the environment before drainage (Anonymous 1989; Garrett et al. 1978).

The only deposition that has taken place on the Malden Plain since its formation has been the deposition of clay in the former channels of the braided-stream surface. Because the topography was created by much greater volumes of water than have been available since, these old "channels" became sloughs and swamps, choked, for the most part, with trees (such as *Nysssa aquatica, Taxodium distichum*) and other vegetation.

Malden Plain Chronology

In many respects this combination of circumstances represents ideal conditions for most kinds of archaeological research. Archaeologists have belatedly begun to realize that one cannot understand functioning systems that were spread out over landscapes from a few holes in some of the densest concentrations of artifacts. If the archaeological record is buried, our understanding of it is destined to be severely limited, because we can obtain only nominal data from excavations. The age of the Malden Plain is such, however, that virtually the entire archaeological record is exposed on the surface; only the very earliest occupation of the region is not so exposed. The current landuse of the region, row-crop agriculture, while damaging the record to a certain degree, also ensures virtually complete access to the record, particularly since drainage has meant that even areas formerly under water are now exposed for examination.

The major impediment to realizing the potential just described is the lack of a detailed chronology. Dating methods that rely upon association are useless. Because of the isolated character of the Malden Plain, it shares few styles with even nearby areas (Dunnell and Feathers 1991; Williams 1954), limiting the utility of typological "dating" (Cottier 1977; Price 1986; Wesler 1991). Even seriation has been of limited use, despite the fact that the Mississippi Valley is one of the heartlands of chronologies based on this method (Phillips et al. 1951). Vessel ceramics are not present much before A.D. 0 and are not abundant enough in assemblages to be of much use until A.D. 500 or so. Furthermore the pottery has few stylistic elements until relatively late.

It was for these reasons that we embarked upon the construction of a TL-based chronology. In addition to vessel ceramics, there are also Poverty Point objects (clay balls used as heating elements, manufactured "rocks" in this stoneless area) that go back at least to 5500 B.P. or so, occasional hunks of burned earth potentially even older, and a tradition of heat-treating lithics that probably begins with the earliest materials found on the surface of Malden Plain.

Much of our immediate effort has been devoted to the Late Woodland/Early Mississippian periods, the time of the emergence of maize-based agriculture. A particularly perplexing problem is the relationship between sand- and shell-tempered potteries, the "markers" for the two periods. The shift from one temper to the other apparently occurred before the shift to a specialized or focal maized-based economy (Lynott et al. 1986). The temper change is accompanied by a suite of other features as well, leading some (such as Morse and Morse 1983, 1990) to suppose that shell-tempered pottery marks a migration. We (Dunnell and Feathers 1986, 1991; Feathers 1990), on the other hand, have argued that technological consequences of the change in temper may well account for all or nearly all of the differences between the shell-tempered and sand-tempered potteries. Furthermore the early shell-tempered potteries have at least as much in common with the preceding sand-tempered potteries as they do with the succeeding, classic Middle Mississippian potteries. Thus it may well be that the sand-tempered/shell-tempered transition is a product of autochthonous evolution, rather than a replacement of cultural tradition. If we are correct, then we would expect that there would be some temporal overlap between the two potteries, albeit rather brief, given that strong selective advantages probably favored shell tempering in vessel formation, firing, and vessel use (Feathers 1990; Feathers and Scott 1989). Unfortunately the latest sand-tempered potteries and the earliest shell-tempered potteries do not occur in spatially segregated assemblages, as the people responsible were either the same or exploited the same niches from the same locations, inextricably mixing the two potteries on the ancient surface. Only a dating strategy that can directly assess the age of individual pieces of ceramics can provide the chronological detail essential to the resolution of this issue.

Equally ambiguous are the tempo and mode of the shift to agricultural economies and the ultimate fate of the specialized agriculturalists. Williams (1983, 1990) has proposed the so-called "vacant quarter hypothesis," in which a large portion of the central Mississippi Valley, including the Malden Plain, is abandoned before contact. This argument is based on the absence of late "marker" types in these areas. But the absence of particular styles, especially given the environmentally conditioned isolation of the Malden Plain, cannot be regarded as conclusive (see Lewis 1982; Wesler 1991). Again direct dating of artifacts is the only definitive way to solve the problem.

Attempts to answer these problems with ^{14}C dating have not been compelling. The need to associate carbon and artifacts has limited the use of this method on the ancient surface of the Malden Plain; the few dates that are available cannot be regarded as representative of either cultural or depositional contexts. Indeed the majority of available ^{14}C dates are from Zebree in northeastern Arkansas (Morse and Morse 1980, 1990).

While Zebree consisted of a churned midden with material representing several occupations, the excavators believed they could separate exclusively sand-tempered and exclusively shell-tempered occupations by dating charcoal associated with pottery in pit features. While some pits contained only sand-tempered ceramics, no pits contained shell-tempered pottery exclusively (Morse 1980). The excavators argued that the sand-tempered pottery in the dominantly shell-tempered associations was of secondary origin (and some of it surely must have been), on the basis of the smaller size of the sand-tempered sherds in these contexts, when compared with those features with only sand-tempered sherds (Anderson 1980). The Zebree ^{14}C dates show considerable temporal overlap between the sand- and shell-tempered groups, despite the sorting procedures described above (Table 6.1; Morse et al. 1980). The overlap was attributed to measurement error in dating. The obvious alternative is that there is a period of time during which both kinds of ceramics were in use.

As shown in Table 6.1, there are a few other ^{14}C dates from the Malden Plain, including a single date from a

Table 6.1. Woodland and Mississippian Radiocarbon Dates from the Malden Plain and Western Lowlands/Eastern Ozarks

Sample	Radiocarbon Age B.P.	Ceramic Association	Maximum Age (A.D.)	Intercepts[a] (A.D.)	Minimum Age (A.D.)
Robards[b]					
RL-1418	1110 ± 130	sa/sh	780	900 902 953	1020
Mangrum[c]					
TX-3074	990 ± 60	sh	990	1021 1043 1105	1150
TX-3073	930 ± 50	sh	1024	1112 1150	1166
Zebree[d]					
SMU-414	1359 ± 74	sa[e]	611	657	763
SMU-415	1121 ± 70	sa[e]	780	890 920 942	991
SMU-432	1087 ± 84	sa[e]	783	980	1019
SMU-433	1140 ± 150	sh[e]	686	892 925 906	1210
SMU-443	1159 ± 61	sh[e]	785	886	963
SMU-445	1133 ± 67	sh[e]	810	893	982
SMU-453	1130 ± 69	sh[e]	810	894	985
SMU-411	1090 ± 54	sh[e]	890	968	1003
SMU-422	1032 ± 48	sh[e]	974	1006	1023
SMU-450	1022 ± 58	sh[e]	974	1012	1029
SMU-426	1002 ± 55	sh[e]	986	1018	1036
SMU-460	938 ± 67	sh[e]	1016	1040	1169
SMU-457	897 ± 60	sh[e]	1031	1160	1218
Lawhorn[e]					
M-1158	750 ± 150	sh	1160	1267	1387
M-1156	625 ± 150	sh	1260	1303 1362 1377	1430
M-1157	375 ± 150	sh	1410	1457	1660
Western Lowlands Sites[f]					
TX-3017	1291 ± 200	sh	560	686 754 757	980
TX-3608	1277 ± 87	sh	654	690 701 709 750 765	863
TX-3607	1218 ± 121	sh	660	777 793 799	980
TX-4090	1041 ± 95	sh	893	994	1148

[a]Stuiver and Reimer (1987).
[b]Dunnell (1982).
[c]Klinger (1982).
[d]Morse et al. (1980).
[e]Moselage (1962).
[f]Price (1986).

Table 6.2. Woodland and Mississippian Thermoluminescence Dates from the Malden Plain and Western Lowlands/Eastern Ozarks

Sample	Ceramic Association	Date
Robards[a]		
Alpha 1268	sa/early shell	A.D. 1040 ± 110
Western Lowlands/Eastern Ozarks[b]		
WU91a2	early shell	A.D. 645 ± 120
Alpha 884b	early shell	A.D. 730 ± 131
WU91a1	early shell	A.D. 755 ± 115
WU101n	early shell	A.D. 830 ± 120
WU91b2	early shell	A.D. 865 ± 105
Alpha 884a	early shell	A.D. 880 + 194

[a]Dunnell (1982).
[b]Price (1986).

pit feature at Robards Farm (Dunnell 1982), that pertain to the same transition as at Zebree, as do a suite of dates from the Western Lowlands and eastern Ozarks as well, both to the west of Crowley's Ridge (these areas are far more similar culturally to the Malden Plain than are remains in the Little River Lowlands, just east of the Malden Plain). Some TL dates are also available for the eastern Ozark localities, as well as a commercial TL date for Robards Farm (Table 6.2).

TL Dating of Malden Plain Surface Deposits

Conventional dating has not led to a comprehensive chronology for the Malden Plain, precisely because the great strength of the Malden Plain archaeological record, its exposure on the surface, also is its major liability. ^{14}C dating requires associations, minimally between a piece of charcoal and some archaeological material; such associations are not possible to extract from surface data. It was because of this that we turned to TL dating. This research was not designed to demonstrate the effectiveness of TL dating in the surface context; it was designed to construct a chronology. Nonetheless some of our results are instructive on this point.

Samples

Our dating efforts have ranged from the Late Archaic forward, but the bulk of concern has focused on the Late Woodland/Early Mississippian and later periods, and these are the data we employ here. We sampled nine locations (see Figure 6.4) that appeared on typological and distributional grounds (that is, single density node) to have the least temporal mixing (Feathers 1990). Later assemblages, however, typically have longer durations. The ceramics were separated into four groups, again on typological grounds, that are at least partly, if not largely, temporal. The "early" group is exclusively sand-tempered and also lacks stylistic markers considered late within sand-tempering, namely, a high frequency of cordmarked surfaces, patterned cordmarking, and folded rims (Dunnell and Feathers 1986, 1991). The second group consists of sand-tempered pottery from assemblages that exhibit the late markers. The third group consists of shell-tempered pottery that has a coarse, oxidized paste, with as much as 80 percent of the sherds being red-slipped on one or both surfaces. Red slipping in high frequency is characteristic of early shell-tempered assemblages throughout much of the Mississippi Valley (Emerson and Jackson 1985; Kreisa 1987; Marshall 1985); red slipping is a fairly minor decorative element in later pottery. The fourth and putatively latest group is composed of classic Middle Mississippian shell-tempered pottery, distinguished by a variety of specialty pastes, mostly shell-tempered, frequently fired in a reduction atmosphere, with handles, and with painted and incised decoration.

TL Results

Thus far 38 samples have been analyzed. Table 6.3 reports these dates as well as the plateau temperature range for each sample. Results with plateaus of less than 125°C are not generally considered reliable. It is apparent in this series, however, that results with no plateaus (Aitken 1989) or very small ones do not differ much or systematically (except for the very earliest samples) from those with good plateaus. Nonetheless, in order that our analysis be as unambiguous as possible, we have restricted ourselves to samples that display plateaus of at least 100°C (Table 6.4); Table 6.4 also supplies additional information (porosity and depth of burial).

The depth-of-burial column in these tables requires some explanation. It records the nominal depth used in calculating ages (see Figure 6.3). Only three samples, the bold-face entries, were actually recovered from a subsurface context; in these cases, depth of burial records the actual depth of sherds recovered from a subsurface pit feature that was excavated. These samples permit us to make unambiguous subsurface/surface contrasts. All other samples were recovered from the surface of tilled fields. One can, however, readily distinguish those sherds that have recently (a few months or years) arrived at the surface from the base of the plowzone from those that have been long-term residents of the plowzone and which could have originated anywhere from the literal surface to the base of the plowzone (Dunnell and Simek 1994). For the former, set in italics in Table 6.4, depth of burial is an accurate measurement of the sample burial depth until recently. In these cases an error of less than 5 cm is indicated, as these fields have been plowed for 100 years or more, and the plowzones are quite mature.

For the remainder of the sherds, the assigned depths of burial represent half the thickness of the plowzone at the find locations. There is no way to know where the actual surface(s) they represent lay with respect to the modern surface before plowing, except to say that it occurred within the modern plowzone. The sherds may have been on the surface (heavily vegetated, of course) until initial tillage between 100 and 150 years ago, or they may have been buried, largely by organic material constituting the O and A soil horizons, to a maximum depth of 20 cm. Analysis of the size distribution of sherds at these localities shows the probability of deep burial to be remote (Dunnell and Simek 1994). The error involved in using the midpoint of the plowzone is thus no more than 10 cm at the maximum and probably much less in most cases. Again it should be emphasized that this uncertainty is much smaller than that which must attend most buried samples, with their complex depositional histories. Additional technical data on the technique employed and on the specific analyses can be found in Feathers (1990).

Discussion

A number of preliminary observations on Table 6.3 bear upon the utility of TL dating in these contexts. First, the general chronological order of the four groups of sherds is clearly confirmed: the early sand-tempered group has a mean dating of A.D. 805 ± 28.2; the late sand-tempered group has a mean of A.D. 882.4 ± 103.2; the early shell-tempered group has a mean of A.D. 1098.9 ± 208.3; and the late shell-tempered group has a mean of A.D. 1397.5 ± 124.6. Of course nothing more should be read into the means or standard deviations, inasmuch as variable numbers of localities, each of variable duration or "purity," were aggregated using "markers" of unknown but variable duration, to make up each group. Nonetheless these results do give some confidence that the TL analyses are indeed delivering chronological information at some scale. The second observation to be made from these data is that while the dates for the early shell-tempered pottery and the sand-tempered pottery do overlap, the

Table 6.3. University of Washington Woodland and Mississippian
Thermoluminescence Dates from the Malden Plain

Sample[a]	Date	Plateau[d]
Sand-Tempered		
CN 427	A.D. 662 ± 125	325–375
CN 421	A.D. 708 ± 109	300–375
CN 420	A.D. 774 ± 123	325–425
CN 249-8	A.D. 782 ± 83	325–450
SP 47	A.D. 803 ± 114	300–425
SP 56	A.D. 828 ± 109	300–425
CS 426	A.D. 839 ± 87	250–425
CN 261-4	A.D. 930 ± 87	none
CN 223-9	A.D. 1004 ± 70	300–375
Late Sand-Tempered		
WF 5	A.D. 762 ± 96	225–425
RB 825-24	A.D. 789 ± 108	325–425
CD 79	A.D. 895 ± 86	300–375
CD 80	A.D. 901 ± 84	225–375
WF 4	A.D. 907 ± 87	350–425
SL 21-1[b]	A.D. 978 ± 93	300–425
SL 26-2[b]	A.D. 982 ± 107	300–400
Early Shell-Tempered		
WF 3	A.D. 203 ± 175	350–425
RB 3517	A.D. 789 ± 156	250–425
RB 3518	A.D. 834 ± 152	300–400
WF 6	A.D. 1066 ± 84	325–450
CD 82	A.D. 1074 ± 75	275–400
RB 825-35	A.D. 1108 ± 79	325–400
RB 825-64	A.D. 1147 ± 125	250–300
RB 825-38	A.D. 1156 ± 96	none
WF 1	A.D. 1210 ± 75	300–400
RB 825-62	A.D. 1261 ± 94	275–425
WF 2	A.D. 1272 ± 57	225–400
RB 825-47	A.D. 1316 ± 74	275–425
Late Shell-Tempered		
LN 884-1[c]	A.D. 1058 ± 105	350–425
LN 1094-1	A.D. 1233 ± 51	250–400
LN 1088	A.D. 1322 ± 51	250–400
CL 347-8[b]	A.D. 1325 ± 92	325–425
LN 1092-3	A.D. 1327 ± 48	275–450
CL 179[b]	A.D. 1370 ± 83	250–375
LN 1092-2	A.D. 1379 ± 46	300–400
CL 179-3	A.D. 1483 ± 41	none
CL 179-7	A.D. 1511 ± 51	250–375
LN 1090	A.D. 1609 ± 34	250–450

[a]Samples are designated by location and sherd number: CN = Cold Water North, CS = Cold Water South, SP = South Pelts, SL = South Langdon, WF = Woodall Farm, RB = Robards Farm, CD = Cude, LN = Langdon, and CL = County Line.
[b]minimum age; fading not measured and/or corrected.
[c]daub, not vessel ceramic.

Table 6.4. Porosity and Depth Data for Table 6.3 Dates, with 100°C or Better Plateaus

Sample[a]	Date	Depth	Porosity[b]
Sand-Tempered			
CN 420	A.D. 774 ± 123	0.20m	16.2%
CN 249-8	A.D. 782 ± 83	0.20m	12.7%
SP 47	A.D. 803 ± 114	0.10m	11.5%
SP 56	A.D. 828 ± 109	0.10m	12.5%
CS 426	A.D. 839 ± 87	0.20m	14.0%
Late Sand-Tempered			
WF 5	A.D. 762 ± 96	0.10m	10.3%
RB 825-24	A.D. 789 ± 108	0.50m	12.7%
CD 80	A.D. 901 ± 84	0.20m	12.1%
SL 21-1	A.D. 978 + 93	0.10m	10.3%
SL 21-2	A.D. 982 ± 107	0.10m	11.7%
Early Shell-Tempered			
RB 3517	A.D. 758 ± 156	0.10m	22.5%
RB 3518	A.D. 834 ± 152	0.10m	25.8%
WF 6	A.D. 1066 ± 84	0.10m	26.6%
CD 82	A.D. 1074 ± 75	0.20m	28.8%
WF 1	A.D. 1210 ± 75	0.10m	31.6%
RB 825-62	A.D. 1261 ± 94	0.50m	64.1%
WF 2	A.D. 1272 ± 57	0.10m	24.4%
RB 825-47	A.D. 1316 ± 74	0.50m	62.7%
Late Shell-Tempered			
LN 1094-1	A.D. 1233 ± 51	0.20m	14.0%
LN 1088	A.D. 1322 ± 51	0.20m	20.8%
CL 347-8	A.D. 1325 ± 92	0.07m	29.3%
LN 1092-3	A.D. 1327 ± 48	0.20m	15.3%
CL 179	A.D. 1370 ± 83	0.07m	19.8%
LN 1092-2	A.D. 1379 ± 46	0.20m	17.3%
CL 179-7	A.D. 1511 ± 51	0.07m	25.8%
LN 1090	A.D. 1609 ± 34	0.20m	14.1%

[a]See Table 6.3 for locality designations.
[b]Porosity is apparent porosity, measured as percent water absorption: saturated weight less dry weight, divided by dry weight.

means are over two hundred years apart, not particularly favorable to an *in situ* development hypothesis, though certainly not falsifying it either.

If we rearrange the data by locality rather than by pottery type (Table 6.5), other instructive patterns are apparent. Where multiple dates from the same locality are available, there is remarkably low variance between dates for particular localities early in the sequence, quite the opposite of what one might expect on the basis of the error terms for the individual dates. While there is some correlation between the number of dates and the variance, this is hardly plausible as an explanation, inasmuch as the variance *characteristic* of the early dates cannot be readily matched, even by picking pairs of dates from the later assemblages.

To an important degree, the variance may reflect duration of occupation. There is, for example, good evidence that the Woodall Farm site (WF) has at least two discrete occupations, one in the Late Woodland/Early Mississippian period and one substantially later, in the

Table 6.5. Means and Standard Deviations for Age and Porosity, by Locality

Locality/Dates	Depth	Temper	Assemblage	Porosity
Cold Water Farm North (CN)			all sa	
774 ± 123	0.20m	sa		16.2%
782 + 83	0.10m	sa		*12.7%*
A.D. 778.0 ± 5.7				14.5 ± 2.5%
South Pelts (SP)			all sa	
803 ± 114	0.10m	sa		11.5%
828 ± 109	0.10m	sa		*12.5%*
A.D. 815.5 + 17.7				12.0 ± 0.7%
South Langdon (SL)			sa/sh	
978 ± 93	0.10m	sa		10.3%
982 ± 107	0.10m	sa		*11.7%*
A.D. 980.0 ± 2.8				11.0 ± 1.0%
Cude Cemetery (CD)			sa/sh	
901 ± 84	0.20m	sa		12.1%
1074 ± 107	0.20m	sh		*28.9%*
A.D. 987.5 ± 112.3				20.5 ± 11.8%
Robards Farm (RB)			sa/sh	
758 ± 156	0.10m	sh		15.4%
789 ± 108	0.50m	sa		12.7%
834 ± 152	0.10m	sh		25.8%
1261 ± 94	0.50m	sh		64.1%
1316 ± 74	0.50m	sh		*62.7%*
A.D. 991.6 ± 273.1				36.1 ± 25.4%
Woodall Farm (WF)			sa/sh	
762 ± 96	0.10m	sa		10.3%
1066 ± 84	0.10m	sh		26.6%
1210 ± 75	0.10m	sh		31.6%
1271 ± 57	0.10m	sh		*24.4%*
A.D. 1077.5 ± 227.3				23.2 ± 9.1%
Langdon (LN)			sh	
1233 ± 51	0.20m	sh		14.0%
1322 ± 51	0.20m	sh		20.8%
1327 ± 48	0.20m	sh		15.3%
1379 ± 46	0.20m	sh		17.3%
1609 ± 34	0.20m	sh		*14.1%*
A.D. 1374 ± 141.5				16.3 ± 2.9%
County Line (CL)			sh	
1325 ± 92	0.07m	sh		29.3%
1370 ± 83	0.07m	sh		19.8%
1511 ± 51	0.07m	sh		*25.8%*
A.D. 1402 ± 97.0				25.0% ± 4.8%

Middle Mississippian, on typological grounds. Strap handles, classic Mississippian pipes, and reduced, unslipped, shell-tempered pottery are present at Woodall Farm but do not occur in Late Woodland/Early Mississippian assemblages elsewhere. Thus a bimodal distribution, one involving only shell-tempered pottery and the other involving both shell-tempered and sand-tempered pottery (assuming no secondary heating), might be expected. The four dates are, of course, inadequate to demonstrate such modality, but they are consistent with it. The Cude (CD) locality was supposed on the basis of distributional studies to represent a single Late Woodland/Early Mississippian occupation, but more recent work indicates that there may have been discrete Woodland and Mississippian occupations, albeit probably not separated by a large amount of time. This might well account for the somewhat greater separation of its two dates.

Likewise Langdon is known on typological grounds to represent a long span of occupation during the Mississippian, so that the array of dates is compatible with other archaeological evidence. County Line (CL), on the other hand, represents a shorter, but still probably substantial, period of occupation toward the later end of the Langdon occupation (see Teltser 1988). Again the typological evidence is in accord with the TL assessments. The Robards (RB) locality, however, is not so clear-cut. Only a handful of artifacts recovered during more than 10 years of work suggest any occupation at all after the Late Woodland/Early Mississippian period. Thus to the extent known, the variance in dates can be rather directly accounted for in terms of duration of occupation; the only clear exception is represented by the Robards dates.

Inspection of the Robards data points to an interesting correlation: there are two modes, an early group of three dates (which are more or less compatible with the single ^{14}C date of 1110 ± 130 B.P. and the Alpha Analytic TL date of 910 ± 110 B.P.) and two other dates that are nearly 500 years later. Both of the later dates are on remarkably porous sherds, suggesting a reason to regard these dates as potentially anomalous. This potential correlation with porosity also prompted a general examination of the relationship between porosity and age. Since the "true" ages of the samples are unknowable, we cannot look at the relationship of porosity to "error" of the mean; however, if error is arising as a consequence of porosity, it should be reflected in a correlation between the standard deviation of mean assemblage porosity and the standard deviation of the age itself. A fairly strong correlation does exist (Figure 6.5), with a Pearson's r or 0.8205. Porosity definitely merits further investigation.

IMPLICATIONS FOR THE USE OF TL IN THE SURFACE CONTEXT

Before taking up possible causes of the relationship between porosity, age, and potential error, we should note that Table 6.4 gives no evidence whatsoever of any relationship between age and surface or subsurface provenance. Both Robards and Cold Water Farm North (CN) provide comparisons between surface- and subsurface-derived samples; in both cases the surface and subsurface dates agree quite closely. Indeed the two problematic Robards dates are on sherds excavated from a subsurface pit representing the ideal (burial at the time of deposit, constant depth since then greater than 0.30 m). Likewise the variance among surface samples from the same location is less than half (79.7 ± 90.2 years vs. 184.5 ± 91.6 years) that of the subsurface samples, although the surface samples are the ones compromised by occupation duration. On these grounds any misgivings about using surface samples should be dispelled.

TL practitioners have traditionally avoided the use of surface samples because of what they supposed would be an uncertainty in the gamma- and cosmic-ray contributions to the annual dose. As noted earlier the simplest context is one in which the sample is surrounded by a uniform matrix. In these circumstances gamma absorption is equal in all directions and the sample is deep enough to treat the cosmic-ray contribution as negligible (Aitken 1985:70–74). As we argued earlier, this is a naive position that fails to take into account the facts that: (1) virtually all deposits are originally on the surface; (2) soil forming processes, the water table, and natural and culturally modified stratigraphy preclude

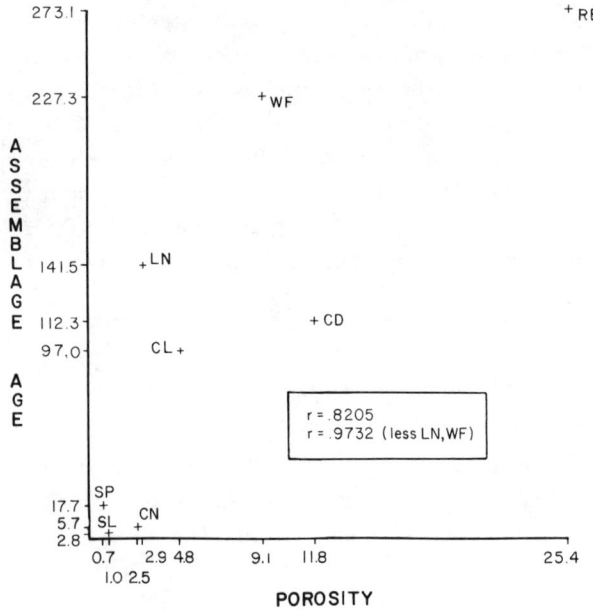

Figure 6.5. Relation of variability in porosity and variability in mean age.

where diffusion is slower and back diffusion more probable. Loss of radon would create a disequilibrium that violates the assumptions used when calculating the dose from contemporary measurements. Again our research does not suggest that radon loss at the surface is measurably different from that in the ground; the consistency between buried and surface samples and among different surface samples from the same locations does not suggest any disequilibrium problems associated with the surface.

It is likely, however, that disequilibrium problems do affect the results reported here. As the dates listed in Table 6.1 show, the TL dates for sand-tempered pottery compare favorably, although they are perhaps younger than anticipated, with ^{14}C dates for similar material at Zebree and elsewhere in the central Mississippi Valley, including the date from the Robards Farm Pit feature that produced most of the TL-dated pottery from that locality. The early shell-tempered pottery is at considerable variance with the ages assigned to this pottery elsewhere on the basis of ^{14}C dates, and its close association on the Malden Plain with the late sand-tempered pottery. While the late shell-tempered dates are possible, they seem overly late. Of course resolution of the vacant-quarter hypothesis is heavily dependent on accurate late dates.

A partial investigation of disequilibrium in six sherds (Feathers 1993) revealed that decay chains in the pottery are in disequilibrium. Although the precise locations of the disequilibria were not determined directly, the daughters in the ^{238}U chain appear enriched relative to the parent, and the daughters in the ^{232}Th chain appear to be depleted. Circumstantially depletion in the ^{232}Th chain is most likely caused by chemical leaching of ^{228}Ra, the only relatively mobile nuclide with a sufficient half-life. Enrichment in the ^{238}U chain is most likely caused by the precipitation of ^{230}Th after the more soluable uranium parents (^{238}U and ^{234}U) have been lost to leaching (Readhead 1984). Some radon and radium loss has probably occurred as well, but it clearly is negligible, compared to leaching. Sherd porosity, in increasing the surface area of samples exposed to interaction with the soil solution, would be expected to be correlated with the effectiveness of leaching. While

the realization of the "homogeneous" matrix condition; and (3) soil forming processes continually change the composition of the sediments surrounding a sample. Thus surficial samples are, all other things being equal, likely to be attended by less uncertainty, not more, in regard to their radiation histories than buried samples. For depths of less than 0.30 m, the traditional cutoff point for TL samples, corrections can be made for the gamma-ray dose (Aitken 1985:72, Appendix H). These procedures have been employed in calculating the dates reported here; the consistency observed between dates for the same localities, regardless of surface or subsurface context, attests to their effectiveness.

Another concern has been that disequilibrium in the uranium and thorium decay chains might occur more readily at the surface (Aitken 1985). Radon (primarily ^{226}Rn in the ^{238}U chain, with a half-life of 3.82 days, and ^{220}Rn in the ^{232}Th chain, with a half-life of 55 seconds), although very short-lived, is more likely to escape from a sample before decaying into a less mobile product through diffusion in air than in the ground,

Table 6.6. Disequilibrium Data and Corrections

Sample	% From Equilibrium[a]		Age (A.D.)[b]	
	^{238}U	^{232}Th	Uncorrected	Corrected
Sand-Tempered				
CF 420	39.5	4.3	774	624
SP 56	73.0	23.5	828	517
Late Sand-Tempered				
CD 80	26.5	26.5	901	826
Early Shell-Tempered				
RB 825-62	180.5	10.5	1261	921
WF 6	66.2	33.4	1066	842
Late Shell-Tempered				
LN 1092-3	99.4	46.4	1327	1175

[a]Calculated by subtracting the activity of the entire chain, as determined by alpha counting, from the activity of the parent, as determined by ICP source mass spectrometry (Feathers 1991), dividing this difference by the activity of the parent, and multiplying by 100.

[b]Uncorrected ages are from Table 6.3. Corrected ages are recalculated assuming that all the disequilibrium in the ^{238}U chain is contributed by the enrichment of ^{230}Th and ignoring any disequilibrium in the ^{232}Th chain.

the sedimentary environment, relation to water table, preferential location of specific ions in grains (that is, near the surfaces), and perhaps composition, as well as absolute age, have a bearing on the effects of leaching, the large differences in porosity seen among samples make this parameter dominant in the case at hand.

Assuming that all disequilibria observed are caused in the manner outlined above, it is possible to recalculate the ages for the six sherds for which parent/daughter data exist. Table 6.6 shows the amount of disequilibrium in each sample and the recalculated age. The more porous sherds are also those with the greatest disequilibria ($r = 0.6416$). While not terribly strong, the correlation between porosity and amount of disequilibrium is a very strong $r = 0.9495$ when one sample, that from South Pelts (SP), is dropped (Figure 6.6). Thus sherd porosity appears to be the dominant factor in all but one sample. It should be noted that the South Pelts sherds are indicative of different diagenetic processes; nearly all are coated with iron-manganese deposits, some nearly enveloped with these concretionary growths. Such structures typically form in horizons that are repeatedly subject to saturation, conditions that would accelerate the leaching of solubles. The recalculated ages are all in good accord with ^{14}C estimates of the sand/shell-temper transition and other temporal indicators.

Summary

The Malden Plain, while offering otherwise remarkable research opportunities, is a chronological nightmare, because of the absence of deposition in the Holocene and the homogenizing effects of tillage on the surficial record. It represents a realistic rather than idealistic set of conditions under which to examine the efficacy of TL dating of surface materials. Although the work described here is still in progress, and the sample size is quite small, the patterns are sufficiently strong as to warrant some clear conclusions. The agreement between dates on materials from surface and subsurface contexts precludes any general problem with surface samples; they yield dates that are at least as consistent

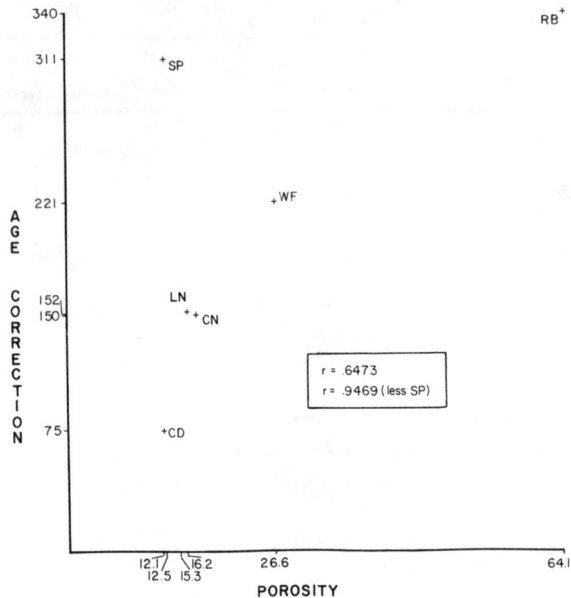

Figure 6.6. Relation of the amount of disequilibrium and sample porosity.

among themselves as are those on subsurface samples. There is no correlation between sample context (surface/subsurface) and disequilibrium. Indeed the major problem detected in this suite of dates relates to disequilibria in decay chains introduced by sample porosity and consequent leaching.

TL dating is clearly capable of resolving the chronological issues posed by this research, even if our work has not progressed to the final answers.

Acknowledgments

We would like to express our appreciation to the several landowners who gave us permission to collect samples, most especially to W. L. Davidson (deceased), E. D. Langdon (deceased), and T. York, as well as to the tenents who farmed the land. We are also endebted to C. Hostetler, who generously allowed us to study his collections from Woodall Farm and who assisted in the collection of the TL samples from that locality. The TL analysis was partly supported by NSF grant BN-58504394A02, to T. G. Stoebe and the senior author, and by the University of Washington Graduate School Research Fund, to the senior author. M. L. Readhead, postdoctoral research associate employed under the NSF grant, developed most of the dating protocols employed in this study and supervised much of the actual work. M. D. Dunnell and C. Beck made valuable editorial suggestions. To all of these people and any we may have inadvertantly omitted, we are deeply grateful.

References Cited

Aitken, M. J.
1985 *Thermoluminescence Dating.* Academic Press, London.
1989 Luminescence Dating: A Guide for Non-Specialists. *Archaeometry* 31:147–59.

Aitken, M. J., and S. J. Fleming
1972 Thermoluminescence Dosimetry in Archaeological Dating. In *Topics in Radiation Dosimetry,* edited by F. H. Attix, pp. 1–78. Academic Press, New York.

Anderson, D. G.
1980 Post-Depositional Modification of the Zebree Behavioral Record. In *Zebree Archeological Project,* edited by D. F. Morse and P. A. Morse, chapter 8. Report submitted to the Memphis District, U.S. Army Corps of Engineers, by the Arkansas Archeological Survey, Fayetteville.

Anonymous
1989 *The Little River Drainage District of Southeast Missouri, 1907–Present.* Little River Drainage District, Cape Girardeau.

Callaghan, R. T.
1986 Analysis of Fluouride Content of Human Remains from the Gray Site, Saskatchewan. *Plains Anthropologist* 31: 317–328.

Chen, R., and S. G. E. Bowman
1978 Superlinear Growth of Thermoluminescence Due to Competition During Irradiation. *PACT* 2:216–232.

Cottier, J. W.
1977 Radiocarbon Dates from the Lilbourn Site and a Check List of Dates from the Eastern Lowlands of Southeast Missouri. *The Missouri Archaeologist* 38:308–314.

Dean, J. S.
1978 Independent Dating in Archaeological Analysis. In *Advances in Archaeological Method and Theory*, edited by M.B. Schiffer, vol. 1, pp. 223–255. Academic Press, New York.

Dunnell, R. C.
1981 Seriation, Groups, and Measurements. In *Manejos de Datos y Métodos Matemáticos de Arqueología*, edited by G. L. Cowgill, R. Whallon, and B. S. Ottaway, pp. 67–90. Unión Internacional de Ciencias Prehistoricas y Protohistóricas, Mexico City.
1982 Current Research, Missouri. *American Antiquity* 47:225–226.

Dunnell, R. C., and W. S. Dancey
1983 The Siteless Survey: A Regional Data Collection Strategy. In *Advances in Archaeological Method and Theory*, vol. 6, edited by M. B. Schiffer, pp. 267–287. Academic Press, New York.

Dunnell, R. C., and J. K. Feathers
1986 Later Woodland Manifestations of the Malden Plain, Southeast Missouri. Paper presented at Southeastern Archaeological Conference, October 16–18, Nashville.
1991 Later Woodland Manifestations of the Malden Plain, Southeast Missouri. In *Late Woodland Stability, Transformation, and Variation in the Greater Southeast*, edited by M. S. Nassaney and C. R. Cobb, pp. 21–45. Plenum, New York.

Dunnell, R. C., and M. L. Readhead
1988 The Relation of Dating and Chronology: Comments on Chatters and Hoover (1986) and Butler and Stein (1988). *Quaternary Research* 39:232–233.

Dunnell, R. C., and J. F. Simek
1994 Artifact Size and Plowzone Process. *Journal of Field Archaeology*, in press.

Emerson, T. E., and D. K. Jackson
1985 The Edelhardt and Lindeman Phases: Setting the Stage for the Final Transition to Mississippian in the American Bottom. In *The Emergent Mississippian*, edited by R. A. Marshall, pp. 172–193. Proceedings of the Sixth Mid-South Archaeological Conference, Cobb Institute of Archaeology, Mississippi State University. Occasional Paper 87-01.

Feathers, J. K.
1990 *Explaining the Evolution of Prehistoric Ceramics in Southeast Missouri*. Ph.D. dissertation, University of Washington, Seattle. University Microfilms, Ann Arbor.
1993 Thermoluminescence Dating of Pottery From Southeastern Missouri and the Problem of Radioactive Disequilibrium. *Archeomaterials* 7:3–20.

Feathers, J. K., and W. D. Scott
1989 Prehistoric Ceramic Composite from the Mississippi Valley. *Ceramic Bulletin* 68:554–557.

Fisk, H. N.
1944 *Geological Investigation of the Alluvial Valley of the Lower Mississippi River*. Mississippi River Commission, Publication 52. Vicksburg.

Garrett, J. D., F. P. Allgood, B. L. Brown, R. B. Grossman, and C. L. Schivner
1978 *Soils of Southeast Missouri*. Extension Division, University of Missouri, Columbia.

Guccione, M. J., R. H. Lafferty III, and L. S. Cummings
1988 Environmental Constraints of Human Settlement in an Evolving Holocene Alluvial System, The Lower Mississippi Valley. *Geoarchaeology* 3:65–84.

Huntley, D. J.
1976 Thermoluminescence as a Potential Means of Dating Siliceous Ocean Sediments. *Canadian Journal of Earth Sciences* 13:593–596.

Ikeya, M.
1978 Electron Spin Resonance as a Method of Dating. *Archaeometry* 20:147–158.

Jones, G. T., and C. Beck

1992 Chronological Resolution in Distributional Archaeology. In *Place, Time, and Archaeological Landscapes,* edited by L. A. Wandsnider and J. Rossignol, pp. 167–192. Plenum, New York.

Kabata-Pendias, A., and H. Pendias
1984 *Trace Elements in Soils and Plants.* CRC Press, Boca Raton.

Klinger, T. C.
1982 *Mangrum.* Arkansas Archeological Survey, Research Series, No. 20. Fayetteville.

Kreisa, P. P.
1987 Late Prehistoric Settlement Patterns in the Big Bottoms of Fulton County, Kentucky. In *Current Archaeological Research in Kentucky,* 1, edited by D. Pollack, pp. 78–99. Kentucky Heritage Council, Frankfort.

Lalou, C., and G. Valladas
1989 Thermoluminescence Dating. In *Nuclear Methods of Dating,* edited by E. Roth and B. Poty, pp. 235–273. Kluwer Academic Publishers, Dortrecht

Lewarch, D. E., and M. J. O'Brien
1981 The Expanding Role of Surface Assemblages in Archaeological Research. In *Advances in Archaeological Method and Theory,* vol. 4, edited by M. B. Schiffer, pp. 297–342. Academic Press, New York.

Lewis, R. B.
1982 *Two Mississippian Hamlets: Cairo Lowland, Missouri.* Special Publication No. 2, Illinois Archaeological Survey, Urbana.

Lynott, M. J., T. W. Boutton, J. E. Price, and D. E. Nelson
1986 Stable Carbon Isotopic Evidence for Maize Agriculture in Southeast Missouri and Northeast Arkansas. *American Antiquity* 51:51–56.

Marshall, R. A.
1985 A Brief Comparison of Two Emergent Mississippian Substage Settlement Patterns in Southeast Missouri and Northwest Mississippi. In *The Emergent Mississippian,* edited by R. A. Marshall, pp. 160–166. Proceedings of the Sixth Mid-South Archaeological Conference, Cobb Institute of Archaeology, Mississippi State University, Occasional Papers 87–01.

McCutcheon, P. T.
n.d. Thermoluminescent Analysis of Burned Bone: Assessing the Problems. Manuscript in possession of the authors.

Morse, D. F.
1980 Stratigraphy and Seriation. In *Zebree Archeological Project,* edited by D. F. Morse and P. A. Morse, chapter 10. Report submitted to the Memphis District, U.S. Army Corps of Engineers, by the Arkanses Archaeological Survey, Fayetteville

Morse, D. F., and P. A. Morse
1980 *Zebree Archeological Project.* Report submitted to the Memphis District, U.S. Army Corps of Engineers, by the Arkansas Archaeological Survey, Fayetteville.
1983 *Archaeology of the Central Mississippi Valley.* Academic Press, New York.
1990 Emergent Mississippian in the Central Mississippi Valley. In *The Mississippian Emergence,* edited by B. D. Smith, pp. 153–173. Smithsonian Institution Press, Washington, D.C.

Morse, D. F., D. Wolfman, and H. Hass
1980 Radiocarbon Dating. In *Zebree Archeological Project,* edited by D. F. Morse and P. A. Morse, chapter 11. Report submitted to the Memphis District, U.S. Army Corps of Engineers, by the Arkansas Archeological Survey, Fayetteville.

Moselage, J. H.
1962 The Lawhorn Site. *Missouri Archaeologist* 24.

Phillips, P., J. A. Ford, and J. B. Griffin
1951 *Archaeological Survey in the Lower Mississippi Alluvial Valley, 1940–1947.* Papers of the Peabody Museum of American Archaeology and Ethnology, Harvard University, vol. 25. Cambridge, Mass.

Poupeau, G., and A. M. Rossi
1989 Electron Spin Resonance Dating. In *Nuclear Methods of Dating,* edited by E. Roth and B. Poty, pp. 275–293. Kluwer Academic Publish-

Price, J. E.
1986 Emergent Mississippian Occupation in the Southeastern Ozarks of Missouri. Paper presented at the 51st Annual Meeting of the Society for American Archaeology, New Orleans.

Readhead, M. L.
1984 *Thermoluminescence Dating of Some Australian Sedimentary Deposits.* Unpublished Ph.D. dissertation, Department of Physics, Australian National University, Canberra.

Royall, P. D.
1988 *Late-Quaternary Paleoecology and Paleoenvironments of the Western Lowlands, Southeast, Missouri.* Unpublished M. A. Thesis, Department of Geology, University of Tennessee, Knoxville.

Saucier, R. T.
1974 *Quaternary Geology of the Lower Mississippi Valley.* Arkansas Archaeological Survey, Research Series, No. 6. Fayetteville.

Schiffer, M. B.
1987 *Formation Processes of the Archaeological Record.* University of New Mexico Press, Albuquerque.

Stuiver, M., and P. J. Reimer
1987 *User's Guide to the Programs CALIB and DISPLAY 2.1.* Quaternary Isotope Lab, University of Washington, Seattle.

Teltser, P. A.
1988 *The Mississippian Archaeological Record of the Malden Plain, Southeast Missouri: Local Variation in Evolutionary Perspective.* Ph.D. dissertation, University of Washington, Seattle. University Microfilms, Ann Arbor.

Tingle, M.
1987 Inferential Limits and Surface Scatters: The Case of Maddle Farm and the Vale of the White Horse Fieldwalking Survey. In *Lithic Analysis and Later British Prehistory,* edited by A. G. Brown and M R. Edmonds, pp. 87–99. BAR, British Series, 162. Oxford.

Wesler, K.
1991 Ceramics, Chronology and Horizon Markers at Wickliffe Mounds. *American Anitquity* 56:278–290.

Williams, S.
1954 *An Archaeological Study of the Mississippian Culture in Southeast Missouri.* Ph.D. dissertation, Yale University, New Haven. University Microfilms, Ann Arbor.
1983 Some Ruminations on the Current Strategy of Research in the Southeast. *Southeastern Archaeological Conference Bulletin* 21:72–81.
1990 The Vacant Quarter and Other Late Events in the Lower Valley. In *Towns and Temples along the Mississippi,* edited by D. H. Dye and C. A. Cox, pp. 170–180. University of Alabama Press, Tuscaloosa.

7
SURFACE EXPOSURE DATING WITH COSMOGENIC NUCLIDES

Mark D. Kurz and Edward J. Brook

Department of Marine Chemistry and Geochemistry
Woods Hole Oceanographic Institution
Woods Hole, Massachusetts

Abstract

Recent developments in accelerator mass spectrometry and noble gas mass spectrometry now allow precise analysis of cosmic-ray produced nuclides in terrestrial materials. Measurement of ^{3}He, ^{21}Ne, ^{10}Be, ^{26}Al, ^{14}C, and ^{41}Ca can be used to determine exposure ages, erosion rates, and burial histories of geological surfaces in favorable situations. The ability to measure surface exposure ages is of particular importance to many aspects of geology, geomorphology, and archeology. In order to calculate the exposure age for a terrestrial surface, the production rates must be well known, the sample must be a closed system for the isotope of interest, and the sample must have had a simple exposure to cosmic rays (no burial or cover). The production rates of all cosmogenic nuclides vary as a function of altitude, latitude, and time, and are critical to all applications; better calibrations of the production rates, by measurements of surfaces of known age, will be necessary to improve the accuracy and precision of surface exposure dating. No single cosmogenic nuclide is applicable to all dating situations; each has its own limitations, related to age of the materials, the half-life of the nuclide, the mineral phases present, and the difficulty of the measurements. Existing data also demonstrate that measurement of more than one cosmogenic nuclide, in the same samples, is extremely useful in evaluating the assumptions inherent to the technique. A number of recent studies demonstrate that surface exposure dating can provide age information for surfaces as young as several thousand years and as old as millions of years. Although many of the successful applications have been within the fields of glacial geology and geomorphology, the technique should also be extremely useful to other fields, such as archaeology. This chapter outlines the assumptions and uncertainties inherent to surface exposure dating with cosmogenic nuclides.

Introduction

ALTHOUGH USING COSMOGENIC NUCLIDES AS A means of dating terrestrial surfaces is not a new idea (see Davis and Schaeffer 1956), the method has received considerable attention recently. This is in large part due to the development of accelerator mass spectrometry (AMS) for the measurement of small amounts of cosmogenic radionuclides (for example, ^{10}Be, ^{26}Al, ^{36}Cl, ^{14}C), making it possible to apply this technique to the low levels found in terrestrial surfaces (see Elmore and Phillips 1987; Litherland 1987; Raisbeck et al. 1987). Prior to this development, dating using cosmogenic nuclides had been applied primarily to studies of meteorites and lunar samples, which are exposed to much higher cosmic-ray fluxes than exist at the earth's surface, and consequently have higher concentrations of cosmogenic nuclides (Eugster 1988; Honda and Arnold 1964; Mazor et al. 1970; Reedy et al. 1983; Vogt et al. 1990). In addition to the radiogenic nuclides mentioned above, two stable cosmogenic noble gas isotopes, ^{3}He and ^{21}Ne, have recently been detected in terrestrial surfaces using conventional noble gas mass spectrometers, instruments that are considerably less expensive than accelerator mass spectrometers (Craig and Poreda 1986; Graf et al. 1991; Kurz 1986a, 1986b; Marti and Craig 1987).

As a result of these technical advances, there are now a number of different cosmogenic nuclides that can be used for dating surfaces, each with its own set of advantages and disadvantages. These techniques have been applied primarily to geological surfaces, such as glacial moraines, striated bedrock, and lava flows, but could also be successfully applied to archeological artifacts and stone buildings. The purpose of this chapter is to review the various methods of using the different nuclides, to summarize the uncertainties that are common to all the methods, and to give several examples that illustrate both the potential and the limitations of the techniques. The emphasis here is on the use of ^{3}He, ^{10}Be, and ^{26}Al because these are the nuclides for which there is the most data, apart from ^{36}Cl which is discussed by Zreda and Phillips (chapter 8 of this volume). New methods based on *in situ* ^{14}C and ^{41}Ca are in development (Fink et al. 1990; Jull et al. 1991) and are discussed briefly.

Principles of Surface Exposure Dating with Cosmogenic Nuclides

The basic principle of surface exposure dating with cosmogenic nuclides is simple. Assuming that the cosmic-ray flux is constant with time, the concentration of accumulated cosmogenic nuclides within surficial rocks is directly related to the time the surface has been exposed. For the purpose of this article, the term "cosmogenic" is intended to refer to any nuclide that is produced by cosmic-ray particles. There are a number of different nuclear reactions that are important in the earth's atmosphere and at the earth's surface, including neutron capture, muon capture, and spallation. The dominant production mechanism within rocks in the top two meters of the earth is neutron-induced spallation, which is simply a collision of a cosmic-ray neutron with a target nucleus, resulting in the breaking apart of the nucleus into fragments. This process is illustrated graphically in Figure 7.1, which shows a spallation event in a photographic emulsion flown at high altitude. The energy threshold for spallation is typically 20 to 50 Mev, and the spallation cross sections are not strongly composition-dependent (because spallation is essentially a collision process). A list of the cosmogenic nuclides that have been most commonly used for surface exposure dating is given in Table 7.1. With the exception of ^{36}Cl, which has a significant production by neutron capture in some rocks (on ^{35}Cl, see Zreda and Phillips, chapter 8 of this volume), and ^{41}Ca, produced dominantly by thermal neutron capture in ^{40}Ca (Fink et al. 1990), spallation is the most important production mechanism for these nuclides. As discussed below there are many parameters that must be considered in calculating exposure ages, and the production rates and age ranges in Table 7.1 are only estimates to be used as general guidelines for the applicability of an isotope to a particular problem.

The basic equation necessary to derive an exposure age for a radioactive cosmogenic nuclide (N), with decay constant λ, relates the amount present in a surface to the processes of production and radioactive decay:

(1) dN/dt = production − loss by radioactive decay
$= P - N\lambda$

where P is the production rate (atoms/g/yr), N is isotope concentration (atoms/g), t is time (years), and λ is the decay constant (yr^{-1}). The solution to this equation is

(2) $$N = \frac{P}{\lambda}\left(1 - e^{-\lambda t}\right).$$

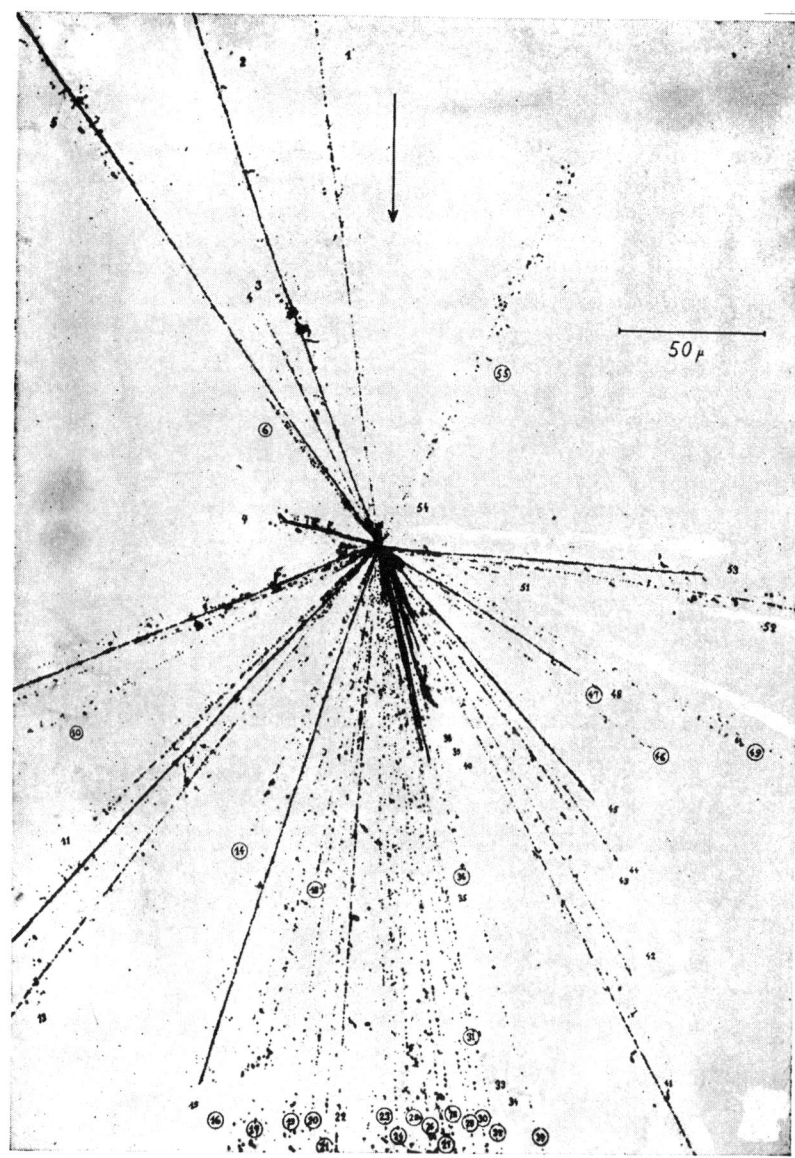

Figure 7.1. A spallation event found in an electron sensitive photographic emulsion, flown near the top of the atmosphere (15 g/cm²) by Le Prince-Ringuet et al. (1949) (reproduced from Rossi 1952). The spallation-inducing particle is infered to be a neutron (arrow). A number of different nucleii and atomic particles are produced by this event; only the charged ones are recorded by the emulsion.

The production rate, P, depends on altitude, latitude, and the depth of the sample below the rock surface. The dependence on rock depth can be described by an exponential,

$$P = P_0 e^{-d/L} \tag{3}$$

Where P_0 is the production rate at the surface, d is the depth below the surface in g/cm², and L is a constant called the apparent vertical attenuation length, with units of g/cm². Units of g/cm² are universally used to normalize for density variations (conversion from these units to distance in cm requires division by the density).

Table 7.1. Some Cosmogenic Nuclides Used for Exposure Dating

Isotope	Half-Life (years)	Measurement Method	Procedural Comments	Approximate Production Rate[a] atoms/g/yr (sea level, >55N)	Approximate Age Range[b]
^{3}He	Stable	Mass Spectrometry	Diffusive loss? high production rate; lowest detection limit; inherited He	160 (olivine)	1 ka to ca. 3 Ma
^{10}Be	1.5×10^6	AMS	Atmospheric contamination	6 (quartz)	3 ka to 4 Ma
^{26}Al	7.16×10^5	AMS	^{27}Al interference (must use Al-poor minerals)	37 (quartz)	5 ka to 2 Ma
^{36}Cl	3.08×10^5	AMS	No mineral separates; composition-dependent (produced by spallation and slow neutrons)	8 (basalt)	5 ka to 1 Ma
^{21}Ne	Stable	Mass Spectrometry	Inherited neon; useful for old samples	45 (olivine)	7 ka to 10 Ma(?)
^{14}C	5,730	AMS	Shortest half-life; atmospheric ^{14}C contamination	20 (basalt)	1 ka to 18 ka
^{41}Ca	103×10^3	AMS	Useful half-life; difficult measurement	?	to 300 ka

[a]References for production rates:
  ^{3}He: Brook and Kurz 1993; Kurz et al. 1990.
  ^{10}Be: Nishiizumi, Winterer, et al. 1989.
  ^{21}Ne: Staudacher and Allegre 1991; Hudson et al. 1991.
  ^{36}Cl: Zreda et al. 1991.
  ^{14}C: Jull et al. 1992.

[b]Age limits calculated using detection limit of 10^6 atoms for nuclides measured by AMS and assuming that 50 grams of sample is processed. Upper limits determined by three times the half-life.

The depth dependence is significant (L is approximately 150–160 g/cm^2, as discussed below), with production rates decreasing by a factor of two in approximately 50 cm in normal rocks; consequently, erosion may in some cases significantly affect exposure ages. A similar equation describes the dependence of the production rate on altitude:

$$(4) \quad P = P_0 e^{(1033-d_a)/L}$$

where 1033 g/cm^2 is the atmospheric depth at sea level, and d_a is the atmospheric depth in units of g/cm^2 (for example, 3 kilometers is 714 g/cm^2). The altitude can be converted to these units using standard tables, or the conversion can be made using a polynomial fit to tabulated data (for example, Lal 1991):

$$(5) \quad d_a = 1033 - 121.95\,(A_{km}) + 5.657\,(A_{km})^2 - 0.1095\,(A_{km})^3$$

where A_{km} is the altitude in kilometers. Equation 4 is an approximation based on cosmic-ray neutron-monitor data. A slightly more complex version of altitude scaling is included in the production rate scaling factors published by Lal (1991), accounting for production by high-energy neutrons, which have a different latitude dependence than the lower-energy component. Production rates must also be scaled for the effects of the earth's magnetic field, which causes production to be somewhat higher at high latitudes than low latitudes. This can be accomplished by using relative latitude effects determined in mobile cosmic ray neutron monitor studies (see Pomerantz and Agarwal 1962; Simpson and Fagot 1956), and are also accounted for by the scaling factors given by Lal (1991). Lal's scaling, presented in polynomial form in Lal (1991), has come to be generally used by a number of workers in this field, and is discussed further below.

The effects of erosion can be included in the above equations; assuming a constant erosion rate, equation 2 becomes

$$(6) \quad N = \frac{P}{\lambda + E/L}(1 - e^{-(\lambda + E/L)t})$$

where E is erosion rate in g/cm²/yr.

For a stable cosmogenic nuclide in a surface with no erosion, the above equations reduce simply to:

$$(7) \quad N = Pt$$

and for a stable cosmogenic nuclide with constant erosion rate:

$$(8) \quad N = \frac{PL}{E}\left(1 - e^{-(E/L)t}\right).$$

The most common issues that must be confronted by a geochronologist when attempting to date any object are the age range and accuracy of the method and its applicability to the sample in question. As discussed below, each of the cosmogenic nuclides in Table 7.1 has advantages and disadvantages, which must be considered individually. In addition surface exposure dating with any cosmogenic nuclide involves a number of common assumptions:

1. The production rates are well known;
2. The sample has been perfectly exposed to cosmic rays (no erosion or cover of any kind), or these parameters must be independently constrained;
3. The sample has not previously been exposed to cosmic rays;
4. The sample has remained a closed system during the exposure (no loss or contamination).

Each of these assumptions must be carefully considered for each geochronological situation. Accurate production rates are important for determining absolute ages, but if relative ages within a sequence of samples is the object of the study, then absolute production rates are less important. If erosion or cover has been important to a particular surface, then any measured age will be a minimum. The magnitude of under estimation is determined by the depth and time dependence of the erosion or cover. The importance of previous exposure will depend on the sample type and age range and in some cases can be evaluated based on field evidence; lava flows, for example cannot have had prior exposure to cosmic rays. If a sample was buried between exposure periods, then measurement of nuclides with different half-lives can place some constraints on the prior exposure history (see Klein et al. 1986). The "closed-system" assumption also depends on the nuclide; diffusive ³He loss is an important issue for some minerals (Brook and Kurz 1993; Cerling 1990; Trull et al. 1991), and addition of atmospheric cosmogenic ^{10}Be and ^{36}Cl can be a problem for some samples (Brown et al. 1991; Zreda et al. 1991). The discussion below is intended to give background information and some examples of each of these assumptions. The reader should keep in mind that simple "dating" of surfaces or exposure ages of objects is not the only application of these techniques that may be relevant to archaeology. As the equations above show, cosmogenic nuclides are sensitive to erosion and burial processes and in favorable cases may provide useful information about erosion histories, histories of previously exposed surfaces and objects now buried and also past sediment or artifact transport in the surface environment.

Production of Cosmogenic Nuclides in Terrestrial Rocks

Interactions of Cosmic Rays with Terrestrial Material

The cosmic-ray energy at ground level is dominantly produced by galactic cosmic rays (GCR), which strike the earth from all directions and whose origin remains one of the great unsolved mysteries of physics. At the top of the atmosphere, the primary GCR flux consists dominantly of positively charged protons, with lesser amounts of alpha particles and heavy nuclei. The energies of these particles are extremely high, up to approximately 10^{19} ev. Solar cosmic rays, which originate from the sun, have significantly lower energy and are not important for *in situ* production at the earth's surface. The GCR strike atoms in the atmosphere, inducing nuclear reactions, such as the spallation event shown in Figure 7.1, which eject particles with sufficient energy to produce further nuclear reactions. By the time the resultant cosmic-ray flux reaches sea level, it is significantly attenuated, having induced many reactions in the atmosphere, and the composition of the particles has changed, so that neutrons are the dominant spallation-inducing particles.

Because the primary GCR particles are charged, the earth's magnetic field deflects them and acts as a filter, keeping out particles with energy lower than that necessary to overcome the magnetic field force vector (referred to in the literature as the "cut-off rigidity"). Because the earth's magnetic field lines are approximately parallel to the surface at the equator and perpendicular to the surface at the poles, this effect is most important at the equator and negligible at latitudes higher than approximately 55° (see Shea et al. 1987). Therefore there is a significant latitudinal variation in cosmic-ray flux and production rates. The sea level cosmic-ray flux varies by approximately 50 percent from the equator to the poles, based on mobile neutron-monitor data (Pomerantz and Agarwal 1962; Rose et al. 1956), a factor that varies with the solar cycle, because the GCR flux is modulated by the solar wind. In surface exposure dating, it is usually reasonable to assume that solar cycle variations average out over periods longer than 10 ka, and the dominant viewpoint in cosmic ray physics is that the flux to the earth has been approximately constant over the last few million years (Reedy et al. 1983).

However, due to the relationship between the earth's dipole moment, the cosmic-ray flux, and temporal changes in the earth's magnetic field, production rates of cosmogenic nuclides may vary as a function of time. It is well documented that the earth's dipole moment has varied significantly in the past (on the 10-ka time scale: McElhinny and Senanayake 1982), and hence the cosmic-ray flux at the earth's surface has also varied. This effect has long been debated with respect to calibration of the ^{14}C time scale, but it is generally recognized that variations in ^{14}C production rate are at least partly due to dipole-moment fluctuations (Damon et al. 1978). With respect to surface exposure dating, changes in production rates due to dipole moment effects are insignificant at high latitude (>55°N), but are a potential complication at low latitudes. The only experimental evidence to document the magnitude of this effect, from Hawaiian lava flows, suggests that the production rate may have varied by up to a factor of two within the last 10 ka (Kurz et al. 1990). However, Kurz et al. (1990) concluded that uncertainties in the experimental data and also in existing estimates for the relationship between dipole moment and sea-level production make it difficult to assess this quantitatively.

Production Rate Calculation

The estimation of cosmogenic nuclide production rates in the earth's atmosphere and in surficial rocks was pioneered by Lal and coworkers (Lal 1958, 1988, 1991; Lal et al. 1958; Lal and Peters 1967). They used a semiempirical approach that involved counting the spallation events in photographic emulsions flown at high altitude in the earth's atmosphere. The nuclear events recorded in such emulsions are often called "stars," based on their appearance; one such event is shown in Figure 7.1 and demonstrates that spallation generates many different nuclear fragments. Based on the number of spallation events counted in photographic emulsions, their appearance, and estimates of the branching ratio for each nuclide, Lal and Peters (1967) estimated production rates in the atmosphere for many cosmogenic nuclides. Using neutron-monitor data from around the world, they then developed curves that allow extrapolation to all latitudes and altitudes. For many isotopes these estimates can also give an approximate value for production rates in surficial rocks, and they have been used by many researchers. The star production rates derived by Lal and Peters (1967) have recently been summarized by Lal (1991) in polynomial form that can be used to scale production rates to any latitude and altitude based on the Lal and Peters (1967) formulation. Production rates can also be estimated using knowledge of nuclear reaction cross sections, target compositions, and the cosmic-ray energy spectrum and flux (Lal 1991; O'Brien 1979; Yokoyama et al. 1977). Such estimates are severely hampered, however, by the lack of appropriate reaction cross sections for neutron-induced spallation.

There are a number of limitations to the above estimates. Much of the data were collected at high altitude during the 1950s, and the latitude and altitude corrections are large. The graphical compilation of these data by Lal and Peters (1967) and the parameterization by Lal (1991) do not readily lend themselves to estimates of the uncertainties in absolute production rates or the altitude/latitude scaling (the original data are not published). Nevertheless the Lal and Peters's (1967) scaling factors for production rates are the most comprehensive and commonly used. More information can be found in Lal and Peters (1967) and Lal (1988, 1991).

Production Rate Calibration

Because production rates are critical to surface exposure dating, and because of the uncertainties in theoretical estimates, a number of workers have attempted to calibrate them (for particular nuclides) against surfaces of known age (Cerling 1990; Kurz 1986a; Kurz et al. 1990; Nishiizumi et al. 1989; Phillips et al. 1986; Zreda et al. 1991). The difficulty with this approach is in finding surfaces that have been accurately dated with other techniques and that have experienced no erosion or cover. Lava flows are ideal, because their surface morphology can be used to evaluate erosion, and there are many that have been dated by ^{14}C. The difficulty here is that the ages of the best flows are very young (<15 ka) and there are relatively small amounts of cosmogenic nuclides in these surfaces. ^{3}He, ^{36}Cl, and ^{21}Ne production rates have been calibrated this way (Cerling 1990; Kurz 1986b, 1987; Kurz et al. 1990; Poreda and Cerling 1992; Zreda et al. 1991). Other attempts to use this type of approach have included glacially polished surfaces for ^{10}Be and ^{26}Al (Nishiizumi, et al. 1989), where the age of glaciation is based on ^{14}C ages of related glacial deposits. The glacial striations and polish demonstrate that the surface has been well preserved, but any previous cover would lower the production rates, and glacial striations are typically better preserved under soil or glacial sediments.

Depth Dependence in Surface Rocks

As mentioned above, production rates vary with altitude, latitude, depth within the surface, and shielding. The variations with depth and altitude are caused by a decrease in cosmic-ray flux as it interacts with matter. The most common form of altitude and depth dependence is an exponential (equation 3 above), with reported values of the attenuation length in the atmosphere (L) between 150 and 220 g/cm^2 (units of g/cm^2 are used to eliminate variations in density). In surface materials this parameter is important, because it controls erosion rate calculations and corrections for overlying material. A number of measurements of L have been made in rock drill cores. Some of these results are summarized in Figure 7.2 (^{3}He from Kurz 1986b; ^{10}Be from Brown, Brook et al. 1992), showing that the production rates decrease by a factor of two with approximately 50 cm depth (e-folding length of approximately 60 cm), demonstrating that it is critical to document the geometry of the sample and to evaluate the impor-

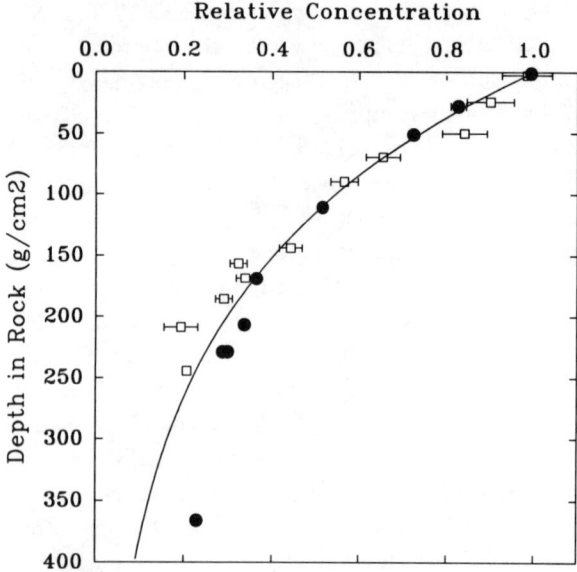

Figure 7.2. Depth profiles in surficial rocks, found by Kurz (1986b) for ^{3}He (solid circles) in a Hawaiian lava flow and Brown, Brook et al. (1992) for ^{10}Be (squares) in an Antarctic sandstone. The data were normalized to the extrapolated concentration in the respective surfaces, to allow direct comparison (that is, concentration in the top of profile defined as 1). Also shown is the profile expected from simple exponential decrease with depth (solid line). The density of both rock types is approximately 2.3 g/cm^3, so the total depth range shown is approximately 1.5 m.

mechanisms also change significantly at greater depths in the rock, and these values are only appropriate near the surface. The deviation of the deepest ^{3}He data in Figure 7.2 from the predicted exponential may be related to an increased contribution from muon-induced reactions (that is, ^{6}Li(n,α)T → ^{3}He; Kurz 1986b). Muons are weakly interacting particles and are not as strongly depth-dependent as neutrons; consequently, below two meters depth, muon-induced reactions become more important relative to spallation (see Lal 1988).

Scaling Problems

In practice determining an absolute surface exposure age requires scaling-calibration data for the latitude and altitude of the sample in question. As an extreme example of the uncertainties that can be introduced into the calculated ages, we consider several different methods to extrapolate existing calibrations for ^{3}He production rates to high latitude. Table 7.2 (from Brook and Kurz 1993) summarizes the reported measurements of ^{3}He production rates (Kurz et al. 1990 at 20°N; Cerling 1990 at 43°N) and the different methods for scaling these data to high latitudes, in addition to available theoretical estimates. The different methods of extrapolation are based on different formulations of the relationship between altitude, latitude, solar cycle effects, and the cosmic-ray neutron flux, and can yield large discrepancies. For example the scaling of Yokoyama et al. (1977) is based on high-altitude neutron measurements (Light et al. 1973), which have a greater latitude dependence than sea level neutrons. The discrepancy between the theoretical ^{3}He production rate estimate and the experimental determinations may result from lack of knowledge of reaction cross sections for neutron-induced spallation (Lal 1991), and perhaps uncertainty regarding the sea level neutron fluxes as well. Further details regarding the table may be found in Brook and Kurz (1993). The important point illustrated in Table 7.2 is that the different formulations give significantly different production rates scaled to sea level and high altitude, and these extrapolations are an important

tance of erosion and soil cover. The values obtained for L using existing drill core data are 165±7 g/cm^2 for ^{3}He, 145 ±7 g/cm^2 for ^{10}Be, and 156±12 g/cm^2 for ^{26}Al (Brown, Brook, et al. 1992; Kurz 1986b); slightly higher values of L have been reported by Olinger et al. (1992) for ^{21}Ne and ^{10}Be (178 and 172 g/cm^2, respectively) in the Bandolier Tuff in New Mexico. Note that because these nuclides are primarily produced by neutron-induced spallation, these values will not apply to nuclides that have other production mechanisms. For example Zreda and Phillips (chapter 8 of this volume) suggest that ^{36}Cl has a more complex depth dependence than that shown in Figure 7.2, due to significant production by thermal neutrons. The production

Table 7.2. Estimates of ^{3}He Production Rates Scaled to Sea Level and above 50° Geomagnetic Latitude, Using Four Scaling Methods Discussed in Text

	Altitude and Latitude Scaling Method[a]			
	1	2	3	4
Measured Production Rates				
Kurz (1987)	156±5	126±4	146±5	352±11
Kurz et al. (1990)	201±48	191±59	221±44	453±109
Cerling (1990)	153±5	153±5	116±4	216±7
Calculated Production Rates				
Lal (1991)			75[b]	
Yokoyama et al. (1977)				219[c]
Lal and Peters (1967)			150[d]	

[a]1 = scaling based on latitude invariant vertical atmospheric attenuation length (160 g/cm^2) and neutron data of Pomerantz and Agarwal (1962) and Rose et al. (1956); 2 = scaling based on Lingenfelter (1963); 3 = scaling based on Lal and Peters (1967); 4 = scaling based on Yokoyama et al. (1977).
[b]Based on cosmic-ray neutron energy spectra and cross sections for proton interactions, calculated for quartz.
[c]Based on ^{3}H production rate, calculated using cross sections for proton interactions and ^{3}H/^{3}He production ratio of Lal and Peters (1967).
[d]Based on cosmic-ray star production/isotope production relationship of Lal and Peters (1967), with a likely uncertainty of approximately 20 percent (Lal, personal communication).

source of uncertainty for numerical-age calculations. In addition the altitudinal and latitudinal variability of production rates may also be energy-dependent, such that cosmic-ray neutron monitor data need corrections to be relevant to nuclide production (Lal 1958; Lal and Peters 1967).

One approach to the problem of altitude and latitude scaling of production rates is to measure production rates in dated surfaces at different altitudes (the latter approach assuming a constant cosmic-ray flux). Where this has been done at one latitude (see Brown et al. 1991; Zreda et al. 1991), results are consistent with the altitude scaling of Lal and Peters (1967), but additional work will be necessary to confirm this conclusion. Another promising approach is to measure cosmogenic nuclides, in experimental targets set out over long periods of time (see Mabuchi et al. 1971). Ultimately this approach, along with results from surfaces of known age, will remove the uncertainties related to altitude and latitude scaling. At present the scaling based on Lingenfelter (1963) or Lal and Peters (1967) seem to be the most comprehensive data available, but they yield significantly different results. Adequate understanding of the scaling problem and recognition of the inherent uncertainties are necessary for the interpretation of *in situ* cosmogenic nuclide data.

^{3}He and ^{21}Ne

^{3}He and ^{21}Ne are both stable nuclides, which is an advantage for dating older surfaces. In addition they can both be measured with a conventional magnetic sector mass spectrometer. However, they also share the disadvantage that a correction must be applied for ^{3}He and ^{21}Ne present in the rock prior to exposure to cosmic rays (referred to here as the "inherited component"). At present there is considerably more data for ^{3}He regarding this problem, and the correction can be made in a relatively simple manner in many cases.

Although the presence of cosmogenic helium in terrestrial rocks was only discovered in 1985, there is now a considerable amount of data for various rock types (Anthony and Poths 1992; Brook and Kurz 1993; Brook et al. 1993; Cerling 1990; Craig and Poreda 1986; Kurz 1986a, 1986b; Kurz et al. 1990; Porcelli et al. 1987). Virtually all of the existing cosmogenic ^{3}He data for igneous rocks is from olivine and clinopyroxene phenocrysts, due to significant loss of ^{3}He from the finer-grained basaltic groundmass (Kurz 1986a). The helium contained within basaltic phenocrysts is a mixture of cosmogenic and magmatic helium. The quantity of cosmogenic ^{3}He can be calculated as follows:

(9) ^{3}He (cosmogenic) = ^{3}He (total) − ^{3}He (inherited).

The quantity of inherited ^{3}He can be calculated as follows:

(10) ^{3}He (inherited) = ^{4}He (total) × (^{3}He/^{4}He) (inherited).

This calculation is valid because only a negligible amount of cosmogenic ^{4}He is produced; that is, the ^{3}He/^{4}He ratios in igneous rocks are typically ca. 10^{-5} and the ^{3}He/^{4}He ratio produced by spallation is ca. 0.2 (Mazor et al. 1970). The inherited ^{3}He/^{4}He ratio is determined by crushing *in vacuo*, which selectively releases the inherited component (dominantly contained by fluid and melt inclusions). The cosmogenic ^{3}He is not released by crushing olivine and clinopyroxene (Kurz 1986a, 1986b), but is released by melting the previously crushed sample.

It is important to note that the simple correction for inherited helium given by equations 9 and 10 does not necessarily apply to other rock types. Brook and Kurz (1993) performed experiments on quartz from Antarctic sandstones and found that significant amounts of cosmogenic ^{3}He were released by crushing in a vaccum, thus demonstrating that the formulation above does not apply to quartz. In this instance they assumed that all the inherited helium is radiogenic, with ^{3}He/^{4}He ratios of ca. 10^{-8} (Andrews 1985; Morrison and Pine 1955), which in this case resulted in a small correction for rocks older than 100 ka. However, it should be emphasized that more data are necessary to evaluate these assumptions for other rock types, and the assumptions regarding inherited helium must be carefully considered.

Due to the low detection limits for ^{3}He (5,000 to 10,000 atoms) and the fact that ^{3}He has the highest production rates of any cosmogenic nuclide (see Table 7.1), helium measurements can be applied to extremely young surfaces, as young as 1,000 B.P. at sea level and potentially younger at higher elevations. Mineral separations are difficult for some rock types and can limit the applicability of the technique, depending on the amount of sample that must be processed, which in turn depends on crystal abundances, detection limits, age, and altitude. For samples older than 1,000 B.P. at sea level, roughly 200 mg of olivine or clinopyroxene is typically adequate for ^{3}He analysis.

The first attempts to calibrate production rates and to test errors in the method were made on a number of Hawaiian lava flows (Kurz 1986a, 1986b; Kurz et al. 1990). These lava flows were dated by ^{14}C (see Rubin et al. 1987), using charcoal from beneath the flows, and they are ideal for ^{3}He dating because olivine is abundant. The published Hawaiian data are summarized in Figure 7.3; they are noteworthy in that they demonstrate that the ^{3}He method can be used for very young ages, in this instance the youngest samples are 1,000 B.P. in age. There is a reasonable correlation between ^{14}C and ^{3}He; both methods yield the same stratigraphy. However, there are some notable deviations from the concordance line in Figure 7.3. This could be partly due to an incorrect production rate (see discussion above), because the concordance line is based on a ^{3}He production rate of 125 atoms/g/yr, derived from the youngest samples because the surfaces are best preserved (note that a best fit to the data yields a lower production rate). Kurz et al. (1990) suggested that some of the deviation, particularly for those samples between 2,000 and 7,000 B.P., could be related to modulation of the cosmic-ray flux by the earth's magnetic field. The decrease in production rate (that is, lower ^{3}He ages) during this period would be consistent with archaeomagnetic evidence for a strong dipole moment (McElhinny and Senanayake 1982) and recent suggestions of strong nondipole fields in Hawaii at this time (Manki-

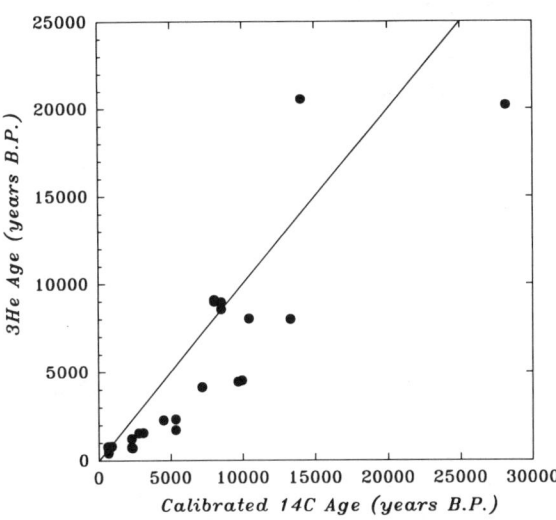

Figure 7.3. Calculated ^{3}He exposure ages from Hawaiian radiocarbon-dated lava flows (assuming a sea level production rate of 125 atoms/g/yr) compared to the ^{14}C ages for the same flows. The helium data are from Kurz et al. (1990), and the radiocarbon dates from Rubin et al. (1987). Note that the line is not a best fit to the data, but is based on the ^{3}He production rate from the youngest samples. The use of a lower ^{3}He production rate would yield better agreement for the samples below the line, but no single production rate explains all the data. One possible explanation is that production rates have fluctuated in the past, due to changes in the earth's magnetic field (Kurz et al. 1990).

nen and Champion 1992). Soil cover and erosion would also lower apparent ^{3}He ages, but Kurz et al. (1990) suggested that these processes are more likely for the older samples. This suite of samples illustrates some of the uncertainties in the method and suggests that the uncertainty in absolute ages is typically 30 percent for this age range. Cerling's (1990) production rate (see Table 7.2) from a single lava flow erupted into a dated shoreline in glacial lake Bonneville is within the error of Kurz et al. (1990) rates, but additional tests will be required to refine production rates and reduce the uncertainties.

Another important issue for using ^{3}He in exposure age dating is diffusive loss from mineral grains. Helium diffusion is extremely slow in olivine and clinopyroxene, making this effect unimportant on time scales less than 10 Ma at surficial temperatures (Hart 1984; Trull et al. 1991). Cerling (1990), based on several attempts to measure helium in four quartz samples, suggested that loss rates are too rapid from this mineral to allow its use for exposure dating. In contrast, Trull et al. (1991) performed diffusion measurements on Antarctic quartz samples that suggest extremely slow diffusive loss. Extrapolation of their diffusion data, which were collected at temperatures in excess of 100°C, to surficial temperatures, suggested that helium loss would be insignificant for time scales less than 2 Ma (Trull et al. 1991). In addition Brook et al. (1993) have reported extremely old ^{3}He exposure ages from Antarctic glacial moraines, discussed further below, which demonstrate that significant quantities of cosmic-ray-produced helium are retained in quartz. However, several aspects of the helium data indicate that the older samples have experienced some loss. Brook and Kurz (1993) demonstrated that the concentration of cosmogenic ^{3}He in quartz grains from a single sample increases significantly with grain size, suggesting a diffusive loss mechanism. Both ^{3}He/^{10}Be and ^{3}He/^{21}Ne ratios in these same samples suggest approximately 40 to 50 percent helium loss in the 2–3 Ma samples (Brook and Kurz 1993; Brown et al. 1991; Staudacher and Allegre 1991). Although the evidence suggests helium losses from quartz over million-year exposure periods, there is also evidence that diffusive loss from quartz is insignificant for shorter exposure periods. Based on the ages obtained from Arena Valley, and particularly the correlation between ^{3}He and ^{10}Be for the younger samples (see Figures 7.4 and 7.5), it seems that ^{3}He will be a useful technique for quartz samples younger than 400 ka. The discrepancy between this conclusion and that of Cerling (1990), who suggested that helium is lost from quartz on time scales shorter than 10 ka, may relate to an inappropriate correction for inherited helium (that is, equation 10) by

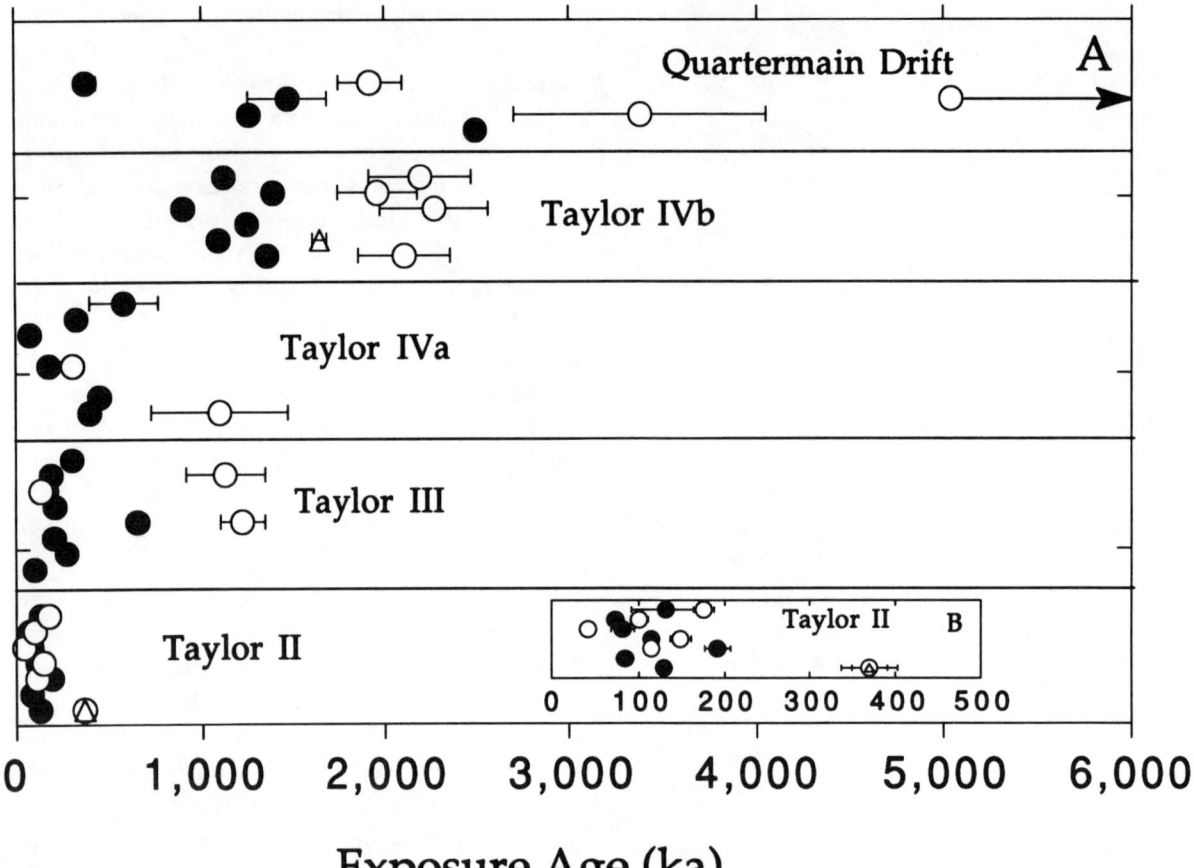

Figure 7.4. ³He and ¹⁰Be age distributions for a set of glacial moraine boulders in Arena Valley, Southern Victoria Land, Antarctica (Brook, Brook, et al. 1993). The solid circles are ³He ages, and the open circles are ¹⁰Be ages; most of the samples are quartz grains from quartz sandstone boulders. The data demonstrate that a single moraine can display a range of exposure ages, requiring detailed sampling of such features. The discrepancy between ³He and ¹⁰Be ages for the older samples is probably related to helium loss from samples older than 500 ka. The inset gives an expanded view of the ages from the youngest moraine; the agreement between ³He and ¹⁰Be ages suggests little loss of ³He in 100 ka.

Cerling (1990), or to differences in sample mineralogy, grain size, or environmental conditions.

²¹Ne has significantly slower diffusion rates from minerals and may be extremely useful, particularly in samples that have undergone helium loss (Graf et al. 1991; Marti and Craig 1987; Staudacher and Allegre 1991). As with ³He, a correction must be made for inherited neon. In young volcanic rocks this correction for magmatic ²¹Ne is analogous to corrections for magmatic ³He. In older rocks a correction also must be made for ²¹Ne produced by (α,n) reactions with thermal neutrons (for example, ^{24}Mg(n,α)^{21}Ne). The importance of the correction depends on the exposure age, the uranium and thorium concentraton (these elements

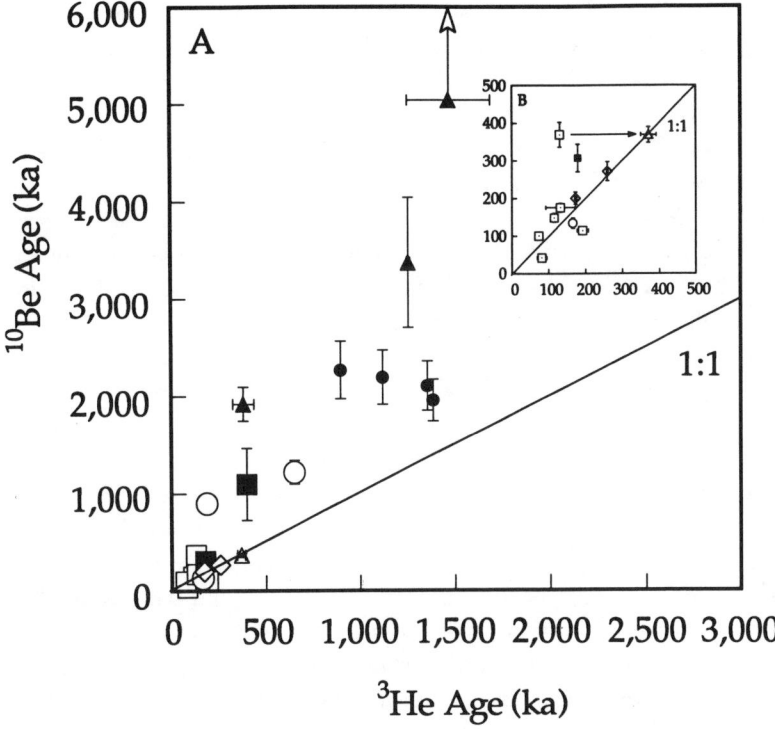

Figure 7.5. ^{3}He and ^{10}Be ages for a subsample of the samples shown in Figure 7.4, calculated with ^{3}He and ^{10}Be production rates of 191 and atoms/g/yr, respectively (Brook et al. 1993). Different symbols indicate the different moraines (see Figure 7.4). Also as demonstrated by Figure 7.4, ^{3}He ages are younger than ^{10}Be ages, due to ^{3}He loss for the older samples. However, the younger samples suggest good agreement between ^{3}He and ^{10}Be ages for samples younger than 400 ka (see inset). The arrow in the inset connects two different grain size fractions from the same sample; the larger grains fall close to the concordance line.

produce alpha particles), and the concentrations of targets for (α,n) reactions. Because neon has three isotopes, discriminating different neon components may be simpler than for helium.

Recently Poreda and Cerling (1992) have undertaken the calibration of ^{21}Ne production rates in olivine and plagioclase in young (< 20 ka) volcanic rocks, finding values of about 45 and 17 atoms/g/yr, respectively, at sea level and high latitude. The difference is due to the different compositions of the minerals. The composition dependence of spallation production has been well studied in meteorites (Eugster 1988; Vogt et al. 1990), and Poreda and Cerling (1992) also studied the compositional dependence of ^{21}Ne production in olivine. More work of this type is needed, but the demonstration that ^{21}Ne can be used in a number of mineral phases is important. For samples with old crystallization ages and short exposure ages, the correction for inherited neon (that is, preexposure, nucleogenic ^{21}Ne) will be important.

Antarctica has been the focus of a number of exposure dating studies (Brown et al.1991; Brook et al. 1993; Cerling 1990; Nishiizumi et al. 1986; Nishiizumi, Kohl, Arnold, et al. 1991; Staudacher and Allegre 1991). In a number of ways, Antarctica is an ideal environment for this technique, because it is a cold desert and erosion is very slow (Brown et al. 1991; Nishiizumi, Kohl, Arnold, et al. 1991). In addition the glacial history of the continent is critical to understanding climatic history, and there are few other methods for dating the glacial deposits. Figure 7.4 shows ^{3}He exposure ages from glacial moraines in Arena Valley, which is adjacent to Taylor Glacier in the Dry Valleys region of Southern Victoria Land (Brook et al. 1993). The moraines record the advance and retreat of Taylor Glacier, which is an outlet glacier from the East Antarctic Ice

Sheet, and have been the subject of a number of glacialogical studies (such as Denton et al. 1989). The data shown in Figure 7.4 are from quartz sandstone moraine boulders and are in good agreement with prior attempts at relative ages of the moraines. Even though the older quartz samples have experienced some ^{3}He loss, as discussed above, they have ^{3}He ages as old as 1.5 Ma. A comparison of ^{3}He with ^{10}Be ages, shown in Figure 7.5, suggests that the loss has been approximately 50 percent of the ^{3}He for the oldest samples (Brook et al. 1993; Brown et al. 1991). Despite the evidence of loss, the stratigraphy obtained using the two techniques is generally consistent.

The data shown in Figures 7.4 and 7.5 illustrate the importance of sampling to any successful application of surface exposure dating. In the case of the moraine boulders, the assumptions of surface exposure dating require that the boulders have not rolled or been covered in the past, and that they have not experienced prior exposure to cosmic rays. The data shown in Figure 7.4 demonstrate that single samples are not adequate to characterize a single moraine. In addition it is important to use several different techniques, rather than limit age determination to one cosmogenic nuclide, because each of the methods provides unique information.

^{10}Be and ^{26}Al

^{10}Be and ^{26}Al are often measured together, because they complement each other in many ways. Both require AMS for measurement because of their low abundances and the presence of isobaric interferences (for example, ^{10}B for ^{10}Be and ^{26}Mg for ^{26}Al). Almost all of the ^{10}Be and ^{26}Al data for terrestrial surface exposure dating are for the mineral quartz, because it has a simple target chemistry, is a ubiquitous mineral in nature, is chemically resistant, and has very low stable aluminum concentrations (typically ca. 100–1000 ppm). The latter two attributes are important from a laboratory standpoint. Contamination of grain surfaces with ^{10}Be produced in the atmosphere can be significant (Brown et al.1991); the use of quartz allows rigorous acid leaching to remove the surface contamination, while leaving interior material intact. In fact this approach has proven extremely successful in eliminating this potential contaminant (Brown et al. 1991; Nishiizumi et al. 1989). In addition, because the quartz matrix is not susceptible to chemical weathering, alteration of the mineral during its exposure history does not affect the results. Because it is not produced in significant quantities in the atmosphere, ^{26}Al does not suffer from similar contamination problems, but the amount of ^{27}Al (the stable isotope) in the sample must be low to obtain reasonable counting statistics for ^{26}Al. For both ^{10}Be and ^{26}Al, the analysis is carried out as a simple isotope dilution. ^{9}Be and ^{27}Al are added to the samples as carriers, and the 26/27 and 10/9 ratios are measured using the AMS. For ^{10}Be analysis of quartz, there is generally not enough naturally occurring ^{9}Be to be of concern, but for ^{27}Al this is not the case (because aluminum is a major constituent of most minerals), and the stable aluminum concentration must be determined prior to chemical purification; then additional ^{27}Al can be added, if necessary. The amount of natural stable aluminum that can be tolerated depends on sample size and the amount of ^{26}Al present, but concentrations greater than a few thousand ppm will make analysis difficult, if not impossible, for most samples. Therefore aluminosilicate minerals, such as feldspars and micas, are unsuitable for ^{26}Al analysis. However, quartz can be separated from other minerals in some rocks by selective acid leaching (see Kohl and Nishiizumi 1992).

The half-lives of ^{10}Be and ^{26}Al (1.5 Ma and 720 ka) are suitable for using the isotopes as a pair, as they both can be used to determine ages of Quaternary deposits. By measuring both isotopes, the internal consistency of the data can be evaluated, since the results should be concordant, and erosion rate constraints are considerably more reliable with two isotopes.

There has been only one calibration of the ^{26}Al and ^{10}Be production rates, by Nishiizumi, Winterer, et al. (1989), who studied glacially polished surfaces on the Sierra Nevada Mountains of California. Their results indicated production rates (at ca. 44° geomagnetic latitude) of 62±3 and 374±28 atoms/g/yr for ^{10}Be and ^{26}Al, respectively (at 3.34 km, or 685 g/cm^2, altitude). This corresponds to production rates of 6 and 37 atoms/g/yr at sea level. These production rates are based, however, on a somewhat uncertain glacial chronology, and the authors indicate additional uncertainties of approximately 10 percent. Another important outcome of this work was the determination of the ^{26}Al/^{10}Be production ratio (ca. 6), a useful parameter that is not greatly affected by altitude or latitude. With improvement in analytical precision, dating based on isotope pairs may be more useful than those based on the absolute concentration of a single isotope, because the use of ratios reduces uncertainties associated with absolute production rates, erosion, and skyline shielding (Brown, Brook, et al. 1992).

^{10}Be and ^{26}Al analyses are possible in other mineral phases, particularly olivine, where some work has been done (Nishiizumi, Klein, et al. 1990), although obtaining enough mineral separate to make an adequate measurement (at least several grams are necessary) is difficult. Calibration of ^{10}Be and ^{26}Al production rates should be possible with lava flow samples, but any comparison of such data with the results for quartz requires understanding the effect of target chemistry on production rates. Although this is fairly well understood in meteorites, it is not clear that it is adequately understood yet in terrestrial rocks. Further work in this area will be necessary. Because ^{10}Be and ^{26}Al are radioactive (with half-lives of 1.5×10^6 and 725,000 yrs respectively), their dating range is limited by their half-lives (see Table 7.1). The lower limits of the potential age range are a function of latitude, altitude, burial depth, and sample size. The practical upper limit is defined by approach to "saturation," where production balances decay and erosional loss.

One aspect of the cosmogenic radionuclides, not yet discussed in this article, is the possibility of using concentrations to place constraints on erosion rates. Over time isotope concentrations reach a steady state with respect to erosion and radioactive decay. The length of time necessary to reach this steady state depends on the half-life of the nuclide and the erosion rate, and if steady state is assumed, a maximum erosion rate can be calculated by setting t equal to infinity in equation 6, yielding:

$$(11) \qquad E = (P/N - \lambda)L.$$

If it is clear that a steady state has been reached, this yields an average erosion rate; otherwise the rate is a maximum value. The ^{26}Al–^{10}Be pair can be useful in this regard; if both yield the same erosion rate, then one can be confident that the samples are at or near steady state. From equation 11, however, it should be obvious that the erosion rate calculation depends on accurate knowledge of production rates, which will be an important source of uncertainty, particularly for low erosion rates. It should also be recognized that these calculations give erosion rates only at particular points on individual surfaces, and using these data to characterize erosion on regional or continental scales may be misleading, depending on the nature of the surfaces sampled, as shown recently by Brown, Stallard et al. (1992). In addition equation 11 assumes a constant erosion rate. More complex scenarios, including variable erosion rates and spalling of discrete thickness of the surface, can be modeled (Lal 1991).

Most of the geological applications of ^{10}Be and ^{26}Al to terrestrial geochronology have been demonstrations of the potential of the technique for determining exposure ages and erosion rates of glacial landforms in Antarctica (for example, Brook et al. 1993; Brown et al. 1991; Nishiizumi, Kohl, Shoemaker, et al. 1991). Earlier work on Libyan desert glass (Klein et al. 1986) demonstrated the power of the technique, and recent work on Meteor Crater in Arizona (Nishiizumi, Kohl, Shoemaker, et al.1991; Phillips et al. 1991) demonstrated excellent agreement between ^{10}Be, ^{26}Al and ^{36}Cl methods. Recent examples of work in Antarctica will demonstrate some of the potential and problems involved in using ^{26}Al and ^{10}Be for surface exposure chronology. Nishiizumi, Kohl, Arnold, et al. (1991) reported ^{10}Be and ^{26}Al data for a number of quartz samples from the Transantarctic Mountains and Alan Hills regions of Antarctica. The data indicated minimum exposure ages ranging from 36 ka to greater than 4 Ma, and they were able to use the data to calculate maximum erosion rates of roughly 10^{-5} cm/yr for their oldest samples. A major result of this work has been the quantification of very low erosion rates of exposed rocks in Antarctica. These low erosion rates make surface exposure dating particularly useful for polar desert regions, since old surfaces of geochronologic interest are so well preserved.

We have initiated efforts to use ^{10}Be and ^{26}Al in conjunction with ^{3}He data, to determine the ages of surficial glacial deposits in the Dry Valleys region of Antarctica, and to use these data to study the Plio-Pliestocene history of the East and West Antarctic ice sheets (Brook, et al. 1993; Brown et al. 1991). Initial efforts have concentrated on dating boulders in Quaternary moraines in the Dry Valleys region, deposits that have been well studied by other workers, who have been hampered by lack of detailed chronology (for example, Bockheim 1992; Denton et al. 1989). One moraine system in Arena Valley, a small hanging valley intruded into in the past by the Taylor Glacier, an outlet glacier of the East Antarctic Ice Sheet, has been studied in detail (Brook et al. 1993; Brown et al. 1991). There are difficulties in dating individual boulders, because they all may have somewhat different exposure histories; but when enough data are accumulated, coherent sets of ages appear to emerge (Brook, et al. 1993; Brown et al. 1991; Phillips et al. 1990; Zreda and Phillips, chapter 8 of this volume) that are consistent with independent evidence. The statistical treatment of such data remains an important question (see also Zreda and Phillips, chapter 8 of this volume). Brook, et al. (1993) chose to take the mean of the measurements shown in Figure 7.4 as the best estimate of the true exposure age of the deposits, while Zreda et al. (1991) assume that maximum ages are the most reliable ones, at least for older deposits. These studies have also verified the low erosion rates reported earlier for many Antarctic samples (Brown et al. 1991; Nishiizumi, Kohl, Arnold et al. 1991). Brown et al. (1991) also developed a statistical treatment of ^{10}Be and ^{26}Al data that indicated that the production rates determined by Nishiizumi, Winterer, et al. (1989), based on a 10-ka exposure age, were consistent with the average rate over the last 10^6 years (with fairly large uncertainties).

The multiple-isotope approach has been useful in these studies. For example potential problems for ^{3}He loss and atmospheric contamination of ^{10}Be can be evaluated by measuring several isotopes in the same samples (for example, Brook et al. 1993; Brown et al. 1991), greatly facilitating the interpretation of age distributions (Figure 7.4), as well as providing new information about the isotope systematics of these nuclides.

From the above discussion, the most important factor in choosing *in situ* ^{10}Be or ^{26}Al for a surface exposure problem relates to the mineral phases present in the material to be dated. Existing studies are primarily confined to quartz, due to the relative ease in obtaining pure mineral separates in large quantities (> 1g), but may be extended to other low-aluminum mineral phases. Glass might also be studied in an archaeological context, although large sample sizes would probably be required. Apart from dating surfaces, other applications of these nuclides are chiefly in estimating the erosion rates of surfaces and sedimentary processes. The latter application has been described in principle by Lal (1987) and employed by Klein et al. (1986) and Nishiizumi, Kohl, Arnold, (1991). The burial and exposure history of individual sedimentary particles or units, as well as the origin of soil or weathering horizons, can be constrained. For example "disequilibrium" in the ^{10}Be–^{26}Al isotopic system can indicate periods of exposure followed by burial, because ^{26}Al and ^{10}Be decay at different rates, producing a burial signal (Klein et al. 1986). The exponential attenuation of production with depth in rocks can be also be employed in studying sedimentary sections. Exposure of material prior to deposition could be distinguished from exposure after deposition by the presence or absence of the exponential decrease. This type of work may prove useful in understanding the timing of deposition versus exposure or determining the origin of sedimentary horizons (deposition versus weathering).

^{14}C and ^{41}Ca

Preliminary work with these two isotopes suggests some interesting and useful applications. Their chief attraction is their relatively short half-lives (5,730 yr for ^{14}C and 103 ka for ^{41}Ca; Klein et al. 1991), resulting in greatest utility for processes on time scales of 0–40 ka and 0–500 ka, and a greater sensitivity to erosion and burial on these time scales than is the case for ^{3}He, ^{21}Ne, ^{10}Be, ^{26}Al, or ^{36}Cl. As are the other spallation-produced nuclides, ^{14}C is produced by the spallation of major elements in a silicate matrix. The production rate should be composition-dependent, and although it has been detected in several terrestrial samples (Jull et al. 1992), ^{14}C production rates have not been systematically calibrated. These measurements are difficult, due to atmospheric contamination and the small quantities of ^{14}C present, but Jull et al. (1992) were able to suggest that previous age estimates (from longer-lived cosmogenic nuclides) for some of their samples were incorrect, because the ^{14}C data suggest significant erosion not resolved by longer-lived cosmogenic nuclides. Clearly more work must be done, but *in situ* ^{14}C dating should prove extremely useful in the future.

^{41}Ca is produced in terrestrial rocks by thermal neutron capture by ^{40}Ca, but *in situ* ^{41}Ca measurements in terrestrial rocks have not, to our knowledge, been reported in the literature. A number of ^{41}Ca measurements have been made with the intention of dating bones, although consistent results have not yet been obtained (Fink et al. 1990; Raisbeck and Yiou 1979). There are a number of difficulties with ^{41}Ca measurements, most notably that the ^{41}Ca/^{40}Ca ratios in most samples are quite low, less than 10^{-14} (Fink et al. 1990). Present AMS backgrounds are at best 5×10^{-16}, so data quality is probably limited at present. Since the half-life of ^{41}Ca is so attractive for studying Quaternary events, progress in ^{41}Ca applications and measurement would be extremely useful.

Summary

It is clear from the discussion presented above that more calibrations of the production rates and of the scaling for altitude and latitude are necessary to reduce the uncertainties in the technique. Calibrations of this kind are underway in a number of laboratories, and it is likely that the precision of surface exposure will therefore improve significantly in the near future.

As with any dating technique, surface exposure dating requires attention to detail in sample collection, laboratory procedure, and evaluation of assumptions. Because the application of the technique is still in its infancy, much of the discussion given before focuses on the outstanding problems. In any application of the technique, careful sample collection and geological constraints on erosion and soil cover are critical. Nevertheless, surface exposure dating is already well enough developed to be of great utility. A good example of the success of the technique is the concordance between several different age determinations on the surfaces of Meteor Crater (Nishiizumi, Kohl, Shoemaker, et al. 1991; Phillips et al. 1991). With the wide range of cosmogenic nuclides given in Table 7.1, surface exposure dating will find many new applications in fields such as archaeology, geomorphology, glacial geology, and volcanology.

Acknowledgments

The authors gratefully acknowledge the collaboration of R. Ackert, G. Denton, D. Lott, D. Kammer, W. Jenkins, E. Brown, G. Raisbeck, and F. Yiou. Some of the work discussed here, and the writing of this manuscript, were supported by grants EAR91–06820 and DPP91–17458 from the National Science Foundation. Erik Brown and Greg Ravizza provided helpful editorial and scientific comments on the manuscript. We also thank Charlotte Beck for her encouragement and patience in the face of adversity.

References

Andrews, J. N.
1985 The Isotopic Composition of Radiogenic Helium and Its Use to Study Ground-Water Movement in Confined Aquifers. *Chemical Geology* 47:339–351.

Anthony, E. Y., and J. Poths
1992 ^{3}He Surface Exposure Dating and Its Implications for Magma Evolution in the Potrillo Volcanic Field, Rio Grande Rift, New Mexico, USA. *Geochimica et Cosmochimica Acta* 56:4105–4108.

Bockheim, J. G.
1992 Properties of a Chronosequence of Ultraxerous Soils in the Trans-Antarctic Mountains. *Geoderma* 28:239–255.

Brook, E. J., and M. D. Kurz
1993 Surface-Exposure Chronology Using *in situ* Cosmogenic ^{3}He in Antarctic Quartz Sandstone Boulders. *Quaternary Research* 39:1–10.

Brook, E. J., M. D. Kurz, R. P. Ackert, Jr., G. H. Denton, E. T. Brown, G. M. Raisbeck, and F. Yiou
1993 Chronology of Taylor Glacier Advances in Arena Valley, Antarctica, Using *in situ* Cosmogenic ^{3}He and ^{10}Be. *Quaternary Research* 39:11–23.

Brown, E. T., E. J. Brook, G. M. Raisbeck, F. Yiou, and M. D. Kurz
1992 Effective Attenuation Lengths of Cosmic Rays Producing ^{10}Be and ^{26}Al in Quartz: Implications for Exposure Age Dating. *Geophysical Research Letters* 19:369–372.

Brown, E. T., J. M. Edmond, G. M Raisbeck, F. Yiou, M. D. Kurz, and E. J. Brook
1991 Examination of Surface Exposure Ages of Antarctic Moraines Using *in situ* Produced ^{10}Be and ^{26}Al. *Geochimica et Cosmochimica Acta* 55:2269–2283.

Brown, E. T., R. F. Stallard, G. M. Raisbeck, and F. Yiou
1992 Determination of the Denudation Rate of Mount Roraima, Venezuela, Using Cosmogenic ^{10}Be and ^{26}Al. *Eos* 73 (43):170.

Cerling, T. E.
1990 Dating Geomorphologic Surfaces Using Cosmogenic ^{3}He. *Quaternary Research* 33:148–156.

Craig, H., and R. Poreda
1986 Cosmogenic ^{3}He in Terrestrial Rocks: The Summit Lavas of Maui. *Proceedings of the National Academy of Sciences* 85:970–974.

Damon, P. E., J. C. Lerman, and A. Long
1978 Temporal Fluctuations of Atmospheric ^{14}C: Causal Factors and Implications. *Annual Review of Earth and Planetary Sciences* 6:457–494.

Davis, R., and O. A. Schaeffer
1956 Chlorine-36 in Nature. *Annals of the New York Academy of Sciences* 62:107–121.

Denton, G. H., J. G. Bockheim, S. C. Wilson, and M. Stuiver
1989 Late Wisconsin and Early Holocene Glacial History, Inner Ross Embayment, Antarctica. *Quaternary Research* 31:151–182.

Elmore, D., and F. M. Phillips
1987 Accelerator Mass Spectrometry for Measurement of Long-Lived Radioisotopes. *Science* 236:543–550.

Eugster, O.
1988 Cosmic-Ray Production Rates for ^{3}He, ^{21}Ne, ^{38}Ar, ^{83}Kr, and ^{126}Xe in Chondrites Based on ^{81}Kr-Kr Exposure Ages. *Geochimica et Cosmochimica Acta* 52:1649–1662.

Fink, D., J. Klein, and R. Middleton
1990 ^{41}Ca: Past, Present and Future. *Nuclear Instruments and Methods in Physics Research* B52:572–582.

Graf, Th., C. P. Kohl, K. Marti, and K. Nishiizumi
1991 Cosmic Ray Produced Neon in Antarctic Rocks. *Geophysical Research Letters* 18:203–206.

Hart, S. R.
1984 He Diffusion in Olivine. *Earth and Planetary Science Letters* 70: 297–302.

Honda, M., and J. R. Arnold
1964 Effects of Cosmic Rays on Meteorites. *Science* 143: 203–212.

Hudson, G. B., M. W. Caffee, J. Beiriger, R. Ruiz, C. P. Kohl, and K. Nishiizumi
1991 Production Rate and Retention Properties of Cosmogenic ^{3}He and ^{21}Ne in Quartz. *Eos* 72(44):575.

Jull, A. J. T., A. E. Wilson, G. S. Burr, L. J. Toolin, D. J. Donahue
1992 Measurements of Cosmogenic ^{14}C Produced by Spallation in High-Altitude Rocks. *Radiocarbon,* 34: 737–744.

Klein, J., D. Fink, R. Middleton, K. Nishiizumi, and J. Arnold
1991 Determination of the Half Life of ^{41}Ca from Measurements of Antarctic Meteorites. *Earth and Planetary Science Letters* 103: 79–83.

Klein, J., R. Giegengack, R. Middleton, P. Sharma, J. R. Underwood, and R. A. Weeks
1986 Revealing Histories of Exposure Using *in-situ* Produced ^{26}Al and ^{10}Be in Libyan Desert Glass. *Radiocarbon* 28:547–555.

Kohl, C. P. and K. Nishiizumi
1992 Chemical Isolation of Quartz for Measurement of *in-situ*-Produced Cosmogenic Nuclides. *Geochimica et Cosmochimica Acta* 56:3583–3587.

Kurz, M. D.
1986a Cosmogenic Helium in a Terrestrial Igneous Rock. *Nature* 320:435–439.
1986b *In-situ* Production of Terrestrial Cosmogenic Helium and Some Applications to Geochronology. *Geochimica et Cosmochimica Acta* 50:2855–2862.
1987 Correction to: *In-situ* Production of Terrestrial Cosmogenic Helium and Some Applications to Geochronology. *Geochimica et Cosmochimica Acta* 51:1019.

Kurz, M. D., D. Colodner, T. W. Trull, R. Moore, and K. O'Brien
1990 Cosmic Ray Exposure Dating with *in-situ* Produced Cosmogenic ^{3}He: Results from Young Hawaiian Lava Flows. *Earth and Planetary Science Letters* 97:177–189.

Lal, D.
1958 *Investigations of Nuclear Interactions Produced by Cosmic Rays*. Unpublished Ph.D. dissertation, Department of Physics, Tata Institute of Fundamental Research, Bombay.
1987 Production of ^{3}He in Terrestrial Rocks. *Chemical Geology, Isotope Geoscience* 66:89–98.
1988 *In-situ* Produced Cosmogenic Isotopes in Terrestrial Rocks. *Annual Review of Earth and Planetary Science Letters* 16:355–388.
1991 Cosmic Ray Labeling of Erosion Surfaces: *In-situ* Nuclide Production Rates and Erosion Models. *Earth and Planetary Science Letters* 104:424–439.

Lal, D., P. K. Malhotra, and B. Peters
1958 On the Production of Radioisotopes in the Atmosphere by Cosmic Radiation and their Application to Meteorology. *Journal of Atmospheric and Terrestrial Physics* 12:306–328.

Lal, D., and B. Peters
1967 Cosmic-Ray Produced Radioactivity on the Earth. In *Handbuch der Physik* 46/2, edited by S. Flugge, pp. 551–612. Springer Verlag, Berlin.

Leprince-Ringuet, L., F. Bousser, H-T. Chang-Fong, L. Jauneau, and D. Morellet
1949 Two Kinds of Very High Energy Cosmic-Ray Stars. *Physical Review* 76:1273–1274.

Light, E. S., M. Merker, H. J. Verschell, R. B. Mendell, and S. A. Korff
1973 Time Dependent Worldwide Distribution of Atmospheric Neutrons and of Their Products. *Journal of Geophysical Research* 78:2741–2762.

Lingenfelter, R. E.
1963 Production of Carbon-14 by Cosmic Ray Neutrons. *Review of Geophysics* 1:35–55.

Litherland, A. E.
1987 Fundamentals of Accelerator Mass Spectrometry. *Philosophical Transactions of the Royal Society of London* A323:5–21.

Mabuchi, H. Y., Y. Gensho, Y. Wada, and H. Hamaguchi
1971 Phosphorous-32 Induced by Cosmic Rays in Laboratory Chemicals. *Geochemical Journal* 4:105–110.

Mankinen, E. A., and D. E. Champion
1992 Latest Pleistocene and Holocene Paleointensity on Hawaii. *Eos* 73(43):145.

Marti, K., and H. Craig
1987 Cosmic-ray Produced Neon and Helium in the Summit Lavas of Maui. *Nature* 325:335–337.

Mazor, E., D. Heymann, and E. Anders
1970 Noble Gases in Carbonaceous Chondrites. *Geochimica et Cosmochimica Acta* 34:781–824.

McElhinny, M. W., and W. E. Senanayake
1982 Variations in the Geomagnetic Dipole 1: The Past 50,000 Years. *Journal of Geomagnetism and Geoelectricity* 34:39–51.

Morrison, P., and J. Pine
1955 Radiogenic Origin of the Helium Isotopes in

Rocks. *Annals of the New York Academy of Sciences* 62:71–92.

Nakamura, Y., H. Mabuchi, and H. Hamaguchi
1972 ^{7}Be Production from Oxygen by Atmospheric Cosmic Rays. *Geochemical Journal* 6:43–47.

Nishiizumi, K., J. Klein, R. Middleton, and H. Craig
1990 Cosmogenic ^{10}Be, ^{26}Al, and ^{3}He in Olivine from Maui Lavas. *Earth and Planetary Science Letters* 98:263–266.

Nishiizumi, K., C. P. Kohl, J. R. Arnold, J. Klein, D. Fink, and R. Middleton
1991 Cosmic Ray Produced ^{10}Be and ^{26}Al in Antarctic Rocks: Exposure and Erosion History. *Earth and Planetary Science Letters* 104:440–454.

Nishiizumi, K., C. P. Kohl, E. M. Shoemaker, J. R. Arnold, J. Klein, D. Fink, and R. Middleton
1991 In situ ^{10}Be-^{16}Al Exposure Ages at Meteor Crater, Arizona. *Geochimica et Cosmochimica Acta* 55:2699–2703.

Nishiizumi, K., D. Lal, J. Klein, R. Middleton, and J. Arnold
1986 Production of ^{10}Be and ^{26}Al by Cosmic Rays in Terrestrial Quartz in situ. *Nature* 319:134–136.

Nishiizumi, K., E. L. Winterer, C. P. Pohl, J. Klein, R. Middleton, D. Lal, and J. Arnold
1989 Cosmic Ray Production Rates of ^{10}Be and ^{26}Al in Quartz from Glacially Polished Rocks. *Journal of Geophysical Research* 94:17,907–17,916.

O'Brien, K.
1979 Secular Variations in the Production of Cosmogenic Isotopes in the Earth's Atmosphere. *Journal of Geophysical Research* 84:423–431.

Olinger, C. T., J. Poths, K. Nishiizumi, C. P. Kohl, R. C. Finkel, M. W. Caffee, J. Southon, and I. Proctor
1992 Attenuation Lengths of Cosmogenic Production of ^{26}Al, ^{10}Be and ^{21}Ne in Bandalier Tuff. *Eos* 73(14):195.

Phillips, F. M., B. D. Leavy, N. O. Jannik, D. Elmore, and P. W. Kubik
1986 Accumulation of Cosmogenic Chlorine-36 in Rocks: A Method for Surface Exposure Dating. *Science* 231:41–43.

Phillips, F. M., M. G. Zreda, S. S. Smith, D. Elmore, P. W. Kubik, R. I. Dorn, and D. J. Roddy
1991 Age and Geomorphic History of Meteor Crater, Arizona, from Cosmogenic ^{36}Cl and ^{14}C in Rock Varnish. *Geochimica et Cosmochimica Acta* 55:2695–2698.

Phillips, F. M., M. G. Zreda, S. S. Smith, D. Elmore, P. W. Kubik, and P. Sharma
1990 Cosmogenic Chlorine-36 Chronology for Glacial Deposits at Bloody Canyon, Eastern Sierra Nevada. *Science* 248: 1529–1532.

Pomerantz, M. A., and A. P. Agarwal
1962 Spatial Distribution of Cosmic Ray Intensity and Geomagnetic Theory. *Philosophical Magazine* 7:1503–1511.

Porcelli, D., J. O. H. Stone, and R. K. O'Nions
1987 Enhanced ^{3}He/^{4}He Ratios and Cosmogenic Helium in Ultramafic Xenoliths. *Chemical Geology, Isotope Geoscience* 66:89–98.

Poreda, R. J., and T. E. Cerling
1992 Cosmogenic Neon in Recent Lavas from the Western United States. *Geophysical Research Letters* 19: 1863–1866.

Raisbeck, G. M., and F. Yiou
1979 Possible Use of ^{41}Ca for Radioactive Dating. *Nature* 277:42.

Raisbeck, G. M., F. Yiou, D. Bourlès, J. Lestringuez, and D. Deboffle
1987 Measurements of ^{10}Be and ^{26}Al with a Tandetron AMS Facility. *Nuclear Instruments and Methods in Physics Research* B29:22–26.

Reedy, R. C., J. R. Arnold, and D. Lal
1983 Cosmic-Ray Record in Solar System Matter. *Annual Review of Nuclear and Particle Science* 33:505–537.

Rose, D. C., K. B. Fenton, J. Katzman, and J. A. Simpson
1956 Latitude Effect of the Cosmic Ray Nucleon and Meson Components at Sea Level. *Canadian Journal of Physics* 34:968.

Rossi, B.
1952 *High Energy Particles.* Prentice Hall, N.J.

Rubin, M., L. K. Gargulinski, and J. P. McGeehin
1987 Hawaiian Radiocarbon Dates. *United States Geological Survey Professional Paper* 1350:213–242.

Shea, M. A., D. F. Smart, and L. C. Gentile
1987 Estimating Cosmic Ray Vertical Cut-Off Rigidities as a Function of the McIlwain L-Parameter for Different Epochs of the Geomagnetic Field. *Physics of the Earth and Planetary Interiors* 48:200–205.

Simpson, J. A., and W. C. Fagot
1956 Properties of the Low Energy Nucleonic Component at Large Atmospheric Depths. *Physical Review* 90:1068–1072.

Staudacher, T., and C. J. Allegre
1991 Cosmogenic Neon in Ultramafic Nodules from Asia and in Quartzite from Antarctica. *Earth and Planetary Science Letters* 106:87–102.

Trull, T. W., M. D. Kurz, and W. J. Jenkins
1991 Diffusion of Cosmogenic ^{3}He in Olivine and Quartz: Implications for Surface Exposure Dating. *Earth and Planetary Science Letters* 103:241–256.

Vogt, S., G. F. Herzog, and R. C. Reedy
1990 Cosmogenic Nuclides in Extraterrestrial Materials. *Reviews of Geophysics* 28:253–275.

Yokoyama, Y., J.-L. Reyss, and F. Guichard
1977 Production of Radionuclides by Cosmic Rays at Mountain Altitudes. *Earth and Planetary Science Letters* 36:44–50.

Zreda, M. G., F. M. Phillips, D. Elmore, P. W. Kubik, P. Sharma, and R. I. Dorn
1991 Cosmogenic Chlorine-36 Production Rates in Terrestrial Rocks. *Earth and Planetary Science Letters* 105:94–109.

8
SURFACE EXPOSURE DATING BY COSMOGENIC CHLORINE-36 ACCUMULATION

Marek G. Zreda
Department of Hydrology and Water Resources
University of Arizona
Tucson, Arizona

Fred M. Phillips
Geoscience Department
New Mexico Institute of Mining and Technology
Socorro, New Mexico

Abstract

The cosmogenic ^{36}Cl accumulation method is a recently developed surface exposure dating technique that allows the direct dating of construction time of geomorphic surfaces. Chlorine-36 is produced in materials exposed at the surface of the earth at a rate proportional to the cosmic-ray intensity and to concentrations of three main target nuclides for ^{36}Cl formation—^{35}Cl, ^{39}K, and ^{40}Ca. Since the production rates of ^{36}Cl from the three target nuclides are known, the measured concentration of cosmogenic ^{36}Cl in a surficial rock can be used to calculate how long a surface has been exposed to cosmic radiation; thus the time of its construction can be determined. Because ^{36}Cl is a long-lived radionuclide (half-life of 301,000 years), the method can be used to date landforms constructed during the last million years; because of the ubiquitous nature of chlorine, the method is applicable to surfaces constructed out of materials of essentially any chemical composition.

The buildup of cosmogenic ^{36}Cl in terrestrial rocks is a function of production rates and radioactive decay. In rocks at the surface, buildup is fastest during the initial period of exposure, decreases with time, and eventually reaches a steady state, when cosmogenic production equals radioactive decay. This idealized buildup pattern may be severely influenced by surficial geological processes that result in calculated apparent ages differing from the landform age. Erosion and gradual exposure at the surface result in variable production rates and usually, but not always, lead to underestimated apparent ages. Intense chemical weathering may lead to a mixing of chlorine in the rock, that contains cosmogenic ^{36}Cl with meteoric chlorine, which has its own ^{36}Cl content, and thus to departure from the ideal buildup curve. Partial and temporal shielding result in underestimated apparent ages because of the reduction in cosmic-ray intensity. These and other factors controlling buildup are considered and appropriate corrections are applied to calculate reliable ^{36}Cl surface exposure ages.

Introduction

Earth scientists have long understood the factors that influence the formation of landforms and have realized that landforms contain valuable information about surficial processes and geological conditions prevailing at the time of their construction. For instance moraines form under cold climatic conditions; therefore the dating of glacial moraines, which results in the establishment of glacial chronologies, yields useful data about changes in local climatic conditions in the past and aids in understanding the nature of global climate changes. Similarly the ages of terrestrial impact craters yield important information on meteorite fluxes, and the dating of fault scarps gives quantitative information about tectonic activity. Landforms are, however, intrinsically difficult to date numerically, because they are generally made of preexisting geological materials; classical radiometric techniques would measure the age of the rock or mineral formation, rather than the age of geomorphic redistribution. Geomorphic surfaces are thus usually not amenable to the standard dating techniques. The last decade has seen the development of alternative dating techniques that can measure how long an object has been exposed at the surface of the earth—surface exposure dating methods. They include methods based on the *in situ* accumulation of cosmogenic nuclides (^{36}Cl, ^{26}Al, ^{10}Be, ^{3}He and ^{14}C) in surficial rocks, the accumulation of organic matter in desert varnish, and physicochemical changes in rock-forming minerals due to weathering processes. In this chapter we describe the cosmogenic ^{36}Cl buildup method and its applications to dating of late Pleistocene landforms.

Chlorine-36 is produced by cosmic rays that interact with several nuclides, predominantly ^{35}Cl, ^{39}K, and ^{40}Ca. In materials exposed at the surface of the earth, cosmogenic ^{36}Cl is produced at a rate proportional to the local cosmic-ray intensity and to the concentrations of the three target nuclides. The concentration of ^{36}Cl can thus be used as a measure of the length of time a material has been exposed to cosmic radiation (Davis and Schaeffer 1955; Phillips et al. 1986). Very low concentrations of ^{36}Cl can now be measured routinely, using accelerator mass spectrometry (Elmore et al. 1979; Elmore and Phillips 1987). Its half-life of 301,000 years makes ^{36}Cl suitable for dating groundwater, geomorphic surfaces, and anthropogenic constructions in the time range from a few thousand years up to about one million years. The ubiquitous character of chlorine and its conservative nature are important attributes that allow the use of the cosmogenic ^{36}Cl buildup method to establish surface exposure age of rocks that originated in various environments and have a very wide range of chemical compositions.

We present in this chapter a state-of-the-art description of the cosmogenic ^{36}Cl buildup method. We begin with a description of the spatial distribution of cosmic radiation in the atmosphere and the top few meters of solid materials. In the next section we characterize mechanisms and rates of cosmogenic ^{36}Cl production and formulate equations for the accumulation of ^{36}Cl in rocks exposed at the surface of the earth and in the shallow subsurface. Then we present two case studies to demonstrate the applicability of the ^{36}Cl method to dating geomorphic surfaces. Finally we examine possible effects of erosion, weathering, and shielding on ^{36}Cl buildup dating and discuss practical aspects of the cosmogenic ^{36}Cl accumulation method.

Spatial Distribution of Cosmogenic Chlorine-36 Production

The intensity of cosmic radiation at the surface of earth is modulated by the earth's magnetic field and by interactions with atmospheric nuclei. As a result of these processes, the highest intensity is at high geomagnetic latitudes and at high elevations. Cosmic-ray neutron measurements at a variety of latitudes and elevations have been used by Lal (1991) to formulate a cubic polynomial equation that allows for the calculation of present-day cosmic-ray intensity at any location relative to any other location (Table 8.1). The validity of this formulation for the late Pleistocene was tested by Zreda et al. (1991), who measured cosmogenic ^{36}Cl in independently dated Hawaiian lava flows and moraines sampled at elevations from 120 to 4,090 m. The exponential curve obtained from the ^{36}Cl data (Figure 8.1) is in excellent agreement with that calculated from Lal (1991). Lal's scaling formulation thus appears to be applicable to surfaces constructed during the late Pleistocene.

Cosmic rays, despite strong attenuation in the atmosphere, reach the surface of the earth, interact with nuclei of minerals in the shallow subsurface, and produce cosmogenic nuclides. Three types of cosmic-ray particles produce most of the ^{36}Cl: secondary fast neutrons (Yokoyama et al. 1977), thermal neutrons (Davis and Schaeffer 1955; Fabryka-Martin 1988; Phillips et al. 1986), and negative slow muons (Fabryka-Martin 1988; Zreda et al. 1990; Zreda et al. 1991); their relative importance is presented in Table 8.2.

Neutrons form the major part of the reactive cosmic-ray flux at high (mountain) elevations. Fast secondary neutrons have high energies (1–30 Mev) and are responsible for the spallation reactions of ^{39}K and ^{40}Ca. They are attenuated both in the atmosphere (Lal 1987; Zreda et al. 1991) and solid materials (Kurz 1986; Lal 1987) according to $exp(-depth/\lambda_n)$ where the attenuation length, λ_n, for the fast component is from 150 to 160 g/cm^2 (Kurz 1986; Lal 1987; Zreda, Phillips, Elmore, et al. 1991).

Thermal neutrons (energies below 0.025 eV) are formed from the fast neutrons that collide with atoms in the atmosphere or within a rock mass and lose energy. In contrast to the spallation component, the distribution of these neutrons in the subsurface cannot be described by a simple exponential term, because of the air-ground boundary effect (O'Brien et al. 1978; Yamashita et al. 1966). The macroscopic thermal neutron absorption cross section of atmospheric gases is much higher than that of common crustal rocks. Therefore neutrons that are produced in the top several centimeters of the rock mass have a propensity to escape out of the rock and into the air above it, where they are absorbed by nitrogen atoms. This leads to the relative depletion of thermal neutrons in the uppermost part of the rock mass. The distribution of thermal neutrons in the top 100 g/cm^2 of a concrete block was measured by Fabryka-Martin et al. (1991), who reported a maximum at the depth of about 45 g/cm^2 (18 cm). Below this depth the intensity of thermal neutrons decreases exponentially, at a rate similar to that for the fast component. Figure 8.2 shows the behavior of the two main components of cosmic radiation, fast and thermal neutrons, in the shallow subsurface (0–1,000 g/cm^2).

At sea level the negative muon stopping rate is comparable to the neutron flux, and in very calcic rocks, slow muon capture by ^{40}Ca becomes a significant cosmogenic ^{36}Cl production reaction (Jha and Lal 1982; Lal and Peters 1967; Rama and Honda 1961). The slow negative muons can penetrate deeper due to their lower reactivity (attenuation length, λ_m of 247 g/cm^2; Conversi 1950; Rossi 1952) and dominate cosmogenic pro-

Table 8.1. Scaling Formulation for Elevation and Geomagnetic Latitude in the Form of a Series of Cubic Polynomials ($y=a+bx+cx^2+dx^3$), Where x Is the Elevation above Sea Level in km and y Is the Scaling Factor, Fitted to the Observed Thermal Neutron Data of Lal (1991)

Geomagnetic latitude	a	b	c	d
0	0.5790	0.4482	0.1723	0.0359
10	0.5917	0.4415	0.1944	0.0363
20	0.6691	0.4764	0.2320	0.0435
30	0.8217	0.6910	0.1712	0.0822
40	0.9204	0.8849	0.2487	0.1031
50	0.9865	1.0298	0.2992	0.1333
60–90	1.0000	1.0889	0.3105	0.1382

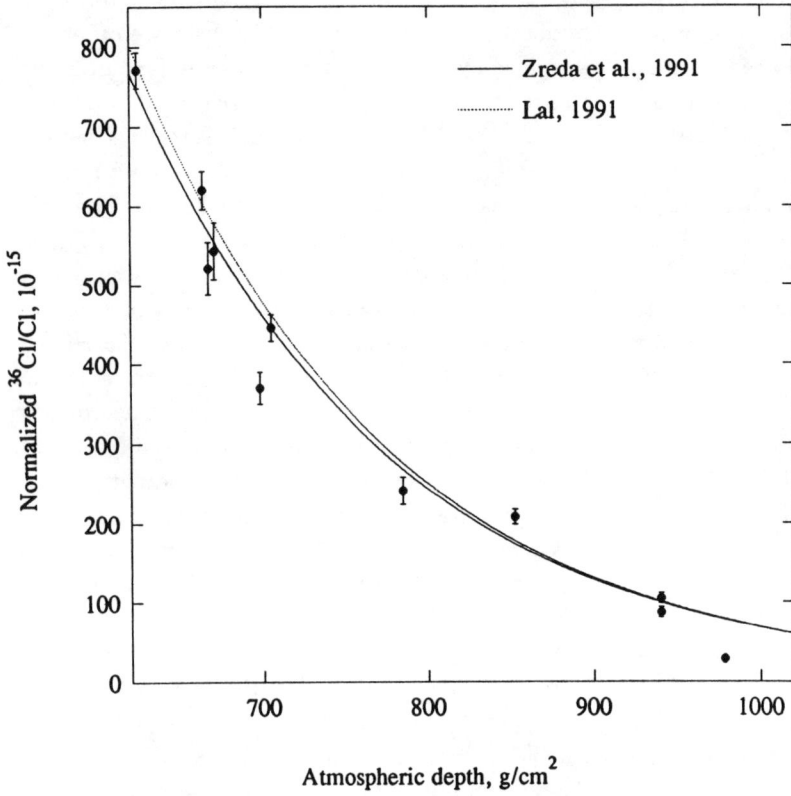

Figure 8.1. Normalized cosmogenic ^{36}Cl at atmospheric depths from 620 g/cm^2 (elevation 4,090 m above sea level) to 1,020 g/cm^2 (elevation 120 m). The intensity of cosmic radiation increases with elevation, due to decreasing atmospheric pressure; this leads to proportionally higher production rates of cosmogenic ^{36}Cl and other nuclides. Therefore relative values of normalized $^{36}Cl/Cl$ ratios at different elevations are indicative of relative cosmic ray intensity. Good agreement between the observed ^{36}Cl data (dots) of Zreda et al. (1991) and the theoretical altitude scaling factors of Lal (1991) indicates the validity of the latter for the late Pleistocene.

duction of ^{36}Cl at depths below about three m of water equivalent (mwe). They can be captured by the nucleus of ^{40}Ca, which results in production of ^{36}Cl. The production from negative muon capture is uncertain and therefore it is lumped together with that due to the spallation of ^{40}Ca (Zreda et al. 1990; Zreda et al. 1991).

Accumulation of *in situ* Chlorine-36 in Surficial Materials

In the idealized case in which a surface is suddenly exposed to cosmic rays and remains in constant position, cosmogenic ^{36}Cl accumulation is a function of the local cosmic-ray intensity, the chemical composition of the sample, and the exposure time. Chlorine-36 is produced at a rate P and radioactively decays at a rate proportional to its abundance and its decay constant, λ_{36}. Its accumulation with time is described by a linear first-order ordinary differential equation:

$$(1) \quad \frac{dN_{36}}{dt} = P - \lambda_{36} N_{36}$$

which has the solution (Bentley et al. 1986)

$$(2) \quad N_{36} = \frac{P}{\lambda_{36}} (1 - e^{-\lambda_{36} t})$$

where N_{36} is the number of atoms of ^{36}Cl and t is the exposure time. For a given chemical composition of material, the production rate P is constant and can be expressed as the sum of the rates of the spallation and thermal neutron activation reactions:

Table 8.2. Relative Contribution of Major Cosmogenic Reactions Leading to the Production of ^{36}Cl in the Top 100 g/cm^2 in Examples of Terrestrial Rocks (Granites, Basalts, Carbonates, and Shales) at Sea Level and High Geomagnetic Latitudes[a]

Reaction Type	Notation	% of Total ^{36}Cl
Spallation of K and Ca	^{39}K(n,2n2p)^{36}Cl	16–80
	^{40}Ca(n,2n3p)^{36}Cl	
Thermal neutron activation of Cl	^{35}Cl(n,γ)^{36}Cl	11–80
Negative muon capture by Ca	^{40}Ca(μ$^-$,α)^{36}Cl	0–10

[a]From Zreda et al. 1990, modified after Fabryka-Martin 1988.

$$(3) \quad P = \psi_{Ca} C_{Ca} + \psi_K C_K + \phi_n \frac{\sigma_{35} N_{35}}{\Sigma \sigma_i N_i}$$

where ψ_{Ca} and ψ_K are the production rates due to spallation of Ca and K per unit concentration of Ca and K, C_{Ca} and C_K are the concentrations of Ca and K, ϕ_n is the thermal neutron absorption rate per unit mass of rock, σ_{35} is the thermal neutron absorption cross section for ^{35}Cl, N_{35} is the number of atoms of ^{35}Cl, σ_i is the thermal neutron absorption cross section for every element i in the rock matrix and N_i is the number of atoms of element i. The production parameters in equation (3) are for rocks on the land surface at sea level and at high geomagnetic latitudes. For materials from other locations, the production rates have to be scaled according to Table 8.1 for elevation and latitude (scaling factor EL) and according to Figure 8.2 for depth below the surface (scaling factor D). It is also convenient to express the concentration of ^{36}Cl in terms of the ratio of ^{36}Cl to the total Cl, because this is the quantity actually measured by accelerator mass spectrometry. The solution to the above differential equation thus becomes

$$(4) \quad R_{36} = ELD \frac{\psi_{Ca} C_{Ca} + \psi_K C_K + \phi_n \frac{\sigma_{35} N_{35}}{\Sigma \sigma_i N_i}}{\lambda_{36} N_{Cl}}$$

$$(1 - e^{-\lambda_{36} t}).$$

In this equation R_{36} is the ^{36}Cl/Cl ratio after the subtraction of background radiogenic ^{36}Cl formed in rocks due to neutrons derived from the decay of uranium and thorium (Andrews et al. 1989; Bentley et al. 1986; Feige et al. 1968; Kuhn et al. 1984), and N_{Cl} is the number of chlorine atoms per unit mass of rock. In commonly used geochemical units, the concentrations of Ca and K are in weight percents of CaO and K$_2$O, the production rates due to spallation are in atoms of ^{36}Cl per weight percent of oxide per kg of rock per year, and the thermal neutron absorption rate is in neutrons per kg of rock per year (Phillips et al. 1986; Zreda et al. 1991). The buildup of cosmogenic ^{36}Cl in rocks with approximately equal production rates due to spallation and thermal neutron activation is graphed in Figure 8.3. The sample has been exposed at the surface since the landform formation. The buildup rate of ^{36}Cl is fastest during the initial period of exposure and decreases with time until the decay rate of ^{36}Cl in the rock asymptotically approaches secular equilibrium with the cosmogenic production rate. We will see in the next section that samples buried below the surface and gradually exposed by erosion of the overlying material have different buildup paths.

The exposure time is obtained by solving the last equation for t

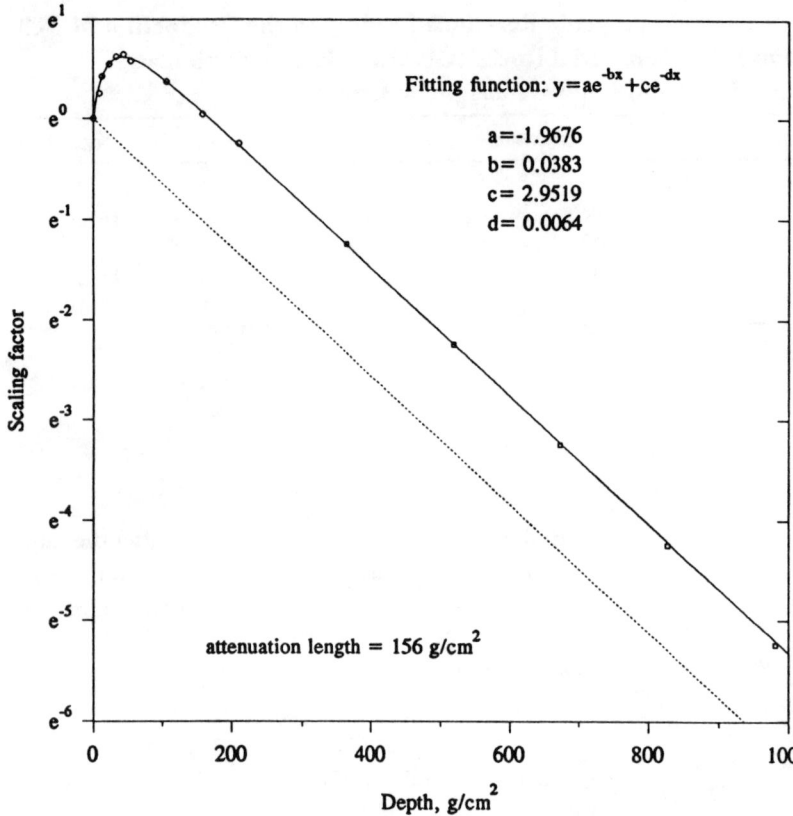

Figure 8.2. Distribution of thermal (solid line) and fast (dashed line) neutrons in the shallow subsurface, normalized to the surface values. The circles are measured thermal neutron intensities (Fabryka-Martin et al. 1991), and the squares are calculated values based on an attenuation length of 156 g/cm². The fitting function is for the thermal component; the fast component can be described by its attenuation length.

$$(5) \quad t = \frac{-1}{\lambda_{36}} \ln \left(1 - \frac{R_{36} \lambda_{36} N_{Cl}}{ELD \left(\psi_K C_K + \psi_{Ca} C_{Ca} + \phi_n \frac{\sigma_{35} N_{35}}{\Sigma \sigma_i N_i} \right)} \right).$$

The error of the exposure time calculation is a combination of (1) analytical errors associated with isotopic and chemical analyses; (2) uncertainties in the production rates; and (3) uncertainties related to the distribution of the cosmic-ray flux in the atmosphere and the shallow subsurface. The analytical error is on the order of 5 to 10 percent and is mainly due to analytical uncertainty in ^{36}Cl measurements by accelerator mass spectrometry; this error is routinely reported as the uncertainty of the age determination (Phillips et al. 1990; Phillips et al. 1991; Zreda et al. 1991; Zreda et al. 1990). Uncertainties in the assessment of the temporal and spatial distribution of the cosmic-ray intensity and also the production rates of cosmogenic ^{36}Cl may add another 10, 20 or more percent to the estimated error of the exposure time, but these errors have not yet been systematically evaluated.

The production rate of ^{36}Cl due to the thermal neutron activation of ^{35}Cl can be calculated based on the thermal neutron absorption rate, the concentration of Cl, and the chemical composition of the sample (Davis and Schaeffer 1955; Phillips et al. 1986). Only a limited number of elements with high thermal neutron absorption cross sections and/or high concentrations (Table 8.3) strongly compete with ^{35}Cl for thermal neutrons; they usually account for more than 98 percent of the absorbed thermal neutrons (Leavy 1987), and therefore

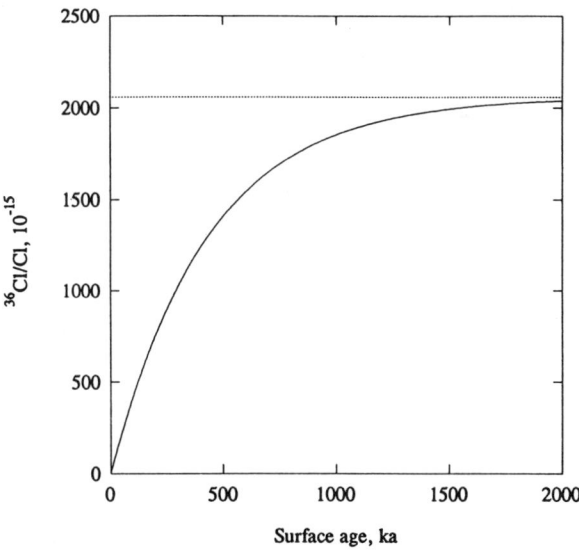

Figure 8.3. Buildup of cosmogenic ^{36}Cl on the surface in rocks. The rocks are instantly exposed at the surface at time $t = 0$ and do not undergo any mass loss due to erosion. The buildup curve is steepest at early times and flattens gradually to reach a steady state at times on the order of several half-lives of ^{36}Cl.

it is not necessary to measure the concentrations of all elements.

The first attempt to use the *in situ* buildup of ^{36}Cl in rocks due to thermal neutron activation was made by Davis and Schaeffer (1955). However, the analytical instruments in the 1950s were not sufficiently sensitive to measure very small quantities of ^{36}Cl, and the idea could not be realized. In addition the total thermal neutron absorption rate was poorly known at that time. A thermal neutron absorption rate varying from 2×10^5 to 4×10^5 neutrons per kg of rock per year was reported by different investigators (Andrews et al. 1986; Hendricks and Edge 1966; Montgomery and Montgomery 1939; Simpson 1951; Yamashita et al. 1966), but the range was too wide to be useful and needed refinement.

Cross sections for the spallation processes are not well known, and their quantification is difficult. For practical purposes we assume that the production of ^{36}Cl due to spallation of ^{39}K and ^{40}Ca is proportional to the concentration of the target elements and their respective production rates. The first theoretical estimates of the production rates of ^{36}Cl from ^{39}K and ^{40}Ca were published by Yokoyama et al. (1977). When applied to ^{36}Cl data from late Pleistocene moraines in the Sierra Nevada, they yielded ages much younger than those indicated by independent geological methods. An empirical determination of the effective production rates from these elements was therefore attempted.

Zreda et al. (1990; see also Zreda et al. 1991) measured ^{36}Cl concentrations in ^{14}C-dated samples and calculated time-integrated (effective) production rates of ^{36}Cl due to spallation of ^{40}Ca and ^{39}K and thermal neutron activation of ^{35}Cl. These are summarized in Table 8.4. These rates were later applied to the dating of several geomorphic surfaces and yielding ages in agreement with those obtained using independent methods (Phillips et al. 1990; Phillips et al. 1991; Zreda et al. 1990; Zreda et al. 1991).

Validation and Applications of the Chlorine-36 Method

For validation and initial applications of the cosmogenic ^{36}Cl dating method, two sites with relatively simple exposure histories and sample geometries and of well-known geomorphological contexts were chosen (Phillips et al. 1990; Phillips et al. 1991; Zreda et al. 1990; Zreda et al. 1991): Meteor Crater, Arizona, where there is a well-preserved meteor impact crater, and Bloody Canyon in the eastern Sierra Nevada, California, where there exists a set of late Pleistocene moraines. In both cases a few fundamental assumptions were made: (1) the investigated rocks were placed instantly at the surface of the landforms at time t=0; (2) the rocks did not contain any inherited ^{36}Cl from previous exposure episodes; (3) the rocks have remained in stable position since their deposition; (4) the surfaces of the rocks did not undergo significant mass loss due to erosion; (5) the rocks have not been shielded from cosmic radiation (for instance, by snow cover or sand dunes) at any time; (6) all measured ^{36}Cl is cosmogenic

Table 8.3. Thermal Neutron Absorption Cross Sections, σ, of the Elements Contributing Significantly to the Total Macroscopic Thermal Neutron Cross Section, $\Sigma \sigma N$. The example chemical composition is that of a monzonite.

Element	σ^a (10^{-24} cm^2)	Composition[b] (g/kg)	N[c] (10^{22}/kg)	σN (cm^2/kg)	% of $\Sigma \sigma N$
Si	0.16	326.70	703	1.125	22.09
Al	0.23	79.40	177	0.407	7.99
Fe	2.55	7.00	7.53	0.192	3.77
Mn	13.3	0.40	0.438	0.058	1.14
Ti	6.1	1.20	1.51	0.092	1.81
Mg	0.063	1.20	3.01	0.002	0.04
Ca	0.43	7.10	10.69	0.046	0.90
Na	0.53	37.10	97.14	0.515	10.11
K	2.1	41.50	64.08	1.346	26.44
P	0.19	0.20	0.389	0.001	0.02
Cl	33.2	0.10	0.170	0.056	1.10
B	759	0.005	0.027	0.205	4.03
Gd	49,000	0.005	0.0019	0.931	18.28
Sm	5,800	0.005	0.0020	0.116	2.28
$\Sigma \sigma N$[d]				5.092	100.00

[a]Thermal neutron absorption cross sections are from Mughaghab and Garber (1973).
[b]Composition of a monzonite from the White Mountains, California (Zreda et al. 1990).
[c]Number of atoms of element per kg of rock, based on composition of the rock.
[d]Macroscopic thermal neutron absorption cross section of the sample.

or radiogenic (that is, there is no meteoric or anthropogenic component present in the measured samples). We will evaluate the above assumptions in the remainder of this chapter, mainly in the light of the results from Meteor Crater and Bloody Canyon.

An iron-nickel meteorite, which fell on the southwest margin of the Colorado Plateau, made a circular impact crater about 1.5 km wide and 170 m deep (Roddy 1978). Initial estimates of the crater's age, based on soil development on the ejecta blanket and lacustrine sediments inside the crater (Shoemaker 1983; Shoemaker and Kieffer 1979), yielded an age of ca. 25 ± 5 ka, whereas the thermoluminescence study of Sutton (1985a, 1985b) on shock-metamorphosed dolomite and quartz indicated that the impact took place 49 ± 3 ka ago. This discrepancy motivated Phillips et al. (1991) to date the crater using the cosmogenic ^{36}Cl method.

During the impact, previously deeply buried dolomites were virtually instantly ejected and exposed to cosmic radiation. The crater thus provides a nearly perfect scenario for surface exposure dating methods. Phillips et al. (1991) sampled five boulders located at the crater rim and measured cosmogenic ^{36}Cl content. Four out of five samples yielded almost identical ages, whereas the fifth sample was much younger (Table 8.5, Figure 8.4). On the basis of the close grouping of the four oldest samples and the markedly different age of the youngest sample, the authors concluded that the present surface of the youngest rock must have been shielded from the cosmic rays after the impact and exposed later than the rest of the sampled boulders. This conclusion is supported by comparison with the data of Nishiizumi et al. (1991), who reported a relative deficit of ^{10}Be very similar to the deficit of ^{36}Cl in the same boulder. The mean age of the four oldest samples, 49.7

Table 8.4. Production Rates of ^{36}Cl from Its Main Target Elements and the Absorption Rate of Thermal Neutrons; Negative Muons Are Included in the Spallation of ^{40}Ca.[a]

Cosmogenic Reaction	Parameter	Effective Production Rate[b]	
Spallation of ^{39}K	ψ_K	1,600 ± 145	7,520 ± 680
Spallation of ^{40}Ca	ψ_{Ca}	520 ± 47	2,900 ± 260
Thermal neutron activation of ^{35}Cl	ϕ_n	(3.14 ± 0.28) × 10^5	

[a]From Zreda 1994.
[b]Production rates due to spallation of ^{39}K and ^{40}Ca are in atoms of ^{36}Cl per kg rock per weight percent of Ca and K per year (first column) and in atoms of ^{36}Cl per mole Ca and K per year (second column). Absorption rate of thermal neutrons is in neutrons per kg of rock per year.

Table 8.5. Concentration of Target Nuclides, Macroscopic Cross Sections, ^{36}Cl/Cl Values, and ^{36}Cl Ages of Meteor Crater[a]

Sample	ELD	$\Sigma\sigma_i N_i$[b] (cm^2/kg)	CaO (wt %)	K$_2$O (wt %)	Cl (ppm)	^{36}Cl/Cl (10^{-15})	Boulder age (ka)
MC-1	3.34	2.28	21.1	0.47	143	1462 ± 44	49.7 ± 1.5
MC-2	3.34	2.37	23.4	0.47	131	1194 ± 39	36.5 ± 1.2
MC-3	3.27	2.65	29.2	0.43	217	1280 ± 57	50.4 ± 2.2
MC-4	3.27	2.73	23.8	0.78	132	1469 ± 71	48.5 ± 2.4
MC-5	3.34	2.50	28.2	0.44	259	1207 ± 38	50.3 ± 1.6
Mean[c]							47.1 ± 6.0
Mean without MC-2[c]							49.7 ± 0.9

[a]From Phillips et al. 1991 and Zreda et al. 1990.
[b]Macroscopic absorption cross section of rock sample; σ_i is the thermal neutron absorption cross section for element i, and N$_i$ is the number of atoms of element i per kg of rock.
[c]Standard deviation of individual sample ages, not from analytical uncertainties.

± 0.9 ka, is in remarkable agreement with two independent age estimates: 49 ± 3 ka based on the thermoluminescence method (Sutton 1985b) and a cosmogenic ^{10}Be/^{26}Al age determination of 48.5 ± 1.3 ka (from Nishiizumi et al. 1991). This study provided support for the accuracy and reliability of the cosmogenic ^{36}Cl method of surface exposure dating and its application to late Pleistocene landforms. It also indicated that even in this nearly perfect scenario for surface exposure dating, there are processes that tend to decrease the apparent ^{36}Cl buildup age: investigators of less suitable landforms should therefore exercise great care during sample collection and evaluation of results. In this connection, Nishiizumi et al. (1991) postulated that the sampled boulders were covered by fine-grained ejecta for the initial few thousand years after the impact and suggested that the age should be corrected by a comparable amount. In the next section we evaluate this possibility and its potential effect on the calculated ^{36}Cl ages.

The second group of landforms initially selected for ^{36}Cl dating are the glacial deposits in Bloody Canyon. These deposits have frequently been investigated because of their good preservation and visibility. Notable studies include those by Blackwelder (1931), Burke and

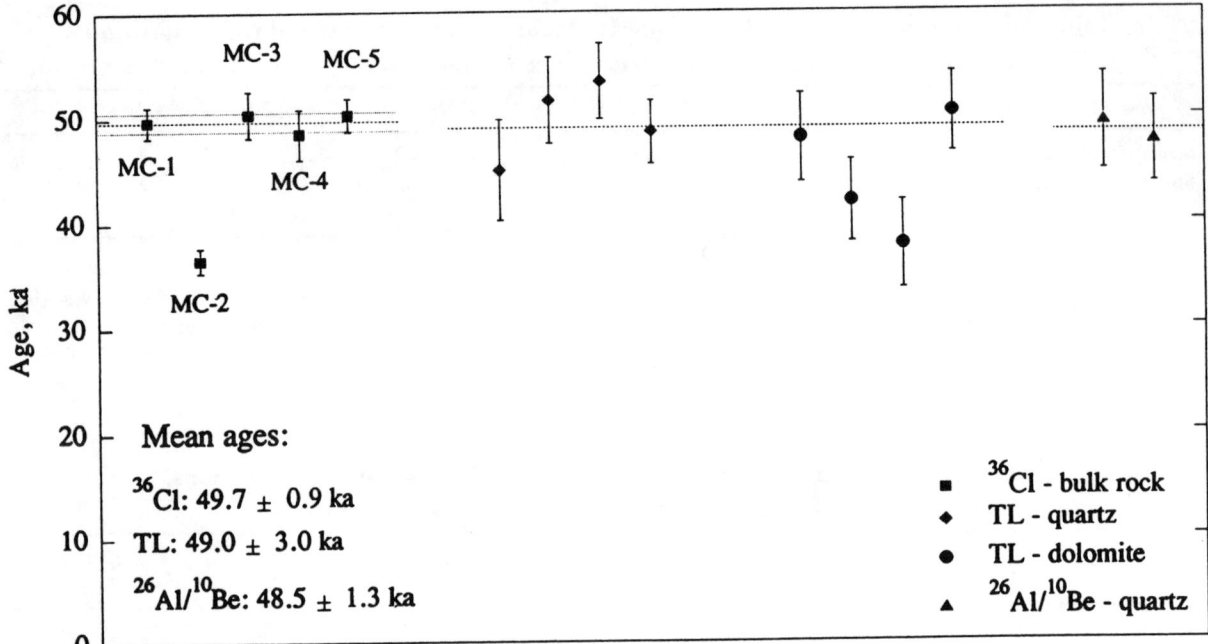

Figure 8.4. Comparison of cosmogenic ^{36}Cl ages (Phillips et al. 1990; Zreda et al. 1990) with thermoluminescence (Sutton 1985a) and selected ^{26}Al/^{10}Be ages (Nishiizumi et al. 1991) for Meteor Crater, Arizona. Sample labels, MC-1 through MC-5, correspond to those in Table 8.5.

Birkeland (1979), and Sharp and Birman (1963); related deposits in other drainages were reported by Atwater et al. (1986), Dorn et al. (1987), Gillespie (1982), Gillespie et al. (1984), and Mezger and Burbank (1986). On the basis of stratigraphic relationships and relative dating criteria, deposits of four glaciations have been distinguished: the Tioga (youngest), Tenaya, Tahoe, and Mono Basin (oldest). Phillips et al. (1990) measured cosmogenic ^{36}Cl in large boulders located on the tops of these moraines and obtained a detailed chronology of the glaciations (Table 8.6, Figure 8.5). The results confirmed the general stratigraphy (with the exception of the Mono Basin deposits) proposed by previous investigators and added numerical constraints to the conventional description of the glacial sequence.

The results indicate that the cosmogenic ^{36}Cl dating technique can indeed be used to distinguish moraines of different ages, even so close to each other as the Tioga and Tenaya. For younger surfaces the individual ages are closely clustered, and the arithmetic average is the best estimate of the time of the glaciation. As the ages become older, the individual boulder ages are no longer clustered, because surficial processes, such as erosion or weathering, result in apparent ages that are generally younger than the true age of the landforms. The authors therefore considered the oldest individual age to be closest to the true age of the moraine (Phillips et al. 1990). In the next section we will show that this heuristic interpretation is correct and also that the gradual exposure of boulder surfaces indeed results in distributions similar to those observed in Bloody Canyon.

Effects of Erosion and Gradual Exposure on ^{36}Cl Ages

In the section above, we assumed that the rocks were deeply buried, then exposed suddenly at the surface and

Table 8.6. Concentration of Target Nuclides, Macroscopic Cross Sections, ^{36}Cl/Cl Values, and ^{36}Cl Ages of the Bloody Canyon Samples[a]

Sample[b]	ELD	$\Sigma\sigma_i N_i$[c] (cm²/kg)	CaO (wt %)	K$_2$O (wt %)	Cl (ppm)	^{36}Cl/Cl (10^{-15})	Boulder age (10^3 years)	Moraine age (10^3 years)
BC86-1-TI	6.34	4.97	0.84	5.09	24	1770	23.1	
BC86-2-TI	6.34	4.06	2.27	2.96	71	402	12.2[d]	Tioga
BC86-3-TI	6.34	4.88	2.12	4.38	103	536	20.4	21.4 ± 1.4
BC86-5-TI	6.34	5.24	2.89	3.44	141	455	20.8	
BC86-6-TE	6.61	4.71	2.14	3.75	34	1350	24.0	
BC86-7-TE	6.14	3.71	3.69	1.68	40	244	5.1[d]	
BC86-8-TE	6.39	4.38	1.47	3.30	67	697	23.3	Tenaya
BC86-9-TE	6.56	4.65	1.94	4.32	74	839	24.4	24.3 ± 0.9
BC86-10-TE	6.14	4.38	1.52	3.96	64	469	13.5[d]	
BC86-11-TE	6.51	5.13	0.98	5.34	26	1951	25.5	
BC86-12-TA	5.57	6.38	7.37	1.06	73	3155	133	
BC86-13-TA	5.75	6.10	2.20	4.37	75	4313	189	Older Tahoe
BC86-14-TA	5.75	4.84	1.19	3.74	49	5736	214	141 ± 11[e]
BC86-15-TA	5.57	5.45	1.46	3.85	76	4211	218	207 ± 16[e]
BC86-16-TA	5.63	6.04	3.82	3.92	115	2790	149	
SC86-17-MB	5.96	4.73	0.56	3.93	57	3123	114	
SC86-18-MB	5.96	4.51	1.22	3.90	122	2001	103	
SC86-19-MB	6.49	5.07	2.40	3.22	113	1959	92	Mono Basin
SC86-20-MB	6.48	4.70	1.18	5.16	28	5289	79[d]	
SC86-21-MB	6.45	4.30	0.66	5.52	26	7031	97	103 ± 11
SC88-1	6.34	5.23	2.36	4.73	76	2848	93	
SC88-2	6.34	5.28	2.64	4.38	111	1916	80[d]	
SC88-3	6.34	5.41	3.41	4.19	157	2266	119	
BC87-1-TA	6.15	4.88	2.02	4.05	74	1638	55.9	
BC87-2-TA	6.15	4.75	0.79	5.57	31	3763	60.6	
BC87-3-TA	6.25	4.46	2.04	3.88	64	1309	38.6[d]	Younger Tahoe
BC87-4-TA	6.35	4.55	2.18	2.48	74	1461	57.0	
BC87-5-TA	6.46	4.79	1.83	4.31	100	1699	65.8	59.8 ± 4.5
BC88-1	6.15	3.89	1.61	4.70	38	315	5.2[d]	
BC88-5	6.15	5.47	2.72	4.41	90	1701	63.2	

[a]From Phillips et al. 1990 and Zreda et al., 1990.
[b]TI=Tioga, TE=Tenaya, TA=Tahoe, MB=Mono Basin.
[c]Macroscopic absorption cross section of rock sample; σ_i is the thermal neutron absorption cross section for element i, and N_i is the number of atoms of element i per kg of rock.
[d]Not used in calculation of mean moraine age.
[e]Younger moraine age is calculated from dates 133 and 149, older from dates 189, 214, and 219 ka.

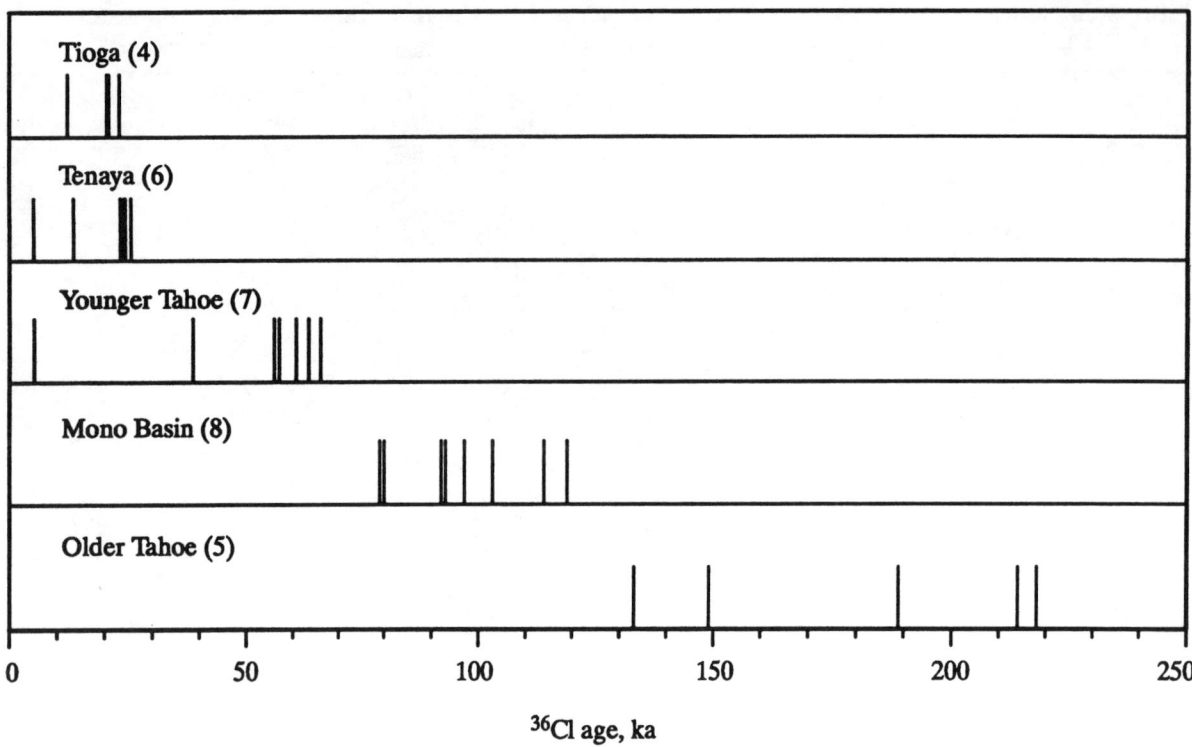

Figure 8.5. Distribution of cosmogenic ^{36}Cl boulder ages among the moraines at Bloody Canyon, Sierra Nevada, California (after Phillips et al. 1990 and Zreda 1990). Names of the moraines correspond to those in Table 8.6. Figures in parentheses indicate number of samples from each surface.

remained there unaffected by erosion until the time of measurements. Most surfaces, however, have undergone removal of some material due to erosion. Therefore the boulders that are now at the surface might have been covered for some period of time and then gradually exposed. The recorded cosmogenic signal will then be different from the signal recorded in rocks that have been exposed at the surface since the landform formation, and so will the apparent age, that is, the age calculated as if the rock has been at the surface since the landform construction. In the following sections, we discuss the gradual exposure model developed and described in more detail by Zreda et al. (1994).

We will model the process of gradual exposure by using the distribution of fast and thermal neutrons in the subsurface (see Figure 8.2), a range of erosion rates, and the maximum amount of soil material covering the boulders. Let us assume that at time $t = 0$ the boulder's surface was at depth x_0 below the ground surface (Figure 8.6). With an erosion rate ε, it will take x_0/ε years for the covering material to be removed and for the boulder to be exposed at the ground surface. At a given depth the production rate due to spallation can be calculated as the surface rate (P_s) multiplied by e^{-x/λ_n}, where x is the depth in g/cm^2 and λ_n is the attenuation length for the spallation component. The production of thermal neutrons is approximated by scaling the surface production (P_n) using the double exponential function $ae^{-b/x} + ce^{-d/x}$ (see Figure 8.2), where a, b, c, and d are the fitted parameters to observed data of Fabryka-Martin et al. (1991).

The differential equation describing the buildup of

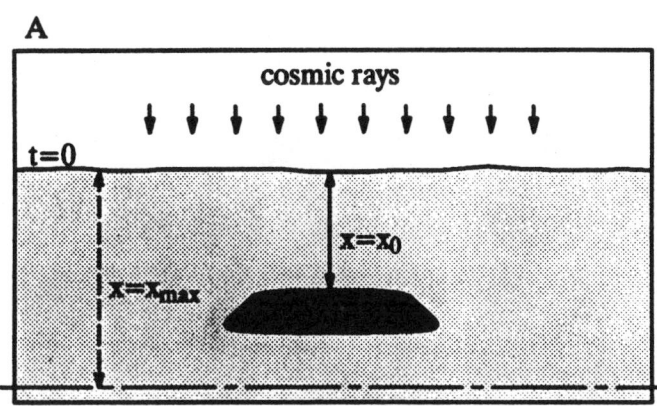
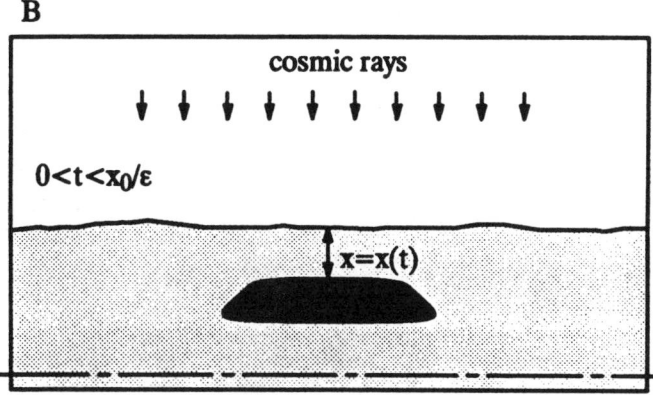
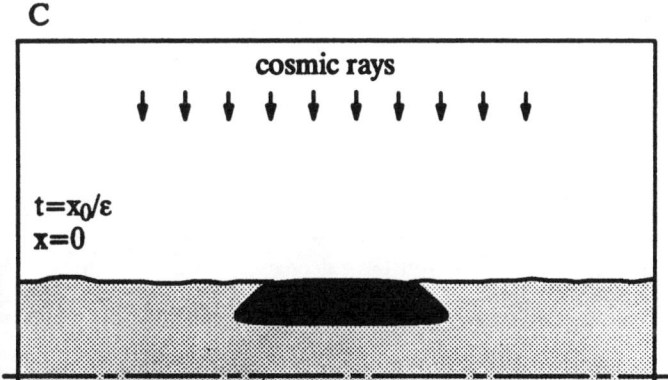
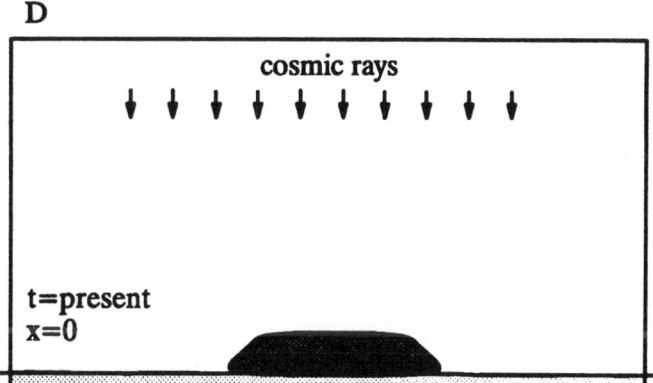

Figure 8.6. Conceptual model for the cosmogenic ^{36}Cl buildup in boulders (dark grey) initially buried in soil (light grey) and gradually exposed at the surface by erosion. Initially (A), the boulder has a cover of thickness $x = x_0$. The cover is removed by erosion at a rate $\varepsilon = x_{max}/t_p$, where t_p is the age of the surface and x_{max} is the erosion depth. At time $0 < t < x_0/\varepsilon$ (B), the boulder is covered by $x = x_0(1-t/t_p)$. At the time of exposure t_e (C), the boulder is exposed at the surface and remains there until the present (D), at which time x_{max} thickness of soil has been removed by erosion. Initial depth values are distributed uniformly between $x = 0$ and $x = x_{max}$, which, for constant erosion rates, leads to uniformly distributed exposure times t_e. The model and figure are modified from Zreda et al. (1994).

cosmogenic ^{36}Cl in gradually exposed surfaces (Zreda et al. 1994) contains depth- and time-dependent production rates $P[x(t)]$

(6) $$\frac{dN_{36}}{dt} = P[x(t)] - \lambda_{36}N_{36}.$$

The time-dependent depth $x(t)$ is represented in terms of the initial depth x_0, the time t, and the erosion rate ε as $x = x_0 - \varepsilon t$. Equation 6, upon substitution for $P[x(t)]$, becomes

(7) $$\frac{dN_{36}}{dt} = EL\left(P_s e^{\frac{-(x_0-\varepsilon t)}{\lambda_n}} + P_n(ae^{-b(x_0-\varepsilon t)} + ce^{-d(x_0-\varepsilon t)})\right) - \lambda_{35}N_{36}.$$

The general solution to this equation is

$$(8) \quad N_{36} = EL \left(\frac{P_s}{\frac{\varepsilon}{\lambda_n} + \lambda_{36}} e^{-\frac{x_0 - \varepsilon t}{\lambda_n}} + \frac{P_n a}{b\varepsilon + \lambda_{36}} e^{-b(x_0 - \varepsilon t)} + \frac{P_n c}{d\varepsilon + \lambda_{36}} e^{-d(x_0 - \varepsilon t)} \right) + C e^{-\lambda_{36} t}$$

where C is the integration constant. The initial condition (t=0, N=0) is appropriate for a landform created out of previously shielded materials. For this condition the solution is

$$(9) \quad N_{36} = EL \left(P_s \frac{e^{\frac{-x_0}{\lambda_n}}}{\frac{\varepsilon}{\lambda_n} + \lambda_{36}} \left(e^{\frac{\varepsilon}{\lambda_n} t} - e^{-\lambda_{36} t} \right) \right.$$

$$+ P_n \frac{a e^{-b x_0}}{b\varepsilon + \lambda_{36}} \left(e^{b\varepsilon t} - e^{-\lambda_{36} t} \right)$$

$$\left. + P_n \frac{c e^{-d x_0}}{d\varepsilon + \lambda_{36}} \left(e^{d\varepsilon t} - e^{-\lambda_{36} t} \right) \right).$$

This formulation will be used to model ^{36}Cl buildup between the time of landform formation (t=0) and the exposure at the surface (t=x_0/ε). After exposure of the rock at the surface, buildup continues according to the following equation:

$$(10) \quad N_{36} = EL \left(N_0 e^{-\lambda_{36} t} + \frac{P_s + P_n}{\lambda_{36}} (1 - e^{-\lambda_{36} t}) \right)$$

if the erosion of the rock surface is negligible, or according to equation 9, with an appropriate erosion rate, if it cannot be neglected. In equation 10, N_0 is the number of ^{36}Cl atoms accumulated previously in the subsurface due to cosmic radiation, (calculated according to equation 9), $N_0 exp(-\lambda_{36} t)$ represents decay of the initial condition N_0, and the last term is new buildup at the surface.

The initial burial depth x_0 and the erosion rate ε determine temporal variability in the production rates of cosmogenic ^{36}Cl in a rock buried in soil for some time and gradually exposed at the surface. Accumulation paths of ^{36}Cl in a rock with approximately equal production rates due to spallation and thermal neutron activation and with the initial burial depth varying from 0 to 300 g/cm² are graphed in Figure 8.7. For samples exposed at the surface all the time (x_0=0) we observe the usual shape of the buildup curve with decreasing accumulation rate with time (solid line; compare with Figure 8.3). The buildup paths of samples buried at shallow depths (two top lines) are above that for the surface sample, because these samples integrate higher than surface production rates (Figure 8.2). Their shapes, however, are similar to that of the surface sample, because with time the samples get closer to the surface and the production rates decrease accordingly. In contrast the accumulation paths of samples buried deeply below the surface (three bottom lines) are placed below that of the surface sample, because of low production rates in deeper subsurface. They are characterized by an increasing buildup rate before the sample reaches the depth of the maximum production rate (see Figure 8.2) and decreasing rate afterwards. The amount of cosmogenic ^{36}Cl accumulated after 100 ka is different for different burial depths x_0 and leads to different apparent cosmogenic ^{36}Cl ages. The distribution of these apparent ages is a function of the erosion depth x_{max} and the landform age, and can thus be used to calculate these two quantities.

We applied the gradual exposure model to Meteor Crater, to evaluate the effects of erosion on apparent ages of the sampled boulders. In those rocks the spallation and thermal neutron-production rates are approximately equal (Phillips et al.1991; Zreda et al. 1990). We assumed maximum thickness of covering material x_0 from 0 to 1,000 g/cm² and erosion rates, such that this cover would be removed in the nominal 49,720 years. We then created, 1,000 uniform random variables in the interval from 0 to x_0 and used the model to

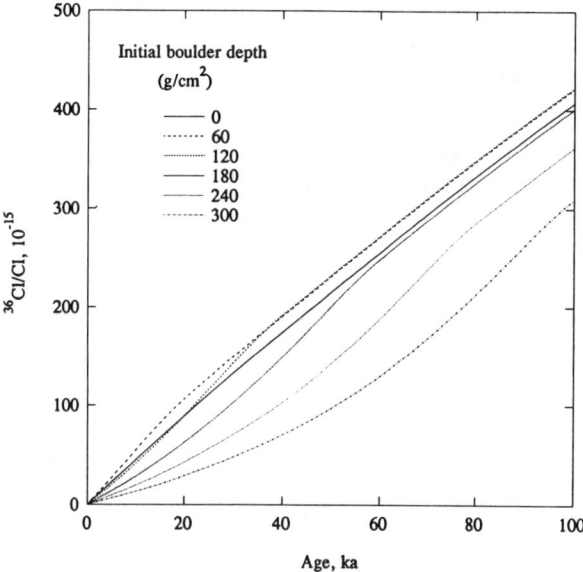

Figure 8.7. Accumulation paths of cosmogenic ^{36}Cl in subsurface rocks in which half of the produced ^{36}Cl is due to spallation of ^{39}K and ^{40}Ca and half due to thermal neutron activation of ^{35}Cl. The rocks are initially buried at depths x_0 less than or equal to the erosion depth x_{max} of 300 g/cm^2. The land surface is constantly eroding downward at a rate $\varepsilon = x_{max}/t_p$, where t_p is the surface age, causing the rock to be exposed at the surface after time $t_e = x_0/\varepsilon$. For $x_0 = 0$ (solid line), the sample has been at the surface all the time, whereas for $x_0 = x_{max} = 300$ g/cm^2, it has been buried until the present. The shapes of the buildup curves depend on initial burial depths x_0 and determine the amount of accumulated cosmogenic ^{36}Cl and thus the calculated apparent age of the rocks.

calculate the apparent ages based on the accumulated ^{36}Cl. The calculated ages were subsequently used to obtain a statistical distribution that we compared with the measured data. For all but negligibly small values of x_0, the distributions of apparent ages show a coefficient of variation much larger than that actually measured (Figures 8.8 and 8.9). This was expected because of the variation of cosmic-ray intensity in the subsurface (see Figure 8.2).

The actual coefficient of variation of samples MC-1 and MC-3 through MC-5 was 0.018. We thus conclude that any covering material on top of the boulders was quickly removed and that the boulders were exposed to cosmic radiation soon after the impact. We also investigated another scenario, in which we assumed that the initial cover of a maximum 300 g/cm^2 was removed after a maximum of 10,000 years from the impact by processes of erosion at the rate of 30 g/cm^2 per 1,000 years and repeated the calculations as described. The obtained distribution was characterized by a very small variance (coefficient of variation of 0.017) and matched the observed data (coefficient of variation of 0.018) almost exactly (Figure 8.10). This result indicates that an initial cover persisting for a maximum of 10,000 years would minimally affect the cosmogenic ^{36}Cl ages and supports the date of 49,700 years for the impact (Phillips et al. 1991). The above calculations demonstrate that the distribution of apparent ages contains valuable information about the erosional history of the investigated surfaces and can be helpful in the evaluation of measured age distributions.

We will now present some modeling results for two surfaces from Bloody Canyon: the Tioga and Tenaya moraines. Again we investigated various scenarios and compared the modeled distributions to the observed

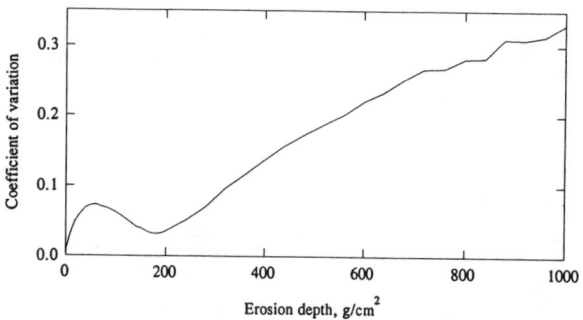

Figure 8.8. Relationship between erosion depth x_{max} and the coefficient of variation calculated for simulated ^{36}Cl buildup ages of sample MC-1 from Meteor Crater, Arizona. The local minimum at $x_{max} = 180$ g/cm^2 is due to a maximum in thermal neutron distribution in the subsurface (see Figure 8.2).

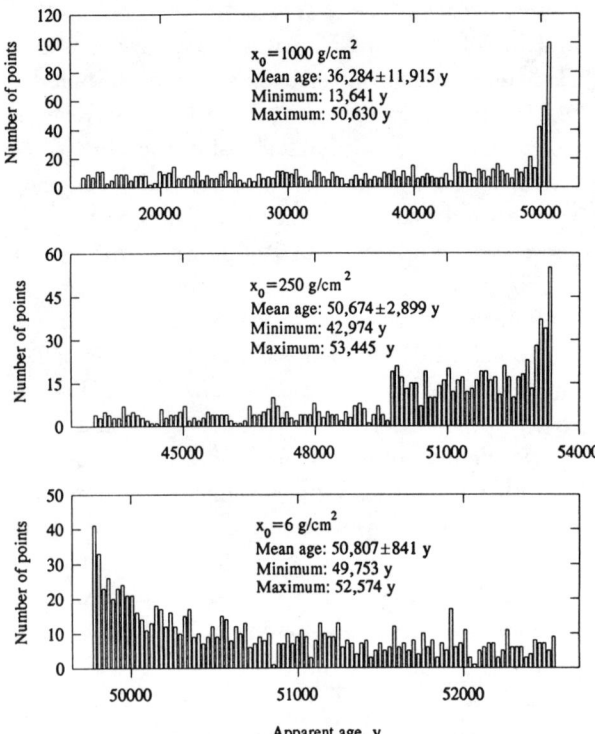

Figure 8.9. Simulation of ^{36}Cl buildup ages for Meteor Crater samples. Erosion depth x_{max} varies from 6 to 1,000 g/cm^2, and the erosion rate is constant for a given x_{max}. Number of samples is 1,000. With decreasing erosion depth, the variance of the distribution decreases.

apparent age distributions. The comparison indicates that the boulders on the Tioga moraine were covered by a material of an average thickness of about 300 g/cm^2, whereas those on the Tenaya moraine had only about 150 g/cm^2 removed since the time of the moraine deposition (Figures 8.11 and 8.12). If the cover had been thicker, the measured data would have been characterized by a larger variance than that reported in Table 8.6. Again we conclude that both the distribution of the calculated ages and the mean values are helpful in interpreting the cosmogenic ^{36}Cl data. Some samples with unusually low measured ^{36}Cl/Cl ratios were excluded from the variance calculations because the low concentration of cosmogenic ^{36}Cl must be due to geological processes other than erosion and gradual exposure (see Phillips et al. 1990).

Lastly we will discuss some general trends for various values of total material eroded and erosion rates. These trends follow from the distribution of the two major cosmic-ray components in the subsurface. In all simulations we assumed approximately equal production from spallation and thermal neutron activation, which is typical for granitic rocks. For minor erosion depth and slow erosion rates (Figure 8.13A), the apparent ^{36}Cl ages slightly overestimate the true age, because the thermal neutron flux increases with depth down to about 45 g/cm^2 (see Figure 8.2). In our example a 10,000-

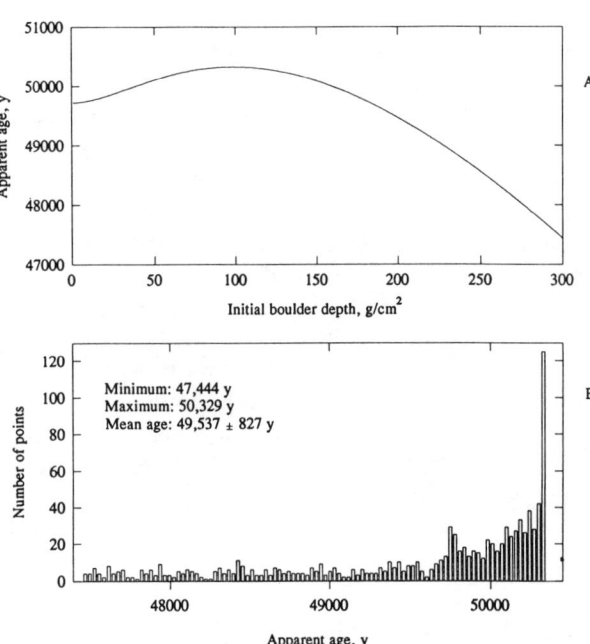

Figure 8.10. Simulation of ^{36}Cl buildup ages in sample MC-1 from Meteor Crater, Arizona. Erosion removes 300 g/cm^2 during the first 10,000 years following the impact; after this time, buildup continues at the surface. Number of points is 1,000. The age of an individual boulder depends on its initial burial depth (A), and the age of the surface is calculated as the mean of the individual boulder ages (B).

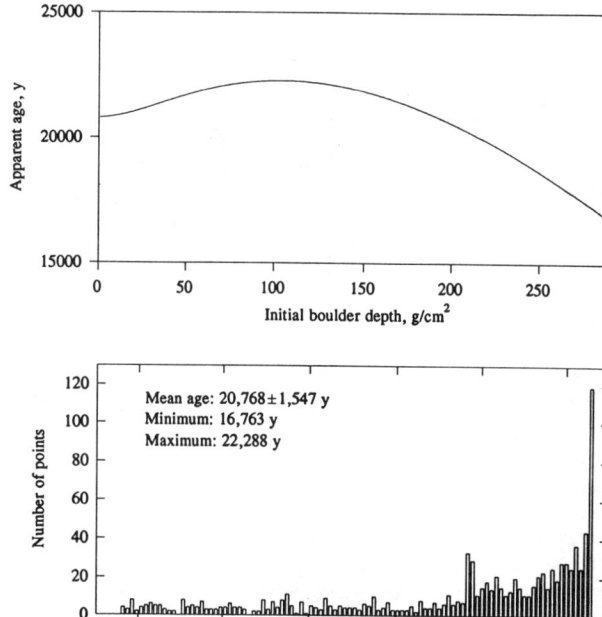

Figure 8.11. Simulation of ^{36}Cl buildup ages for the Tioga moraine, Bloody Canyon, Sierra Nevada, California. The simulation was performed using an erosion depth of 291 g/cm^2 and constant erosion rate of 0.014 g/cm^2/yr. Number of samples is 1,000. (A) dependence of individual boulder age on its initial burial depth; (B) age of the surface calculated as the mean of the individual boulder ages.

For soils thicker than about 200 g/cm^2, we observe a monomodal distribution again, with the majority of the ages close to the actual age, but tailing toward the younger ages (Figure 8.14A–C). In such cases most of the apparent ages underestimate the true age of the landform (independent of the age and the erosion rate) and, therefore, the oldest measured age should be chosen as the age of the landform formation. In practice we will rarely have a sufficient number of ^{36}Cl samples to construct a completely reliable distribution, but we can proceed by using sample variances calculated from the individual boulder ages. The variance has a tendency to increase with age and, consequently, with erosion depth

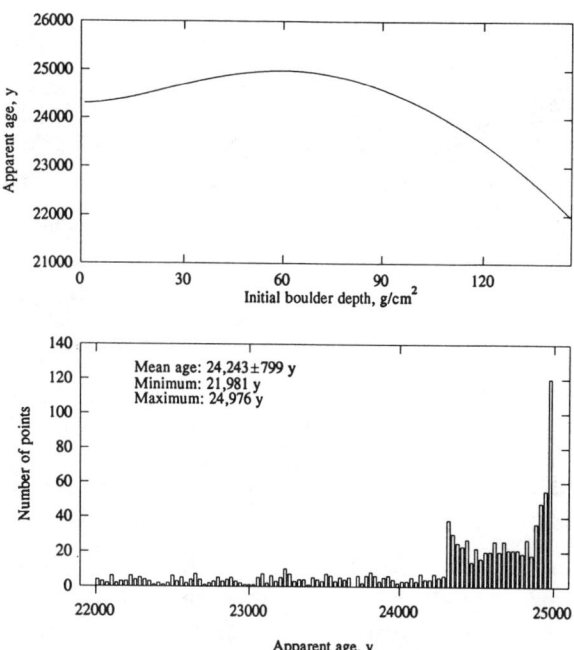

Figure 8.12. Simulation of ^{36}Cl buildup ages for the Tenaya moraine, Bloody Canyon, Sierra Nevada, California. An erosion depth of 145.8 g/cm^2 and a constant erosion rate of 0.006 g/cm/yr were used. Number of points is 1,000. (A) dependence of individual boulder age on its initial burial depth; (B) age of the surface calculated as the mean of the individual boulder ages.

year-old surface yielded ages between 10,000 and 11,000 years, with the majority falling in the interval between 10,000 and 10,250 years. If we increase the erosion depth to 100 g/cm^2, the distribution is shifted even more toward the older ages (Figure 8.13B) and becomes bimodal, with many samples close to either 10,000 years or 12,000 years and with fewer between the two extremes. If we assume the same total erosion depth, but decrease the erosion rate (thus increasing the landform age), this bimodal distribution becomes slightly less well defined, and calculated ages all fall in the interval between the actual age and one about 25 percent older.

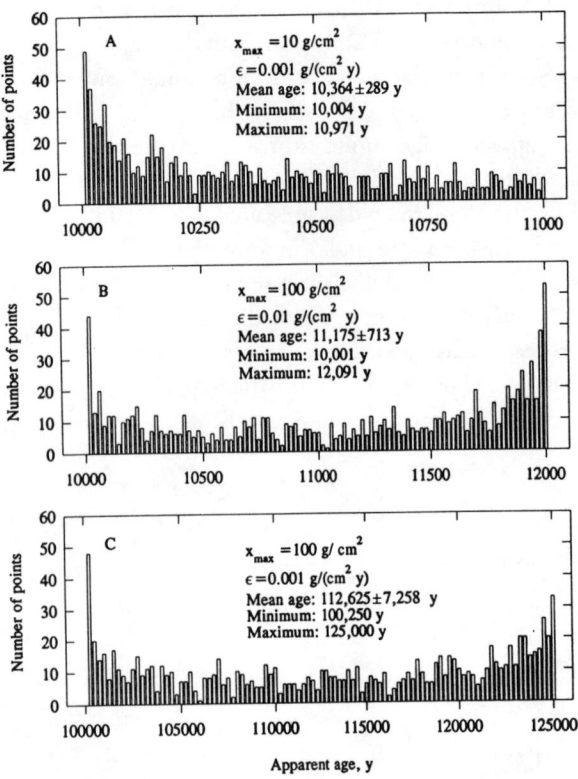

most obvious is weathering and the formation of secondary minerals that replace original crystals. If weathering removes both ^{36}Cl and stable chlorine at approximately the same rate, the $^{36}Cl/Cl$ ratio, and thus the calculated age, will be negligibly affected. However, water is the major agent of weathering processes, and it can also transport dissolved chlorine into the rock. This chlorine, having its own ^{36}Cl content, can possibly replace or be added to the chlorine in the rock and change its isotopic characteristics. We encountered this problem in studies of cosmogenic ^{36}Cl in basalts from Lathrop Wells Cone, Nevada (Zreda et al. 1993). Oliv-

Figure 8.13. Distributions of apparent ^{36}Cl buildup ages for surfaces of actual ages of 10 ka (A, B) and 100 ka (C), with different values of erosion depth x_{max} and the erosion rate ε. Each simulation was performed with 1,000 points.

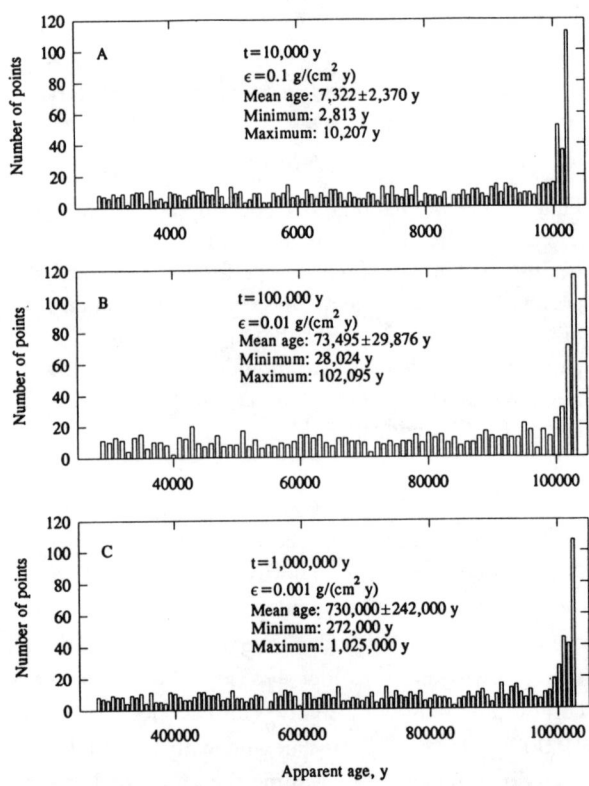

x_0. Therefore from the mean and the sample variance, we can estimate both the true age of the landform and its erosional history. For more details on the modeling of ^{36}Cl buildup ages, we refer the reader to the recent paper by Zreda and coworkers (Zreda et al. 1994).

Other Factors Affecting Buildup

There exist other factors that also affect the cosmogenic ^{36}Cl buildup in terrestrial materials. One of the

Figure 8.14. Distributions of apparent ^{36}Cl buildup ages for a surface with an erosion depth x_{max} of 1,000 g/cm² and three sets of values of the actual age t and the erosion rate ε. For fixed x_{max}, the shape of the distribution is independent of the landform age. Each simulation was performed with 1,000 points.

ines (containing 300–1,500 ppm of igneous Cl) were replaced by iddingsite (1,500–3,300 ppm of secondary, meteoric Cl), and a strongly weathered sample yielded an age about 30 percent higher than unweathered samples from the same surface. The higher apparent age was due to the high $^{36}Cl/Cl$ ratio in the meteoric water (about 400×10^{-15}), combined with the low cosmogenic $^{36}Cl/Cl$ in unweathered rocks (about 300×10^{-15}). Other possible sources of meteoric Cl are vesicular secondary carbonates, common in arid climates, and clay minerals (such as kaolinite), which are common products of weathering in moderate to cold climatic zones. Both can be removed during sample preparation; carbonates by leaching in nitric acid and clay minerals by removing fractions smaller than 20 μm.

Partial and temporally variable shielding can reduce the intensity of cosmic rays and result in apparent ages younger than the true age; partial shielding can be caused by topographic features blocking part of the incoming radiation. The required correction $F(\Theta)$ is a function of a slope Θ of a line connecting the top of the shielding object and the sampled surface, and can be calculated as $(sin\Theta)^{2.3}$ (Nishiizumi et al. 1989). The production rates should be multiplied by $F(\Theta)$, averaged over all horizontal directions. This correction is usually small and approaches 15 percent for angles close to 45° (Figure 8.15).

In addition to temporally variable shielding by soil, shielding can also be provided by water, if snow or rain can persist for significant periods of time at the surfaces of boulders. Snow cover may be an important factor in high mountains and in colder climates. The shielding power of water is very high, because hydrogen has very high thermal neutron absorption and scattering capability. Experiments conducted by Fabryka-Martin et al. (1991) indicated that 18 cm of water reduces the thermal neutron production rate by about 40 percent. To reduce the potential problem with water shielding, samples can be taken from the tops of the tallest boulders, which are likely to have been swept free of snow by the wind.

Practical Aspects of the Cosmogenic Chlorine-36 Method

Sample collection and preparation are the two most critical steps in applications of the cosmogenic ^{36}Cl to dating geomorphic surfaces; therefore they should be very carefully planned and conducted. In the field sample selection should be performed based on three criteria: the degree of preservation of original surfaces, the geometry of the sampled rock and surrounding topographic features, and the extent of chemical weathering. We seek samples with indications of original surfaces, such as glacially polished morainal boulders or bedrock, boulders with heavy coatings of rock varnish, lava flows with preserved flow-surface textures, and slickensides along faults. By finding these kinds of features, we partially satisfy the condition that the geometry of the investigated surface not have changed, for example, due to erosion, since the landform's formation. To fully satisfy this condition, we also desire information about the stability of boulders; that is, whether they have remained in their present position since emplacement or have rolled over at some time. Generally boulders found on horizontal or subhorizontal surfaces are preferred,

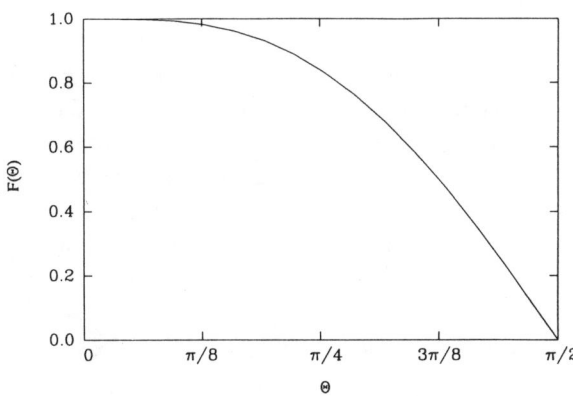

Figure 8.15. Topographic correction calculated as a function of the angle θ between the sampling point and the top of the topographic feature partially blocking cosmic rays. Production parameters should be multiplied by F(θ) averaged over horizontal directions (2π). Calculated using the formulation from Nishiizumi et al. (1989).

because small topographic gradients provide strong assurance of boulder stability.

The geometry of boulders and the surrounding topography has important implications for the cosmic-ray flux reaching sampled surfaces. The distribution of cosmic-ray-induced nuclear transformations is not uniform in boulders. There is a strong edge effect, which causes a leakage of thermal neutrons out of boulder edges and corners and into the atmosphere. The edge effect can be important for boulders smaller than the attenuation length for neutrons (50–60 cm) and for rough surfaces, such as pressure ridges in basalt lavas; required corrections may be 30 percent or higher, depending on the angularity of the boulder, but they are not well established. Samples should thus be taken from the centers of large boulders, as far from the edges as possible. Where samples from flat surfaces are harder to obtain, such as in the case of the pressure ridges in lava flows, corrections for the thermal neutron flux need to be implemented. Surrounding topography is also an important factor, because the blockage of part of the cosmic-ray flux affects ^{36}Cl production rates and consequently leads to underestimated apparent ages. Corrections for topography can easily be performed (see Figure 8.15), if the angles between the sampling point and the tops of the topographic features are measured.

The third criterion for sample selection is the extent of chemical weathering of the sampled rock surfaces. Fresh-looking, unweathered, or physically weathered rocks are preferred, because they are more likely to contain only unaltered cosmogenic ^{36}Cl. If there is no choice, and strongly altered samples must be collected, separation of secondary minerals from primary ones by means of chemical or physical techniques can be attempted. Some types of secondary minerals, for instance vesicular carbonates in basalts, are easily separable, and cleaned samples yield correct ages. Others, such as iddingsite replacing olivines in basalts, are so strongly integrated with the original crystals that their removal is very difficult, if not impossible. Such samples can still yield useful results, but they require performing additional analytical procedures and solving a nonlinear buildup equation.

Summary

In this chapter we have described the cosmogenic ^{36}Cl accumulation method, one of several new dating methods based on cosmogenic nuclide accumulation in materials exposed to cosmic radiation. This method has been under development since the early 1980s and has undergone significant changes, including advancements in techniques of sample collection, preparation, and measurement, as well as new approaches to the evaluation of results.

Although the method has proved to be a suitable tool for the dating of late Pleistocene simple constructional and degradational landforms, it is still under development, because our present knowledge of the processes contributing to the distribution of chlorine isotopes in nature is incomplete. Initial efforts focused on the calibration of the production rates and the assessment of their temporal and spatial variability, and applications were limited to simple cases of negligible erosion and weathering, constant production rates, and ideal geometry. Clearly most of the actual cases of geological interest fall outside of this group, and therefore other, nonideal scenarios should be considered. Future research may focus on such topics as the steady and intermittent degradation of landform surfaces at constant or variable erosion rates, the presence of sources (or sinks) for ^{36}Cl and their effect on calculated surface exposure ages, spatial and temporal variability of the cosmic-ray flux and the resulting variable production rates of cosmogenic nuclides, and so on. For a full understanding of the complexity of these processes, collective, multidisciplinary research efforts are needed, not only in the field of chlorine isotope geochemistry, but also in such related fields as cosmic-ray physics, geomorphology, geochemistry, palaeoclimatology, geology, and hydrology.

References

Andrews, J. N., S. N. Davis, J. Fabryka-Martin, J.-Ch. Fontes, B. E. Lehmann, H. H. Loosli, J.-L. Michelot, H. Moser, B. Smith, and M. Wolf

1989 The *in situ* Production of Radioisotopes in Rock Matrices with Particular Reference to the Stripa Granite. *Geochimica et Cosmochimica Acta* 53:1,803–1,815.

Andrews, J. N., J.-Ch. Fontes, J.-L. Michelot, and D. Elmore
1986 *In-situ* Neutron Flux, ^{36}Cl Production and Groundwater Evolution in Crystalline Rocks at Stripa, Sweden, *Earth and Planetary Science Letters* 77:49–58.

Atwater, B. F., D. P. Adam, R. M. Bradbury, R. K. Forester, W. R. Mark, W. R. Lettis, G. R. Fisher, K. W. Gobalet, and S. W. Robinson
1986 A Fan Dam for Tulare Lake, California, and Implications for the Wisconsin Glacial History of the Sierra Nevada. *Geological Society of American Bulletin* 97:97–109.

Bentley, H. W., F. M. Phillips, and S. N. Davis
1986 Chlorine-36 in the Terrestrial Environment. In *Handbook of Environmental Isotope Geochemsitry*, vol. 2, *The Terrestrial Environment*, B, edited by P. Fritz and J.-Ch. Fontes, pp. 427–480. Elsevier, New York.

Blackwelder, E.
1931 Pleistocene Glaciation in the Sierra Nevada and Basin Ranges. *Geological Society of America Bulletin* 42:865–922.

Burke, R. M., and P. W. Birkeland
1979 Reevaluation of Multiparameter Relative Dating Techniques and Their Application to the Glacial Sequences along the Eastern Escarpment of the Sierra Nevada, California. *Quaternary Research* 11:21–51.

Conversi, M.
1950 Experiments on Cosmic-Ray Mesons and Protons at Several Altitudes and Latitudes. *Physics Reviews* 79:749–767.

Davis Jr., R., and O. A. Schaeffer
1955 Chlorine-36 in Nature. *Annals of the New York Academy of Science* 62:105–122.

Dorn R. I., B. D. Turrin, A. J. T. Jull, T. W. Linick, and D. J. Donahue
1987 Radiocarbon and Cation-Ratio Ages for Rock Varnish on Tioga and Tahoe Morainal Boulders of Pine Creek, Eastern Sierra Nevada, California, and Their Paleoclimatic Implications. *Quaternary Research* 28:38–49.

Elmore D., B. R. Fulton, M. R. Clover, J. R. Marsden, H. E. Gove, H. Naylor, K. H. Purser, L. R. Kilius, R. P. Beukins, and A. E. Litherland
1979 Analysis of ^{36}Cl in Environmental Water Samples Using an Electrostatic Accelerator. *Nature* 277:22–25.

Elmore, D., and F. M. Phillips
1987 Accelerator Mass Spectrometry for Measurement of Long-Lived Radioisotopes. *Science* 236:543–550.

Fabryka-Martin, J. T.
1988 *Production of Radionuclides in the Earth and Their Hydrogeologic Significance, with emphasis on Chlorine-36 and Iodine-129*. Ph.D. dissertation, University of Arizona, Tucson. University Microfilms, Ann Abor.

Fabryka-Martin, J. F., M. M. Fowler, and R. Biddle
1991 Study of Neutron Fluxes Underground. *Isotope and Nuclear Chemistry Division Quarterly Report* October 1–December 31, 1990, 82–85.

Feige Y., B. G. Oltman, and J. Kastner
1968 Production Rates of Neutrons in Solids Due to Natural Radioactivity. *Journal of Geophysical Research* 73:3,135–3,142.

Gillespie, A. R.
1982 *Quaternary Glaciation and Tectonism in the Southern Sierra Nevada, Inyo County, California*. Ph.D. dissertation, California Institute of Technology. University Microfilms, Ann Arbor.

Gillespie, A. R., J. C. Huneke, and G. J. Wasserburg
1984 Eruption Age of a 100,000-year-old Basalt From ^{40}Ar-^{39}Ar Analysis of Partially Degassed Xenoliths. *Journal of Geophysical Research* 89:1,033–1,048.

Hendricks, L. D., and R. D. Edge
1966 Cosmic-Ray Neutrons Near the Earth. *Physics Reviews* 145:1,023–1,025.

Jha, R., and D. Lal
1982 On Cosmic Ray Produced Isotopes in Surface Rocks. In *Natural Radiation Environment*, ed-

ited by K. G. Vohra et al., pp. 629–635. Proceedings of Second Special Symposium on Natural Radiation Environment, Halsted Press.

Kuhn, M. W., S. N. Davis, H. W. Bentley, and R. Zito
1984 Measurements of Thermal Neutrons in the Subsurface. *Geophysical Research Letters* 11:607–610.

Kurz, M.
1986 Cosmogenic Helium in a Terrestrial Igneous Rock. *Nature* 320:435–439.

Lal, D.
1987 Cosmogenic Nuclides Produced *in situ* in Terrestrial Solids. *Nuclear Instruments and Methods in Physics Research* B29:238–245.
1991 Cosmic Ray Labelling of Erosion Surfaces: *in situ* Production Rates and Erosion Models. *Earth and Planetary Science Letters* 104:424–439.

Lal, D., and B. Peters B.
1967 Cosmic Ray Produced Radioactivty on Earth. In *Encyclopedia of Physics,* edited by S. Fluegge, vol. 46/2, *Cosmic Rays II,* edited by K. Sitte, pp. 551–612. Springer Verlag, Berlin.

Leavy, B. D.
1987 *Surface-Exposure Dating of Young Volcanic Rocks Using the in situ Buildup of Cosmogenic Isotopes.* Unpublished Ph.D. dissertation, Geoscience Department, New Mexico Institute of Mining and Technology, Socorro.

Mezger, L., and D. Burbank
1986 The Glacial History of the Cottonwood Lakes Area, Southeastern Sierra Nevada. *Geological Society of America Abstracts with Programs* 18:157.

Montgomery, C. G., and D. D. Montgomery
1939 The Intensity of Neutrons of Thermal Energy in the Atmosphere at Sea Level. *Physics Reviews* 56:10–12.

Mughaghab, S. F., and D. I. Garber
1973 *Neutron Cross Sections,* vol. 1, *Resonance Parameters.* Brookhaven National Laboratory.

Nishiizumi, K., C. P. Kohl, E. M. Shoemaker, J. R. Arnold, J. Klein, D. Fink, and R. Middleton
1991 ^{10}Be-^{26}Al Exposure Ages at Meteor Crater, Arizona. *Geochimica et Cosmochimica Acta* 55:2,699–2,703.

Nishiizumi, K., E. L. Winterer, C. P. Kohl, J. Klein, R. Middleton, D. Lal, and J. R. Arnold
1989 Cosmic Ray Production Rates of ^{10}Be and ^{26}Al in Quartz From Glacially Polished Rocks. *Journal of Geophysical Research* 94:17,907–17,915.

O'Brien, K., H. A. Sandmeier, G. E. Hansen, and J. E. Campbell
1978 Cosmic Ray Induced Neutron Background Sources and Fluxes for Geometries of Air Over Water, Ground, Iron, and Aluminum. *Journal of Geophysical Research* 83:114–120.

Phillips, F. M., B. D. Leavy, N. D. Jannik, D. Elmore, and P. W. Kubik
1986 The Accumulation of Cosmogenic Chlorine-36 in Rocks: A Method for Surface Exposure Dating. *Science* 231:41–43.

Phillips, F. M., M. G. Zreda, S. S. Smith, D. Elmore, P. W. Kubik, R. I. Dorn, and D. Roddy
1991 Age and Geomorphic History of Meteor Crater, Arizona, from Cosmogenic ^{36}Cl and Rock Varnish ^{14}C. *Geochimica et Cosmochimica Acta* 55:2,695–2,698.

Phillips, F. M., M. G. Zreda, S. S. Smith, D. Elmore, P. W. Kubik, and P. Sharma
1990 A Cosmogenic Chlorine-36 Chronology for Glacial Deposits at Bloody Canyon, Eastern Sierra Nevada, California. *Science* 248:1,529–1,532.

Rama and M. Honda
1961 Cosmic-Ray-Induced Radioactivity in Terrestrial Materials. *Journal of Geophysical Research* 66:3,533–3,539.

Roddy, D. J.
1978 Pre-Impact Geologic Conditions, Physical Properties, Energy Calculations, Meteorite and Initial Crater Dimensions and Orientations of Joints, Faults and Walls at Meteor Crater, Arizona. *Proceedings of the 9th Lunar and Planetary Sciences Conference,* pp. 3,891–3,930.

Rossi, B.
1952 *High Energy Particles.* Prentice Hall, N.J.

Sharp, R. P., and J. H. Birman
1963 Additions to Classical Sequence of Pleistocene Glaciations, Sierra Nevada, California. *Geological Society of America Bulletin* 74:1,079–1,086.

Shoemaker, E. M.
1983 Asteroid and Comet Bombardment of the Earth. *Annual Reviews of Earth and Planetary Science* 11:461–494.

Shoemaker, E. M., and S. Kieffer
1979 *Guidebook to the Geology of Meteor Crater.* Arizona State University.

Simpson, J. A.
1951 Neutrons Produced in the Atmosphere by the Cosmic Radiations. *Physics Reviews* 83:1,175–1,188.

Sutton, S. R.
1985a Thermoluminescence Measurements on Shock-Metamorphosed Sandstone and Dolomite from Meteor Crater, Arizona: 1. Shock Dependence of Thermoluminescence Properties. *Journal of Geophysical Research,* 90:3,683–3,689.
1985b Thermoluminescence Measurements on Shock-Metamorphosed Sandstone and Dolomite from Meteor Crater, Arizona: 2. Thermoluminescence Age of Meteor Crater. *Journal of Geophysical Research* 90:3,690–3,700.

Yamashita, M., L. D. Stephens, and H. W. Patterson
1966 Cosmic-Ray-Produced Neutrons at Ground Level: Neutron Production Rate and Flux Distribution. *Journal of Geophysical Research* 71:3,817–3,834.

Yokoyama, Y., J.-L. Reyss, and F. Guichard
1977 Production of Radionuclides by Cosmic Rays at Mountain Altitudes. *Earth and Planetary Science Letters* 36:44–50.

Zreda. M. G.
1994 *Cosmogenic ^{36}Cl Chronology of Late Quaternary Glaciations: Glacial History, Correlations, and Paleoclimatic Implications.* Unpublished Ph.D. dissertation, Department of Geoscience, New Mexico Institute of Mining and Technology, Socorro.

Zreda, M. G., F. M. Phillips, and D. Elmore
1994 Cosmogenic ^{36}Cl Accumulation in Unstable Landforms: II. Monte Carlo Simulations and Experimental Observations on Eroding Glacial Moraines. *Water Resources Research,* in press.

Zreda, M. G., F. M. Phillips, D. Elmore, P. W. Kubik, P. Sharma, and R. I. Dorn
1991 Cosmogenic ^{36}Cl Production Rates in Terrestrial Rocks. *Earth and Planetary Science Letters* 105:94–109.

Zreda, M. G., F. M. Phillips, P. W. Kubik, P. Sharma, and D. Elmore
1993 Eruption Age at Lathrop Wells, Nevada, from Cosmogenic ^{36}Cl Accumulation. *Geology* 21:57–60.

Zreda, M. G., F. M. Phillips, and S. S. Smith
1990 *Cosmogenic ^{36}Cl Dating of Geomorphic Surfaces.* Hydrology Program Report 90–1, New Mexico Tech.

9

LICHENOMETRIC DATING: A REVIEW WITH PARTICULAR REFERENCE TO 'LITTLE ICE AGE' MORAINES IN SOUTHERN NORWAY

John A. Matthews

Department of Geography
University of Wales at Swansea
Singleton Park
Swansea, United Kingdom

Abstract

'Little Ice Age' moraine ridges in southern Norway have been the sites of numerous lichenometric dating studies since the late 1950s. These studies are used to illustrate the principles, potential, and problems of lichenometric dating in surface context. Data collection, the construction of lichenometric dating curves, and dating at local and regional scales are analyzed. Applications to different types of surface and in other locations are briefly reviewed. The variety of possible applications requires a range of appropriate lichenometric dating techniques.

Indirect lichenometric dating, whereby lichenometric dating curves are constructed from surfaces of known age (control points), has been widely applied as a calibrated-age dating technique (Colman et al. 1987). The results obtained by different workers under favorable conditions at Nigardsbreen are critically assessed, with the conclusion that recent results, based on the use of families of curves, probably attain an accuracy of ca. 10 percent on the 'Little Ice Age' time scale. All applications depend on the reliability of available control points, the sparsity of which normally leads to much less accurate dates on older surfaces. Because of greater environmental heterogeneity among surfaces, regional lichenometric dating is also likely to be less accurate.

Preliminary results are presented of direct lichenometric dating, whereby lichen growth curves are constructed from direct measurements of lichen growth over several years. An estimated maximum growth rate for the *Rhizocarpon* subgenus at Nigardsbreen of 1.10 mm/yr, and the resulting linear growth curve, are not immediately compatible with the results of dating by the indirect approach. Perhaps due to the effects of competition on older surfaces, direct measurements of lichen growth rates appear a long way from providing a biological justification for the indirect approach.

Introduction

LICHENOMETRIC DATING—THE DATING OF SURfaces using measurements of lichen size or other indices of lichen growth—has developed considerably since publication of the first systematic account of lichenometry in the Austrian Alps, over four decades ago (Beschel 1950, 1973). Then as now lichenometric dating was most widely applied in environments above and beyond tree limits in alpine and polar regions and, in particular, to the dating of moraine ridges on recently deglaciated terrain (glacier forelands) (see reviews in Beschel 1957 1961; Innes 1985a; Locke et al. 1979; Mottershead 1980; Reger and Péwé 1969; Webber and Andrews 1973a; Worsley 1990). Indeed with applications from New Zealand (Birkeland 1981; Burrows et al. 1990; Burrows and Lucas 1967; Burrows and Orwin 1971; Gellatly 1982, 1983), Antarctica (Birkenmajer 1980a; Curl 1980; Lindsay 1973), the former Soviet Union (Golodkovskaya 1982; Serebryanny et al. 1979; Serebryanny et al. 1984; Serebryanny and Solomina 1989; Solomina and Golodkovskaya 1989), China (Zhou et al., 1991), Africa (Mahaney 1990; Mahaney and Spence 1993; Spence and Mahaney 1988), and South America (Rodbell 1992), in addition to many from Europe, North America, and the North Atlantic region (see citations elsewhere in this contribution), the lichenometric dating of moraines has become a topic of worldwide interest.

The existence of progressively older moraines at increasing distances from a retreating glacier provides not only an opportunity to apply lichenometric dating, but also suitable conditions for testing and improving approaches and techniques. In this chapter, therefore, "Little Ice Age" moraine sequences are exploited to illustrate the principles, potential, and problems of lichenometric dating in surface context. Most attention is given to examples from southern Norway (Figure 9.1), a region that has proved well suited to the development and application of lichenometric dating techniques (for example, Andersen and Sollid 1971; Bickerton and Matthews, 1992, 1993; Erikstad and Sollid 1986; Innes 1985a, 1986a; Matthews 1974, 1975; Mottershead and White 1972, 1973). Lichenometric dating appears to have been more successful in southern Norway than in the Alps (see Belloni 1973; Beschel 1950, 1973; Burga 1987; Holzhauser 1984; Orombelli and Porter 1983), and surfaces of known age (necessary for calibrating lichenometric dating curves) are more common than in most other arctic-alpine environments. However, other studies are considered where appropriate, and a brief survey is made of the range of possible applications.

Principles

Lichenometric dating as a calibrated-age dating technique is based on the establishment of a numerical relationship between surface age and an index of lichen growth. Normally the index of growth is a measure of the thallus size of a readily identifiable lichen species or group, the growth form of which is circular or eliptical, and the growth rate of which is appropriate in the context of the dating problem. A wide range of lichen species or groups have been used or suggested for use in lichenometry (see, for example, Locke et al. 1979), although yellow-green specimens of the *Rhizocarpon* subgenus have been most commonly and successfully used. Specimens of this subgenus tend to be abundant, colonize rock surfaces early after exposure, and grow slowly—all characteristics that favor the use of the group for dating purposes. In relatively dry areas, where growth rates are extremely low, it has been suggested that the temporal range of lichenometric dating may exceed 9,000 years (Miller and Andrews 1972). However, this is an extreme example; in the majority of cases, lichenometry as a calibrated-age dating technique has a useful range of less than 500 years (Innes 1985a).

Simple axial measurements are usually preferred, although measurements of thallus area, percentage cover, and species composition have also been employed. Beschel (1950, 1961) maintained that only the single largest lichen on a surface should be used for dating purposes, on the grounds that it is likely to be the oldest individual, growing under optimal environmental conditions (see also Webber and Andrews 1973b). If the largest individual colonized soon after the surface was formed, its age would provide a close minimum age for the surface. Smaller lichens do not indicate the age of their substrate, because they are either younger (later colonizers) or are growing in a suboptimal environment. In practice, however, the important feature of Beschel's technique was not the use of the single largest

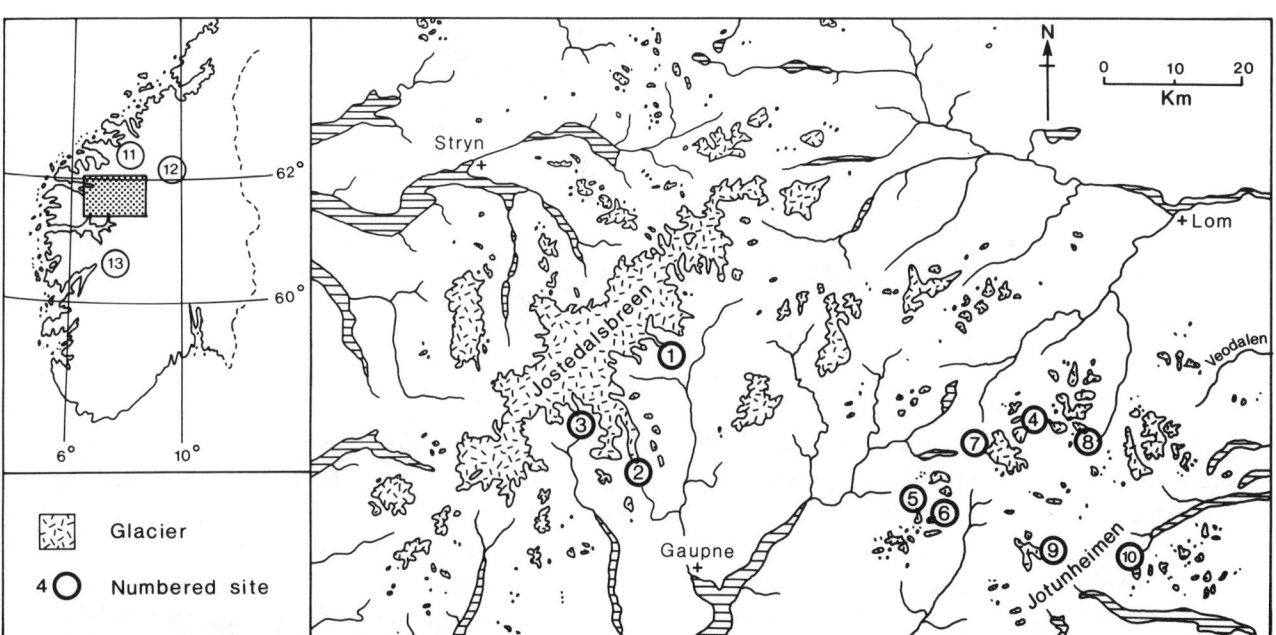

Figure 9.1. Locations of lichenometric dating studies in southern Norway: (1) Nigardsbreen, (2) Tunsbergdalsbreen, (3) Austerdalsbreen, (4) Storbreen, (5) Styggedalsbreen, (6) Gjertvassbreen, (7) Bøverbreen, (8) Bukkeholsbreen, (9) Mjølkedalsbreen, (10) Slettmarkbreen, (11) Nordvestlandet, (12) Rondane, (13) Hardangerjøkulen.

lichen per surface as such, but rather the control of environmental variation that was introduced by using this attribute. Other attributes of lichen populations, ranging from the mean size of several largest lichens to the entire lichen size-frequency distribution, have proved to be useful indices of surface age for dating. Likewise other ways of controlling for environmental variation are available. Confusion seems to have arisen because the assumptions underlying lichenometric dating are not the same as those involving lichenometry for the study of lichen growth rates (Matthews 1974).

There are two fundamentally different approaches to lichenometric dating: the so-called indirect and direct approaches. These differ in the method used to relate lichen size to surface age. In the indirect approach, a correlation is established between lichen size and surface age, based on measurements of the size of lichens growing on surfaces of known age at one point in time. The numerical relationship between lichen size and surface age is expressed by a "lichenometric dating curve," the purpose of which is to predict the age of surfaces of unknown age from the size of the lichens growing on them. This approach is purely empirical; it does not require the age or growth rate of the lichens to be known and provides only an indirect approximation to lichen growth rates (Platt and Amsler 1955; Rydzak 1961). The direct approach involves measurement of individual lichen thalli over several years, providing lichen growth rates that can be used for establishing a "lichen growth curve" (Andrews and Webber 1969; Aplin and Hill 1979; Armstrong 1974, 1975, 1983; Benedict and Nash 1990; Haworth et al. 1986; Hill 1981; G. H. Miller 1973; Proctor 1983; Rogerson et al. 1986; Schroeder-Lanz 1983). Lichen growth curves, which describe the expected size of individual lichens through time, can be used subsequently to date surfaces of unknown age from the age of the lichens growing on them.

Both approaches assume that the surface to be dated was lichen-free on exposure to lichen colonization, or that anomalous thalli can be recognized later. Anomalously large lichens may reach a surface by such processes as dumping from a medial moraine (Griffey 1978; Innes 1985a; Matthews 1973). Although it is possible to construct numerical rules for the rejection of large thalli that deviate markedly from some norm (Calkin and Ellis 1980; Innes 1983c; Rapp and Nyberg 1981), nonarbitrary rejection requires independent evidence, such as geomorphic evidence of disturbances.

Both approaches also assume that once ecesis (establishment) has occurred, lichen size increases in a regular, monotonic fashion. The direct approach assumes in addition that ecesis takes place immediately, or at least that the time required for ecesis is known; the indirect approach makes no such assumption. Because growth measurements are normally available only for a short time interval relative to the age of the surface to be dated, the direct approach effectively assumes a constant environment during the history of the surface. In contrast the indirect approach assumes that the environmental history of the surface parallelled the environmental history of surfaces of known age. Clearly, however, both approaches require comparability in environmental conditions between those pertaining to the curves (of whichever type) and those relating to the surfaces of unknown age. As environmental conditions vary within and among surfaces, over space and through time, lichenometric dating techniques must contrive to reduce the extent to which such variations are effective, so that measured lichen size becomes primarily a function of surface age.

In principle the direct approach to lichenometric dating is more widely applicable than the indirect approach, because there is no requirement for surfaces of known age (control points or fixed points for curve calibration). There is also a firmer basis in the theories of population biology for the direct approach (cf. Webber and Andrews 1973b). However, there are many uncertainties about lichen growth, particularly in relation to the slow-growing species of interest for dating purposes, and the direct approach is much more time consuming, requiring a longer-term research commitment. Consequently the indirect approach has been widely applied, despite the necessity for surfaces of known age, and the direct approach is still in the early stages of development.

Data Collection

Many aspects of data collection are of critical importance, including: lichen taxonomy, lichen attributes for measurement, measurement techniques, the number of lichens to be measured, where to search, the area of surface to be searched, the search procedure, operator error, and the recognition of anomalous specimens. Recent research in southern Norway on aspects of lichenometric methodology provides a wealth of information relevant to the choice of appropriate procedures (Haines-Young 1983, 1985; Innes 1982, 1983b, 1983c, 1984a, 1985a, 1985b, 1985c, 1985d, 1986a, 1986b, 1986c). Attention is therefore given here to the dating of "Little Ice Age" moraines in this region, which has, in general, fared well in light of this scrutiny.

In common with the majority of applications, yellow-green specimens of the *Rhizocarpon* subgenus (commonly termed *Rhizocarpon geographicum* agg.) have been employed. These have not usually been identified to the species level, although sometimes section *Rhizocarpon* and section *Alpicola* have been differentiated (Innes 1985b; see also Benedict 1988; King and Lehmann 1973; Poelt 1988). Although there is evidence that these two sections grow at different rates, use of the aggregate has little effect on dating the southern Norwegian moraines, because *Rhizocarpon* section *Rhizocarpon* predominates on all the dated surfaces, which are not sufficiently old to be unduly influenced by the faster rates of growth of later-colonizing individuals of section *Alpicola* (Bickerton and Matthews 1992; Innes 1982, 1983c).

Various axial measurements of lichen size have been employed. Bornfeldt and Österborg (1958), the first to employ lichenometric dating in southern Norway, used the longest axis, as did Andersen and Sollid (1971), Bickerton and Matthews (1992), Matthews (1974, 1975, 1977), Matthews and Shakesby (1984), and Mottershead and White (1972, 1973). Hole and Sollid (1979) and Erikstad and Sollid (1986) used a mean of the longest and shortest axes. Although Locke et al. (1979) recommended the "largest inscribed circle," which is equivalent to the shortest axis, Innes (1986c) has argued that measurement of the longest axis is preferable. Although there appears to be no great advantage over use of the shortest axis, the most convincing reason for using the long axis is that the shortest axis may reflect restricted lichen growth. Whereas a mean of both axes may more closely reflect thallus area, it is more time-consuming, less reproducible, and again, confers no significant benefits (cf. Griffey 1977). More complex measures, including thallus area, do not appear justified for indirect lichenometric dating, as other sources of potential error are much more important.

Similarly any random measurement errors introduced by, for example, use of a ruler (rather than calipers) appear to be unimportant (Innes 1985a). Between-operator variation can be much more significant than within-operator error (Innes 1985a, 1985c), particularly where student operators are used (as in most published southern Norwegian applications). However, Erikstad and Sollid (1986) reported no appreciable difference between operators, and between-operator variation can be reduced by cross-checking.

Southern Norwegian applications pioneered the use of a mean of several largest lichens (rather than the single largest) and also the use of multiple subplots (searching a set of areas of uniform size, rather than searching the whole surface or relying on one small part of that surface). The use of a mean of the several largest lichens has been discussed by Matthews (1974), who concluded that it is unexceptionable. This procedure avoids reliance on the use of a single lichen, which may be unreliable. In practice a mean of the five largest lichens (each from a separate subplot) was found to be optimal in detailed investigations at Storbreen, Jotunheimen, where both the single largest lichen and a mean of the ten largest lichens appear to underestimate surface age (Matthews 1975; see also Gordon and Sharp 1983; Innes 1984a).

Size of area to be searched and location of subplots both have a major effect on recorded lichen sizes. It is generally agreed that the use of large surface areas is likely to produce more realistic results, mainly because lichen size tends to vary greatly over a moraine surface, both along the length of the moraine (see especially Matthews's data from moraines at Storbreen, published as Figure 20 in Innes 1985a) and across it (see especially Haines-Young 1983, 1985). Consequently the probability of finding a larger "largest" lichen increases with the area searched. In a detailed investigation of this problem, Innes (1984a) has shown that the use of means and subplots tends to reduce the variability of the lichen-size index recorded from a particular surface. Hence the use of means and subplots should lead to more reliable dates. Innes concluded that where a complete search of a surface is impractical, at least 10 subplots of no less than 400 m^2 should be searched and that at least the 10 largest lichens should be measured in each subplot. Southern Norwegian applications have all tended to place most emphasis on a mean of the five largest lichens but have used a diverse range of subplot areas and sizes, with total areas searched ranging from 300 m^2 (Bornfeldt and Österborg 1958) to the whole moraine surface (Matthews 1975). Although some of the areas involved are smaller than Innes's guidelines, this has often been mediated by preliminary searches to locate areas of the surface where lichens tend to be largest.

The southern Norwegian studies have to some extent controlled for within-plot, within-surface, and within-foreland environmental variability. This has been achieved *de facto* by measuring the largest lichens, which, almost by definition, tend to be found in optimal environments for lichen growth (see above). Searching whole surfaces is of course the only way to ensure that optimal growth environments are found. The alternative approach to achieving environmental control is to restrict the search to particular environments. This approach was used by Griffey (1977), who limited his search to moraine crests. However, the use of moraine crests alone includes a very wide range of environments (related, in particular, to moraine size and snow depth), defeating the object of the exercise as well as reducing drastically the available search area. A more appropriate environment, in the southern Norwegian context at least, would be moraine bases, which tend to include the optimal environment for lichen growth (the "green zone") (Haines-Young 1983, 1985; Innes 1985d; Matthews 1977).

The overall effect of using different techniques of data collection is well illustrated by comparing lichen sizes recorded by different workers on moraine surfaces of known age at Nigardsbreen (Figures 9.2 and 9.3). The independent documentary and observational evidence of moraine age is here better established than at any other southern Norwegian glacier (Bogen et al. 1989; Grove 1985, 1988; Østrem et al. 1976). Each point on the graph in Figure 9.3 represents a mean of the five largest lichens (each from a separate site) on a moraine of known age. Nine separate data sets, each relating to at least one of four moraines (respectively dating from A.D. 1750, 1873, 1909, and 1930) are involved.

For each surface the largest lichens were recorded by those workers who searched the largest areas (Bickerton and Matthews 1992; Erikstad and Sollid 1986; Innes 1986a; Matthews et al. 1979). There is relatively good agreement between the sizes recorded by these workers. The smallest lichen sizes were recorded as a result of searching small areas and/or moraine crests (Griffey 1977; Haines-Young 1983). Haines-Young's results demonstrate a major effect of slope position, with lichens consistently 10–15 mm larger near the base of moraine slopes than on moraine crests. Despite large differences among data sets, a consistent increase in lichen size with surface age is exhibited within each data

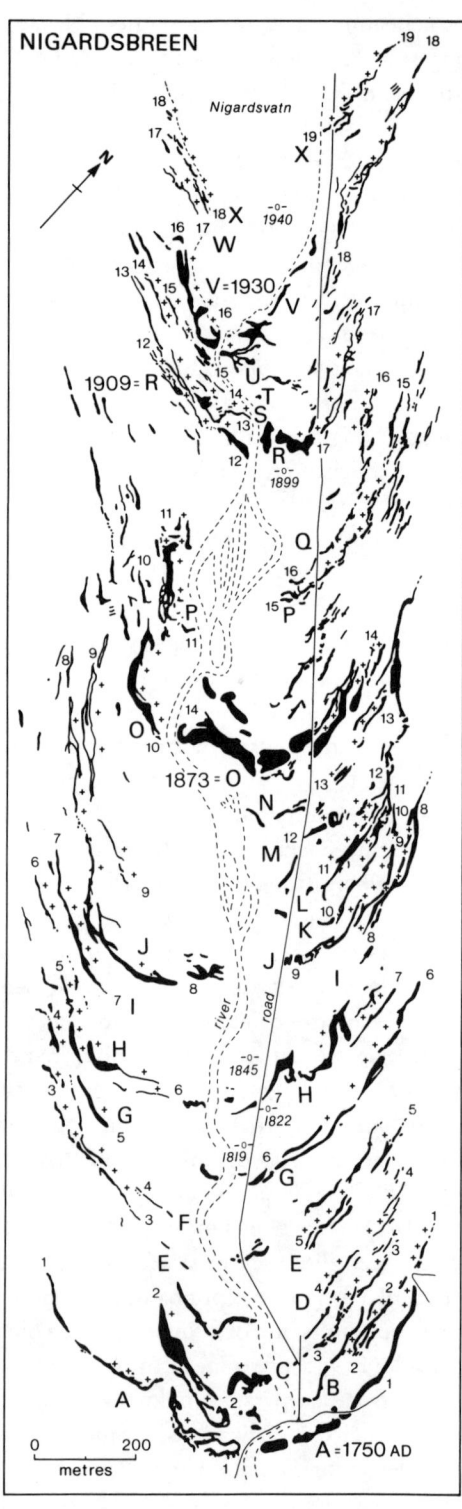

Figure 9.2. Map of moraine ridges (numbered and lettered A–X) on the glacier foreland of Nigardsbreen. Dates refer to moraines or glacier positions of known age; crosses indicate sites where lichen-size measurements were made (after Bickerton and Matthews 1992).

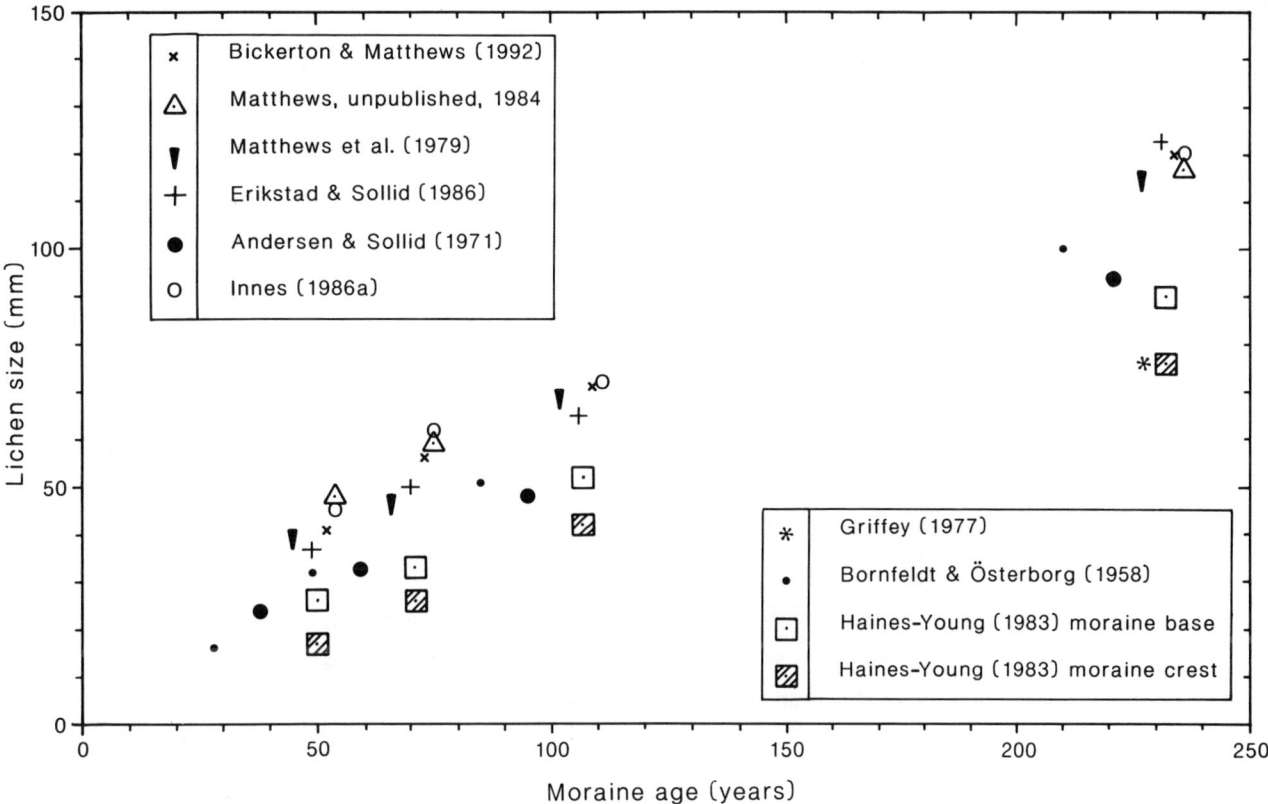

Figure 9.3. Lichen sizes on moraine surfaces of known age at Nigardsbreen. Data points represent a mean of the five largest lichens (each from a separate site) at the time the lichen measurements were made. Symbols refer to particular workers. For further information, see text.

set. A consistent pattern is required for the construction of a lichenometric dating curve. However, the differences between data sets clearly demonstrate the importance of adopting the same techniques for data collection from all surfaces, of both known and unknown age.

Lichenometric Dating Curves

Selected lichenometric dating curves based on surfaces of known age at southern Norwegian glaciers are shown in Figure 9.4. Early curves, such as that produced by Bornefeldt and Österborg (1958) at Nigardsbreen (Jostedalsbreen) were drawn by eye. Mottershead and White (1972, 1973) demonstrated the usefulness of statistical curve-fitting to the construction of a lichenometric dating curve at Tunsbergdalsbreen (Jostedalsbreen); it is the revised form of their curve (Mottershead and Collin 1976) that is shown in Figure 9.4. The use of statistical procedures for fitting curves through the small number of fixed points was criticized by Worsley (1973). However, objective curve fitting is important precisely because curve form is so sensitive to the position of the control points when they are small in number. Mottershead and White (1972) introduced the principle of using best-fit lines to define lichenometric dating curves, a practice that has been continued

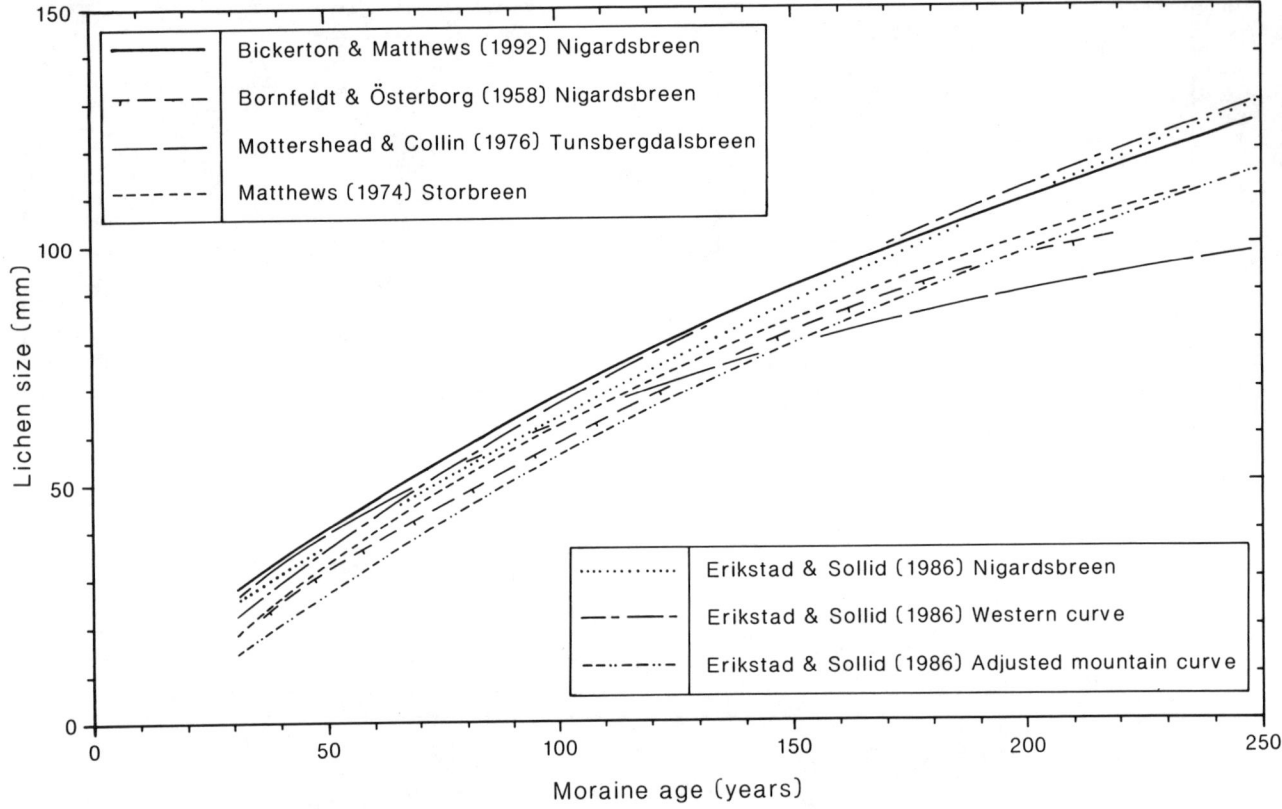

Figure 9.4. Selected lichenometric dating curves from glacier forelands in southern Norway. All curves are based on a mean of the five largest lichens (5.1). Regression equations (y = moraine age; x = lichen size): Bickerton and Matthews (1992), $\log(y + 144) = 2.1411 + 0.0036x$ (Nigardsbreen, 5.1); Erikstad and Sollid (1986), $\ln(y + 380) = 5.9119 + 0.0041x$ (Nigardsbreen, 5.1); Erikstad and Sollid (1986), $\ln(y + 150) = 5.0309 + 0.0074x$ (Western Curve); Erikstad and Sollid (1986), $\ln(y + 160) = 5.1382 + 0.0076x$ (Adjusted Mountain Curve); Mottershead and Collin (1976), $\log(y + 28) = 1.52 + 0.0094x$ (Tunsbergdalsbreen); Matthews (1974), $\log(y + 70) = 1.9072 + 0.0052x$ (Storbreen, 5.1); Bornfeldt and Österborg (1958), curve fitted by eye.

in more recent applications. The same procedure was followed by Erikstad and Sollid (1986) to construct curves for Nigardsbreen and various glaciers in the Jostedalsbreen, Jotunheimen, and Nordvestlandet regions. The curve for Storbreen (Jotunheimen) is one of a family of curves, each constructed using a similar procedure by Matthews (1974) (see below). The other curve for Nigardsbreen is one of a similar family of curves constructed by Bickerton and Matthews (1992).

It was the small amount of information used in the construction of most lichenometric dating curves that led Matthews (1974, 1975) to develop techniques to test the accuracy of lichenometric dates at Storbreen. In the absence of sufficient independent evidence of moraine age, those techniques are based on reproducibility. There are essentially two approaches, both producing sets or families of lichenometric dating curves. The first approach (Matthews 1974) involves the construction of a set of separate curves, each based on a different number of largest lichens per surface and coded according to the number of subplots per surface and the number of lichens measured per subplot, respectively. Thus the curve for Storbreen shown in Figure 9.4 (one curve from a family of curves) is coded 5.1, as it is based on five subplots and the largest lichen in each of these. Surfaces of unknown age are dated by each curve separately. Use of the whole family of curves produces a range of predicted dates for each surface, and frequency histograms can be drawn showing the distribution of predicted dates for each surface (Figure 9.5A). Mean or median predicted dates are then used instead of a single prediction from an individual curve, and the range of dates gives a measure of reliability.

The second approach (Matthews 1975) overcomes a problem of the first approach, namely the nonindependence of curves within the family. Independence is achieved by the random sampling of subplots from each surface, both for constructing the lichenometric dating curves and for dating moraines of unknown age. Histograms of predicted dates for the surfaces of unknown age derived by this approach (Figure 9.5B) can be used to produce mean predicted ages with statistical confidence intervals. Although the range of individual predicted dates produced by the randomized approach is very wide, confidence intervals derived in this way appear to provide a more realistic and reliable measure of the accuracy of the dates than other types of confidence interval, including statistical confidence intervals around individual predicted dates (see Matthews 1974; Mottershead and White 1972) and less rigorously defined error limits (see Calkin and Ellis 1984).

The randomized approach as developed by Matthews (1975) requires a large number of subplots. Where moraine surface areas are small or there is insufficient time to search large areas, families of curves are more appropriately constructed by the first approach (Matthews 1974), although it is possible that the nonindependence of the curves may lead to biased results. However, the good agreement at Storbreen between the mean predicted ages produced by the two approaches (see Figure 9.5A and B) suggests that the first approach has produced reliable results here.

Table 9.1 compares lichenometric dating results from four studies of the Nigardsbreen moraine se-

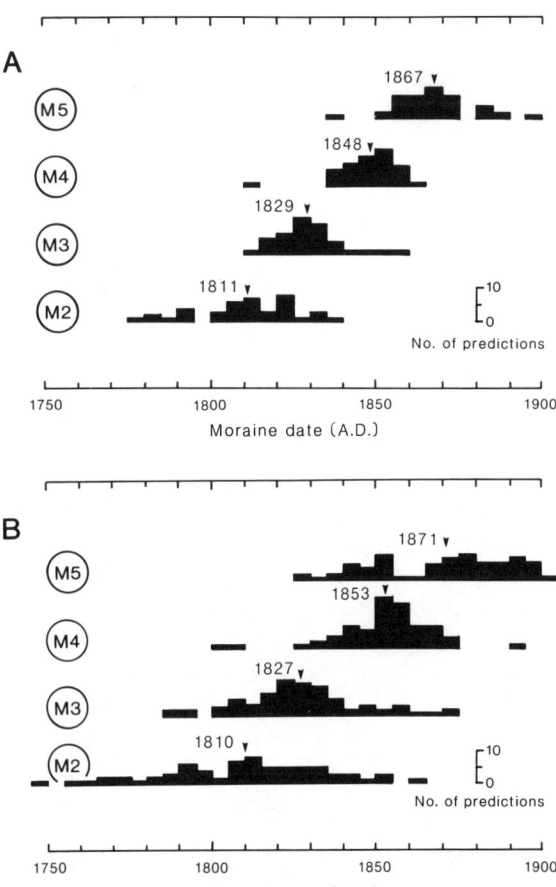

Figure 9.5. Lichenometric dates for four moraines of unknown age on the Storbreen glacier foreland, Jotunheimen. Histograms represent dates derived from: (A) families of lichenometric dating curves based on different numbers of largest lichens and different numbers of subplots per surface; (B) the randomized approach to the generation of families of curves. Arrows indicate mean predicted dates (after Matthews 1975).

quence shown in Figure 9.2. The most recent of these employed families of lichenometric dating curves using the first approach outlined above (Bickerton and Matthews 1992). Results are given for the *Rhizocarpon* subgenus and separately (in parentheses) for section *Rhizocarpon* alone. The other studies employed single curves and the five largest lichens per surface; Andersen and

Table 9.1. Lichenometric Dates for Moraine Ridges at Nigardsbreen, Southern Norway

Moraine ridge[a]			Lichenometric dates			
(1)	(2)	Historical date (A.D.)	Bickerton and Matthews (1992)	Erikstad and Sollid (1986)	Innes (1986)	Andersen and Sollid (1971)
X̄	o	1940[b]	1940 (1938)[d]	—	—	—
W	—	—	1941 (1941)	—	—	—
V	n	1930	—	—	—	—
U	—	—	1919 (1919)[d]	—	—	—
T	m	—	1914 (1914)[d]	1913 (1914)	—	—
S	—	—	1915 (1915)	—	—	—
R	l	1909	—	—	—	—
Q	k	1899[c]	1912 (1913)[d]	—	—	—
P	j	—	1891 (1892)	1899 (1902)	—	1890
O	i	1873	—	—	—	—
N	—	—	1875 (1875)[d]	—	—	—
M	—	—	1869 (1868)[d]	—	—	—
L	h	—	1866 (1865)	1857 (1862)	—	—
K	—	—	1867 (1871)[d]	—	1847	—
J	g	—	1852 (1849)	1850 (1856)	1843	1860
I	—	—	1842 (1839)	—	—	—
H	f	—	1839 (1835)	1842 (1848)	1835	1850
G	e	—	1822 (1815)	1834 (1840)	1820	1840
F	—	—	1826 (1818)[d]	—	1810	—
E	d	—	1807 (1805)	1831 (1837)	1803	—
D	—	—	1805 (1795)	—	1795	—
C	c	—	1795 (1789)	1812 (1818)	—	—
B	b	—	1780 (1775)[d]	1766 (1769)	1789	1790
A	a	1750	—	—	—	—

[a]Moraine ridge codes: (1) (A–X) Bickerton and Matthews (1992) (see Figure 9.2), (2) (a–o) Erikstad and Sollid (1986). Dates in brackets are based on: Bickerton and Matthews's (1992) use of section *Rhizocarpon* alone and Erikstad and Sollid's (1986) "Western Curve."
[b]Used as a fixed point only by Erikstad and Sollid (1986).
[c]Used as a fixed point by Erikstad and Sollid (1986) and Andersen and Sollid (1971).
[d]Dates based on lichen measurements from less than five plots per moraine.

Sollid (1971) and Innes (1986a) used curves fitted by eye, whereas Erikstad and Sollid (1986) used a statistical best-fit curve. The studies used the same fixed points, although neither Innes nor Bickerton and Matthews used the A.D. 1899 and 1940 moraines as fixed points, because they considered the independent evidence to be equivocal. It should be pointed out that Erikstad and Sollid (1986) also dated these moraines, using their regional "Western Curve" (see Figure 9.4; dates in parentheses in Table 9.1), which incorporates additional fixed points from other glacier forelands, considered by them to lie in the same climatic region (see below).

The differences in predicted dates obtained by the

different workers for the same moraines give a clear indication that inaccuracies arise even where good independent evidence exists for the establishment of local lichenometric dating curves. In the case of one moraine (moraine E), predicted dates differ by 28 years (34 years if the result based on Erikstad and Sollid's regional curve is included); in seven other cases (moraines B, C, F, G, H, J, and K), the difference is 15–25 years. Bickerton and Matthews (1992) suggest that the accuracy of lichenometric dating under favorable conditions for its use on the 'Little Ice Age' time scale of ca. 230 years may be ca. 15 percent. However, results from the careful use of families of curves are likely to be more accurate than this, and may attain an accuracy of ca. 10 percent (± 20 years for the oldest moraines and ± 5 years for the youngest) (Bickerton and Matthews 1992).

Although greater levels of accuracy may be attainable where more control points are available, results may be much less accurate where fixed points are of poorer quality. A good illustration of this is provided by the dispute over the age of the outermost moraine ridges in Jotunheimen (Erikstad and Sollid 1988; Matthews 1987). Lichenometric dating at Storbreen (see Figures 9.4 and 9.5) has been carried out by assuming the outermost moraine (A) to date from A.D. 1750. There is, however, only meager local evidence to justify this assumption. Erikstad and Sollid (1986) therefore used lichen size data from mine waste tips (and other data) to adjust their results, even though the mines were located outside the region and the waste was characterized by relatively small lichens (in relation to those growing on moraines of the same age). Use of their "Adjusted Mountain Curve" (see Figure 9.4) suggests that the outermost moraine at Storbreen dates from A.D. 1787, that is 37 years younger than previously proposed.

Matthews (1977) used a randomized experimental approach to produce lichenometric dating curves from the reliable (young) fixed points only and dated the outermost moraine by extrapolation. Mean predicted ages were A.D. 1785, 1757, and 1774, based on the single largest, the five largest, and the ten largest lichens, respectively. However, 95 percent confidence limits extend from A.D. 1743 to 1770, in the case of the five largest lichens, and the lower age limits for the estimate based on single largest lichens suggests that a date as young as A.D. 1797 is possible. Thus the test was unable to differentiate between the alternative views, and the dispute remains.

Regional Lichenometric Dating

Most of the examples discussed above have involved local lichenometric dating; that is, lichenometric dating curves have been constructed and used on particular glacier forelands with local fixed points. However, a lack of suitable fixed points often necessitates the use of fixed points from a wider area. Erikstad and Sollid's (1986) "Western Curve" (see Figure 9.4) is the best example of a regional lichenometric dating curve from southern Norway. This curve was derived from fixed points at Nigardsbreen, Austerdalsbreen, and two glaciers in western Jotunheimen (Styggedalsbreen and Gjertvassbreen). However, problems increase where applications are attempted at a regional level.

The most important problem is that of environmental heterogeneity. The sensitivity of lichen growth to numerous abiotic and biotic environmental factors and the importance of this sensitivity for lichenometric dating has been pointed out many times (for example, Benedict 1967, 1990, 1991; Innes 1985a, 1985d; Jochimsen 1966, 1973; Webber and Andrews 1973b). Moisture supply, snow cover, temperature, lithology, and inter- and intraspecific competition appear to be particularly influential in southern Norway. Major differences in these environmental factors between forelands, which differ in altitude, aspect, continentality, or in other ways, will introduce variations in lichen size unrelated to surface age. Regional lichenometric dating curves constructed from control points characteristic of a heterogeneous collection of environments will be less reliable than local curves, because relatively large environmental differences will be reflected in the scatter of points. There is likely to be an even more heterogeneous collection of environments associated with the surfaces to be dated, introducing the possibility of further errors. In relation to dating by largest lichens, the largest errors will occur where the local optimum conditions for lichen growth do not reflect the regional optimum (Matthews 1987).

At Nigardsbreen the predicted ages of moraines dated using the regional "Western Curve" are up to about six years younger than those derived from the local Nigardsbreen curve (Table 9.1). These differences reflect the introduction of fixed points derived from western Jotunheimen. Such small differences between the two sets of predicted ages probably reflect the fact that data from Nigardsbreen comprise the major input to the "Western Curve." Greater differences and larger errors would be expected, were the form of the "Western Curve" not so closely controlled by the fixed points from Nigardsbreen. This is illustrated by the dating of moraines at Austerdalsbreen (a neighboring outlet of the Jostedalsbreen ice cap), where application of the "Western Curve" suggests that the outermost moraine dates from A.D. 1800 (Erikstad and Sollid 1986). These authors consider that relatively poor growth conditions on this moraine are responsible for an underestimate of age by about 50 years. The possibility of such large errors in the application of regional lichenometric dating has led Matthews (1987) to doubt the validity of the distinct moraine chronologies proposed by Erikstad and Sollid (1986) for different regions of southern Norway.

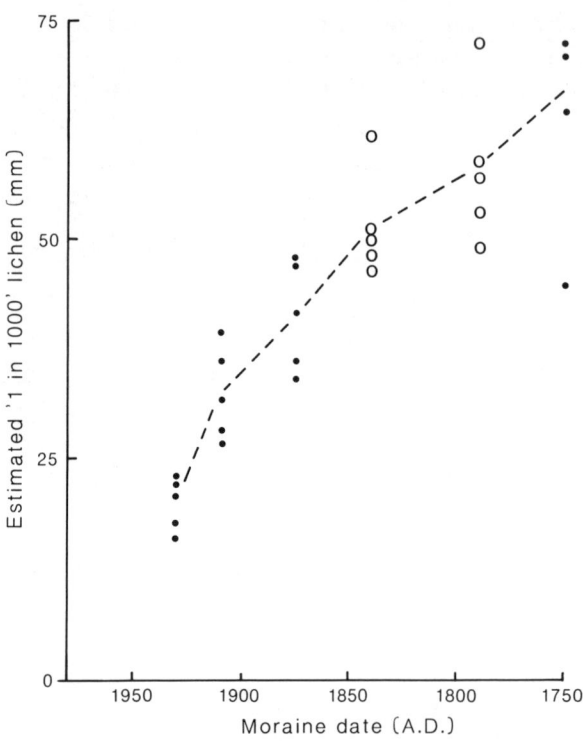

Figure 9.6. The size of the "one in a thousand" lichen for different subplots on moraines of various ages at Nigardsbreen. Each point represents the "one in a thousand" lichen derived by size-frequency analysis of a sample of 1,000 lichens. Closed circles are historically dated fixed points; open circles represent moraines dated by lichenometric methods (after Innes 1983b).

Additional Techniques

It has been proposed that other characteristics of the lichen size population can be employed for dating purposes as well as, or instead of, largest lichens (Benedict 1985; Caseldine 1991; Gellatly 1982; Locke et al. 1979; Smirnova and Nikonov 1990). Such characteristics have been little used for dating moraines in southern Norway, although Andersen and Sollid (1971) and Erikstad and Sollid (1986) used size-frequency curves effectively to identify anomalously large lichens at Nigardsbreen. Furthermore Innes (1983b, 1983c) has tested the recommendation of Locke et al. (1979) that an estimate of the size of the "one in a thousand" lichen, derived from a lichen size-frequency curve, is preferable to the use of the largest lichen present as an index of surface age.

Innes (1983b) found the "one in a thousand" lichen to vary greatly on surfaces of known age at Nigardsbreen (Figure 9.6). This may reflect not only the degree of fit of the data to the lichen size–log frequency model but also variations in the lichen-size population in response to differences in the physical environment, competition and postdeposition disturbance of the surface (see Haines-Young 1988; Innes 1983b, 1985a, 1986c, 1986d). The main implication of this for lichenometric dating is that the "one in a thousand" lichen is not always a reliable index of surface age. Measurement of the whole population of lichens on a surface or within subplots is also a very time-consuming operation. Widespread adoption of this index cannot therefore be recommended for dating purposes, although other indices derived from the size-frequency distribution may prove more effective (see Smirnova and Nikonov 1990).

Although attempting to date surfaces independently by more than one species is desirable (see Andrews and Webber 1964; Beschel 1957, 1973; Calkin and Ellis 1984; Orombelli and Porter 1983; Smirnova and Nikonov 1990; Winchester 1984), apart from the early attempt of Bornefeldt and Österborg (1958) this approach has been neglected in southern Norway. The difference in growth rates between *Rhizocarpon* section *Rhizocarpon* and *Rhizocarpon* section *Alpicola*, which has been established by Innes (1983a, 1983c, 1985b), suggests that these two lichen groups could be used for independent dating, although Haines-Young (1983) found that section *Alpicola* has a more patchy distribution, and Bickerton and Matthews (1992) note that it is more difficult to separate from section *Rhizocarpon* on younger surfaces. Other species either do not appear to be common enough for dating or grow so fast that they would only be useful for dating relatively young moraines. Finally, because the *Rhizocarpon* subgenus has been applied so successfully, there has been no need to employ faster-growing lichens for establishing their growth rates using lichen-size ratios (see Andrews and Webber 1964, 1969; Locke et al. 1979).

Direct Measurements of Lichen Growth Rates

Although Schroeder-Lanz (1983) has presented a theoretical discussion of the direct approach to lichenometric dating in the context of southern Norway, and four other researchers (R. W. Bickerton, R. H. Haines-Young, J. L. Innes and J. A. Matthews) have set up sites for the direct measurement of lichen growth rates, no results have yet been published. Some preliminary results are presented here for a site of apparently optimal growth on the outer moraine at Nigardsbreen. Mean annual growth rates of individual thalli of the *Rhizocarpon* subgenus, which were marked out and measured by Bickerton in 1981 and remeasured by Matthews in 1986, are shown in Figure 9.7. The long axes of well-defined thalli were measured on each occasion using Mitutoyo dial calipers (precision 0.01 mm). All specimens were separate from other lichens and therefore not influenced by competition.

The data indicate very large variations in growth rate between thalli of approximately the same size, with no suggestion of a decline in growth rate with increasing lichen size. The statistical distribution of growth rates is approximately normal. It is possible that the smallest lichens (diameter < 5–10 mm) are growing at a slower rate, as was found by Armstrong (1983) for *Rhizocarpon geographicum* and by Benedict and Nash (1990) for different species. However, the scatter in the data does not justify the use of a growth rate other than one calculated for all specimens. The mean growth rate is 0.66 mm/yr with a standard deviation of 0.26 mm/yr. The fastest recorded growth rate is 1.58 mm/yr, but this was exceptional, with the second fastest individual growing at 1.12 mm/yr. The estimated maximum growth rate given in Figure 9.7 (1.10 mm/yr) is the value likely to be exceeded by the fastest-growing 5 percent of the sample ($\bar{x} + t.\hat{\sigma}$; n = 63). This estimated maximum growth rate has been used to produce a lichen growth curve (Figure 9.8, curve A) for comparison with the lichenometric dating curves constructed by the indirect method (Figure 9.8, curves C and D). The origin of the direct curve allows no delay for ecesis or the possibility of a slower growth rate initially.

The most interesting feature of these results is that the direct-growth measurements predict much larger lichens on the older moraine surfaces than those observed. Although the growth curve shown in Figure 9.8 has limitations, due to the variability in the data, there is no doubt that maximum recorded growth rates are greatly in excess of those expected from the size of lichens on the older moraines, and that the largest lichens measured exhibit no signs of the decline in growth rate that was expected from the shape of the indirect lichenometric dating curve. There are four possible rea-

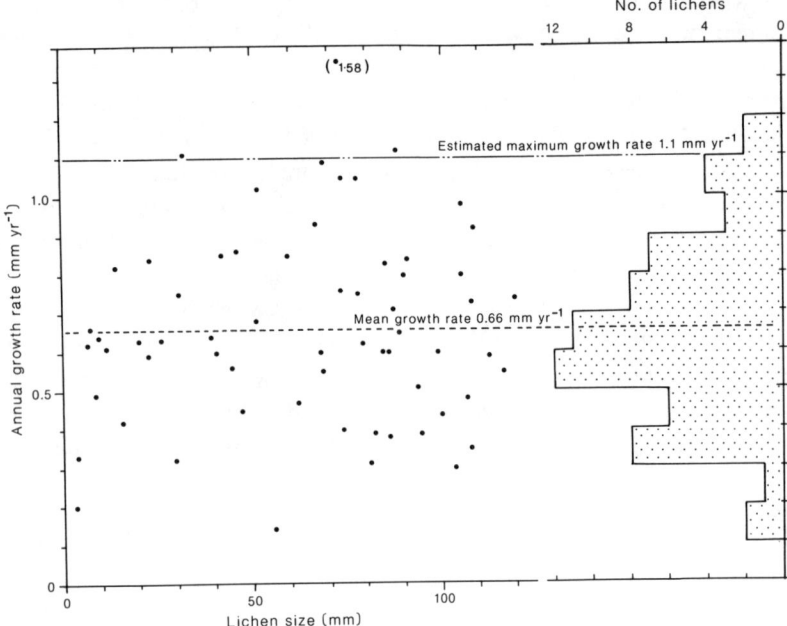

Figure 9.7. Direct growth measurements of the *Rhizocarpon* subgenus at Nigardsbreen. Each point represents the mean annual growth rate of an individual thallus over a five-year interval (1981–1986). The mean growth rate for the 63 thalli, an estimate of the maximum growth rate likely to be exceeded by 5 percent of the population, and the frequency distribution of individual growth rates (shaded) are shown.

sons for the divergence of the direct and indirect curves. First, the moraines could be younger than supposed. Second, the lichens on the older moraines could be younger than the surfaces on which they are growing. Third, the lichens on the older moraines could be growing slower, due to competition. Fourth, lichen growth rates could have been slower in the past. The first explanation is not possible at Nigardsbreen, because the moraines are of known age. Although none of the other explanations can be ruled out, the third is considered most likely, with maximum growth rates being prevented on the older surfaces by increasing competition from other lichens (see Haines-Young 1983, 1985, 1988; Innes 1986d; Matthews 1977, 1987).

Unfortunately, because of such competition effects, there appears to be no simple way of using the direct lichen growth curve based on maximum growth rate for dating the largest lichens on the moraines of unknown age. Similar difficulties have been encountered by Haworth et al. (1986) in the Brooks Range, Alaska. There appears to be a closer relationship between the indirect lichenometric dating curve and a growth curve based on the mean growth rate (Figure 9.8, curve B). However, the use of this curve for dating purposes is difficult to justify. Until more data are available on the growth rates and controls on the growth rates of the *Rhizocarpon* subgenus, the indirect approach to lichenometric dating seems destined to remain more important than the direct approach.

Some Other Applications from Southern Norway

Although the dating of moraines has been the major application for lichenometric dating, some other studies have been carried out, all using the *Rhizocarpon* subgenus. Some of these have involved different types of surfaces on glacier forelands; others have not been confined to recently deglaciated terrain.

Maizels and Petch (1985) dated intermoraine areas on the glacier foreland of Austerdalsbreen (Jostedalsbreen) using a variety of lichen size indices. Their aim was to date the palaeochannels of abandoned outwash

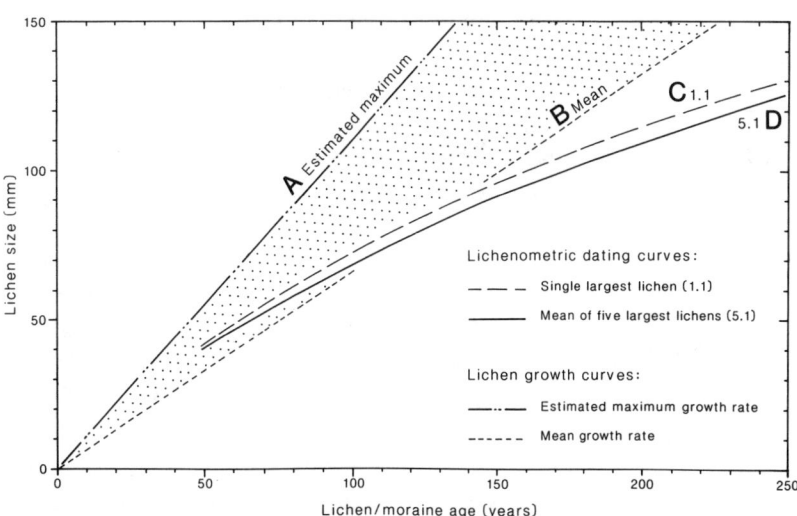

Figure 9.8. Preliminary direct lichen growth curves for Nigardsbreen, based on the data in Figure 9.7, in relation to indirect lichenometric dating curves: (A) growth curve based on the maximum growth rate; (B) growth curve based on the mean growth rate; (C) lichenometric dating curve based on the single largest lichen; (D) lichenometric dating curve based on the five largest lichens. The shaded area depicts lichen growth rates between the mean and the maximum.

plains (*sandar*) and to reconstruct the drainage pattern associated with glacier retreat. They were able to date the formation and abandonment of distinct palaeo-channel systems, each reflecting a complex sequence of geomorphological events. Matthews et al. (1986) dated the drainage of a "Little Ice Age" ice-dammed lake at Bøverbreen, Jotunheimen, to about A.D. 1826, by the application of lichenometric dating on both the relict shoreline and the youngest moraine into which the shoreline was etched. Lichens on the shoreline were less than 100 mm in diameter. The former ice-dammed lake produced a distinct lichen trimline, above which lichens were up to three times larger. Another example related to an ice-dammed lake has been provided by Shakesby (1985), who dated boulder deltas formed by jökulhlaups (floods released by catastrophic ice-dammed lake drainage) at Mjølkedalsbreen, Jotunheimen.

Debris flows were dated by Innes (1985e) on three colluvial fans in the Jotunheimen-Jostedalsbreen region, using *Rhizocarpon* section *Alpicola*. Section *Rhizocarpon* dating curves were used after converting section *Alpicola* diameters with reference to size ratios. Two periods of enhanced debris-flow activity were detected (A.D. 1670–1720 and 1790–1860). Lichen sizes have also been used for the relative-age dating of a catastrophic landslide (*sturzström*) (Dawson et al. 1986), protalus ramparts, and talus-foot rock glaciers (Shakesby et al. 1987) in Rondane, central southern Norway. All of these landforms were characterized by maximum diameters of section *Rhizocarpon* between 250 and 480 mm. In the light of available lichenometric dating curves from southern Norway (Figure 9.3), these landforms were certainly in existence well before the "Little Ice Age." A much younger rock glacier that had developed from a lateral moraine at Bukkeholsbreen, Jotunheimen, was shown by Vere and Matthews (1985), on the basis of lichen sizes, to have begun its development in the eighteenth century, shortly after the glacier deposited its outer moraine during the "Little Ice Age."

In a different kind of application, Ballantyne and Matthews (1982) and Cook-Talbot (1991) have used lichenometric dating to estimate the time elapsed since stabilization of sorted circles, a type of periglacial patterned ground. On the glacier foreland of Slettmarkbreen, Jotunheimen, Ballantyne and Matthews (1982) found that the largest lichens on sorted circles were never more than 30 mm smaller than those growing on adjacent moraines unaffected by periglacial activity.

They concluded that the circles were formed and stabilized in the ice-marginal zone within 50 years of deglaciation. In her detailed study of sorted circles on much older terrain in the Veodalen area of eastern Jotunheimen, Cook-Talbot (1991) used largest lichens and size-frequency techniques. By use of inflection points in size-frequency curves, she demonstrated that the circles experienced widespread reactivation between about A.D. 1640 and 1740 (during the most severe phase of the "Little Ice Age"). There was also less-widespread evidence for an earlier phase of reactivation around the twelfth and thirteenth centuries.

Applications Elsewhere

The wide range of possible applications of lichenometric dating is summarized in Table 9.2. Most applications have been made in arctic-alpine environments, using *Rhizocarpon* subgenus *Rhizocarpon*. Widespread application in arctic-alpine environments probably reflects the dominance of lichen growth forms and the lack of competition from other plants on rock surfaces. In southern Norway dense growths of dwarf shrubs or trees often prevent the growth of the *Rhizocarpon* subgenus at lower altitudes, and the growth of moss on boulder surfaces has a similar effect in some western districts characterized by high precipitation.

Suitable rock surfaces are needed in addition to the presence of a suitable species. The area of surface is important as well as its quality. A minimum surface area is required for search purposes (see above) and, on sedimentary deposits, clast size may affect the maximum size a thallus can attain (Orwin 1972). Rock surface texture and chemical composition also influence lichen colonization and growth rates. For example Innes (1985a) reported that on gravestones, greatest *Rhizocarpon* growth is frequently on a surface other than the polished one (see also Benedict 1967). Almost all species within the *Rhizocarpon* subgenus grow best on acidic lithologies (Runemark 1956) and hence cannot be used on calcareous rocks. However, it may be possible to use other species, such as *Xanthoria elegans* (Osborn and Taylor 1975) or *Aspicilia calcarea* (Winchester 1988) in such situations.

Almost all the examples in Table 9.2 are based wholly on the indirect approach to lichenometry. Hence they are dependent on the existence of suitable fixed points of known age. In almost all cases this, not lichen senescence, restricts lichenometric dating to surfaces formed or exposed during the last few hundred years. Where lichenometric dating curves have been constructed for up to several thousands of years (for example, Benedict 1967, 1981, 1985; Calkin and Ellis 1980, 1984; Karlén 1973, 1979), using a small number of radiocarbon-dated surfaces as fixed points, the dating control has been relatively poor, leading to large and poorly defined levels of inaccuracy. In this respect the recent studies of raised boulder beaches along the coast of the Gulf of Bothnia in northern Sweden (Broadbent 1987; Broadbent and Bergqvist 1986; Sjöberg 1990) are exceptional. Here it is possible to obtain a relatively large number of fixed points that are relatively accurately dated by means of land-uplift rates. Broadbent and Bergqvist (1986) present section *Rhizocarpon* lichenometric dating curves for two local areas, Grundskataräften and Bjuröklubb, which are based respectively on 10 and 12 fixed points and extend from 200 to 950 B.P. and from 300 to 1500 B.P. Over these time intervals, the curves have a linear form, even though lichen diameters increase to over 350 mm at the second locality. Both data sets are in very good agreement, and the combined curve provides a uniquely well-founded lichenometric dating curve for the last 1,500 years. They suggest that it will be possible to construct large numbers of curves for different localities and that this will have a major impact on dating historical and archaeological structures, including stone churches and runestones.

Two distinct types of application can be recognized in the lichenometric dating of surfaces. First, the more common type assumes a monogenetic surface and the objective is to find its date of formation or exposure. The dating of moraines, raised beaches, and river terraces is of this type, because, perhaps after a short interval of stabilization, the surface remains essentially unchanged. The second type of application involves

Table 9.2. Applications of Lichenometric Dating Excluding Moraines

Type of Surface	Location	Reference
Fluvial and Lacustrine Landforms		
Active river channels	Australia	Gregory (1976)
Abandoned channels and bars	England	Macklin (1986); Milne (1982); Macklin et al. (1993)
Flood plain zones	England	Harvey et al. (1984)
Sandar/river terraces	Iceland	Maizels and Dugmore (1985); Thompson and Jones (1986)
Sandar surfaces	southern Norway	Maizels and Petch (1985)
Lake Shorelines		
Boulder deltas	southern Norway	Shakesby (1985)
Lake shorelines	Baffin Island	Andrews and Barnett (1979)
Lake shorelines	southern Norway	Matthews et al. (1986)
Coastal Features		
Raised beaches	Finnmark	Donner et al. (1977)
Raised beaches	Antarctica	Birkenmajer (1981)
Raised beaches	Spitsbergen	André (1985, 1986)
Raised beaches	Gulf of Bothnia	Broadbent (1987); Sjöberg (1990)
Periglacial Surfaces		
Rock glaciers	Colorado, U.S.A.	Birkeland (1973); C. D. Miller (1973)
Rock glaciers	Swiss Alps	Haeberli et al. (1979)
Rock glaciers	southern Norway	Vere and Matthews (1985)
Protalus ramparts	southern Norway	Shakesby et al. (1987)
Block stream	Colorado, U.S.A.	Carrara and Andrews (1973)
Patterned ground	Scotland	King (1971)
Patterned ground	southern Norway	Ballantyne and Matthews (1982)
Patterned ground	southern Norway	Cook-Talbot (1991)
Talus	Spitsbergen	André (1985, 1986)
Rapid Mass-movement Phenomena		
Debris flows	Swedish Lappland	Nyberg (1985); Rapp and Nyberg (1981)
Debris flows	Tatras, Poland	Jonasson (1991); Jonasson et al. (1991)
Debris flows	Scotland & Norway	Innes (1983a, 1983d, 1985e)
Landslides	Italian Alps	Porter and Orombelli (1981)
Landslide/sturzström	southern Norway	Dawson et al. (1986)
Avalanche deposits	southern Norway	McCarroll and Matthews (personal communcation)
Archaeological Structures		
Polynesian statues	Easter Island	Follmann (1961)
Stone walls	England	Laundon (1980)
Game-drive structures	Colorado, U.S.A.	Benedict (1985)

(continues)

Table 9.2. Continued.

Type of Surface	Location	Reference
Archaeological Structures		
Cairns/fish-net posts	northern Sweden	Broadbent and Bergqvist (1986)
Stone cairns, oven, etc.	northern Sweden	Broadbent (1987)
Megalithic stone circles	England	Winchester (1984, 1988)
Tectonic and Volcanic Surfaces		
Earthquake-induced landslides/ disruptions	Tadjikistan Tien Shan/Pamirs	Nikonov and Shebalina (1979) Smirnova and Nikonov (1990)
Earthquakes/faults	New Zealand	W. B. Bull (personal comm.)
Volcanic surfaces	Antarctica	Birkenmajer (1980b)
Exhumed fault scarp	southern Italy	Mudge (personal comm.)
Other Surfaces		
Snowpatch fringes	Greenland	Pitman (1973)
Limestone pavements	Eire	Trudgill et al. (1979)

polygenetic surfaces, which do not remain stable after formation; the objective here is to date the disturbance history. This may require the use of different techniques, such as size-frequency analysis, to distinguish different populations of lichen sizes. This approach, originally used by Benedict (1967, 1985) to distinguish lichens that survived Indian wall-building activity in Colorado, is well illustrated by the work of Cook-Talbot (1991) on periglacial sorted circles (described above). It may find wide application in archaeological contexts to differentiate structures that were moved, rebuilt, or otherwise disturbed. It is possible, however, to recognize disturbance without using size-frequency methods, as shown by Winchester (1984, 1988), who dated the megaliths in the stone circles of Avebury (Wiltshire), Rollright (Oxfordshire), and Castlerigg (Cumbria). Dates obtained from individual megaliths indicated that many were moved or emplaced at various times, some of which coincided with known excavations or other activities at the sites of these historic monuments.

Conclusion

In the light of the detailed research reported from southern Norway, and the increasingly diverse range of apparently successful applications of lichenometric dating worldwide, I take an optimistic view of its present status and future prospects. Lichenometric dating is the best available technique for dating rock surfaces in many situations, particularly in arctic-alpine environments, where lichen growth is relatively unaffected by competition from other plant groups. This contrasts with the negative conclusions of Jochimsen (1966, 1973) and the scepticism of Worsley (1981, 1990), but continues the traditional optimism of the practitioners, such as Webber and Andrews (1973b), Locke et al. (1979), and Mottershead (1980). However, this does not mean that lichenometric dating is a panacea. Like all dating techniques, there are limitations and restrictions on its use, and the critical appraisal of its performance is necessary in the context of each application.

It is particularly important to recognize that lichenometric dating involves several different approaches, which vary in their applicability to specific cases. At one extreme, exemplified by the dating of moraines in southern Norway, this method provides calibrated ages. Over the short time scale of the last few centuries, and with sufficient independent dating control, the best applications of the indirect approach have achieved this status. Indeed the various published age estimates for the moraines at Nigardsbreen, southern Norway, formed since the mid-eighteenth century, probably attain an accuracy of ca. 10–15 percent (Bickerton and Matthews 1992; see also Bickerton and Matthews 1993). At the other extreme, without any fixed points, only relative-age estimates can be made. Many applications, especially those involving time scales of thousands of years, provide age estimates that are not well founded, because they are based on fixed points of insufficient quality and/or quality.

The lack of surfaces of known age often leads to the use of different kinds of surfaces as fixed points, such as mine waste tips, roads, bridges, canals, quarries, building foundations, historic monuments, walls, cairns, railway embankments, balloon (rockpile) anchors, tombstones, rockfalls, landslides, and debris flows (see Benedict 1967, 1981; Erikstad and Sollid 1986; Innes 1983d, 1984b; Karlén 1973, 1979; Kugelmann 1990; Orombelli and Porter 1983; Smirnova and Nikonov 1990; Werner, 1990). This will result in dating inaccuracies, unless conditions for lichen growth are the same as on the surfaces to be dated. Regional lichenometric dating curves, with a relatively large number of fixed points, may appear to be based on firmer foundations than local curves based on a smaller number. However, they are more likely than local curves to conceal a high degree of environmental heterogeneity, which may become prohibitive as the spatial scale of the investigation increases. Even if a regional lichenometric dating curve is a true reflection of regional optimum conditions for lichen growth, dating accuracy will be affected where local conditions for lichen growth do not correspond to regional optimal conditions. Combined with the tendency for the availability of reliable fixed points to decline rapidly for older surfaces, this lead to the conclusion that indirect lichenometric dating is most suited to local studies involving the historical period.

The direct approach to lichenometric dating has so far produced disappointing results. Direct measurements have shown that the growth rates of the slow-growing species used for dating purposes are extremely variable. This, combined with the small number of thalli measured over a small number of years to obtain the growth-rate estimates, has led to an inability to determine accurately the form of the lichen growth curves. Furthermore the small number of studies that have proceded as far as to construct lichen growth curves from direct growth measurements have produced conclusions that conflict with the results of the indirect approach (see Figure 9.8). In southern Norway the most important cause of this conflict appears to be increasing competition between lichens as surface age increases. Unless such effects can be taken into account, there would seem to be little prospect of the direct approach to lichenometric dating graduating from a relative-age to a calibrated-age dating technique. Webber and Andrews (1973b) saw the direct approach as providing the biological justification for the indirect approach to lichenometric dating. While this may remain true in the long-term, the present justification for the indirect approach remains the results achieved in applications where best practice has been adopted under favorable conditions.

Finally, with an increasing range of applications for lichenometric dating, any call for standardization of technique is premature. There is no reason to believe that the same techniques are appropriate for different applications. For example, where the aim is to date the disturbance history of polygenetic surfaces, size-frequency techniques may be more appropriate than those found useful for estimating moraine age. Similarly, techniques emphasizing extensive searches of large areas of surface are clearly inappropriate for many geomorphic and archaeological applications. A detailed, explicit statement of the methods used, combined with a critical assessment of the results in terms of possible sources of error and likely accuracy levels, is far more important than standardization.

Acknowledgments

My research on lichenometric dating in southern Norway continues as part of the research programme of the Jotunheimen Research Expeditions; this review constitutes Jotunheimen Research Expeditions Contribution No. 98. I am grateful to all those who, over the years, have assisted with the fieldwork, sponsored the expeditions, or supported the work in other ways. I am particularly grateful to the following members of the expeditions for discussions on lichenometry and/or comments on the manuscript: Richard Bickerton, Dr. Judith Cook-Talbot, Dr. Alastair Dawson, Dr. Nigel Griffey, Dr. Roy Haines-Young, Dr. Danny McCarroll, Dr. James Petch, Dr. Richard Shakesby, and Dr. Diana Vere. I would also like to record my appreciation of the work of three other groups who have worked independently in the same region: Dr. Derek Mottershead and others, based at Portsmouth Polytechnic, who introduced precise statistical curve-fitting techniques; Dr. John Innes, who, then based in the Geography Section at University College, Cardiff, made an unprecedented contribution to lichenometric methodology generally; and Professor J. L. Sollid, Dr. Lars Erikstad, and others, based in Oslo, who have made important advances in the application of lichenometric dating at the regional level. The progress made in the lichenometric dating of moraines in southern Norway owes much to mutual stimulation.

References Cited

Andersen, J. L., and J. L. Sollid
1971   Glacial Chronology and Glacial Geomorphology in the Marginal Zones of the Glaciers Midtdalsbreen and Nigardsbreen, South Norway. *Norsk Geografisk Tidsskrift* 25:1–38.

André, M. F.
1985   Lichénométrie et Vitesses d'Evolution des Versants Arctiques Pendant l'Holocène (Région de la Baie du Roi, Spitsberg, 79°N). *Revue de Géomorphologie Dynamique* 34:49–72.

1986   Dating Slope Deposits and Estimating Rates of Rock Wall Retreat in Northwest Spitsbergen by Lichenometry. *Geografiska Annaler* 68(A):65–75.

Andrews J. T., and D. M. Barnett
1979   Holocene (Neoglacial) Moraine and Periglacial Lake Chronology, Barnes Ice Cap, North West Territories, Canada. *Boreas* 8:341–358.

Andrews, J. T., and P. J. Webber
1964   A Lichenometric Study of the Northwestern Margin of the Barnes Ice Cap: a Geomorphological Technique. *Geographical Bulletin* 22:80–104.

1969   Lichenometry to Evaluate Changes in Glacial Mass Budgets: As Illustrated from North-Central Baffin Island, N.W.T. *Arctic and Alpine Research* 1:181–194.

Aplin, P. S., and D. J. Hill
1979   Growth Analysis of Circular Lichen Thalli. *Journal of Theoretical Biology* 78:347–363.

Armstrong, R. A.
1974   Growth Phases in the Life of a Lichen Thallus. *New Phytologist* 73:913–918.

1975   Studies on the Growth Rates of Lichens. In *Lichenology: Progress and Problems,* edited by D. H. Brown, D. L. Hawksworth, and R. H. Bailey, pp. 309–322. Academic Press, London and New York.

1983   Growth Curve of the Lichen *Rhizocarpon geographicum. New Phytologist* 94:619–622.

Ballantyne, C. K., and J. A. Matthews
1982   The Development of Sorted Circles on Recently Deglaciated Terrain, Jotunheimen, Norway. *Arctic and Alpine Research* 14:341–354.

Belloni, S.
1973   Ricerche Lichenometriche in Valfurva e Nella Valle di Solda. *Bolletino del Comitato Glaciologico Italiano* 21:19–33.

Benedict, J. B.
1967   Recent Glacial History of an Alpine Area in the Colorado Front Range, U.S.A. I. Establishing a Lichen-Growth Curve. *Journal of Glaciology* 6:817–832.

1981   The Fourth of July Valley: Glacial Geology and Archaeology of the Timberline Ecotone. *Center for Mountain Archaeology, Ward, Colorado, Research Reports* 2:1–139.

1985   Arapaho Pass: Glacial Geology and Archaeology at the Crest of the Colorado Front Range. *Center for Mountain Archaeology, Ward, Colorado, Research Reports* 3:1–197.

1988   Techniques in Lichenometry: Identifying the Yellow Rhizocarpons. *Arctic and Alpine Research* 20:285–291.

1990   Experiments on Lichen Growth. I. Seasonal Patterns and Environmental Controls. *Arctic and Alpine Research* 22:244–254.

1991   Experiments on Lichen Growth. II. Effects of a Seasonal Snow Cover. *Arctic and Alpine Research* 23:189–199.

Benedict, J. B., and T. H. Nash III
1990   Radial Growth and Habitat Selection by Morphologically Similar Chemotypes of *Xanthoparmelia*. *The Bryologist* 93:319–327.

Beschel, R. E.
1950   Flechten als Altersmasstab Rezenter Moränen. *Zeitschrift für Gletscherkunde und Glazialgeologie* 1:152–161.

1957   Lichenometrie im Gletschervorfeld. *Jahrbuch des Vereins zum Schutze der Alpenpflanzen undtiere* (München) 22:164–185. [Translation by William Barr, University of Saskatchewan, 1968]

1961   Dating Rock Surfaces by Lichen Growth and Its Application to Glaciology and Physiography (Lichenometry). In *Geology of the Arctic*, vol. I, edited by G. O. Raasch, pp. 1044–1062. University of Toronto Press, Toronto. [Proceedings of the 1st International Symposium on Arctic Geology]

1973   Lichens as a Measure of the Age of Recent Moraines. *Arctic and Alpine Research* 5:303–309. [Translation, by William Barr, of Beschel 1950]

Bickerton, R. W., and J. A. Matthews
1992   On the Accuracy of Lichenometric Dates: An Assessment Based on the 'Little Ice Age' Moraine Sequence at Nigardsbreen, Southern Norway. *The Holocene* 2:227–237.

1993   'Little Ice Age' Variations of Outlet Glaciers from the Jostedalsbreen Ice-Cap, Southern Norway: A Regional Lichenometric-Dating Study of Ice-Marginal Moraine Sequences and Their Climatic Significance. *Journal of Quaternary Science* 8:45–66.

Birkeland, P. W.
1973   Use of Relative-Age Dating Methods in a Stratigraphic Study of Rock Glacier Deposits, Mt. Sopris, Colorado. *Arctic and Alpine Research* 5:401–416.

1981   Soil Data and the Shape of the Lichen Growth-Rate Curve for the Mt. Cook Area. *New Zealand Journal of Geology and Geophysics* 24:443–445.

Birkenmajer, K.
1980a   Lichenometric Dating of Glacier Retreat at Admiralty Bay, King George Island (South Shetland Islands, West Antarctica). *Bulletin de l'Académie Polonaise des Sciences, Série des Sciences de la Terre* 27:77–85.

1980b   Age of the Penguin Island Volcano, South Shetland Islands (West Antarctica) by the Lichenometric Method. *Bulletin de l'Académie Polonaise des Sciences Série des Sciences, de la Terre* 27:69–76.

1981   Lichenometric Dating of Raised Marine Beaches at Admiralty Bay, King George Island (South Shetland Islands, West Antarctica). *Bulletin de l'Académie Polonaise des Sciences, Série des Sciences, de la Terre* 29:119–127.

Bogen, J., B. Wold, and G. Østrem
1989   Historic Glacier Variations in Scandinavia. In *Glacier Fluctuations and Climatic Change*, edited by J. Oerlemans, pp. 109–128. Kluwer, Dordrecht.

Bornfeldt, F., and M. Österborg
1958   Lavarter som Hjälpmedel för Datering av Ändmoräner vid Norska Glaciärer. *Stockholms*

Högskola, *Geografiska Proseminariet* 403:1–37. [Unpublished seminar paper]

Broadbent, N. D.
1987 Lichenometry and Archaeology. Testing of Lichen Chronology on the Swedish North Bothnian Coast. *Centre for Arctic Cultural Research, Umeå University, Research Reports* 2:1–61.

Broadbent, N. D., and K. I. Bergqvist
1986 Lichenometric Chronology and Archaeological Features on Raised Beaches: Preliminary Results from the Swedish North Bothnian Coastal Region. *Arctic and Alpine Research* 18:297–306.

Burga, C. A.
1987 *Gletscher- und Vegetationsgeschichte der Südrätischen Alpen seit der Späteiszeit.* Birkhäuser Verlag, Basel.

Burrows, C. J., K. W. Duncan, and J. R. Spence
1990 Aranuian Vegetation History of the Arrowsmith Range, Canterbury II. Revised Chronology for Moraines of the Cameron Glacier. *New Zealand Journal of Botany* 28:455–466.

Burrows, C. J., and J. Lucas
1967 Variations in Two New Zealand Glaciers During the Past 800 Years. *Nature* 216:467–468.

Burrows, C. J., and J. Orwin
1971 Studies on Some Glacial Moraines in New Zealand—I. The Establishment of Lichen-Growth Curves in the Mount Cook Area. *New Zealand Journal of Science* 14:327–335.

Calkin, P. E., and J. M. Ellis
1980 A Lichenometric Dating Curve: Its Application to Holocene Glacier Studies in the Central Brooks Range, Alaska. *Arctic and Alpine Research* 12:245–264.
1984 Development and Application of a Lichenometric Dating Curve, Brooks Range, Alaska. In *Quaternary Dating Methods,* edited by W. C. Mahaney, pp. 227–246. Elsevier, Amsterdam.

Carrara, P. E., and J. T. Andrews
1973 Problems and Application of Lichenometry to Geomorphic Studies, San Juan Mountains, Colorado. *Arctic and Alpine Research* 5:373–384.

Caseldine, C. J.
1991 Lichenometric Dating, Lichen Population Studies and Holocene Glacial History in Tröllaskagi, Northern Iceland. In *Environmental Change in Iceland: Past and Present,* edited by J. K. Maizels and C. J. Caseldine, pp. 219–233. Kluwer, Dordrecht.

Colman, S. M., K. L. Pierce, and P. W. Birkeland.
1987 Suggested Terminology for Quaternary Dating Methods. *Quaternary Research* 28:314–319.

Cook-Talbot, J. D.
1991 Sorted Circles, Relative-Age Dating and Palaeoenvironmental Reconstruction in an Alpine Periglacial Environment, Eastern Jotunheimen, Norway: Lichenometric and Weathering-Based Approaches. *The Holocene* 1:128–141.

Curl, J. E.
1980 A Glacial History of the South Shetland Islands, Antarctica. *Institute of Polar Studies, Ohio State University, Columbus, Ohio, Reports* 63:1–129.

Dawson, A. G., J. A. Matthews, and R. A. Shakesby
1986 A Catastrophic Landslide (Sturzstrom) in Verkilsdalen, Rondane National Park, Southern Norway. *Geografiska Annaler* 68(A): 77–87.

Donner, J., M. Eronen, and H. Jungner
1977 The Dating of the Holocene Relative Sea-Level Changes in Finnmark, North Norway. *Norsk Geografisk Tidsskrift* 31:103–108.

Erikstad, L., and J. L. Sollid
1986 Neoglaciation in South Norway Using Lichenometric Methods. *Norsk Geografisk Tidsskrift* 40:85–105.
1988 Neoglaciation in South Norway Using Lichenometric Methods: Reply to Matthews. *Norsk Geografisk Tidsskrift* 42:62.

Follmann, G.
1961 Estudios liquenométricos en los monumentos prehistóricos de la Isla de Pascua. *Revista Universitaria. Anales de la Academia Chilena de Ciencias Naturales* 24:149–154.

Gellatly, A. F.
1982 Lichenometry as a Relative-Age Dating Method in Mount Cook National Park, New Zealand. *New Zealand Journal of Botany* 20:343–353.
1983 Revised Dates for 2 Recent Moraines of the Mueller Glacier, Mt. Cook National Park. *New Zealand Journal of Geology and Geophysics* 26:311–315.

Golodkovskaya, N. A.
1982 Dynamics of Glaciers on the Southern Slope of the Central Caucasus for the Last 700 Years (Based on Lichenometric Data). *Materialy Glyatsiologicheskikh Issledovanii Khronika Obsuzhdeniya* 45:76–84. [In Russian]

Gordon, J. E., and M. Sharp
1983 Lichenometry in Dating Recent Glacial Landforms and Deposits, Southeast Iceland. *Boreas* 12:191–200.

Gregory, K. J.
1976 Lichens and the Determination of River Channel Capacity. *Earth Surface Processes* 1:273–285.

Griffey, N. J.
1977 A Lichenometric Study of the Neoglacial End Moraines of the Okstindan Glaciers, North Norway, and Comparisons with Similar Recent Scandinavian Studies. *Norsk Geografisk Tidsskrift* 31:163–172.
1978 Lichen Growth on Supraglacial Debris and Its Implications for Lichenometric Studies. *Journal of Glaciology* 20:163–172.

Grove, J. M.
1985 The Timing of the Little Ice Age in Scandinavia. *The Climatic Scene,* edited by M. J. Tooley and G. M. Sheail, pp. 132–153. George Allen and Unwin, London.
1988 *The Little Ice Age.* Methuen, London.

Haeberli, W., L. King, and A. Flotron
1979 Surface Movement and Lichen-Cover Studies of the Active Rock Glacier Near the Grubengletscher, Wallis, Swiss Alps. *Arctic and Alpine Research* 11:421–441.

Haines-Young, R. H.
1983 Size Variation of *Rhizocarpon* on Moraine Slopes in Southern Norway. *Arctic and Alpine Research* 15:295–305.
1985 Discussion of 'Size Variation of *Rhizocarpon* on Moraine Slopes in Southern Norway': a Reply. *Arctic and Alpine Research* 17:212–216.
1988 Size-Frequency and Size-Density Relationships in Populations from the *Rhizocarpon* Subgenus Cern. on Moraine Slopes in Southern Norway. *Journal of Biogeography* 15:863–878.

Harvey, A. M., R. W. Alexander, and P. A. James
1984 Lichens, Soil Development and the Age of Holocene Valley Floor Landforms: Howgill Fells, Cumbria. *Geografiska Annaler* 66(A):353–366.

Haworth, L. A., P. E. Calkin, and J. M. Ellis
1986 Direct Measurement of Lichen Growth in the Central Brooks Range, Alaska, U.S.A., and Its Application to Lichenometric Dating. *Arctic and Alpine Research* 18:289–296.

Hill, D. J.
1981 The Growth of Lichens with Special Reference to the Modelling of Circular Thalli. *The Lichenologist* 13:265–287.

Hole, N., and J. L. Sollid
1979 Neoglaciation in Western Norway—Preliminary Results. *Norsk Geografisk Tidsskrift* 33:213–215.

Holzhauser, H.
1984 Zur Geschichte der Aletschgletscher und des Fieschergletschers. *Physische Geographie* 13:1–448.

Innes, J. L.
1982 Lichenometric Use of an Aggregated *Rhizocarpon* 'Species.' *Boreas* 11:53–57.
1983a Lichenometric Dating of Debris-Flow Deposits in the Scottish Highlands. *Earth Surface Processes and Landforms* 8:579–588.
1988b Size Frequency Distribution as a Lichenometric Technique: An Assessment. *Arctic and Alpine Research* 15:285–294.
1983c Use of an Aggregated *Rhizocarpon* 'Species' in Lichenometry: An Evaluation. *Boreas* 12:183–190.
1983d Development of Lichenometric Dating Curves for Highland Scotland. *Transactions of the*

        Royal Society of Edinburgh, Earth Sciences 74:23–32.
1984a The Optimal Sample Size in Lichenometric Studies. *Arctic and Alpine Research* 16:233–244.
1984b Lichenometric Dating of Moraine Ridges in Northern Norway: Some Problems of Application. *Geografiska Annaler* 66(A):341–352.
1985a Lichenometry. *Progress in Physical Geography* 9:187–254.
1985b A Standard *Rhizocarpon* Nomenclature for Lichenometry. *Boreas* 14:83–85.
1985c Replication of Lichenometric Data: Errors Associated with Variations in Operator Search Efficiency. *Area* 17:221–232.
1985d Moisture Availability and Lichen Growth: The Effects of Snow Cover and Streams on Lichenometric Measurements. *Arctic and Alpine Research* 17:417–424.
1985e Lichenometric Dating of Debris-Flow Deposits on Alpine Colluvial Fans in Southwest Norway. *Earth Surface Processes and Landforms* 10:519–524.
1986a The Use of Percentage Cover Measurements in Lichenometric Dating. *Arctic and Alpine Research* 18:209–216.
1986b Dating Exposed Rock Surfaces in the Arctic by Lichenometry: The Problem of Thallus Circularity and Its Effects on Measurement Errors. *Arctic* 39:253–259.
1986c Influence of Sampling Design on Lichen Size-Frequency Distributions and Its Effect on Derived Lichenometric Indices. *Arctic and Alpine Research* 18:201–208.
1986d The Size-Frequency Distributions of the Lichens *Sporastata testudinea* and *Rhizocarpon alpicola* through Time at Storbreen, South-west Norway. *Journal of Biogeography* 13:283–291.

Jochimsen, M.
1966 Ist die Grosse des Flechtenthallus Wirklich ein Grauchbarer Masstab zur Latierung von Glazidmorphologischen Relikten. *Geografiska Annaler* 48A:157–164.

1973 Does the Size of Lichten Thalli Really Constitute a Valid Measure for Dating Glacial Deposits? *Arctic and Alpine Research* 5:417–424.

Jonasson, C.
1991 Holocene Slope Processes of Periglacial Mountain Areas in Scandinavia and Poland. *Uppsala Universitet, Naturgeografisk Institutionen (UNGI) Report* 79:1–156.

Jonasson, C., M.. Kot, and A. Kotarba
1991 Lichenometrical Studies and Dating of Debris Flow Deposits in the High Tatra Mountains, Poland. *Geografiska Annaler* 73(A):141–146.

Karlén, W.
1973 Holocene Glacier and Climatic Variations, Kebnekaise Mountains, Swedish Lapland. *Geografiska Annaler* 55(A):29–63.
1979 Glacier Variations in the Svartisen Area, Northern Norway. *Geografiska Annaler* 61(A):11–28.

King, R. B.
1971 Boulder Polygons and Stripes in the Cairngorm Mountains, Scotland. *Journal of Glaciology* 10:375–386.

King, L., and R. Lehmann
1973 Beobachtung zur Oekologie und Morphologie von *Rhizocarpon geographicum* (L.) DC. und *Rhizocarpon alpicola* (Hepp.) Rabenh. im Gletschervorfeld des Steingletschers. *Berichte der Schweizerischen Botanischen Gesellschaft* 83:139–147.

Kugelmann, O.
1990 Datierung Neuzeitlicher Gletschervorstosse im Svarfadardalur/Skidadalur (Nordisland) mit Einer Neu Erstallten Flechtenwachstumskurve. *Münchener Geographische Abhandlungen Reche B* 8:36–58.

Laundon, J. R.
1980 The Use of Lichens for Dating Walls at Bradgate Park, Leicestershire. *Transactions of the Leicester Literary and Philosophical Society* 74:11–30.

Lindsay, D. C.
1973 Estimates of Lichen Growth Rates in the Mari-

time Antarctic. *Arctic and Alpine Research* 5:341–346.

Locke, W. W., J. T. Andrews, and P. J. Webber
1979 A Manual for Lichenometry. *British Geomorphological Research Group, Technical Bulletin* 26:1–47.

Macklin, M. G.
1986 Channel and Floodplain Metamorphosis in the River Nent, Cumberland. In *Quaternary River Landforms and Sediments in the Northern Pennines, England: Field Guide,* edited by M. G. Macklin and J. Rose, pp. 19–33. British Geomorphological Research Group/Quaternary Research Association, London.

Macklin, M. G., B. T. Rumsby, and T. Heap
1993 Flood Alluviation and Entrenchment: Holocene Valley Floor Development and Transformation in the British Uplands. *Geological Society of America Bulletin,* in press.

Mahaney, W. C.
1990 *Ice on the Equator: Quaternary Geology of Mount Kenya.* Wm. Caxton, Sister Bay, Wisconsin.

Mahaney, W. C., and J. R. Spence
1993 Lichenometry of Neoglacial Moraines in Lewis and Tyndall Cirques on Mount Kenya, East Africa. *Zeitschrift für Gletscherkunde und Gletschergeologie,* in press.

Maizels, J. K., and A. J. Dugmore
1985 Lichenometric Dating and Tephrochronology of Sandur Deposits, Sólheimajökull Area, Southern Iceland. *Jökull* 35:69–77.

Maizels, J. K., and J. R. Petch
1985 Age Determination of Intermoraine Areas, Austerdalen, Southern Norway. *Boreas* 14:51–65.

Matthews, J. A.
1973 Lichen Growth on an Active Medial Moraine, Jotunheimen, Norway. *Journal of Glaciology* 12:305–313.
1974 Families of Lichenometric Dating Curves from the Storbreen Gletschervorfeld, Jotunheimen, Norway. *Norsk Geografisk Tidsskrift* 28:215–235.
1975 Experiments on the Reproducibility and Reliability of Lichenometric Dates, Storbreen Gletschervorfeld, Jotunheimen, Norway. *Norsk Geografisk Tidsskrift* 29:97–109.
1977 A Lichenometric Test of the 1750 End-Moraine Hypothesis: Storbreen Gletschervorfeld, Southern Norway. *Norsk Geografisk Tidsskrift* 31:129–136.
1987 A Comment on 'Neoglaciation in South Norway Using Lichenometric Methods.' *Norsk Geografisk Tidsskrift* 41:61–67.

Matthews, J. A., R. Cornish, and R. A. Shakesby
1979 'Saw-Tooth' Moraines in Front of Bødalsbreen, Southern Norway. *Journal of Glaciology* 22:535–546.

Matthews, J. A., A. G. Dawson, and R. A. Shakesby
1986 Lake Shoreline Development, Frost Weathering and Rock Platform Erosion in an Alpine Periglacial Environment, Jotunheimen, Norway. *Boreas* 15:33–50.

Matthews, J. A., and R. A. Shakesby
1984 The Status of the 'Little Ice Age' in Southern Norway: Relative-Age Dating of Neoglacial Moraines with Schmidt Hammer and Lichenometry. *Boreas* 13:333–346.

Miller, C. D.
1973 Chronology of Neoglacial Deposits in the Northern Sawatch Range, Colorado. *Arctic and Alpine Research* 5:385–400.

Miller, G. H.
1973 Variations in Lichen Growth from Direct Measurements: Preliminary Curves for *Alectoria miniscula* from Eastern Baffin Island, N.W.T., Canada. *Arctic and Alpine Research* 5:333–339.

Miller, G. H., and J. T. Andrews
1972 Quaternary History of Northern Cumberland Peninsula, East Baffin Island, North West Territory, Canada. Part VI: Preliminary Lichen Growth Curve. *Geological Society of America Bulletin* 83:1133–1138.

Milne, J. A.
1982 River Channel Change in the Harthorpe Valley, Northumberland, Since 1897. *University of Newcastle-upon-Tyne, Department of Geography, Research Series* 13:1–39.

Mottershead, D. N.
1980 Lichenometry—Some Recent Applications. In *Timescales in Geomorphology,* edited by R. A. Cullingford, D. A. Davidson, and J. Lewin, pp. 95–108. Wiley, Chichester.

Mottershead, D. N., and R. L. Collin
1976 A Study of Flandrian Glacier Fluctuations in Tunsbergdalen, Southern Norway. *Norsk Geografisk Tidsskrift* 56:413–436.

Mottershead, D. N., and I. D. White
1972 The Lichenometric Dating of Glacier Recession, Tunsbergdal, Southern Norway. *Geografiska Annaler* 54(A):47–52.
1973 Lichen Growth in Tunsbergdal—a Confirmation. *Geografiska Annaler* 55(A):143–145.

Nikonov, A. A., and T. Yu. Shebalina
1979 Lichenometry and Earthquake Determination in Central Asia. *Nature* 280:675–677.

Nyberg, R.
1985 Debris Flows and Slush Avalanches in Swedish Lappland, Northern Scandinavia. *Meddelanden från Lunds Universitets Geografiska Institution, Avhandlingar* 97:1–222.

Orombelli, G., and S. C. Porter
1983 Lichen Growth Curves for the Southern Flank of the Mont Blanc Massif, Western Italian Alps. *Arctic and Alpine Research* 15:193–200.

Orwin, J.
1972 The Effect of Environment on Assemblages of Lichens Growing on Rock Surfaces. *New Zealand Journal of Botany* 10:37–47.

Osborn, G., and J. Taylor
1975 Lichenometry on Calcareous Substrates in the Canadian Rockies. *Quaternary Research* 5:111–120.

Østrem, G., O. Liestøl, and B. Wold
1976 Glaciological Investigations at Nigardsbreen, Norway. *Norsk Geografisk Tidsskrift* 30:187–209.

Pitman, G. T. K.
1973 A Lichenometrical Study of Snow Patch Variation in the Frederikshåb District, South-West Greenland, and Its Implications for Studies of Climatic and Glacial Fluctuations. *Meddelelser om Grønland* 192:1–31.

Platt, R. B., and F. P. Amsler
1955 A Basic Method for the Immediate Study of Lichen Growth Rates and Succession. *Journal of the Tennessee Academy of Science* 30:177–183.

Poelt, J.
1988 Rhizocarpon Ram. em. Th. Fr. subgen. *Rhizocarpon* in Europe. *Arctic and Alpine Research* 20:292–298.

Porter, S. C., and Orombelli, G.
1981 Alpine Rockfall Hazards. *American Scientist* 69:67–75.

Proctor, M. C. F.
1983 Sizes and Growth-Rates of Thalli of the Lichen *Rhizocarpon geographicum* on the Moraines of the Glacier de Valsorey, Valais, Switzerland. *The Lichenologist* 15:249–261.

Rapp, A., and R. Nyberg
1981 Alpine Debris Flows in Northern Scandinavia. *Geografiska Annaler* 63(A):183–196.

Reger, R. D., and T. L. Péwé
1969 Lichenometric Dating in the Central Alaska Range. In *The Periglacial Environment,* edited by T. L. Péwé, pp. 223–247. McGill-Queen's University Press, Montreal.

Rodbell, D. T.
1992 Lichenometric and Radiocarbon Dating of Holocene Glaciation, Cordillera Blanca, Perú. *The Holocene* 2:19–29.

Rogerson, R. J., D. J. A. Evans, and W. D. McCoy
1986 Five-year Growth of Rock Lichens in a Low-Arctic Mountain Environment, Northern Labrador. *Géographie Physique et Quaternaire* 40:85–91.

Runemark, H.
1956 Studies in Rhizocarpon II. Distribution and Ecology of the Yellow Species in Europe. *Opera Botanica* 2:1–150.

Rydzak, J.
1961 Investigations on the Growth Rate of Lichens. *Annales Universitatis Mariae Curie-Sklodowska, Section C* (Lublin) 16:1–13.

Schroeder-Lanz, H.
1983 Establishing Lichen Growth Curves by Repeated Size (Diameter) Measurements of Lichen Individua in a Test Area—A Mathematical Approach. In *Late- and Postglacial Oscillations of Glaciers: Glacial and Periglacial Forms,* edited by H. Schroeder-Lanz, pp. 393–409. Balkema, Rotterdam.

Serebryanny, L. R., N. A. Golodkovskaya, and E. O. Ilvesidr
1979 Fluctuations of Mountainous Caucasus Glaciers in Historical Time (by Lichenometric and Radiocarbon dating). *Isvestiya Vsesoyuznogo Geograficheskogo Obshchestva* 111:11–18. [In Russian]

Serebryanny, L. R., N. A. Golodkovskaya, A. V. Orlov, E. S. Malyasova, and E. O. Illvesidr
1984 *Glacier Variations and Moraine Accumulation Processes in the Central Caucasus.* Nauka, Moscow. [In Russian]

Serebryanny, L. R., and O. N. Solomina
1989 Glacial Changes in the Tien Shan Mountains as Revealed by Bioindicators: Time-Series Analysis and Interpretation. *International Association for Scientific Hydrology Publication* 183:81–87.

Shakesby, R. A.
1985 Geomorphological Effects of Jökulhlaups and Ice-Dammed Lakes, Jotunheimen, Norway. *Norsk Geografisk Tidsskrift* 39:1–16.

Skakesby, R. A., A. G. Dawson, and J. A. Matthews
1987 Rock Glaciers, Protalus Ramparts and Related Phenomena, Rondane, Norway: A Continuum of Large-Scale Talus-Derived Landforms. *Boreas* 16:305–317.

Sjöberg, R.
1990 Measurement and Calibration of Weathering Processes and Lichenometric Investigations on a Wave Washed Moraine, Bådamalen, on the Upper Norrland Coast, Sweden. *Geografiska Annaler* 72(A):319–327.

Smirnova, T. Tu., and A. A. Nikonov
1990 A Revised Lichenometric Method and Its Application: Dating Great Past Earthquakes. *Arctic and Alpine Research* 22:375–388.

Solomina, O. N., and N. A. Golodkovskaya
1989 Lichenometric Method. In *Moraines as a Source of Glaciological Information,* edited by L. R. Serebryanny, A. V. Orlov, and O. N. Solomina, pp. 149–164. Nauka, Moscow. [In Russian]

Spence, J. R., and W. C. Mahaney
1988 Growth and Ecology of *Rhizocarpon* section *Rhizocarpon* on Mount Kenya, East Africa. *Arctic and Alpine Research* 20:237–242.

Thompson, A., and A. Jones
1986 Rates and Causes of Proglacial River Terrace Formation in Southwest Iceland: An Application of Lichenometric Dating Techniques. *Boreas* 15:231–246.

Trudgill, S. T., R. W. Crabtree, and P. J. C. Walker
1979 The Age of Exposure of Limestone Pavements—A Pilot Lichenometric Study in Co. Clare, Eire. *Transactions of the British Cave Research Association* 6:10–14.

Vere, D., and J. A. Matthews
1985 Rock Glacier Formation from a Lateral Moraine at Bukkeholsbreen, Jotunheimen, Norway: A Sedimentological Approach. *Zeitschrift für Geomorphologie N.F.* 29:397–415.

Webber, P. J., and J. T. Andrews
1973a Lichenometry: Dedicated to the Memory of the Late Roland E. Beschel. *Arctic and Alpine Research* 5:293–432.
1973b Lichenometry: A Commentary. *Arctic and Alpine Research* 5:295–302.

Werner, A.
1990 Lichen Growth Rates for the Northwest Coast of Spitsbergen, Svalbard. *Arctic and Alpine Research* 22:129–140.

Winchester, V.
1984 A Proposal for a New Approach to Lichenometry. *British Geomorphological Research Group, Technical Bulletin* 33:3–20.

1988   An Assessment of Lichenometry as a Method for Dating Recent Stone Movements in Two Stone Circles in Cumbria and Oxfordshire. *Botanical Journal of the Linnean Society* 96:57–68.

Worsley, P.
1973   An Evaluation of the Attempt to Date the Recession of Tunsbergdalsbreen, Southern Norway, by Lichenometry. *Geografiska Annaler* 55(A):137–141.
1981   Lichenometry. In *Geomorphological Techniques*, edited by A. Goudie, pp. 302–305. George Allen and Unwin, London.
1990   Lichenometry. In *Geomorphological Techniques*, 2d ed., edited by A. Goudie, pp. 422–428. Unwin Hyman, London.

Zhou, S. Z., F. H. Chen, B. T. Pan, J. X. Cao, J. J. Li, and E. Derbyshire
1991   Environmental Change During the Holocene in Western China on a Millennial Timescale. *The Holocene* 1:151–156.

10
USING DENDROCHRONOLOGY FOR THE DATING OF LAND SURFACES

Olavi Heikkinen

Department of Geography
University of Oulu
Oulu, Finland

Abstract

Dendrochronology studies the annual rings of trees for various purposes; dendrogeomorphology, one of its subfields, employs tree-ring counts to investigate geomorphic processes and to date landforms and soil surfaces that may be erosional or depositional in character. Geomorphic processes taking place in the habitats of trees regulate growth rates and impose peculiar growth forms on trunks, roots, and branches.

Separate ring-width series collected from living trees and dead wood material can often be matched together by crossdating techniques to construct a long master chronology that makes it possible to date old land surfaces and historical and archaeological finds containing wood. Thus tree-ring evidence also helps to solve many geological and cultural problems.

Introduction

Dendrochronology is a science that makes use of the annual rings of trees primarily for the dating of wooden objects and of changes in ecological conditions. The systematic dating and analysis of tree rings also enables us to trace climatic variations and to solve other environmental problems related to geomorphic processes (see Alestalo 1971; Fritts 1976; Heikkinen 1987; Schweingruber 1983, 1989).

Advances and specialization in dendrochronology have led to its division into several subfields, each covering different uses of tree-ring data. This subdivision is fairly arbitary, however, and many dendrochronological investigations fall into more than one category.

The oldest and probably the most frequently practiced subfield is *dendroclimatology* (Fritts 1976; Hughes et al. 1982; Schweingruber 1983), which investigates past and present climatic conditions as deduced from the measured widths, densities, or other characteristics of the annual rings of trees. *Dendrohydrology* involves the analysis of tree-ring series in order to shed light on changes in stream flows, water levels, and other hydrological phenomena related to tree growth at times before instrumental observations were being made (see Smith and Stockton 1981). *Dendroecology* studies variations in the width or other parameters of annual tree rings, in order to interpret specific ecological events that resulted in changes in the ability of trees to photosynthesize and fix carbon (Kienast 1985). One must remember, however, that all factors affecting the growth of trees are actually ecological in character; that is, they have some impact on the ability of trees to maintain their vital functions.

The final subfield of dendrochronology, and the one to which the present article refers, is *dendrogeomorphology*, in which annual rings in the trunks, roots, and branches of trees are used to investigate geomorphic processes and to date land surfaces and landforms (Alestalo 1971; Schweingruber 1983, 1989; Shroder 1980).

It is important for the purposes of dendrochronology to know how trees normally grow and how they respond to burial and exposure processes or other edaphic changes in their habitats. A knowledge of the basic growth processes of trees makes it possible in many cases to give approximate dates to the ground surface where germination took place and enables the dating of any soil accumulation or erosion processes that the trees may have experienced in their lifetime. It is also possible in many cases to date exhumed dead trees and identify changes in the land surface that took place during their lifetimes, by relating the tree-ring series of such dead trees to those of living trees in nearby areas. This procedure of tree-ring matching is called cross-dating.

Because of the importance of understanding normal tree growth as well as peculiar growth responses to environmental changes, I will discuss these issues at the very beginning. Furthermore, because the collecting and handling of tree-ring data is important, I will also consider sampling strategies and laboratory techniques before entering upon the main theme of this chapter: the dating of land surfaces by dendrochronological means.

Normal Tree Growth

The life of a tree generally begins when its seed comes into contact with the soil, whereupon it receives the water it needs to germinate and the nutrients to enable it to grow roots and other organs. The borderline between the roots and stem, known botanically as the root collar or organological base, develops at approximately ground level. The level of the root collar, whose relation to the land surface can alter with time as a consequence of geomorphic processes, indicates the position of the ground level at the time when the tree started growing (Alestalo 1971:34, 1987:67).

Every year the cambium of a living tree produces a new wood layer around the cylinder formed in previous years. This annual wood layer or tree ring is formed not only in the stem but also in the branches and roots of the tree (Figure 10.1).

The major part of each ring consists of the large-celled early wood, or spring wood, which develops at the beginning of the growing season, while a darker, smaller-celled late wood, or summer wood, is produced toward the end of the season. The boundary between the late wood of one growing season and the early wood of the following one is usually very clear in conifers. Due to the cell structure of the wood of deciduous trees, their annual rings are sometimes difficult to identify. The longest absolutely dated tree-ring chronology of all, however, which extends back to the year 7938 B.C., has been developed from the German oak (*Quercus robur, Quercus petraea*) (Becker et al. 1991).

In some years growing conditions may be so poor that a tree is unable to form a ring in all portions of its stem. If this is the case, a specimen bored from a tree may not contain a continuous tree-ring series, as some rings are missing in the sampled segment or sector of the stem. These incompletely formed annual rings are called missing, partial, or locally absent rings (see Figure 10.1).

Sometimes a growing season that has started well is interrupted by a severe night frost or some other hazardous event, with the consequence that the trees start producing smaller, darker cells. When favorable conditions are restored, the tree again forms larger cells with thinner walls. The growth reduction indicated by the small, dark cell layer is called a false ring, multiple ring, or intra-annual growth band (Fritts 1976:20–22; Stokes and Smiley 1968).

In order to obtain accurate dates for past occur-

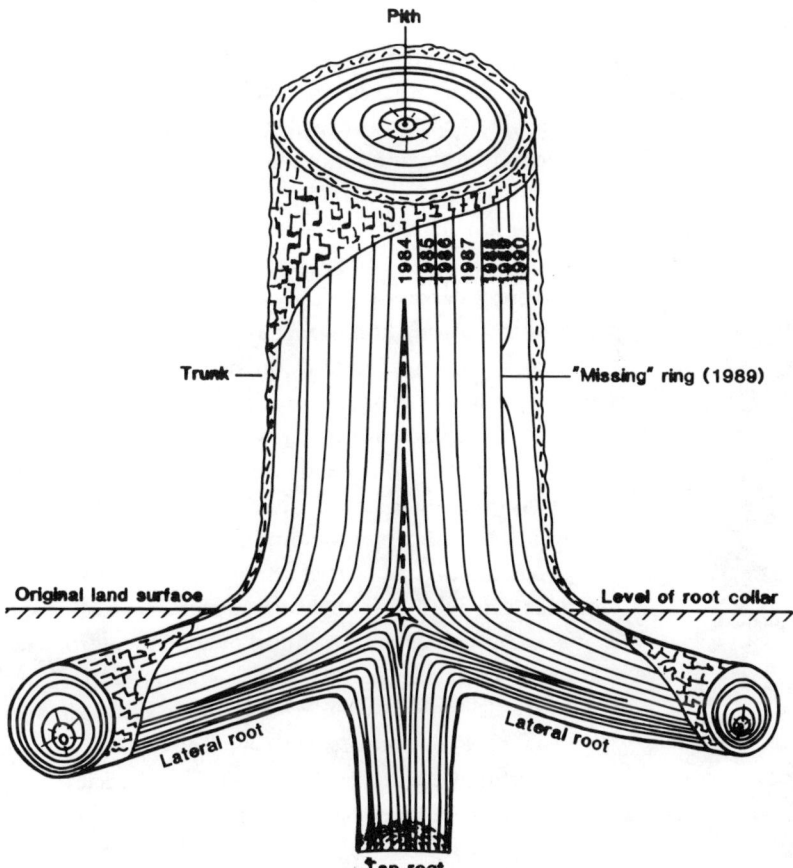

Figure 10.1. Generalized anatomy of the base and upper root system of the tree.

rences, both missing rings and false rings must be spotted, located, and dated. This can be done by the cross-dating technique (see below).

Excluding the very first years, the growth of a tree is usually relatively rapid in its first decades, after which this growth curve, which is partly dependent on genetic factors, turns downwards at an almost exponential rate. The life span of a tree depends largely on the species. Many of the longest-lived tree species are found in North America. The bristlecone pine (*Pinus longaeva*) can achieve an age of 5,000 years (Figure 10.2), while the giant sequoia (*Sequoiadendron giganteum*) can live for 4,000 or 4,500 years, and the coastal redwood (*Sequoia sempervirens*) for more than 2,000 years. The life spans of some junipers in the same area can reach 3,000 years, and the Douglas fir (*Pseudotsuga menziesii*), ponderosa pine (*Pinus ponderosa*), Alaska yellow cedar (*Chamaecyparis nootkatensis*) and western red cedar (*Thuja plicata*) are also long-lived trees, being able to survive for more than 1,000 years. Generally the life span of a tree is less than 1,000 years, quite often only 200 to 500 years (see Brubaker 1982).

Longevity is a good characteristic of trees as far as the tracing of past landform processes is concerned, because long tree-ring chronologies built up from individual living trees often give a more comprehensive picture of

Figure 10.2. The bristlecone pine (*Pinus longaeva*), the longest-lived tree in the world, has been a treasure-house of information for dendrochronologists. This tough individual grows in the Schulman Grove (White Mountains, California) and is called Pine Alpha, because it is the first tree proved to be older than 4,000 years. Photographed by Olavi Heikkinen in 1986.

environmental changes than do chronologies constructed from trees of different generations.

Trees Suitable for Dendrochronological Purposes

It is important in dendrochronology that the tree rings be annual ones and that they be visible. In addition the trees must be "sensitive" to climatic fluctuations, so that there is a distinct year-to-year variation in ring widths. Otherwise the cross-dating or matching of rings in one specimen with the corresponding rings in another is difficult, if not impossible.

When the growth of a tree is predominantly limited by some macroclimatic factor, such as precipitation rate or temperature, annual variations in ring widths are rather similar over a wide geographical region. The trees of this relatively homogeneous region tend to produce narrow rings in climatically unfavorable years and wider rings in more favorable years, making cross-dating easier. If the ring-width patterns of some individual trees deviate markedly from the regional pattern, one can suspect that these growth anomalies are caused by local agents, probably by geomorphic events.

Numerous tree species throughout the world produce quite visible annual rings, but there are some species whose rings are not annual or are difficult to determine, especially in the tropics and subtropics, and partly also outside these regions. Some species in such regions are too short-lived to allow any cross-dating to be performed with certainty, while other species growing under stable climatic and soil conditions produce "complacent" tree-ring series, in which the annual rings are so similar that it makes cross-dating difficult. Such regions also have some tree species that tend to have lobate or wedge-forming radial growth patterns, and partly for this reason they feature many false and missing rings. Trees of this kind are not suitable for dendrochronological analysis.

On the other hand, trees growing in regions where there is a regular alternation between summer and winter or a wet and a dry season develop distinct annual rings. Coniferous gymnosperms have been used more frequently than deciduous trees (angiosperms), since their rings are usually easier to define. Problems and strategies associated with the selection and utilization of different taxa in dendrochronology are discussed by Fritts (1976) and LaMarche et al. (1982).

It has turned out in practice that the annual rings of trees living in temperate, cold or dry regions are often datable and yield information on past and present environmental conditions. Although many characteristics of tree rings can be utilized when studying climatic fluctuations, ring widths are the most suitable parameter when the dendrochronological method is employed to trace soil processes such as mass movements of substrate and depositional or erosional changes in the ground.

Collecting Ring-Width Data

Sampling

Depending upon the problems to be solved, the dendrogeochronologist can collect material for tree-ring analysis from living or dead trees. If the selected material is fragile charcoal or decayed wood, special treatment is necessary (Stokes and Smiley 1968:27).

Sometimes the material required for analysis may be obtained by cutting discs from the trunk with a saw. One advantage of this approach is that a disc shows the annual radial growths of the tree in all directions. In most cases, however, it is difficult or impossible to fell trees for this purpose, and less harmful or less destructive techniques must be used.

Samples are usually taken by means of a special tool known as an increment borer, which is designed to remove a narrow core about 5 mm in diameter from a living tree without causing noticeable injury. Most increment borers are hand-operated, although battery-driven borers have also been developed. It is often useful to core a tree at different heights and on different sides of the trunk (at least on the uphill and downhill sides), in order to reveal any eccentricity and other irregularities in growth. The core specimens are numbered and inserted into soda straws or taped onto corrugated cardboard for transportation to the laboratory.

Exact field notes should be made on the trees and sites sampled, including species, state and growth form of the tree, location, altitude, exposure, slope and soil of the site, and date of the sampling, all of which may prove important for subsequent analysis and interpretation (Ferguson 1970; Fritts 1976:247–248; Stokes and Smiley 1968).

Preparation of Samples

The discs and cores are taken to the laboratory for the dating and measurement of the annual rings. Certain preparations are required, however, before the specimens can be analyzed.

The sawn surface of a disc is too rough to show all the tree rings and their structures clearly, and thus its cross section has to be polished with sandpaper. Sometimes only a few lines across the disc surface need to be prepared for microscopic analysis, in which case the tree rings and cell walls can be made visible by cutting the wood surface down to the lines carefully with a razor blade. Discs can be used to investigate the whole rings visible in the cross sections of the tree, which makes it easier to detect local absences, double (false) rings, and other characteristics.

Cores are often fragile and must therefore be mounted before surfacing with sandpaper or a razor blade. They should be mounted (that is, glued onto grooved wood sticks) so that the ends of the originally vertical tracheids, or xylem cells, are exposed to the observer. In many cases the visibility of the cells can be improved if the core is rotated slightly from this vertical position (Ferguson 1970; Fritts 1976:249; Stokes and Smiley 1968).

Dating and Measurements

Once the specimens have been prepared, their annual rings can be dated. As it is not always certain that all the rings of a specimen will be determinable or visible, dating calls for the cross-dating procedure, in which cores extracted from the same and different trees are systematically correlated with each other or with a tree-ring chronology previously constructed from the area. The purpose is to date accurately all the annual rings present in the specimens collected (Figure 10.3).

Cross-dating makes use of obvious similarities in the ring-width patterns of trees growing in the same climatic area, since trees form abnormally narrow rings, for instance, in years when the climate is anomalously dry, too cold, or otherwise unfavorable. Exceptionally

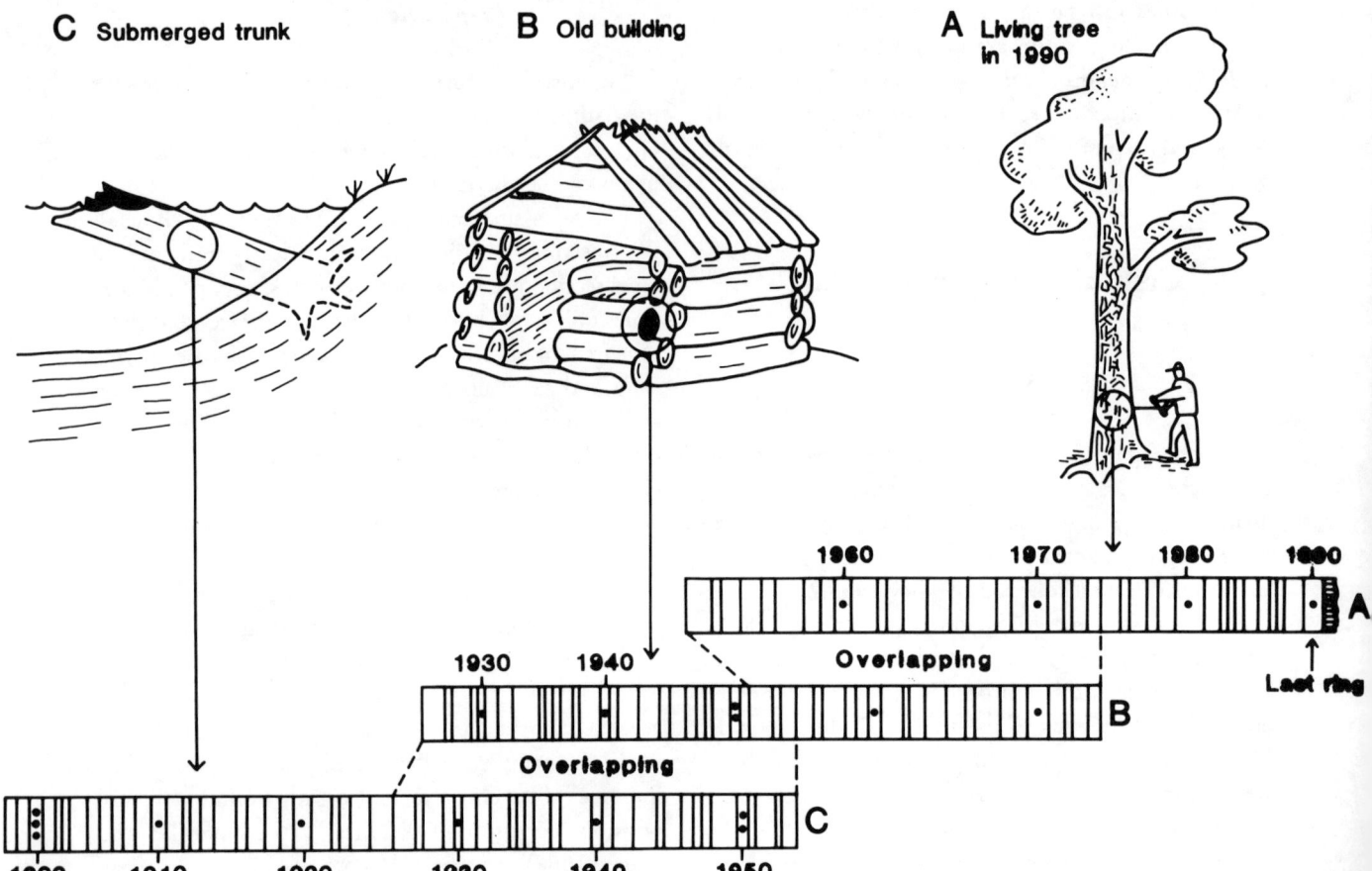

Figure 10.3. Principle for constructing a long chronology by cross-dating and matching separate ring-width series.

narrow rings are the best clues of all in cross-dating, enabling this process to point to missing and false rings in specimens and to give exact dates for many environmental phenomena.

It is also common to measure tree rings and present them graphically before attempting any cross-dating. This often facilitates the determination of problematic years and final dating.

Once the dating has been performed, the tree rings are measured to an accuracy of 0.01 mm and depicted as columns or a broken line on a diagram, with the value for the youngest ring on the right. Following this tradition makes it easier to cross-date and compare different chronologies.

Construction and Use of Chronologies

The ring widths measured from one increment core make up a single ring-width series or absolute ring-width chronology. When building an areally representative chronology, the measured ring widths for each individual series are often converted to relative indices by a procedure called standardization (Fritts 1976; Graybill 1982). The primary purpose of this procedure is to remove nonclimatic variations, such as biological growth trends and tree disturbances, and to scale the mean of the indices for each single ring-width series to a value of approximately 1.0. The standardized ring-width indices for all the cores obtained from one area can then be averaged year by year to produce a mean or site chronology. Due to its relatively strong macroclimatic signal, a site chronology is useful for cross-dating and for reconstructing past climates.

Site chronologies have also been constructed using measured ring-width values themselves, instead of standardized indices. This means that the trees are not weighted equally, since fast-growing trees will have greater influence than slow-growing ones, although it is in fact often the latter that carry stronger climatic signals in their tree-ring patterns.

The increment cores used to construct a site chronology must be taken from at least 10 individual trees of the same species. If the external conditions under which the sampled trees are growing are similar, their common macroclimatic signal will be strong; that is, all the ring-width series will resemble each other very closely.

A reliable site chronology based on living trees provides an opportunity to cross-date ring-width series constructed from dead trees or archaeological material that stems from earlier periods. Cross-dating the ring-width series of an older wooden object with the site chronology is likely to succeed if the two tree-ring series to be compared overlap sufficiently in time. If this is so, the older object can be dated, that is, its annual rings can be assigned to precise calendar years. In addition the ring-width series of the dated object can be incorporated into the site chronology, and the latter used as a "master chronology." By combining overlapping tree-ring series of different ages through cross-dating, the master chronology can be extended back thousands of years into the past (Ferguson 1970; Stokes and Smiley 1968). The longest continuous chronology, developed from oak in Germany, goes back more than 9,900 years (Becker et al. 1991), and the longest bristlecone pine chronology built up in the United States, about 8,700 years (Ferguson and Graybill 1983). The principle of cross-dating is presented in Figure 10.3.

In addition to the continuous site or master chronologies, dendrochronologists have constructed "floating chronologies" from old wood remnants such as snags, buried logs, and archaeological wood material. Chronologies are referred to as "floating" if they have not yet been combined with continuous chronologies based on precisely dated tree rings. Trees from whose annual rings the floating chronologies have been constructed may still give useful information about the environmental changes that took place during their lifetimes.

Wood materials from which floating tree-ring chronologies are derived can be dated by radiocarbon analysis to give approximate dates that help us to match these chronologies with each other or even with continuous chronologies. Even if radiocarbon dates do not serve to link chronologies, they will very probably show the location and duration of the missing tree-ring series between the separate chronologies. This information in turn can probably help us to find wood material whose tree-ring series cover secular gaps and finally make it possible to link floating chronologies together and with calendar years. One could say, in principle at least, that the longer the continuous site chronology is, the older the geomorphic processes that can be interpreted and dated dendrochronologically.

Dendrochronologists investigating palaeoclimatic changes in certain areas try in particular to develop and utilize long continuous mean chronologies whose sensitive year-to-year variations include a clear macroclimatic signal. Since these serve as suitable master chronologies when dating tree-ring series constructed from wood material of unknown age, they are also of great importance to researchers who are attempting to trace past landform processes in forested areas or to date archaeological specimens.

In many cases dendrogeomorphologists are more interested in anomalies than in the general features of chronologies, although it is often difficult to know what features in a tree-ring pattern are anomalous irregularities before one has compared them with a standard (site, mean, or master) chronology. Prehistoric natural hazards such as floods and volcanic eruptions have sometimes been dated simply by counting tree rings in trees that were affected but survived, but because of potential missing rings, the dates obtained in this way are probably inaccurate. The cross-dating procedure eliminates mistakes of this kind (see Yamaguchi 1985).

When dendrochronological investigations are focused on landform development and disturbances influencing the growth of trees, one can make use not only of tree trunks but also of the branches and roots of trees. Growth forms and the annual rings in roots, in particular, may yield very valuable information about the geomorphic processes that shaped the local land surface during the lifetimes of the trees.

Trees as Records of Landform Processes

Age of Living Trees

Natural processes often cause drastic changes in the environment, and new, virgin soil is created on which trees will germinate in time. A minimum age for such a soil may be derived from the ages of the first trees to become rooted, if these are still alive at the time of investigation. This kind of dating is done by determining the number of rings in discs or increment cores collected from the tree bases.

Virgin soils can be produced in a variety of ways. For instance new soils are created when the surface layer and its vegetation are eroded by wind or water. Such soils may also develop when aeolian or fluvial processes cause new material to accumulate upon the old vegetation. Similarly, volcanic eruptions or mass movements, such as mudflows, destroy the original vegetation and create a new soil surface. Correspondingly an ice margin advancing into the forest zone and then retreating in response to climate change will leave a new soil surface in which trees can become established. New seedlings were shown to become established on young terminal moraines at Mt. Baker in Washington State, for example, in one to five years if soil conditions were favorable, and in about 20 years in less-favorable habitats (Heikkinen 1984a). Finally new soil may emerge from beneath water in the course of land uplift or because of a drop in water level. A good example of this is the shoreline displacement of as much as several of kilometers per century on the coast of Finland, caused by glacioisostatic uplift, deriving from the melting of the Fennoscandian Ice Sheet. Land can also become available for the growth of trees as a result of catastrophic discharges of water from lakes or the intentional lowering of their water levels.

All the above cases allow the age of the soil to be evaluated dendrochronologically and an approximate age to be calculated for settlements established on this newly emerged land. The maximum age of soils that can be dated by this method is dependent on how long the tree species and individuals growing in the area can live. This means in practice (for example, at Mt. Rainier in Washington State) that till soils with fairly reliable ages calculated from the annual rings of the oldest trees seldom date back more than 600 years (Sigafoos and Hendricks 1972). In most parts of the world, the ages obtained by this method are much younger, due to the shorter life span of the local trees.

The ages obtained for a given soil are in any case minimum ones, as there are at least four possible sources of error in the use of dendrochronological calculations. The first of these is the ecesis time (that is, the time delay between the exposure of the land and the commencement of tree growth in the area), which is dependent on the stabilization rate and fertility of the soil, the proximity of seeding trees, and climatic factors (Heikkinen 1984a; Sigafoos and Hendricks 1969). The ecesis time usually varies from zero to some decades. Unfortunately it is rather difficult to give any close aproximation ecesis times in each case, although observations of local natural forest reestablishment rates provide some help in this dilemma (Figure 10.4).

A second source of error concerns the fact that the oldest existing tree may not have been found after all (Lawrence 1950). Although the largest trees are usually considered the oldest, there is not always a positive correlation between size and age. Similarly the third error factor is that the oldest living trees cannot be proved to represent the first generation. Such doubts are justified particularly when the soil and the trees growing on it are relatively old and only dendrochronological dates are available for determining soil age. In any case if only

Figure 10.4. Under favorable conditions trees may invade new land surfaces in a matter of a few years. Here the topsoil was removed in 1982, and the first pine seedlings were established in 1984. Oulu, Finland; photographed by Olavi Heikkinen in 1991.

old relicts, such as rotten stumps, are found, the method based on the age of living trees cannot be used to date the soil surface concerned.

The final factor can be termed "coring loss," that is, the earliest tree rings may not have been calculated, as the core may have been taken from too high a position in the tree or the drill may not have reached the pith (Heikkinen 1984a; Helley and LaMarche 1973:7; Sigafoos and Hendricks 1972). Coring loss can be prevented by cutting through the tree at the base, that is, at the original root collar from which the tree began to grow.

As stated above the age of a living tree never indicates more than the minimum age of the soil on which the tree is growing. Unless the tree is known to represent a pioneering species on a new soil, tree ring calculations provide no relevant data on the actual age of the soil concerned.

Living trees are often encountered with their roots covered by aeolian, alluvial, or volcanic material (see Alestalo 1971; Schweingruber 1983, 1989; Shroder 1980). In such cases the ages of the youngest buried trees provide the most exact maximum age for the beginning of the accumulation event. Should new trees have become rooted on the accumulated material, the oldest of these will indicate the latest date by which the accumulation process must have ended (Figure 10.5).

Changes in Radial Growth

The accumulation and erosion of soil in the immediate environment of trees, as well as fluctuations in soil level caused by these processes, can be dated by examining quantitative changes in radial growth. When a tree becomes buried rapidly to a considerable depth, its radial growth will slow down suddenly, assuming that the tree survives at all, for it is difficult for the root system and radial growth of the trunk to recover from such a drastic change. Phenomena such as volcanic eruptions and mudflows cause material to accumulate very rapidly, in which case it is often possible to point to an exact time when the trees became buried, and particularly the time at which the process began.

The eruptions of Mt. St. Helens in Washington State, for example, have frequently covered the surrounding areas with tephra, layers of which have been dated from living Douglas firs that survived the ash fallout. The Wn tephra stratum was deposited between the growing seasons of A.D. 1479 and 1480 and the We tephra between those of A.D. 1481 and 1482. The exact dates of the eruptions were determined by an extremely meticulous cross-dating procedure, in which control material was also obtained from trees growing outside the ash layer zone. The dating indicated that there are numerous partly missing and very narrow rings in the trees covered by layers of tephra, corresponding to the years immediately following the eruptions (Yamaguchi 1985).

Even when a tree becomes buried rapidly, though not very deeply, the radial growth of its trunk may actually increase in the first few years after the event. A series of lahar-type mudflows from Mt. Rainier occurred in October of 1947, which destroyed the forest and created a new soil surface on the lower course of Kautz Creek. The radial growth of many buried trees was even greater in 1948 than in the preceding year, however, apparently due to the fact that the lahars also eliminated many of the trees competing with them for light, etc. The shock effect then reduced radial growth for the following five years, after which growth again exceeded the previous level, possibly due to the adjustment of the roots to the overlying lahar and the fertilizing effect of the buried organic matter (Heikkinen 1984b).

Soil material sometimes accumulates gradually on roots, as in the case of aeolian processes, some fluvial processes, and even mass movements (Hupp et al. 1987:3), and here again radial growth may increase at first, as in dunes, where the gradually accumulating matter is often well aerated, fairly dry, and rich in nutrients. This gives the roots the time and opportunity to penetrate into the new, fertile soil layer (Alestalo 1971:54–55; Wolfe 1932).

When trees become buried deeply enough in dune sand, even at a more gradual rate, their radial growth decreases and the conditions surrounding the roots become less propitious. A tree-ring analysis of pines buried to a depth of seven meters in a shore dune at Kalajoki, Finland, on the coast of the Gulf of Bothnia (Figure 10.5), indicated that the trees had adjusted relatively well to the slow accumulation of sand over several decades, even though their radial growth had gradually decreased and they were doomed to a premature death (Heikkinen and Tikkanen 1987).

Soil erosion is reflected in the growth of trees in the same way as is accumulation. Fairly rapid fluvial erosion has been found to reduce growth, as there is not enough time for the tree to adapt by extending its roots deeper into the ground (LaMarche 1966:85). Once the erosion slows down or stops altogether, growth will revive.

The difficulties involved in dating soil accumulation or erosion by means of ring-width series are partly due to the fact that both burial and exposure can sometimes hamper growth and sometimes promote it. Furthermore it may be difficult to know whether some variations in radial growth are caused by geomorphic processes or by diseases or pests. False interpretations can be eliminated by examining the geomorphic features of the area and comparing the radial growth of the buried trees with that of trees growing in nearby "unaffected" areas.

Abnormal Growth Forms of Trees

Many abnormal growth patterns and forms of trunks, branches, and roots may sometimes provide quite exact data on the magnitude and rate of the changes in soil level that have taken place at the growing

Figure 10.5. This mobile coastal dune has been burying pines on its slipface side. Some of the pines stand about seven meters deep in sand. The ages of the buried trees give relevant maximum ages for the beginning of sand accumulation, and the tree-ring pattern of the trees would provide information on the progress of the accumulation process. New seedlings became established on the sand surface when aeolian activity slowed down (Heikkinen and Tikkanen 1987). Kalajoki, Finland; photographed by Olavi Heikkinen in 1986.

sites of trees during their lifetimes. The growth reactions caused by aggradation and degradation are divided here into five categories: barrel-shaped growth, eccentricity of radial growth and curvature of trunk, height and age of adventitious roots, modifications of branches, and corrasion scars.

Barrel-Shaped Growth

The radial growth of the trunk of a tree is always greatest at ground level, decreasing both downwards and upwards from this point, hence the phrase "barrel-shaped growth." The reduced radial growth in the underground part is due partly to the lack of bending stress and partly to weakened metabolism. This manner of growth also affects exposed roots and reflects the accumulation and deflation that take place around a tree, especially one growing in aeolian material (Alestalo 1971:46–50, 1987; Heikkinen and Tikkanen 1987:261).

When a tree becomes buried in sand, the zone of most rapid radial growth will gradually shift upward, as the bending stress imposed on the trunk by wind, which affects the regulation of radial growth, is strongest at ground level. Correspondingly, when

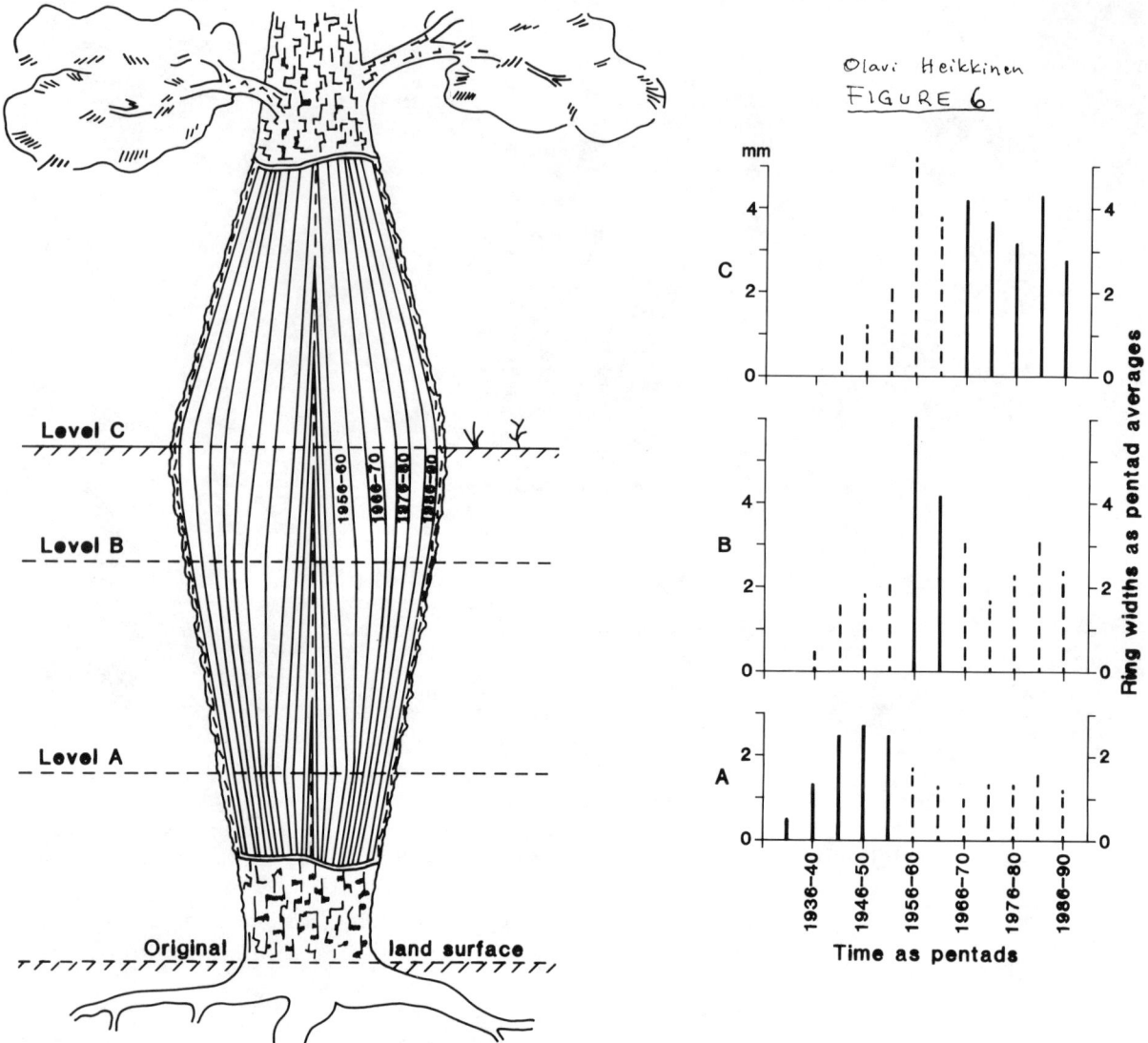

Figure 10.6. Idealized scheme depicting barrel-shaped growth of a pine buried in dune sand in three stages. The solid lines refer to the pentads of greatest radial growth, which always takes place at ground level.

the thickness of the accumulation layer is reduced by erosion, the level of maximum radial growth moves downward.

Basically each tree ring in the trunk is widest at the point that corresponded to ground level at the time when the ring developed. This means that a set of tree-ring series obtained from samples taken from various heights will provide a fairly good idea of the history of ground-level changes around the tree during its lifetime (Figure 10.6).

The above principle can also be used to some extent to date erosion that has advanced to a level below the

Figure 10.7. Degradation has caused barrel-shaped growth in the exposed roots of a pine. Dendrochronological form-growth analyses of buttress roots would allow the calculation of the erosion rate of this land surface in the past. Kalajoki, Finland; photographed by Olavi Heikkinen in 1991.

root collar. As the roots become exposed, their growth improves and they are better able to support the tree (Figure 10.7). The uppermost lateral roots, starting from the main root, will die if they are exposed completely, however, and their year of death can also be determined dendrochronologically. Thus root forms and tree rings obtained from these can also be used to define and specify the points in time at which the ground level dropped, once the tree had become seeded (Alestalo 1971:38–42). Bare roots of a growing tree are themselves signs of degradation and its net quantity during the tree's lifetime.

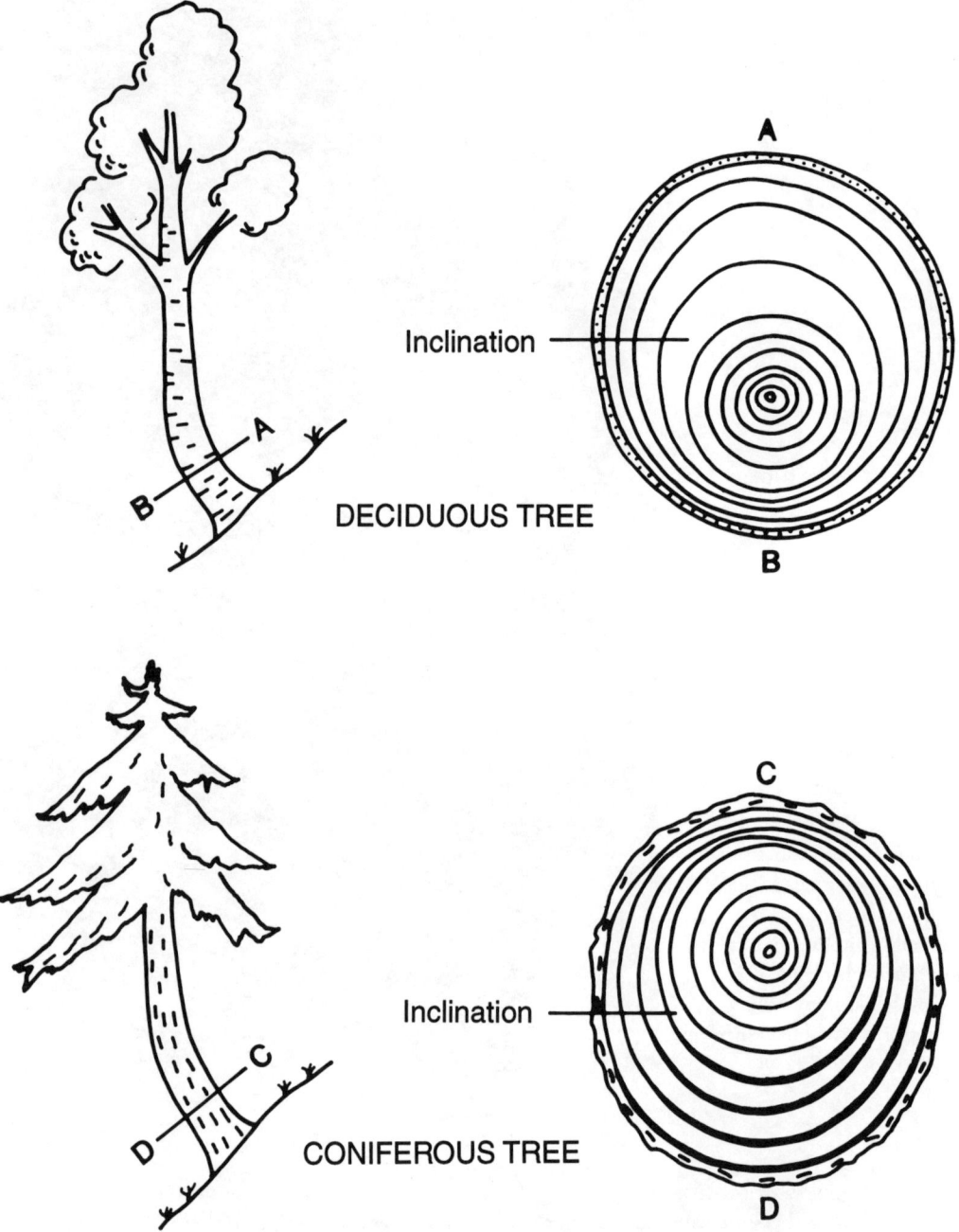

Figure 10.8. The inclination of trees can be dated from the tree rings, which become eccentric after tilting. The eccentricity of inclined coniferous trees is the opposite to that of deciduous ones.

Eccentricity of Radial Growth and Curvature of Trunk

When a tree is tilted by geomorphic processes, its manner of growth will change. Having lost its balance, the tree begins to straighten itself by a process of geotropical curvature and develops asymmetric tree rings during the first growth season. The widest rings occur on the lower side of the inclined trunk of a coniferous tree but on the upper side in a deciduous tree (Figure 10.8). This reaction wood, which serves to support the tree, is termed compression wood in coniferous trees and tension wood in deciduous ones (Fritts 1976:220–221; Lawrence 1950). Both the tree rings and the trunk become eccentric in cross section as a result of the development of reaction wood, and the trunk becomes bent up to the level to which the crown reached when the tree began to incline.

The year of inclination can be determined by measuring the widths of the tree rings in samples taken from different sides of the tree and comparing the results to identify the point from which the eccentric growth originated and the time when this process began. A number of conclusions can be drawn regarding the nature of geomorphic disturbances that must have affected the tree as well as the magnitude of any soil displacements, their orientation, and time of occurrence by carefully analyzing the shapes of the trunk and roots and their growth rings (Alestalo 1971:24–34).

Sudden tiltings in trees are often caused by landslides, avalanches (Carrara 1979), and other gravitational mass movements, as well as the flooding of rivers (Butler 1979), all of which may give rise to marked local upheavals and the development of new soil surfaces. Trees may also incline rapidly as the result of an earthquake (Page 1970) or the advance of a glacier into a forest (Lawrence 1950). Heikkinen (1984a) gives a detailed description of how the Coleman Glacier on Mt. Baker tilted and damaged coniferous trees that are still alive, during its maximum readvances in the winters of 1886/87 and 1978/79. Soil level changes and the bending of trees take place gradually in other cases, such as where aeolian sand carried from a given direction accumulates against their trunks. Similarly, tilting and bending usually occur slowly when littoral forces or other forms of erosion cause the substrate to be eroded on one side only (Alestalo 1971:25).

Many geomorphic processes that cause the inclination of trees, such as ice thrust against shores, frost heave, and minor movements on unstable slopes, usually create only small patches of new soil. These movements may even cause trees to incline in various directions. Zoltai (1975), who studied inclination directions in trees growing on hummocky permafrost terrain in Northern Canada, subject to active ground heave movements, noticed that some trees showed as many as nine periodic tiltings in different directions, as indicated by the reaction wood. In such cases, as with the gradual inclination of trees, the growth of reaction wood and the bending of the trunk constitute a complicated process that is difficult to date exactly (Shroder 1980:166).

Height and Age of Adventitious Roots

When material accumulates around a tree, adventitious roots often sprout from the dormant buds or cambium of the buried part of the trunk, as in the case of most deciduous trees and genera such as *Abies, Larix, Juniperus, Picea,* and *Sequoia*. The age of the roots can be determined from their tree rings (Figure 10.9). As adventitious roots sprout in a layer immediately below the ground level, their age and their height on the trunk indicate exactly the amount of material that has accumulated at the growing site at various stages during the tree's lifetime (Alestalo 1971:37, 45–46, 1987). The spruce (*Picea*), which has a shallow root system, reacts extremely quickly, by establishing its adventitious roots in an accumulation layer only a few centimeters thick (Strunk 1989).

Adventitious roots are highly suitable for tracing the age of deposition of peat, dune sand, and even finer sediments. The roots grow rapidly only in their first years under conditions of continuous accumulation, for as they become buried more deeply, soil conditions will deteriorate and root growth will decrease, even though it may continue for decades (Alestalo 1987).

Adventitious root layers can also be used to examine the deposition of material by floods and mass movements in mountain areas, and to date debris flows, the

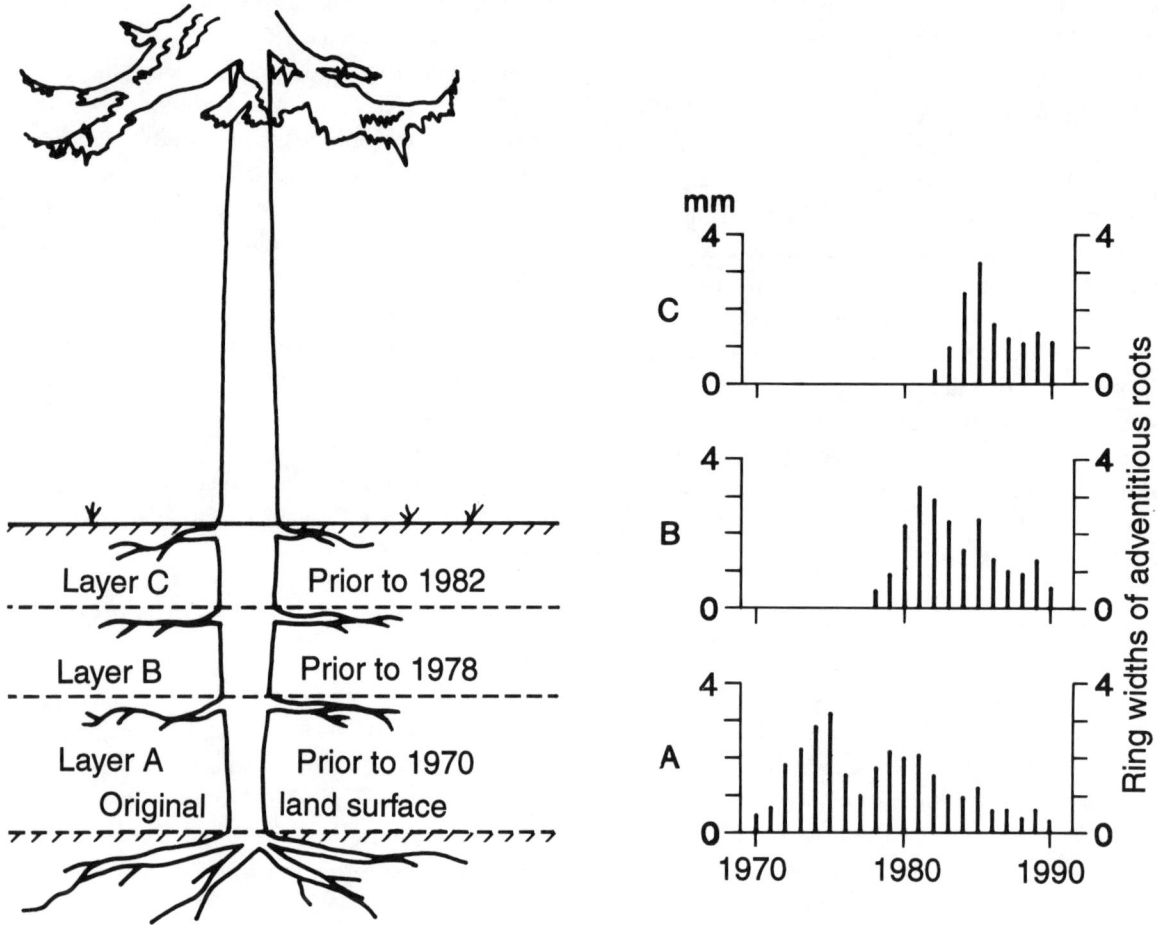

Figure 10.9. Schematic representation of the development and radial growth of adventitious roots.

burial of cultural deposits, and the destruction of settlements possibly caused by these processes over a matter of centuries. One of the difficulties with such dating procedures, however, is that not all adventitious roots sprout immediately after the cambium or dormant buds become buried, but may involve a delay of some years or even decades. In addition the bases of adventitious roots, that is, their oldest parts, gradually become embedded in the growing trunk, and the first rings are thus lost in routine sampling (Strunk 1989).

Modifications of Branches

The growth forms of branches, their heights, numbers of rings, and ring-width patterns reflect the course of the accumulation process of such airborne substances as volcanic ash or aeolian sand (Alestalo 1971:51–53). As a result of more catastrophic events (such as landslips, slides, and avalanches), accumulation may sometimes reach branch level and result in the burial or inclination of trees. Avalanches in particular also frequently break treetops. These natural processes, which create new soil surfaces, can often be dated from the growth reactions in the branches.

Branches sometimes die when they become buried by accumulating material, in which case the years of death and their heights on the trunk provide approximate data on the progress of accumulation. The year of death can be determined dendrochronologically and anatomically from a vertical section of the trunk through the center of the base of the branch to be analyzed.

A branch is often only partially buried, so that its end remains visible above the soil surface. In the case of *Pinus* and *Picea,* such a branch may become a layer, its buried part possibly developing adventitious roots, while the unburied end bends geotropically into a vertical position, and its stem and branches adopt the shape of an ordinary tree. When many branches are converted into layers, a multistem, partly buried "candelabrum tree" is created (Figure 10.10A).

A layer developed from a branch differs from an ordinary branch in its manner of radial growth. An ordinary branch, which grows laterally from the trunk, usually bends upwards geotropically, as a result of which eccentric tree rings develop. When a branch changes into a layer, however, the radial growth of the buried part gradually changes from eccentric to concentric, while the segment of the layer located approximately at the soil level develops a steep curve to reach a vertical position. Thus this part of the branch assumes a still more eccentric mode of radial growth, as indicated by the considerable development of reaction wood (see Figure 10.10A). Both the time of accumulation and that of the resulting layering can be determined by dating the point at which the radial growth of the buried part reverted from eccentric to concentric, when the first tree rings of the adventitious roots of the layer were created, or when the part of the layer leading it into a vertical position began to grow even more eccentrically.

Many dormant and adventitious buds on the trunks and branches of *Salix* species develop into sprouts, particularly at the soil surface (see Figure 10.10B). The progress of soil accumulation in time can thus be traced back using the altitude and rings of branches that developed out of these buds (Alestalo 1971).

If a tree trunk is severed by a landslide or an avalanche, but the tree survives, one of its branches will become a new leader, that is, it will begin to grow vertically and finally form a new crown. Having once adopted this role, it begins to increase its radial growth and develop reaction wood on either side, indicated by wider rings that become eccentric. This enables the mass movement that severed the trunk to be dated (Carrara 1979:776–777).

Corrasion Scars

Various geomorphic processes that alter the soil surface can cause mechanical erosion or corrasion of trunks, branches, and roots. Rocks carried by mass movements, for instance, may cause fractures of the branches or trunk or leave deep scars on the trunk, whereas finer matter such as aeolian or alluvial sand will only cause abrasion scars (Alestalo 1971:21–24). Because the material that causes corrasion usually moves on or near the land surface, the heights at which the scars occur provide some data on the position of the land surface when they were created.

When determining the year in which a branch was broken by mass movements, a section must be cut to examine how the annual rings of the branch continue in the trunk. This will indicate how many rings have developed in the stem since the death of the branch. The geomorphic process that caused the fracture may be dated by determining the time at which the branch was broken, although the height of the land surface created cannot be dated directly or exactly.

Any severe damage caused by mass movements or ice thrust is indicated by a decrease in annual radial growth. This can be verified by comparing the growth of damaged trees with that of undamaged ones at the same site.

A good way of dating corrasion is to examine the cross-section of the tree at the scar, which facilitates the detection of possible destruction of tree rings caused by a blow or subsequent decay (Figure 10.11). The rings formed before corrasion are of a normal concentric kind and of normal width, whereas a scarred tree develops a

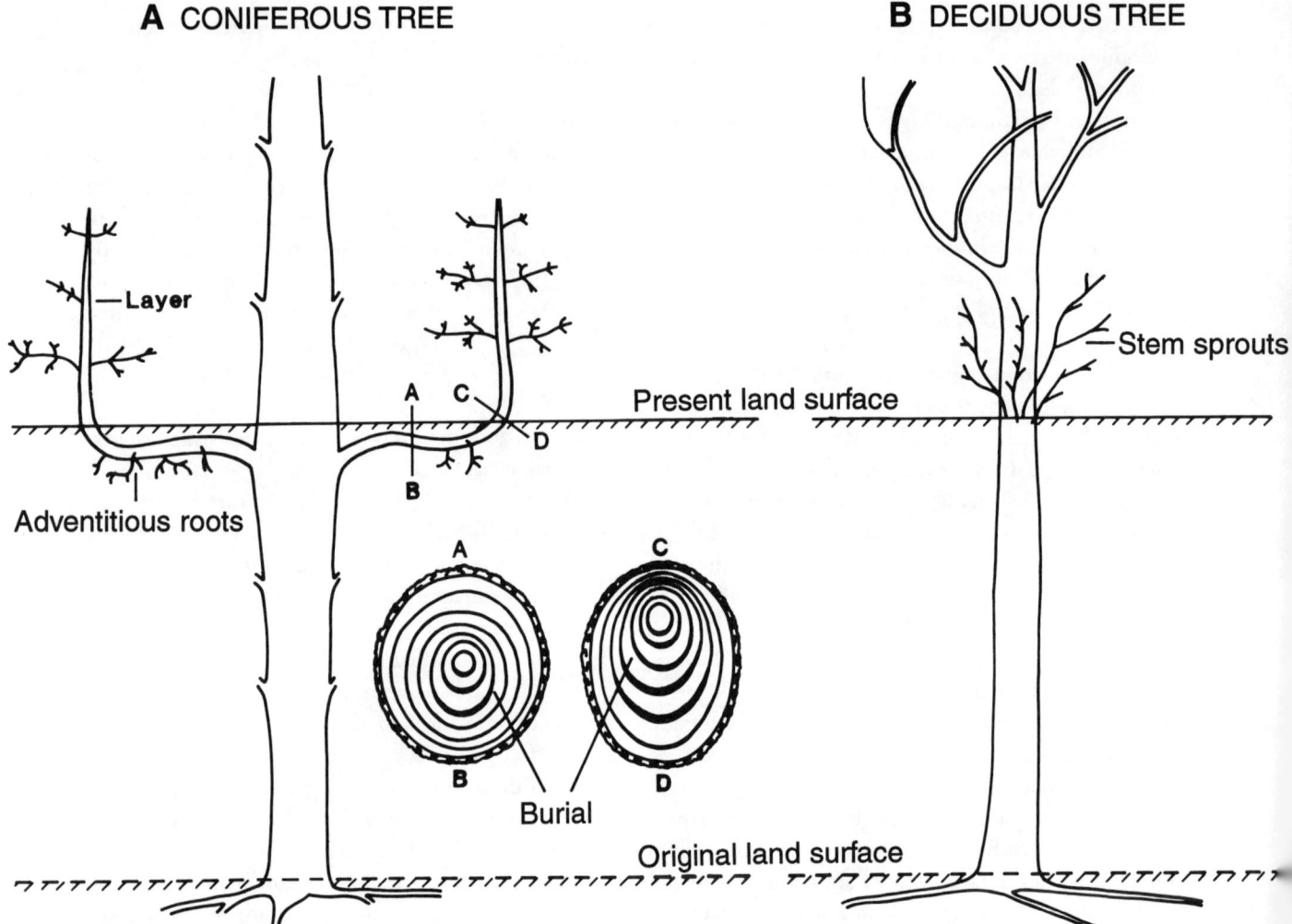

Figure 10.10. The development of layers and a candelabrum tree (A) and the formation of stem sprouts (B). Largely based on Alestalo (1971, Figure 20).

callous margin with irregular tree rings around the wound of the trunk. When a tree is subjected to a hard blow, this often pushes its trunk over, causing eccentric radial growth and the development of reaction wood. The scar may sometimes heal, after which it is no longer visible externally (Carrara 1979). Both corrasion and the soil level changes that caused it can be dated by calculating the number of tree rings in the callous margin, as these developed after those which originated in the ordinary manner. It is important to make sure, however, that the scars were not caused by animals or fire.

Even corrasion that is so weak that it leads only to a thinning of the bark can affect the functioning of the cambium. This form of corrasion is common in cases where trees are chafed by aeolian sand. The inadequately protected cambium on the side subjected to

Dendrochronology / 231

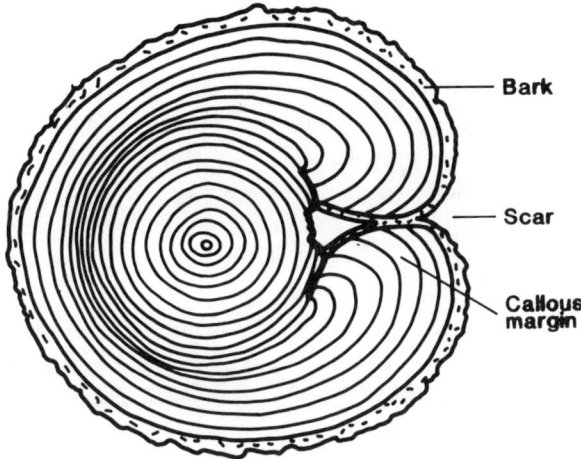

Figure 10.11. The age of a scar on a living tree can be determined by counting the annual rings of the callous margin.

such corrasion will suffer from temperature variations and increased evaporation, so that narrower tree rings will develop on that side. In addition, false rings, related to "frost rings," also tend to develop on this unprotected side under cool conditions. Temporal variations in the surface of a sandy soil can be detemined by examining the age and altitude of such asymmetrical rings in trunks growing in dune areas (Alestalo 1971:24).

Age of Dead Trees

A methodological discussion is provided above of the dendrochronological means by which fluctuations in land surface level and soil age can be determined from living trees. It is often possible to date soils and land surfaces by applying the same methods to dead trees, although it is more difficult to determine whether a ring width or frequency variation was caused by geomorphic or other factors. In addition it is difficult to connect tree-ring series observed in dead trees to calendar years by the cross-dating technique, unless there is a sufficiently long, reliable master chronology available.

The relative ages of dead trees, for example, buried ones, can be determined by radiocarbon dating, which always facilitates the process of combining tree-ring series into long chronologies, even if it is not yet possible to date them dendrochronologically. The reliability of soil dating based on dead trees is also highly dependent on whether the trees are still standing *in situ* and in possession of their roots, or whether they have been moved to their present location from somewhere else.

Dead Trees *in situ*

Buried trees may be found in sediments that accumulated in water or bogs, in dune sand, or in volcanic sediments; in addition to which trees may be found *in situ* under layers of till transported by glaciers and the debris accumulated by avalanches. Erosion or the withdrawal of water from an area may reveal buried trees, which provide data on how and when the soil they once grew in became covered by new material (Schweingruber 1983).

It is sometimes difficult from the point of view of soil dating to identify whether the trees died during the burial process or some time afterward. This problem can often be solved by analyzing their growth reaction from the annual rings, a simultaneous death suggesting that all the trees succumbed upon burial. In drowned forests on subsidence shores, there are no young tree generations, as the flood water will have prevented trees from becoming rooted (Alestalo 1971:68). It may be difficult to date exactly the geomorphic process that led to such destruction and the death of the tree, even if the tree-ring series can be absolutely dated, as buried trees have often lost their bark and an unknown number of their outermost rings.

In cases where trees are known to have become buried only after their death, it may be difficult to define the time interval between death and burial. A tree that has remained on land will decay rapidly under warm, humid conditions, whereas the small-celled wood of bristlecone pine snags is preserved for millennia under the cool, dry conditions of the California mountains.

Numerous buried trunks can be found *in situ* in rivers and on seashores. A large number of oaks buried in river beds in southern Germany have been examined and dendrochronological dating schemes thus extended back for nearly 10,000 years. It has thus been possible to examine the development of the river network and of landforms in the area from the point of view of the alternation between erosion and sedimentation. A long tree-ring chronology can also be used to date wooden bridges, palisades, and other wooden objects, perhaps dating back thousands of years (Schweingruber 1983:178–181).

A large number of oak and pine trunks have been found in sediments near the present shoreline and below it on the northwest coast of the British Isles. These date back over 8,000 years, as indicated by radiocarbon dating and dendrochronological analyses. The altitudes at which the roots of the trees are located provide data on shoreline displacements that may have resulted from eustatic fluctuations in ocean level, isostatic subsidence of the earth's crust in nonglaciated areas after the Ice Age, and vertical tectonic movements (Heyworth 1978; Schweingruber 1983).

Dead Trees in Secondary Position

Trunks or other parts of dead trees found on land, in soil, or in water have often become detached from their roots, as in the case of driftwood that has been transported thousands of kilometers to the shores of arctic areas where no forest grows. Driftwood may be found on those ancient shores that rose from the sea during the Holocene, that is, during the last 10,000 years, as a result of glacioisostatic land uplift. One example is Svalbard in the Arctic Ocean, where driftwood trunks dating back about 10,000 years now lie at an altitude of over 50 m above sea level (Häggblom 1982).

Determination of the altitude and year of death of a driftwood trunk will indicate the time at which the high-water limit was at the altitude concerned and the period during which the land area between the dated driftwood and the recent driftwood zone rose from the sea. When numerous dates are available for driftwood located at different altitudes, these can be used to depict postglacial land uplift in the area as a function of time.

The species and area of origin of a driftwood trunk must be known in order to determine its exact age, as its tree-ring series can only be related to the master chronology of its own growth area and species (Bartholin and Hjort 1987). Unfortunately, since a suitable and sufficiently long comparative chronology is seldom found, if it even exists, at least the oldest driftwood has to be dated by the radiocarbon method (Häggblom 1982). Some aboriginal peoples such as the Eskimos, who live in areas where no trees survive, have traditionally used driftwood as a building material, which may provide a field of investigation for archaeologists using dendrochronology.

Uprooted trees also tend to float along inland water systems and may today be found on dry land near lakes and rivers. The altitudes and years of death of such trees provide data on fluctuations in water level and the channel network.

Trees and their parts are also carried off by rapid mass movements. The age of the new soil and land surface created by these movements and the time at which the old land surface became buried can be determined dendrochronologically by defining the year of death of the trees.

Wood left on the land surface by humans usually provides a minimum age for the soil horizon concerned, while wood buried by volcanic, aeolian, fluvial, or littoral material is older than the material covering it, except in the case of that buried or submerged in bogs or sediments. If the age of a land surface or soil layer can be dated dendrochronologically from the wood found in it, the age of archaeological finds of other materials from the site can also be assessed.

The close relation between dendrochronology and archaeology can be attributed to the work of Andrew Ellicott Douglass, a pioneer dendrochronologist, in the American Southwest in 1914. It was mainly thanks to him that in 1929 a floating tree-ring chronology collected from the ruins of prehistoric Indian dwellings in the area could be connected by cross-dating to an absolute tree-ring series that extended up to the present (1929). Thus Douglass obtained a tree-ring record that extended from A.D. 700 to 1929. The tree-ring dating method, which had thus proved to be an excellent tool for archaeological investigation, spread rapidly, and new applications were proposed (Baillie 1982; Bannister and Robinson 1975; Dean 1978).

Archaeological investigations usually include an attempt to date any wood discovered and possibly to determine its origin. The dating of archaeological objects, also other than wooden ones, that may be found on the land surface and in buried horizons is facilitated by the many applications of dendrochronological and dendrogeomorphic methods available.

Summary

A minimum age for a new soil surface may be derived from the numbers of annual rings of pioneer trees, if these are still alive. The ages of partially buried living trees provide information about the progress of accumulation processes in the area concerned.

Changes in the widths of annual rings often reveal the aggradation and degradation of soil in the immediate vicinity of trees. Both burial and exposure usually reduce the growth of trees, although in certain circumstances they promote it.

Abnormal growth forms of trunks, branches, and roots and the associated anomalies in annual rings are generally the responses of trees to geomorphic processes such as mass movements and floods, as well as to the deposition and deflation of aeolian sand. The first tree rings related to the growth responses usually date the geomorphic processes affected, or the beginning of those processes if they are slow in character.

It is almost always easier to date land surfaces created by geomorphic events that took place during the lifetimes of trees still alive. Even so soil ages can be determined also with the aid of dead trees, if an appropriate and sufficiently long master chronology is available. In many cases, however, even the approximate dating of land surfaces or soil horizons using dead trees also demands other dating techniques in addition to dendrochronological methods.

References Cited

Alestalo, J.
1971 Dendrochronological Interpretation of Geomorphic Processes. *Fennia* 105:1–140.
1987 The Dendrochronology of Accumulation Processes. *Annales Academiae Scientiarum Fennicae, Series A III, Geologica-Geographica* 145:67–77.

Baillie, M. G. L.
1982 *Tree-Ring Dating and Archaeology.* Croom Helm, London and Canberra.

Bannister, B., and W. J. Robinson
1975 Tree-Ring Dating in Archaeology. *World Archaeology* 7:210–225.

Bartholin, T. S., and C. Hjort
1987 Dendrochronological Studies of Recent Driftwood on Svalbard. In *Proceedings of the Task Force Meeting on Methodology and Dendrochronology: East/West Approaches* (June 2–6, 1986, Kraków, Poland), edited by L. Kairiukstis, Z. Bednarz, and E. Feliksik, pp. 207–219. Warsaw.

Becker, B., B. Kromer, and P. Trimborn
1991 A Stable-Isotope Tree-Ring Timescale of the Late Glacial/Holocene Boundary. *Nature* 353:647–649.

Brubaker, L. B.
1982 Western North America. In *Climate from Tree Rings,* edited by M. K. Hughes, P. M. Kelly, J. R. Pilcher, and V. C. LaMarche, Jr., pp. 118–126. Cambridge University Press, Cambridge.

Butler, D. R.
1979 Dendrogeomorphological Analysis of Flooding and Mass Movement, Ram Plateau, Mackenzie Mountains, Northwest Territories. *The Canadian Geographer* 23:62–65.

Carrara, P. E.
1979 The Determination of Snow Avalanche Frequency through Tree-Ring Analysis and Historical Records at Ophir, Colorado. *Geological Society of America Bulletin* 90:773–780.

Dean, J. S.
1978 Tree-Ring Dating in Archeology. *Anthropological Papers: Miscellaneous Collected Papers* 24:129–163. University of Utah Press, Salt Lake City.

Ferguson, C. W.
1970 Concepts and Techniques of Dendrochronology. In *Scientific Methods in Medieval Archaeol-*

ogy, edited by R. Berger, pp. 183–200. University of California Press, Berkeley.

Ferguson, C. W., and D. A. Graybill
1983 Dendrochronology of Bristlecone Pine: A Progress Report. In *Radiocarbon* 25:287–288.

Fritts, H. C.
1976 *Tree Rings and Climate.* Academic Press, London

Graybill, D. A.
1982 Chronology Development and Analysis. In *Climate from Tree Rings,* edited by M. K. Hughes, P. M. Kelly, J. R. Pilcher, and V. C. LaMarche, Jr., pp. 21–28. Cambridge University Press, Cambridge.

Häggblom, A.
1982 Driftwood in Svalbard as an Indicator of Sea Ice Conditions. *Geografiska Annaler* 64(A):81–94.

Heikkinen, O.
1984a Dendrochronological Evidence of Variations of Coleman Glacier, Mount Baker, Washington, U.S.A. *Arctic and Alpine Research* 16:53–64.
1984b Laharit, Tulivuorten Tuhovirrat (Lahars, Volcanic Devastators). *Terra* 98:45–59.
1987 Dendroclimatology and Dendroecology: Global and Regional; Problems and Questions. *Annales Academiae Scientiarum Fennicae,* Series A III, *Geologica-Geographica* 145:19–36.

Heikkinen, O., and M. Tikkanen
1987 The Kalajoki Dune Field on the West Coast of Finland *Fennia* 165:241–267.

Helley, E. J., and V. C. LaMarche, Jr.
1973 Historic Flood Information for Northern California Streams from Geological and Botanical Evidence. *U.S. Geological Survey Professional Paper* 485-E:1–16.

Heyworth, A.
1978 Submerged Forests around the British Isles: Their Dating and Relevance as Indicators of Post-Glacial Land and Sea Level Changes. In *Dendrochronology in Europe,* edited by J. Fletcher. *British Archaeological Research Series* 51:279–288.

Hughes, M. K., P. M. Kelly, J. R. Pilcher, and V. C. LaMarche, Jr. (editors)
1982 *Climate from Tree Rings.* Cambridge University Press, Cambridge.

Hupp, C. R., W. R. Osterkamp, and J. L. Thornton
1987 Dendrogeomorphic Evidence and Dating of Recent Debris Flows on Mount Shasta, Northern California. *U.S. Geological Survey Professional Paper* 1396-B:1–39.

Kienast, F.
1985 *Dendroökologische Untersuchungen an Höhenprofilen aus Verschiedenen Klimabereichen.* Juris Drukt Verlag, Zürich.

LaMarche, Jr., V. C.
1966 An 800-year History of Stream Erosion as Indicated by Botanical Evidence. *U.S. Geological Survey Professional Paper* 550-D:83–86.

LaMarche Jr., V. C., E. R. Cook, and M. G. L. Baillie
1982 Sampling Strategies. In *Climate from Tree Rings,* ed. by M. K. Hughes, P. M. Kelly, J. R. Pilcher, and V. C. LaMarche, Jr., pp. 2–8. Cambridge University Press, Cambridge.

Lawrence D. B.
1950 Estimating Dates of Recent Glacier Advances and Recession Rates by Studying Tree Growth Layers. *Transactions, American Geophysical Union* 31:243–248.

Page, R.
1970 Dating Episodes of Faulting from Tree Rings: Effects of the 1958 Rupture of the Fairweather Fault on Tree Growth. *Geological Society of America Bulletin* 81:3085–3094.

Schweingruber, F. H.
1983 *Der Jahrring.* Paul Haupt, Bern.
1989 *Tree Rings.* English edition of *Der Jahrring.* Kluwer Academic Publishers, Dordrecht.

Shroder Jr., J. F.
1980 Dendrogeomorphology: Review and New Techniques of Tree-Ring Dating. *Progress in Physical Geography* 4:161–188.

Sigafoos, R. S., and E. L. Hendricks
1969 The Time Interval between Stabilization of Al-

pine Glacial Deposits and Establishment of Tree Seedlings. *U.S. Geological Survey Professional Paper* 650-B:B89–B93

1972 Recent Activity of Glaciers of Mount Rainier, Washington. *U.S. Geological Survey Professional Paper* 387-B:B1–B24.

Smith, L. P., and C. W. Stockton

1981 Reconstructed Stream Flow for the Salt and Verde Rivers from Tree-Ring Data. *Water Resources Bulletin, American Water Resources Association* 7:939–947.

Stokes, M. A., and T. L. Smiley

1968 *An Introduction to Tree-Ring Dating.* University of Chicago Press, Chicago.

Strunk, H.

1989 Dendrogeomorphology of Debris Flows. *Estratto da "Dendrochronologia"* 7:15–25.

Wolfe, F.

1932 Annual Rings of *Thuja occidentalis* in Relation to Climatic Conditions and Movement of Sand. *Botanical Gazette* 93:328–335.

Yamaguchi, D. K.

1985 Tree-Ring Evidence for a Two-Year Interval between Recent Prehistoric Explosive Eruptions of Mount St. Helens. *Geology* 13:554–557.

Zoltai, S. C.

1975 Tree Ring Record of Soil Movements on Permafrost. *Arctic and Alpine Research* 7:331–340.

INDEX

Aluminum-26 dating, 142, 152–54
Anderson, D. S., 23
Anderson, L. W., 23
Arnold, J. R., 168–69

Ballantyne, C. K., 199–200
Bates, J. K., 52
Bergqvist, K. I., 200
Beryllium-10 dating, 142, 146, 150, 151, 152–54
Bierman, P., 93, 96
Birkeland, P. W., 4, 23
Black Rock obsidian source, Utah, 56, 57, 58
Bloody Canyon, California, 169–70, 171, 172, 175–77
Broadbent, N. D., 38–39, 200
Brook, E. J., 149
Browns Bench obsidian source, Nevada/Idaho, 56, 57, 58, 61, 62, 63, 64, 65, 66, 67, 70, 71, 72n2
Bull, W. B., 106
Butler, D. R., 23
Butte Mountain obsidian source, Nevada, 56, 57, 58, 61, 62, 63, 64, 65, 66
Butte Valley, Nevada: continuity and duration of occupation in, 61, 63–65; map of, 55; obsidian hydration dating in, 56–57, 59–66, 70–71; obsidian types found in, 56, 57, 58, 62, 65, 66–67, 68, 69–70; projectile points in, 66–67, 69, 70–71; temperature and humidity in, 57, 59

Cahill, T. A., 93, 96
Calcium-41 dating, 142, 155
Carbon-14 dating. *See* Radiocarbon dating
Carroll, T., 23, 24
Casa Diablo obsidian source, California, 49
Cation-ratio dating: advantages of, 106; in archaeology, 101; blind tests of, 99–101; cation-leaching curve and, 84–85; cation-leaching studies and, 85–89; controversies in, 92–96; in geomorphology, 105; methods for, 89–92
Cerling, T. E., 149–50, 151
Chinn, T. J. H., 19, 21–22

Chlorine-36 dating, 142; in geomorphology, 168–70, 171, 172; principles of, 162–67; problems affecting, 172–79; sample collection and preparation for, 179–80
Clast-sound velocity method, 25–26
Cold Water Farm site, Missouri, 119, 120, 130, 131
Colman, S. M., 4, 17, 18, 24, 25
Colodner, D., 148, 149
Colorado River geoglyphs, California, 96–97, 102
Cook-Talbot, J. D., 200
Cosmogenic nuclide dating, 7, 107–8, 139–40; aluminum-26 method, 142, 152–54; assumptions, 143, 144–47; beryllium-10 method, 142, 146, 150, 151, 152–54; calcium-41 method, 142, 155; carbon-14 method, 142, 154–55; in geomorphology, 148–49, 150, 151–52, 153–54; helium-3 method, 142, 146, 147–50, 151; neon-21 method, 142, 150–52; principles of, 140–43. *See also* Chlorine-36 dating
Cougar Mountain point, 69
County Line site, Missouri, 130, 131
Crook, R., Jr., 25–26
Cude Cemetery site, Missouri, 130, 131

Dating in archaeology, 7–10, 115–16; of bone, 118, 155; of burned daub, 118; of ceramics, 116–34; of glass, 154; of obsidian artifacts, 48–71; of petroglyphs, 98, 99–101, 102, 103; of stone artifacts, 102; of stone features and monuments, 102, 201–2, 203; using diagnostic artifacts, 48; of wooden artifacts, 232–33
Dating in geomorphology, 4–7; of alluvial fans, 25–26, 100, 105, 106; of bedrock, 104–5, 106; chronofunction approach to, 5; chronosequence approach to, 5; of colluvium, 104–5, 106; of debris flows, 104–5, 106, 199, 201; of dunes, 222; of glacial polish, 100, 145, 152–53; of glaciofluvial surfaces, 24; of groundwater, 162; of intermoraine areas, 198–99; of lake shorelines, 32, 104–5, 199, 201; of landslide deposits, 19, 22, 32, 38, 199, 201, 202; of lava flows, 86, 87, 146, 148, 149, 153, 162–63; of Meteor Crater, 155, 168–69, 170, 174–75, 176; of moraines, 19, 22–23, 25–26, 31–32, 40, 100, 103, 106, 150, 151–52, 154, 167, 169–70, 171, 172, 175–77, 186, 190–95, 196, 199, 203, 220; of mud-

flows, 222; of protalus ramparts, 32, 199, 201; of raised shorelines, 200, 201, 220, 232; of river deposits, 21, 22, 25–26, 201, 228–29, 231–32; of rock coatings, 77–99, 102–8; of rock glaciers, 32, 199, 201; rock exposure-based, 139–55, 162–80; of soils and sediments, 154, 220, 222, 227–28, 231; of sorted rock features, 199–200, 201, 202; of talus, 201; of tephra, 222; tree-based, 214–33; weathering-based, 5, 15–27, 30–32, 38–42

Dating methods. *See* Cation-ratio dating; Chlorine-36 dating; Cosmogenic nuclide dating; Dendrochronology; Lichenometric dating; Obsidian hydration dating; Radiocarbon dating; Rock varnish dating; Rock weathering dating; Thermoluminescence dating

Dawson, A. G., 199

Dendrochronology, 6, 213; in archaeology, 232–33; constructing chronologies for, 218–20; cross-dating in, 214, 218, 219; data collection for, 217–18; in geomorphology, 219–32; tree growth, abnormal, and, 222–31; tree growth, normal, and, 214–16; use of dead trees in, 231–33; use of living trees in, 220–30

Dendroclimatology, 213
Dendroecology, 213–14
Dendrogeomorphology, 214, 219–32
Dendrohydrology, 213
Desert Side-Notched point, 70, 71
Dorn, R. I., 85–86, 87, 101, 168
Douglass, A. E., 232

Ebert, W. L., 52
Elko Side-Notched point, 67, 70, 71
Elmore, D., 168, 172–74
Erikstad, L., 194, 195

Fink, D., 168–69
Friedman, I., 48, 49, 50, 51, 52

Gillespie, A. R., 25–26, 93, 96

Hall, M. C., 53, 54
Helium-3 dating, 142, 146, 147–50, 151
Hughes, R. E., 49
Humboldt point, 70

Innes, J. L., 189, 196, 199

Jackson, R. J., 53, 54
Jenkins, W. J., 149

Kane Spring obsidian source, Nevada, 56, 57, 58
Karolta site, South Australia, 100
Klein, J., 168–69
Knuepfer, P. L. K., 21–22

Kohl, C. P., 168–69
Krinsley, D. H., 87
Kubik, P. W., 168
Kurz, M. D., 148, 149

Lal, D., 143, 144–45, 147, 162–63
Langdon site, Missouri, 130, 131
Leonard, P. M., 101
Lichenometric dating, 185; in archaeology, 7–8, 201–2; data collection for, 188–91, 196–97; dating curves, 191–96, 200, 203; direct measurement of growth rates for, 197–98, 203; in geomorphology, 6, 186, 190–96, 198–203; principles of, 186–88
"Little Ice Age", 31, 186, 199
Loendorf, L. L., 99–100
Long, W., 51

Maizels, J. K., 198–99
Malad obsidian source, Idaho, 56, 57, 58
Malden Plain, Missouri, 122–23; ceramics, 123–24, 126–27, 129, 131; chronology, 123–26; thermoluminescence dating in, 126, 127–33, 134
Matthews, J. A., 30–31, 189, 192–93, 195, 199–200
Mazer, J. J., 52
McCarroll, D., 5, 32
McGlone, W. R., 101
McSaveney, M. J., 21–22
Meteor Crater, Arizona, 168–69, 170, 174–75, 176
Michels, J. W., 52–53
Middleton, R., 168–69
Moore, R., 148, 149

Nazca geoglyphs, Peru, 96–97, 101–2
Nelson, C. M., 52–53
Neon-21 dating, 142, 150–52
Nigardsbreen, Norway, 190–91, 192, 193–94, 196, 197–98, 199
Nishiizumi, K., 168–69

O'Brien, K., 148, 149
Obsidian hydration dating, 6; effect of chemical composition on, 49; effect of humidity on, 52; effect of temperature on, 50–51; rate for, 48, 50; in surface archaeology, 9, 53–54, 56–57, 59–66, 70–71; testing assemblage contemporaneity with, 65–66; used to calibrate rock-weathering rates, 24

Panaca Summit obsidian source, Utah, 56, 57, 58, 62, 64, 65, 66, 67, 70, 71
Pancake Mountain obsidian source, Nevada, 56, 57, 58
Petch, J. R., 198–99
Peters, B., 145, 147
Phillips, F. M., 168, 172–74

Pierce, K. L., 4, 17, 18, 24, 25
Pinto point, 70, 71
Point site, Colorado, 100
Poreda, R. J., 151
Porter, S. C., 22–23
Pumice Hole obsidian source, Utah, 56, 57, 58

Radiocarbon dating: cosmogenic, 142, 154–55; dipole-moment fluctuations and, 144; disadvantages of, 116; in geomorphology, 15–16; of organic matter in rock varnish, 96–99, 101–2, 103, 105, 106; used to calibrate obsidian hydration rates, 52–53; used to calibrate rock-weathering rates, 18, 23, 38; used to check cation-ratio dates, 99–100, 101, 145, 149; used to check cosmogenic isotope dates, 100; from Woodland/Mississippian period sites, 124–26
Raymond, A. W., 61
Ridings, R., 53
Robards Farm site, Missouri, 125, 126, 130, 131
Rock coatings, 77–78. *See also* Lichenometric dating; Rock varnish dating
Rock surface hardness. *See* Schmidt hammer
Rock varnish dating: in archaeology, 8, 9, 101–2, 103; cation-ratio method, 84–96, 99–101, 105, 106; collection procedures for, 84; future of, 106–8; in geomorphology, 6–7, 102–6; methods, 79, 89–92; radiocarbon method for, 96–99, 101–2, 103, 105, 106; sampling for, 80, 83–84; varnish types, 78, 80–84. *See also* Cation-ratio dating
Rock weathering dating: in archaeology, 8, 26–27; calibration of rates for, 18–19, 21, 23, 24, 25; in geomorphology, 5, 19–26; principles of, 16–18; sampling for, 18; in subsurface contexts, 22, 24; in surface contexts, 19, 21–24. *See also* Schmidt hammer
Roddy, D., 168

Schmidt hammer, 5, 29–30, 40–42; operation, 30, 31; sources of error for, 32–38; use in numerical age dating, 38–40, 41; use in relative age dating, 30–32; use in weathering studies, 30
Shakesby, R. A., 30–31, 199
Shoemaker, E. M., 168–69
Sjöberg, R., 38–39
Smith, R. L., 48, 49, 50, 52
Smith, S. S., 168
Sollid, J. L., 194, 195
South Australian petroglyphs, 88, 96–97, 98, 101, 102, 103
South Pahroc obsidian source, Nevada, 56, 58
Stevenson, C. M., 52
Storbreen glacier, Norway, 34–36, 38, 40, 41
Surface contexts: dating of, 3–4; prejudice against in archaeology, 115–16. *See also* Dating in archaeology; Dating in geomorphology

Thermoluminescence dating, 6; advantage of, 116; in archaeology, 9, 119–21, 122, 126, 127–33; principles of, 116–21; sources of error in, 131, 132–33
Topaz Mountain obsidian source, Utah, 56, 57, 58, 62, 64, 65, 66, 67
Torlesse greywacke, New Zealand, 19–21
Tremaine, K. J., 54, 66
Trull, T. W., 148, 149
Tsong, I. S. T., 52–53

Western Stemmed Tradition, 56, 67
Whitehouse, I. E., 21–22
Wildhorse obsidian source, Utah, 56, 57, 58, 62, 64, 66, 67
Williams, S., 124
Woodall Farm site, Missouri, 129
Wyoming petroglyphs, 88, 101

Zebree site, Arkansas, 124, 125
Zeier, C. D., 52
Zookeeper site, Colorado, 100
Zreda, M. G., 168, 172–74

ERRATA

Two figures in Chapter 3 (pp. 38 and 40) and two in Chapter 4 (pp. 60 and 64) were mistakenly transposed. They are shown here with their correct captions.

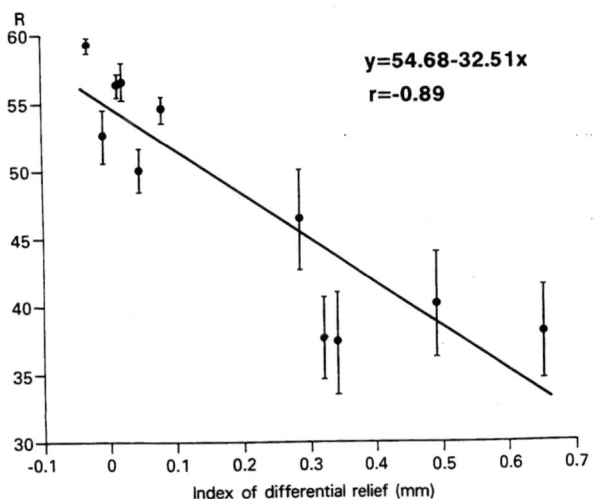

Figure 3.7. The relationship between Schmidt hammer R-values and a measure of degree of weathering of a gabbro surface in Leirdalen, southern Norway. The index of differential relief represents the mean height of pyroxene grains relative to adjacent feldspar grains on a transect. Bars represent two standard errors of the mean.

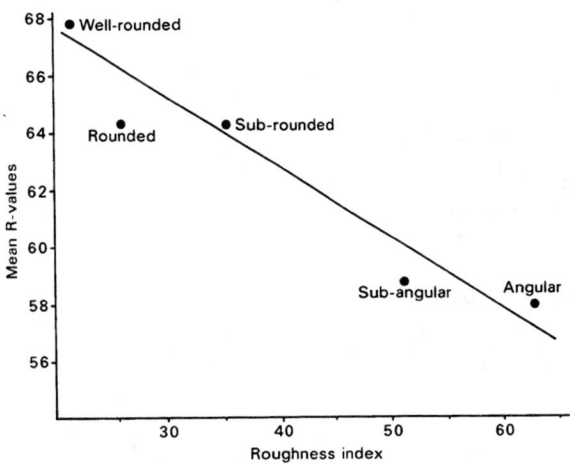

Figure 3.9. Comparison of mean R-values and roughness values (index A of Figure 3.8) obtained from boulders grouped according to roundness.

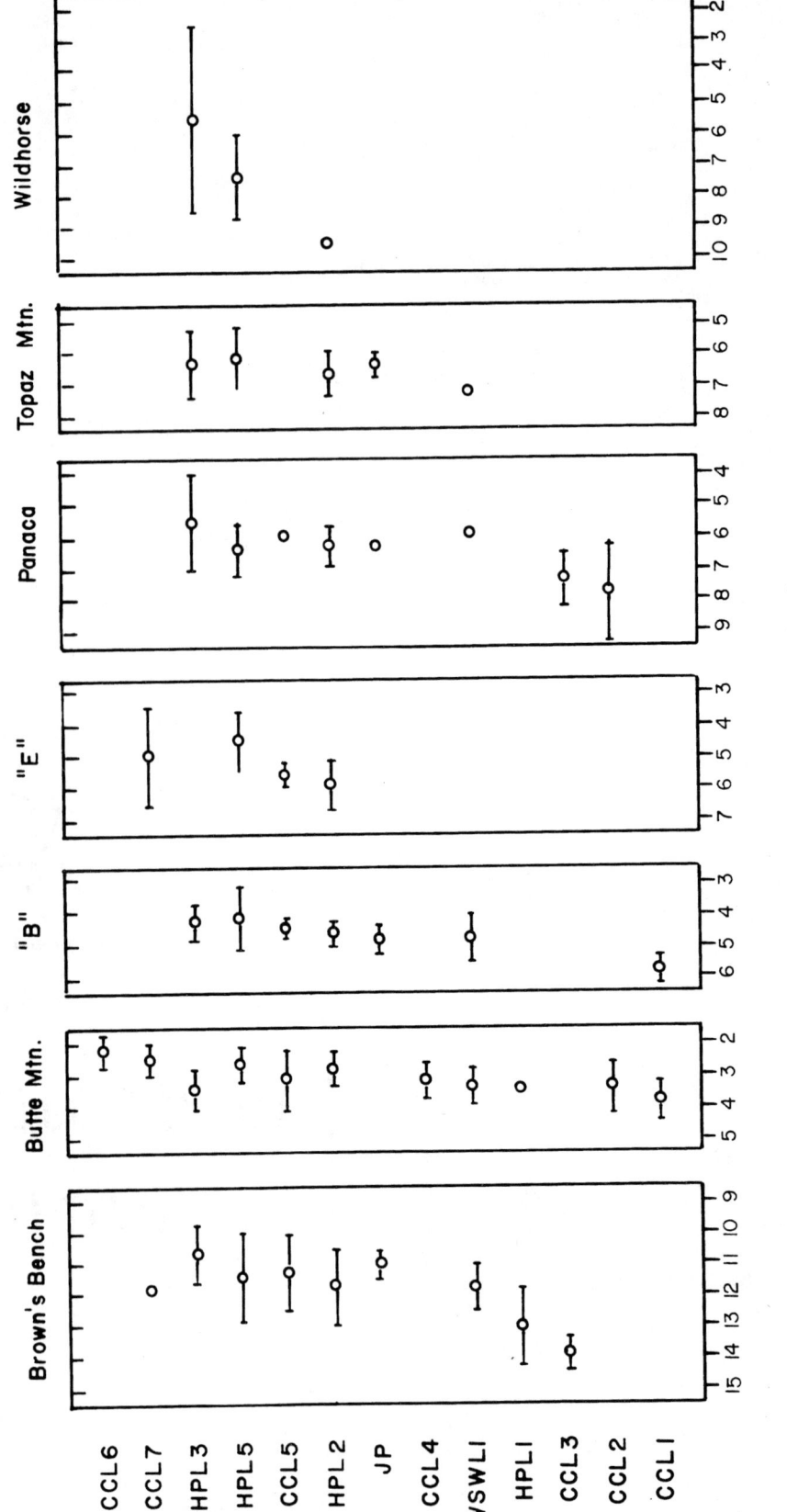

Figure 4.3. Serial order of 13 Butte Valley assemblages, based on mean hydration values for the seven most prevalent obsidians. Means based on three or more values are accompanied by standard deviations.

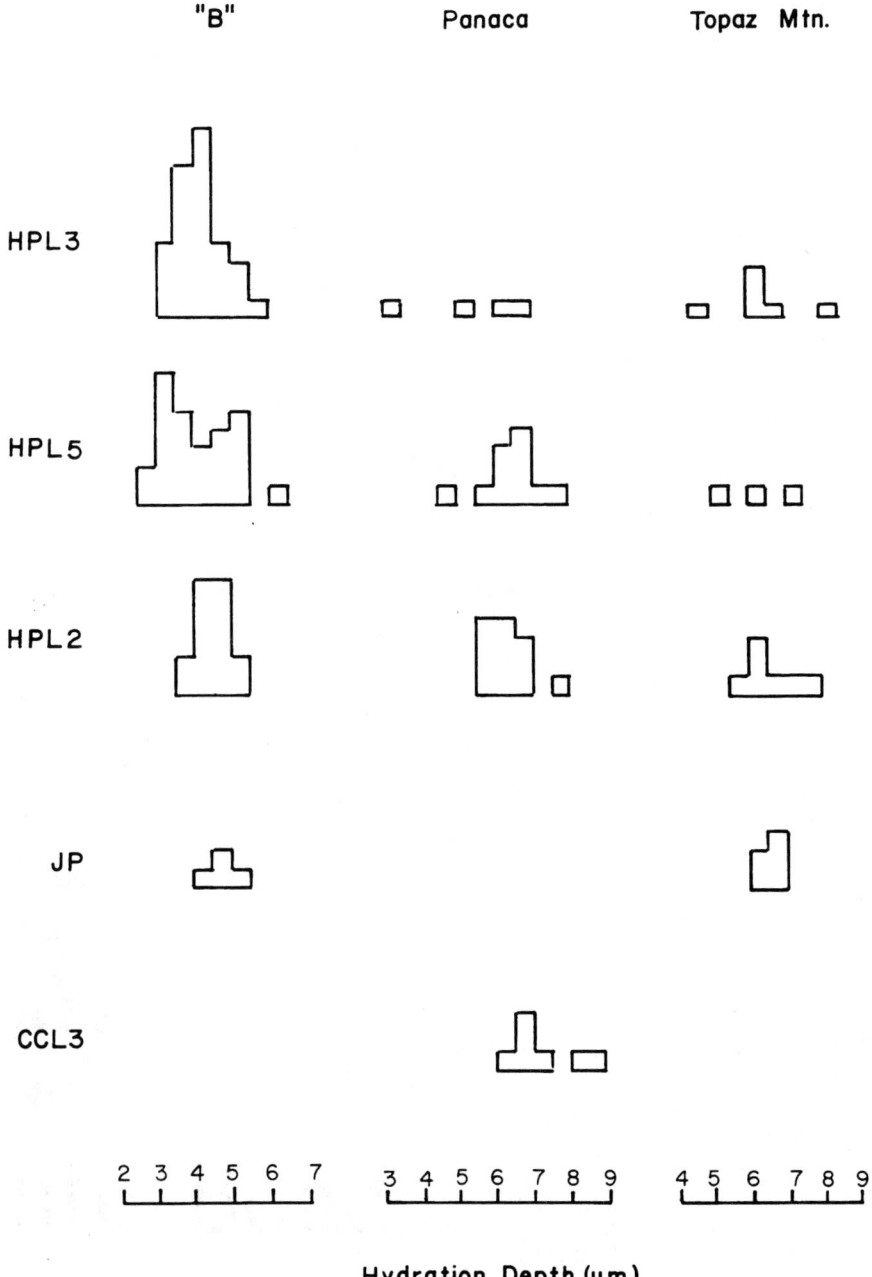

Figure 4.5. Distribution of hydration values for "B," Panaca, and Topaz Mountain obsidians in each of the Butte Valley assemblages. Only those assemblages with six or more values are graphed; values for remaining assemblages can be seen in Table 4.3.